Mapping the Chinese and Islamic Worlds

Long before Vasco da Gama rounded the Cape of Good Hope en route to India, the peoples of Africa, the Middle East, and Asia engaged in vigorous cross-cultural exchanges across the Indian Ocean. This book focuses on the years 700 to 1500, a period when powerful dynasties governed both the Islamic and Chinese regions, to document the relationship between the two worlds before the arrival of the Europeans. Through a close analysis of the maps, geographic accounts, and travelogues compiled by both Chinese and Islamic writers, the book traces the development of major contacts between people in China and the Islamic world and explores their interactions on matters as varied as diplomacy, commerce, mutual understanding, world geography, navigation, shipbuilding, and scientific exploration. When the Mongols ruled both China and Iran in the thirteenth and fourteenth centuries, their geographic understanding of each other's society increased markedly. This rich, engaging, and pioneering study offers glimpses into the worlds of Asian geographers and mapmakers, whose accumulated wisdom underpinned the celebrated voyages of European explorers like Vasco da Gama.

Hyunhee Park is an assistant professor of history at CUNY John Jay College of Criminal Justice in New York City, where she teaches Chinese history, global history, and justice in the non-Western tradition. She currently serves as an assistant editor of the academic journal *Crossroads – Studies on the History of Exchange Relations in the East Asian World*.

For my parents

Mapping the Chinese and Islamic Worlds

Cross-Cultural Exchange in Pre-modern Asia

HYUNHEE PARK
City University of New York

CAMBRIDGE
UNIVERSITY PRESS

CAMBRIDGE
UNIVERSITY PRESS

University Printing House, Cambridge CB2 8BS, United Kingdom

Cambridge University Press is part of the University of Cambridge.

It furthers the University's mission by disseminating knowledge in the pursuit of education, learning and research at the highest international levels of excellence.

www.cambridge.org
Information on this title: www.cambridge.org/9781107547834

First published 2012
First paperback edition 2015

A catalogue record for this publication is available from the British Library

Library of Congress Cataloguing in Publication data
Park, Hyunhee, 1972–
Mapping the Chinese and Islamic worlds : cross-cultural exchange in pre-modern Asia / Hyunhee Park.
p. cm.
Includes bibliographical references and index.
ISBN 978-1-107-01868-6 (hardback : alk. paper)
1. China – Civilization – 960–1644. 2. Islamic Empire – Civilization. 3. China – Relations – Islamic Empire. 4. Islamic Empire – Relations – China. 5. Discoveries in geography – History – To 1500. 6. Cartography – History – To 1500. I. Title.
DS750.72.P37 2012
303.48′251017670902–dc23 2012015544

ISBN 978-1-107-01868-6 Hardback
ISBN 978-1-107-54783-4 Paperback

Contents

List of Maps and Illustrations — *page* vi
Acknowledgments — ix
Abbreviations — xiii
Timeline — xvii
Glossary of Chinese Characters — xix
Note on Transliteration — xxv

Introduction — 1
1. From Imperial Encounter to Maritime Trade: Chinese Understanding of the Islamic World, 750–1260 — 20
2. The Representation of China and the World: Islamic Knowledge about China, 750–1260 — 56
3. Interpreting the Mongol World: Chinese Understanding of the Islamic World, 1260–1368 — 91
4. Beyond Marco Polo: Islamic Knowledge about China, 1260–1368 — 124
5. Legacy from Half the Globe before 1492: Chinese Understanding of the Islamic World and Islamic Knowledge about China, 1368–1500 — 161

Conclusion: Lessons from Pre-modern Sino-Islamic Contact — 191

Notes — 203
Works Cited — 243
Index — 269

Maps and Illustrations

Maps

1. China and the Islamic World, circa 800 — *page* xxvi
2. China and the Islamic World, circa 1340 — xxvii
3. China and the Islamic World, circa 1420 — xxviii

Figures

0.1. Al-Idrīsī's map of the world (1154) — 3
0.2. *The Map of Integrated Regions and Terrains and of Historical Countries and Capitals* (1402) — 4
1.1. Archaeological sites containing Chinese ceramics dated 8th–10th centuries — 30
1.2. The route from Guangzhou to foreign countries as envisioned by Jia Dan (circa 800) — 31
1.3. Ink-line sketch of *The Tracks of Yu* (top) and *The Map of Chinese and Non-Chinese Territories* (bottom) (1136) — 36
1.4. The "Map of the States in the Western Regions in the Han Dynasty" (top) and the "Map of the Five Indian States in the West" (bottom) (circa 1270) — 39
1.5. The "Geographic Map of the Land of China to the East" (circa 1270) — 42
1.6. The five great seas described by Zhou Qufei (1178) — 49
2.1. The seven seas described by al-Mas'ūdī (circa 947) — 72
2.2. Al-Iṣṭakhrī's world map (10th century) — 74
2.3. Al-Bīrūnī's sketch of the distribution of land and sea (1029) — 79

2.4. Al-Idrīsī's map of the world with place-names (top), and the sectional maps put together (bottom) (1154) 85
3.1. Four Khanates of the Mongol Empire (top); a geographical map from *The Encyclopedia of Yuan Dynasty Institutions* (circa 1330) 101
3.2. *The Kangnido* (1402) with place-names 104
3.3. Comparing depictions of the Mountains of the Moon Al-Khwārizmī's picture of the Nile (left); a depiction in al-Idrīsī's world map (top, right); and a depiction in the *Kangnido* (bottom, right) 106
3.4. "Map of the World's Regions" (1360) 108
4.1. Al-Qazwīnī 's sketch of the distribution of land and sea (late 13th century) 130
4.2. Comparison of Ḥamd Allāh Mustawfī al-Qazwīnī's map of the Iranian-Turkestan area (circa 1330) and the geographical map from *The Encyclopedia of Yuan Dynasty Institutions* (circa 1330) 143
4.3. Ḥamd Allāh Mustawfī's world map (circa 1330) 145
4.4. The world map of Caliph al-Ma'mūn from Ibn Faḍlallāh al-ʿUmarī (1301–1349) 149
5.1. *The Comprehensive Map of the Great Ming Empire* (14–15th centuries) 164
5.2. The "Map of Foreign Lands in Southeast Sea" (right) and the "Map of Foreign Lands in Southwest Sea" (left) (1541) 166
5.3. Reconstructed sea charts of Zheng He's maritime route in Mao Yuanyi, *The Treatise of Military Preparation* (circa 1621) 173
5.4. Star charts from the Zheng He sea charts. The first page (right) and the fourth page (left) 175

Acknowledgments

This book covers a wide scope of time and space, and it utilizes specialized knowledge of geography that could never have been studied without the generous support of numerous people. My deepest gratitude goes first to Valerie Hansen of Yale University, who inspired and guided me through my PhD dissertation, the initial study from which this book stemmed. Beatrice Gruendler has provided unfailing advice and encouragement throughout the journey of learning Arabic and Islamic scholarship. I was also fortunate to receive guidance from Jonathan Spence, whose valuable suggestions, insights, and warm encouragement throughout my years at Yale have enriched my thoughts and motivated my passion for studying history as a guide for life. Morris Rossabi of CUNY Queens College has been an equally inspiring mentor for my study of this challenging topic, the Mongol empire, and provided me with exceptional advice and support for turning the dissertation into a book.

Several colleagues read my manuscript closely and gave me valuable feedback on specific details, including those in Persian sources that I was not yet able to read in the original. These include Morris Rossabi, Ralph Kauz of Universität Bonn, Muhammad B. Vosoughi of Tehran University, Peter Bol of Harvard University, and Qiu Yihao of Peking University. I also thank the two anonymous readers for the Press, whose suggestions, corrections, and bibliographic help saved me from many embarrassing mistakes. The responsibility for any remaining gaffes and blunders is entirely my own.

I would also like to thank many other scholars who read parts of my book or dissertation manuscript and gave me important advice and comments; special mention is due for their generous support and sharing of ideas and resources: Sugiyama Masaaki and Miya Noriko of Kyoto University; Yuba Tadanori of Kyoto Tachibana University; Yamagata Kinya in Tokyo; Michal Biran, Raphael Israeli, Yuri Pines, Reuven Amitai-Preiss, and Ben-Ami Shillony of the Hebrew University of Jerusalem; Kim Hodong, Yi Eunjeung, and Seol Paehwan of Seoul National University; Shim Jae-hoon and Jung Su-il of Dankook University; Yang Bokyung of Sungshin Women's University; Chen Gaohua of the Chinese Academy of Social Sciences in Beijing; Li Xiaocong and Lee Myunghee of Peking University; Lu Xiqi of Xiamen University; Billy K. L. So of Hong Kong University of Science and Technology; and Zvi Ben Dor and Joanna Waley-Cohen of New York University. In addition, Andreas Kaplony of Universität Zürich, who generously agreed to become an outside reader for my dissertation at the last moment, read my entire draft in less than a month and gave me extensive, probing commentary.

Organizers of several specialized seminars and colloquiums invited me to share my ideas about my book manuscript and provided me with invaluable opportunities to discuss my topic from broader perspectives and to receive feedback from many different angles. These seminars and workshops include: the "Small Cities" conference at Ball State University convened by Kenneth Hall and Kenneth Swope; a colloquium on Eurasian Influences on Yuan China convened by John Chaffee of Binghamton University; a conference on Scientific and Philosophical Heritage of Nasir al-Din al-Tusi sponsored by the Written Heritage Research Centre in Tehran; a colloquium about the Selden Map of China convened by David Helliwell of Bodleian Library; and the History and Philosophy of Science speaker series of McGill University led by Nicholas Dew and Jamil Ragep. I also thank Angela Schottenhammer of the University of Ghent for inviting me to work as an assistant editor of *Crossroads – Studies on the History of Exchange Relations in the East Asian World*, which greatly encouraged me to work more deeply on the history of the cross-cultural contact.

I am deeply indebted to earlier scholars in this field who did pioneering work. I have benefited, in particular, from translations of many core passages of major sources done by these scholars, including Donald Daniel Leslie, Gabriel Ferrand, and W. M. Thackston. I have checked most of their translations against the original (except for Persian sources for which I relied on different translations), and updated the Romanization, but have often found that I cannot improve on their translations.

I also wish to express many thanks to my colleagues at John Jay College, in particular Allison Kavey, James De Lorenzi, David Munns,

Michael Pfeifer, and Fritz Umbach, for their manifold assistance, advice, and friendship. Deep gratitude also goes to colleagues in many libraries and museums, including the East Asian Library at Yale University. Financial support was kindly provided by the Yale Council of East Asian Studies, the Yale Center for International and Area Studies, the Yale-Beida exchange program at Peking University, the Richard Light Fellowship, and PSC-CUNY grants. The CUNY Faculty Fellowship Publications Program allowed me to participate in a writing seminar where I was able to receive inspirational, critical, and encouraging feedback on the book manuscript from other FFPP Fellows, including our advisor of the group, Virginia Sanchez-Korrol.

Finally, I wish to express my profound gratitude to all members of my family and friends. My study could not have been made possible without the continuous encouragement given to me by my parents, Park Dongho and Choi Bonghwa. I would like to thank my husband, Fumihiko Kobayashi, who has accompanied me everywhere since we first met in Jerusalem in 2000 and who always cheers and entertains me with all kinds of fascinating stories from his studies in Japanese and comparative folklore. My little brother Junhee and sister-in-law Yeonjeong and my in-laws in Japan were also a source of truthful encouragement. My friends Mary and Timothy Min also gave me gracious support for my study and living in the United States. Last, I cannot miss thanking my English editor, Danielle McClellan, whose intelligent and knowledgeable advice allowed me to present high-quality English academic writing with confidence.

Abbreviations

Bretschneider	Bretschneider, E. *Mediaeval Researches from Eastern Asiatic Sources*. London: Routledge & Kegan, 1910 [1888]. 2 vols.
EI2	*Encyclopedia of Islam*, 2nd edition.
HC1 / *HC2:1* / *HC2:2*	Harley, J. B. and David Woodward, eds. *The History of Cartography:* Volume One, *Cartography in Prehistoric, Ancient and Medieval Europe and the Mediterranean*; Volume Two, Book One, *Cartography in the Traditional Islamic and South Asian Societies*; Volume Two, Book Two, *Cartography in the Traditional East and Southeast Asian Societies*. Chicago, 1987–1994.
Ibn Baṭṭūṭa	Ibn Baṭṭūṭa. *Voyages d'Ibn Batoutah: texte arabe, accompagné d'une traduction*. Paris, 1853–1858.
Ibn Baṭṭūṭa/Gibb	Ibn Baṭṭūṭa. *The Travels of Ibn Battuta A.D. 1325–1354*. Translated, revised, and annotated by H. A. R. Gibb, 5 vols. Cambridge, 1958, 1961, 1971, 1994, 2000.
Ibn Mājid	Aḥmad b. Mājid al-Najdī. *Kitāb al-fawāʾid fī uṣūl ʿilm al-baḥr wa-l-qawāʾid* [The Book of Profitable Things Concerning the First Principles and Rules of Navigation]. Dimashq, 1971.
Ibn Mājid/Tibbetts	Aḥmad b. Mājid al-Najdī. *Arab Navigation in the Indian Ocean before the Coming of*

	the Portuguese, being a translation of Kitāb al-fawā'id fī uṣūl 'ilm al-baḥr wa-l-qawā'id of Aḥmad b. Mājid al-Najdī. Translated by G. R. Tibbetts. London, 1971.
JT	Rashīd al-Dīn. *Rashiduddin Fazlullah's Jamiʿu't-tawarikh: Compendium of Chronicles*. Translated by W. M. Thackston. Cambridge, 1998.
JTS	Liu Xu. *Jiu Tangshu* [Old History of the Tang]. Beijing, 1975.
Ma Huan	Ma Huan. *Ming chaoben "Yingyai shenglan" Jiaozuo* [Ming-period manuscript of "Yingyai shenglan," with annotations and footnotes]. Edited by Wan Ming. Beijing, 2005.
Ma Huan/Mills	Ma Huan. *Ying-yai Sheng-lan: The Overall Survey of the Ocean's Shores*. Translated by J. V. G. Mills. London, 1970.
Miller	Miller, Konrad. *Mappae Arabicae: Arabische Welt- und Länderkarten*. Frankfurt am Main, 1994. 2 vols.
Muqaddimah	Ibn Khaldūn. *Al-Muqaddimah* [The Introduction]. Al-Dār al-Bayḍa (Casablanca). 3 vols.
Muqaddimah/ Rosenthal	Ibn Khaldūn. *Muqaddimah, an Introduction to History*. Translated by Franz Rosenthal. Princeton, 1967. 3 vols.
NQ1 / *NQ2*	Ḥamd Allāh Mustawfī al-Qazwīnī. *Geographical Part of the Nuzhat al-Qulub composed by Hamd-Allah Mustawfi of Qazwin in 740 (1340)*. Vol.1 in Persian and Vol.2 in English. Leyden, 1919.
QZZJSK	Wu Wenliang. *Quanzhou zongjiao shike* [Religious inscriptions in Quanzhou]. Beijing, 2005.
Reinaud	Abū-Zayd Ḥasan al-Ṣīrāfī. *Relation des voyages faits par les Arabes et les Persans dans l'Inde et à la Chine dans le IXe siècle de l'ère chrétienne, Arabic text with French translation and commentary*. Translated by M. Reinaud. Osnabruck, 1988.
Renaudot	Abū-Zayd Ḥasan al-Ṣīrāfī. *Ancient Accounts of India and China by Two Mohammedan*

	Travellers, Who Went to Those Parts in the 9th Century. Translated by Eusebius Renaudot. London, 1733.
Sauvaget	*Aḫbār aṣ-Ṣīn wa l-Hind. Relation de la Chine et de l'Inde rédigée en 851*. Translated by Jean Sauvaget. Paris, 1948
XTS	Ouyang Xiu. *Xin Tangshu* [New History of the Tang]. Beijing, 1975.
YS	Song Lian. *Yuanshi* [The History of the Yuan]. Beijing, 1976.
ZGDJ/Ming	Cao Wanru et al. *Zhongguo gudai ditu ji: Ming* [An Atlas of Ancient Maps in China – the Ming Dynasty (1368–1644)]. Beijing, 1994.
ZGDJ/Yuan	Cao Wanru et al. *Zhongguo gudai ditu ji*: Zhanguo – Yuan [An Atlas of Ancient Maps in China – From the Warring States Period to the Yuan Dynasty (476 BCE–1368 CE)]. Beijing, 1990.
Zhufan zhi	Zhao Rugua. *Zhufan zhi jiaoshi* [Description of the Foreign Lands, with annotations and footnotes]. Beijing, 1996.
Zhufan zhi/Fujiyoshi	Zhao Rugua. *Shoban shi* [Description of the Foreign Lands]. Translated by Fujiyoshi Masumi. Osaka, 1991.
Zhufan zhi/Hirth	Zhao Rugua. *Chau Ju-Kua: his work on the Chinese and Arab trade in the twelfth and thirteenth centuries entitled Chu-fan-chi (Description of foreign peoples)*. Translated by Friedrich F. Hirth and W. W. Rockhill. St. Petersburg, 1911.

Timeline

Middle East	China
• Achaemenid Empire (circa 550–330 BCE)	• Qin Dynasty (221–206 BCE)
• Seleucid Empire (312–63 BCE)	• Han Dynasty (206 BCE–221 CE)
• Parthian Empire (238 BCE–226 CE)	• Six Dynasties (222–589)
• Sassanid Empire (224–651)	• Tang Dynasty (618–907)
• Muslim Conquest (622–750)	• Five Dynasties (907–960)
• Umayyad Caliphate (661–750)	• Song Dynasty (960–1276)
• ʿAbbāsid Caliphate (750–1258)	• Liao Dynasty: the Khitan rule (916–1125)
• Il-Khanate: the Mongol rule (1260–1335)	• Jin Dynasty: the Jurchen rule (1115–1234)
• Mamlūk Dynasty (1250–1517)	• Yuan Dynasty: the Mongol rule (1271–1368)
• Timurid Dynasty (1369–16th century)	• Ming Dynasty (1368–1644)
• Ottoman Empire (1299–1923)	

Glossary of Chinese Characters

Ajuluo	亞俱羅
A-la-bi	阿剌壁
Anguo	安國
Anxi	安息
Atabei	阿塔卑
Baida	白達
baochuan	寶船
Baoda	報達
baohuo	寶貨
Baoying	寶應
Beidi	北狄
bohuo	舶貨
Boluo	孛羅
Bosi	波斯
Cengba	層拔
Chana	察那
Chang De	常德
Chen Cheng	陳誠
chengxiang	丞相
Chenqing zhan	宸慶展
chi	尺
Congling	葱嶺
cun	寸
Dadu/Daidu	大都
Daming hunyi tu	大明混一圖
Daoyi zhi	島夷志

Daqin	大秦
Dashi	大食
Dayuan	大苑
Dayuan da yitong zhi	大元大一統志
dili	地理
Ding Jiezhai	丁節齋
Dingsi	丁巳
Dong Dashi hai	東大食海
Dongnan haiyi tu	東南海夷圖
Dongyi	東夷
Dong zhendan dili tu	東震旦地理圖
Du Huan	杜環
Dunhuang	敦煌
Du You	杜佑
Fei Xin	費信
Fengtian	奉天
Fozu tongji	佛祖統紀
Fuda	縛達
Fujian dao	福建道
Fulila	弗利剌
Ganpu	澉浦
Goguryeo	高句麗
Go Seonji	高仙芝
guanben chuan	官本船
Guanglun jiangli tu	廣輪疆理圖
Guangxi	廣西
Guang yutu	廣輿圖
Guangzhou tong haiyi dao	廣州通海夷道
Gujin huayi quyu zongyao tu	古今華夷區域摠要圖
Guo Kan	郭侃
guoyang qianxing tu	過洋牽星圖
Guo Ziyi	郭子儀
Gwon Geun	權近
Hacihasundacihan	哈刺哈孫答刺罕
Haiguo tuzhi	海國圖志
haijin	海禁
Hainei huayi tu	海內華夷圖
haiyun	海運
haiyun fu qianhu	海運副千戶
Hanghai waiyi	航海外夷

Hanshu	漢書
Han xiyu zhuguo tu	漢西域諸國圖
Helifa	合里法
Honglu si	鴻臚寺
Honil gangli yeokdae gukdo jido	混一疆理歷代國都之圖
Huang Chao	黃巢
Huayi tu	華夷圖
Huihui Guozijian	回回國子監
Huihui li	回回曆
Huihui Sitiantai	回回司天臺
Hunyi jiangli tu	混一疆理圖
Hyecho	慧超
Jia Dan	賈耽
Jicini	吉慈尼
Jin	金
Jinshi	進士
Jishui tan	積水潭
Kai-a-bai	愷阿白
Kim Sahyung	金士衡
Kuolifusi	闊里扶思
la nama	剌那麻
li	里
Lidai dili zhizhang tu	歷代地理指掌圖
Limu	里木
Lingnan	嶺南
Lingshan	靈山
Lin Zhiqi	林之奇
Liu Yu	劉郁
Li Zemin	李澤民
Loulan	樓蘭
Lumei	盧眉/蘆眉
Luo Hongxian	羅洪先
Ma Huan	馬歡
Majia	麻嘉
Maliba	麻離拔
Maomen	茂門
Mao Yuanyi	茅元儀
Meilugudun	眉路骨惇
Min	閩
Minhai	閩海

Mojia	默茄
Moluo	末羅
mubiezi	木鱉子
Mulanpi	木蘭皮
Na Huai	那懷
Nanman	南蠻
peijinfu	佩金符
Pei Xiu	裵秀
Puluohong	蒲囉吽
Pu Shougeng	蒲壽庚
Pu Ximi	蒲希密
Qilier	訖立兒
qilin	麒麟
Qingjing	清淨
Qing Jun	清濬
qinwang	親王
Qiuci	龜玆
Qi Yuli	契玉立
Saidianchi Shansiding	賽典赤 贍思丁
Sanfoqi	三佛齊
Sanshan	三山
Shache	莎車
Shanhai jing	山海經
Shengjiao guangbei tu	聲教廣被圖
Shenzhong	神宗
Shepo	闍婆
Shi	石
shibosi	市舶司
Shiji	史記
Shijie mingti zhi	世界名體志
Shi Nawei	施那幃
Shisu	十宿
Shoushi li	授時曆
suoxing ban	索星板
suoxing shu	索星術
Taiping yulan	太平御覽
Tang Taizong	唐太宗
Tianbao	天寶
Tianfang	天方
Tian Shan	天山

Tiantang	天堂
Tianzhu	天竺
Tiaozhi	條枝/條支
Tilaluhua	提羅盧和
Tongdian	通典
Tufan	吐蕃
tujing	圖經
Wang Dayuan	汪大淵
Wang Xuance	王玄策
Wang Yinglin	王應臨
Wannian li	萬年歷
Wei Yuan	魏源
Wengman	瓮蠻
Wuba	勿拔
Wubei zhi	武備志
Wui	嫣
Wu Jian	吳鑒
Wula	烏剌
Wusili	勿斯離/勿斯里
Wusun	烏孫
Wuwei	武威
Xiaozong	孝宗
Xia Xiyang	下西洋
Xi Dashi hai	西大食海
Xihai	西海
Xinan haiyi tu	西南海夷圖
Xingcha shenglan	星槎勝覽
xing mishujianshi	行秘書監事
xing Quanfu si	行泉府司
Xinya Tuoluo	辛押陀羅
Xirong	西戎
Xishi ji	西使記
Xitu wuyin zhi tu	西土五印之圖
Xiyang	西洋
Xiyu	西域
Xiyu fanguo zhi	西域番國志
Xiyu xingcheng ji	西域行程記
Xuanzang	玄奘
xuejie	血碣
Xumi shan	須彌山

Yada	啞靼
Yang Shu	楊樞
Yongle	永樂
Yongle dadian	永樂大典
Yuan Jingshi dadian dili tu	元經世大典地理圖
Yu ditu	輿地圖
Yugong tu	禹貢圖
Yuhai	玉海
Yuji tu	禹跡圖
Yumen	玉門
Zhamaluding	扎馬魯丁
Zhanbu zhou	瞻部洲
zhang	丈
Zhang Qian	張騫
Zheng Sixiao	鄭思肖
Zhengyi	正議
zhenlu	針路
Zhenxi	鎮西
Zhigu	直沽
Zhipan	志磐
zhiyong yuan	致用院
Zhiyuan	至元
zhongguo	中國
zhongshu xing	中書省
zhongxian xiaowei	忠顯校尉
Zhou-da-er	紂答兒
Zhou Mi	周密
Zhufan tu	諸蕃圖
zhuju shibosi	提舉市舶司
Zhunian	注輦
Zhu Siben	朱思本
Zhu Yuanzhang	朱元璋
Zou Yan	鄒衍

Note on Transliteration

The book gives dates according to the Gregorian calendar and does not give *Hijri* and Chinese dates specifically. The book follows the *pinyin* system to transliterate Chinese names and terms, and the system of the Library of Congress to transliterate Arabic names and terms. Names and terms of Persian origin have also been transliterated as if they were Arabic. Common words and place names, such as caliph and Baghdad, are written in the generally accepted English form without diacritics. Unlike Arabic and Persian writings that use phonetic alphabets, Chinese writing consists of morphosyllabic characters, and therefore, the book provides a glossary of Chinese characters. Names and terms of Mongolian origin have been transliterated according to Antoine Mostaert's scheme as modified by F. W. Cleaves except for these deviations: č is rendered as ch; š as sh; γ is gh, q is kh, and ǰ is j.

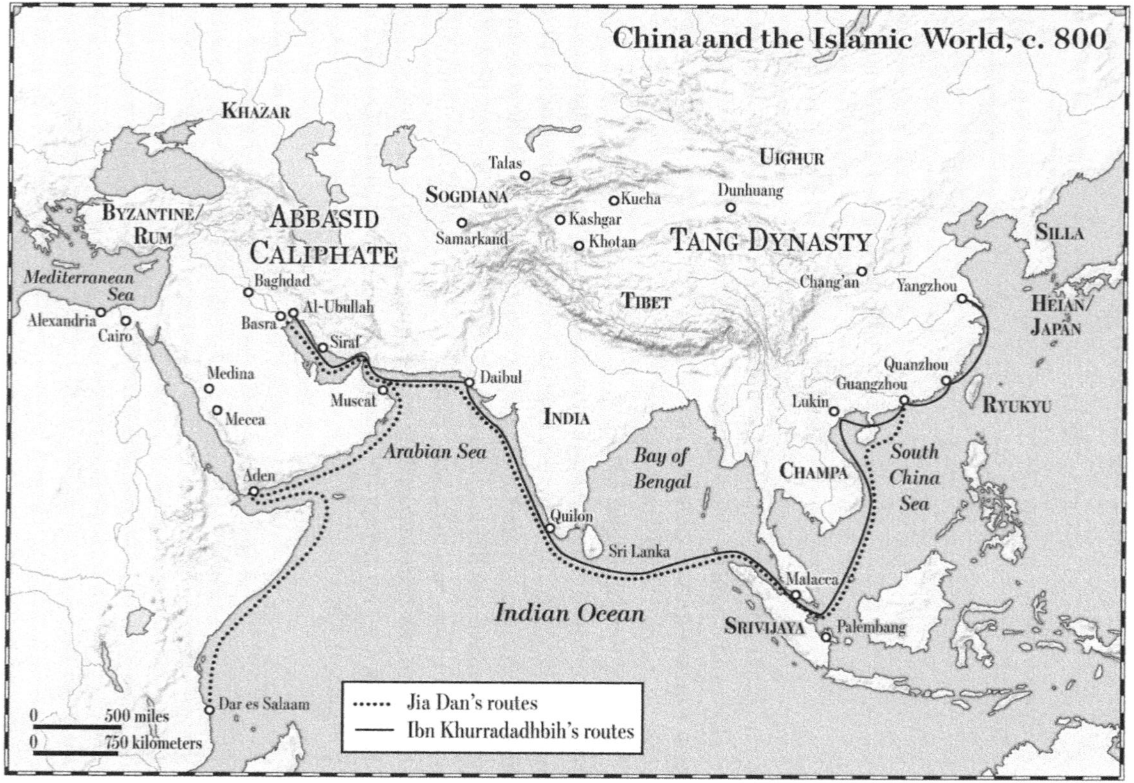

MAP 1 China and the Islamic World, circa 800.

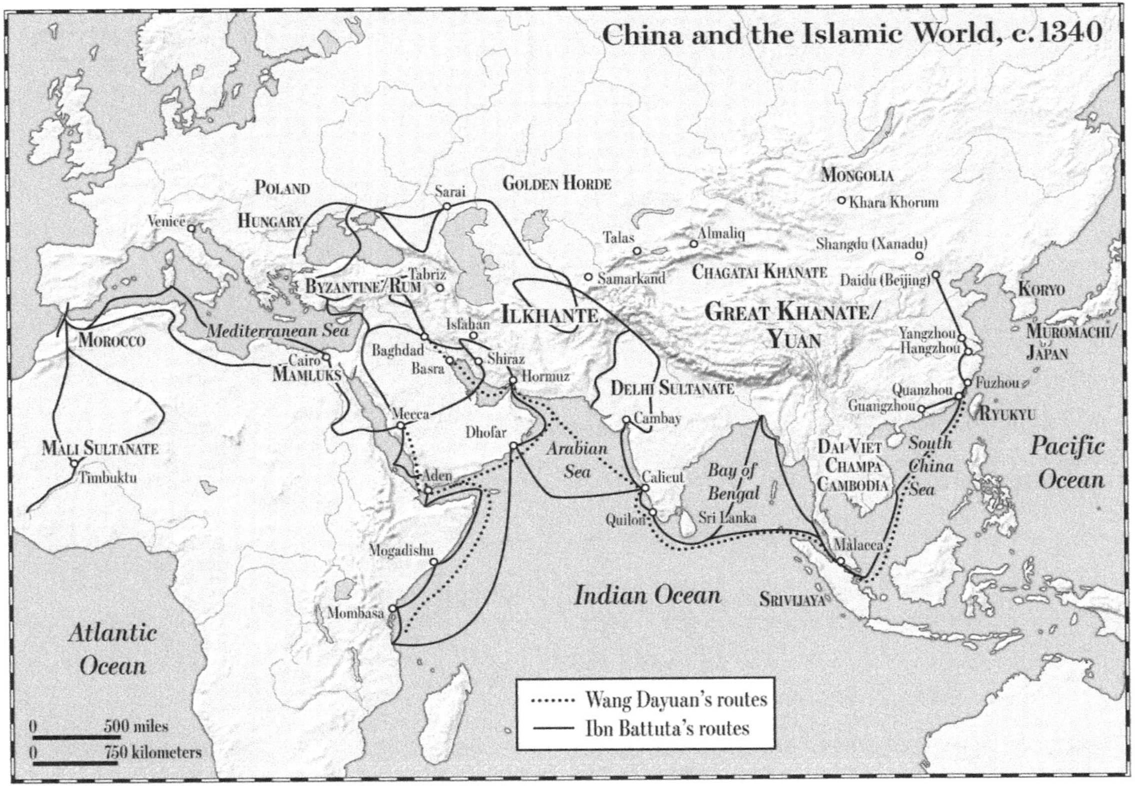

MAP 2 China and the Islamic World, circa 1340.

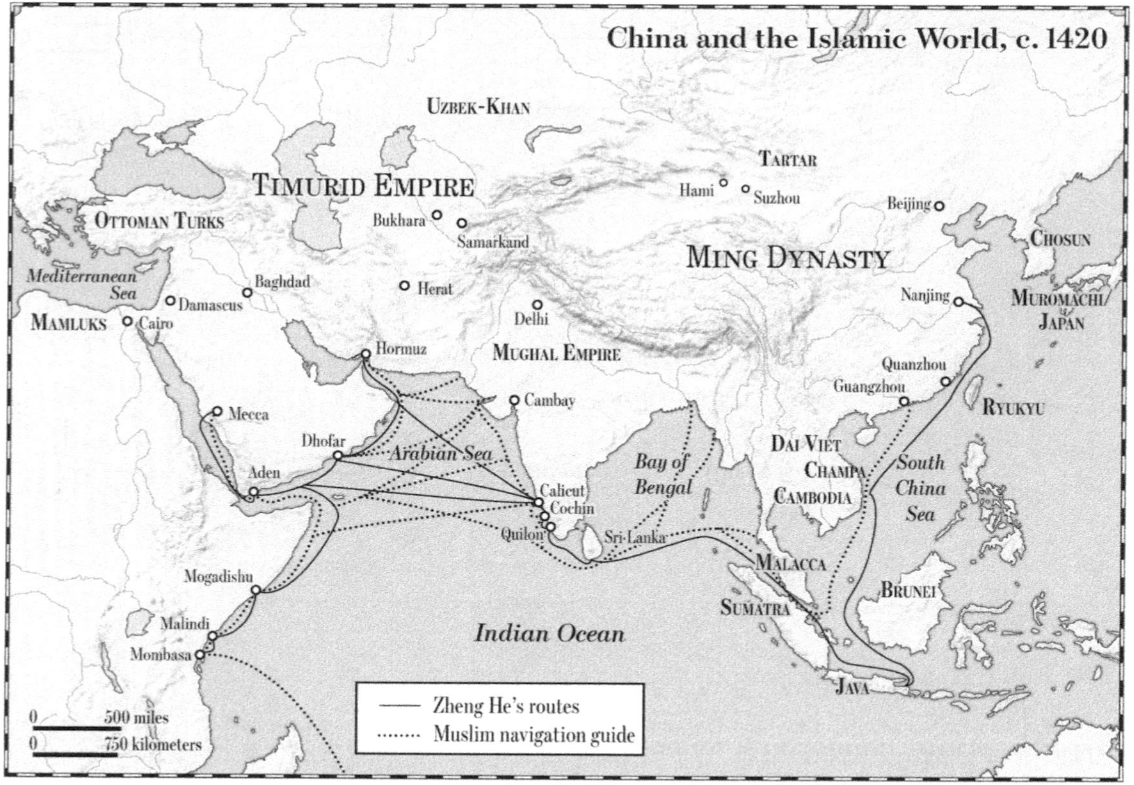

MAP 3 China and the Islamic World, circa 1420.

Introduction

In 1497, Vasco da Gama set sail from Portugal, seeking an eastern route to Asia and its fabled lands of gold and spices. As he ventured south along Africa's western coast, da Gama traveled in waters previously unknown to Europeans – and little known to Muslim and Chinese geographers as well.[1] This was no longer the case, however, from the moment he rounded the Cape of Good Hope and passed into the Indian Ocean. Once there, the Portuguese explorer and his crew found themselves on the world's longest sea trade route in regular use to date – a series of passages that linked the peoples of East Africa, the Arabian Peninsula, India, Southeast Asia, and ultimately, China.

Da Gama did find the route to India, but his success depended largely on the expertise of a Muslim navigator familiar with the sea routes that led to Calicut. What da Gama himself knew about his world does not concern us in this book, but rather the knowledge of his navigator. This book seeks to understand the extent of the geographic knowledge that existed between two of the principal actors that created this interconnected world of Asia, namely China and the Islamic world, as well as the processes by which they gained this knowledge over centuries of continuous contact. We will, in effect, try to see the world as it looked through the eyes of da Gama's navigator and those of the Asian geographers, mapmakers, and others whose accumulated wisdom would prove so vital to European explorers such as da Gama on their celebrated voyages.

This book challenges the prevalent Eurocentric approach to world history – which continues to see the year 1492 as the initial moment of interaction between distant cultures – by examining the eight centuries of contact and exchange prior to 1492 involving two of the world's major cultures: China and the Islamic world.[2] From around 700 to 1500, each society enjoyed similarly high levels of economic and cultural development. Hubs of information ran parallel to their rich markets for goods. As the Chinese sought spices and fragrances from the Middle East, they also gained knowledge about advanced astronomy, mathematics, engineering, and medicine. As merchants from the Islamic world purchased silks and porcelains from China, they in turn adopted various technological inventions pioneered by the Chinese, such as the art of papermaking and the compass. This activity also naturally resulted in the increase of mutual geographic knowledge. Mapmakers and writers recorded this new geographic information, thanks to the rich literary traditions of both societies. By 1500, the Chinese learned significantly more about the Islamic world, and the Muslims of West Asia and North Africa knew a great deal more about China, than either society had known about each other in the eighth century. During these eight centuries preceding Vasco da Gama, a great metamorphosis occurred: Asia's most affluent and powerful societies, each located at the extreme end of the other's known world, transformed their understanding of each other, turning *terra incognita* into *terra cognita*.

In 750, maps of China did not exist in the Islamic world, nor did the Chinese possess maps of the Islamic world. Chinese geographers knew about *Dashi*, the Chinese term for the Arabs or Arabia (and later for the Muslims in general),[3] but had little idea about their region's geographic shape. Similarly, their counterparts in the Islamic world in the early years of Islam had only a vague notion of China, a country at the eastern end of the Silk Road from which merchants returned with silks and other goods, but whose precise location was not well-defined. In the ensuing centuries, merchants, diplomats, and travelers from both spheres acquired and disseminated a great deal of knowledge about the histories, customs, and religious practices of other societies. Scholars then recorded their accounts, and based on their data, cartographers drew increasingly more detailed maps of the two regions and the lands that linked them (see Figures 0.1 and 0.2).

Figure 0.1 shows the world map drawn by the Muslim geographer al-Idrīsī in the mid-twelfth century. Placing the Arabian Peninsula at the center, al-Idrīsī presents a very accurate depiction of the Mediterranean coastline to the west and the Indian Ocean and seas reaching China to the east. Figure 0.2 shows a map drawn in Korea in 1402 that, according to its Korean authors, was based on maps drawn in China during the fourteenth century. The 1402 map therefore reveals the level of Chinese

FIGURE 0.1. Al-Idrīsī's map of the world from his *Pleasure of He who Longs to Cross the Horizons* (*Nuzhat al-mushtāq fī ikhtirāq al-āfāq*, dated to 1154), copy of 1553. By permission of the Bodleian Library, University of Oxford (Ms. Pococke 375, fols. 3b–4a). The original map placed the south on top; the map is reversed here for clarity.

understanding about the world at the time, which included accurate knowledge of the contours of the Arabian Peninsula and Africa. This leap from no maps to fairly precise geographic depictions, as evidenced in these two maps, is the direct result of the lively exchange of geographic and cartographic knowledge between the Chinese and Islamic worlds.[4]

The state of European geographic knowledge during this period stands in clear contrast to the elaborate, systematic, and accurate descriptions of the world that Asian contemporaries produced thanks to continuous and open contact. Although the Europeans aspired to understand and engage the lands to the east from which exotic goods came, their knowledge

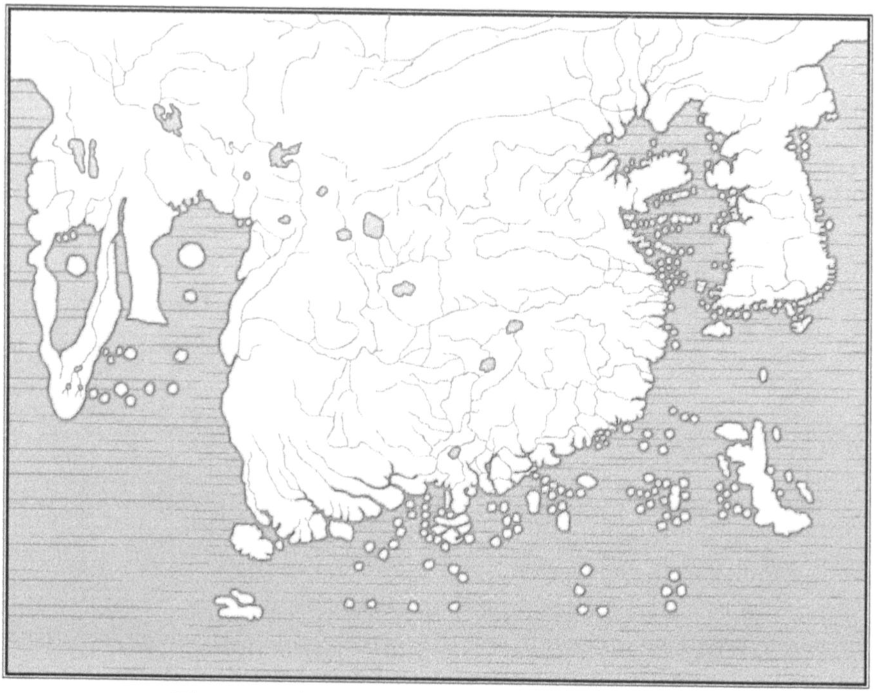

FIGURE 0.2. *The Map of Integrated Regions and Terrains and of Historical Countries and Capitals* (*Honil gangni yeokdae gukdo jido*, or shortly the *Kangnido*) – the world map drawn in Korea in 1402 based on maps drawn in China during the Mongol period. This copy of the Korean original is dated 1470 and held in Ryūkoku University, Kyoto, Japan. Redrawn after the original image.

remained largely circumscribed by a simplistic world view, represented by the "T-in-the-O" map: this image accounted for the Middle East but depicted distant places such as China as little more than fabled lands of monsters and the original Garden of Eden.[5] One of the first important sources of information was the travelogue of Marco Polo, who claimed to have journeyed to and from China between 1271 and 1295. Its contents constituted a sum of all geographic knowledge circulating throughout Asia in the fourteenth century. Da Gama's predecessors, Henry the Navigator and Christopher Columbus, were each said to have read the travelogue. In other words, the geographic knowledge of the world gradually accumulated in China and the Islamic world and communicated through Marco Polo (as well as other geographic and travel accounts) helped open the way to the age of European exploration and discovery in the sixteenth century.[6]

Although an enormous number of secondary sources about pre modern Sino-Islamic relations already exist in many languages,[7] this book is the first to treat both sides of the exchange equally, using a comparative analysis of major primary sources in Chinese, Arabic, and Persian. These sources taken together provide enough data to trace the cross-cultural exchange of geographic knowledge that took place between these two societies, which, as we have just seen, would have powerful implications for world history.

China and the Islamic World: Connected by Land and Sea

To define what we mean by "China" and "the Islamic world," this study uses geographic markers that reflect the two societies' perceptions of each other during the pivotal eight centuries. "China" refers to the river valleys of the Yellow, Yangzi, and Pearl Rivers, which, in our period of study, was sometimes under Han Chinese rule and sometimes not.[8] "The Islamic world" refers to the regions of modern-day Iraq and Iran as well as North and East Africa and Turkestan. For practical purposes, this study does not include other parts of the world where Muslim populations predominated, such as Southeast Asia. People living in these geographic regions of China and the Islamic world came to share similar cultures and traditions after a long process of intraregional political interactions.[9] As they did, writers within that region gradually defined their own societies and differentiated them from other societies.

The earliest people to call themselves Chinese established the first Chinese states on the North China Plain along the Yellow River sometime between 1500 and 200 BCE. They called their states the "Middle Kingdom" (*zhongguo*) to contrast them with their "barbarian" neighbors, according to their world view. Gradually the whole of China proper was unified, both politically and culturally, and the Chinese maintained and accentuated their cultural distinction over the centuries under successive ruling dynasties.[10] One of China's earliest contacts with peoples to the west was with the pre-Islamic Sassanid empire of Iran (226–651). The means of contact was the overland routes of the Silk Road, but because of the huge distances and many natural obstacles, the exchange typically took place via relays. Traders such as the famous Sogdian merchants, who made their home in what is now Uzbekistan, would travel back and forth in short circuits, passing commodities from one market to another. These goods would then move along another stretch of the overland route via another set of carriers.[11] We can assume that some basic knowledge about the land and people of China was transmitted from one merchant to another along with the goods they traded, and eventually made its way to the Arabian Peninsula. It is important to note that this information was probably more substantial than that transmitted to the Roman empire, for Roman writers tell us only about a place called *Serica* [*Sērikē*], the country of silk. The Indo-Iranian term for China that circulated in Central and West Asia at this time was *Chīn*, probably derived from the name of the first Chinese empire, Qin (221–210 BCE). The Arabs subsequently borrowed this term to create their own word for China, *al-Ṣīn*.[12] They continued to use the name, even several centuries after the fall of the Qin dynasty.

In 622, a new force intervened in the established trading routes linking China and West Asia. A new religion, Islam, began to rise as a strong political power under the Arabs, who swiftly conquered West Asia and soon after asserted their political dominance over Central Asia, North Africa, and Southern Europe, creating the political and cultural unity known as *ummah* (the Community of the Muslim Believers). The Umayyad caliphate's expansion into Central Asia reached as far as Kashgar, the oasis city located at the western end of contemporary China. As the western side of Eurasia experienced political upheaval, a new, strong, and outward-looking dynasty – the Tang – came to power in China, establishing itself in the year 618.

A few extant sources reveal that contacts between the Tang dynasty (618–907) and the Islamic caliphates existed during this early period. Even if we exclude the legendary story about the visit of Muḥammad's close relative Saʿd b. Abī Waqqās to Guangzhou (Canton) in the seventh century, official Chinese histories mention thirty-three Arab diplomatic missions to keep peaceful relations with the Tang dynasty between 651 and 750. Unfortunately, Arabic sources corroborate very few of these accounts,[13] and we do not know how many of these missions were dispatched by the Islamic rulers. Merchants from western Asia, including Sogdians and Persians, continued to visit China in large numbers along the Silk Road as they had even before the rise of the Tang dynasty, and many undoubtedly provided the Chinese with information about their native lands as well as neighboring countries. At the same time, Chinese geographers learned about the rise of Islam from people traveling to West Asia such as Buddhist monks. The earliest surviving Chinese source that mentions Dashi (the Arabs) is an account by the Korean monk Hyecho [Chinese: Huichao] (704–787), who traveled from China to India and Central Asia. His narrative contains a brief sentence about the Arab invasion of Iran (651), which indicates that the Chinese knew about the event.[14]

Around 750, the histories of the two societies entered a new, dramatic phase. After a successful rebellion in Central Asia (Khorasan/Transoxania), the ʿAbbāsids replaced the Umayyad caliphate (661–750). Continuing its eastward push, the ʿAbbāsid caliphate (750–1258) soon collided with the westward expanding Tang dynasty. This first full-scale contact between the Chinese and Islamic societies took the form of clashes over political and military supremacy in Central Asia. As we will see in Chapter 1, soon after contest, the conditions of overland routes gradually worsened and Silk Road trade dwindled. Their decline, however, stimulated the development of ocean routes. By the eighth century, sea travel in the Indian Ocean became the predominant mode of contact, both direct and indirect, between China and the Islamic world.

According to the first-century Greek text *The Periplus of the Erythraean Sea*, it was the Greeks who pioneered the sailing route from the Red Sea to the Indian Ocean, which they called the Erythraean Sea, during the mid-first century CE.[15] The account details navigation itineraries and the kinds of goods traded in ports along the way, but provides only a vague description of a country beyond India called *Thīnai* (*Sinae*), from which silks came.[16] After the *Periplus*, western sources mostly fall silent about routes in the Indian Ocean. A few archaeological sources reveal activity by Persians who sailed through the Indian Ocean and into East Asia.[17] Chinese official histories before 750 (sources are few for the contemporary Islamic world) record a long-term development of Chinese maritime trade with Southeast and South Asian merchants.[18] Here lay an opportunity, it seems, for Chinese and West Asians to meet somewhere in the Indian Ocean's midst. However, middlemen from South and Southeast Asia primarily conducted trade on both ends, and therefore, the scale of the trade and contact was limited.

Sources, in both Chinese and Arabic, testify to a dramatic – and soon becoming steady – growth in scale of maritime contact between China and the Islamic world after 750. This study focuses primarily on maritime contacts in order to contrast it with the more familiar narratives about China's contact with the western regions through the famous overland Silk Routes. By the 1500s (when Europeans were initiating active contact with Asian markets), political fragmentation of the Islamic world – such as the establishment of the Shi'i Savavid empire that served as a block between the Sunni kingdoms (Uzbeks and Ottomans) – was disrupting overland trade. At the same time, maritime trade operated continuously even in the face of strife. And so, Europeans in the 1500s traveled to Asia along the maritime routes, including those between Iraq and China that Arab-Persian Muslims and Chinese had pioneered in earlier times.

Despite our maritime emphasis here, it is crucial to also examine the important diplomatic channels conducted through overland routes. In fact, maritime and overland societies experienced political integration during the thirteenth and fourteenth centuries under the Mongols, who conquered most of Eurasia and reopened overland routes that had been in decline for centuries. Even during this period, however, Sino-Islamic contacts grew most through maritime commercial channels. Only recently have scholars begun to pay attention to the significance of maritime trade during the Mongol period, which the nomadic Mongol rulers supported more vigorously than anyone had suspected.[19]

During the several centuries of continuous Sino-Islamic contact, scholars and geographers in both societies began to write about each other. Most of these accounts contain information about trade goods, local products and inventions, sailing routes, history, and customs – knowledge intended to facilitate trade relations. When this commercially-oriented information circulated between the two societies, other forms of knowledge such as science and technology (including cartographic techniques) traveled with it. Thus, Sino-Islamic exchange led to an overall growth in cross-cultural knowledge, which served to encourage further contact. How well we can calibrate this growth depends on our ability to interpret the geographical and cartographical evidence before us.

Source Materials

Specialists in comparative history realize that it is not easy to find equivalent sources from both sides of an encounter. Such is the case when studying Sino-Islamic contacts. Fortunately, China and the Islamic world, arguably the world's two most advanced societies between 750 and 1500, both produced abundant texts on a variety of subjects. By 750, the Chinese literary tradition was already over a thousand years old, and by the eleventh century, the Chinese were producing texts on a mass scale thanks to the innovation and spread of wood-block printing. As a result, more books from China survive in their complete forms than from any other culture of this period. Literature in the Islamic world, in contrast, did not blossom until the creation of the Qur'ān in the seventh century, which initiated the standardization of written Arabic, a necessary precursor to the evolution of Arabic literature.[20] From the eighth century onward, the number of Arabic literary genres increased dramatically, but manuscripts would continue to be hand copied for a millennium, as printing would not be introduced until the nineteenth century. Despite the disparities in the quantity and quality of written sources, both Chinese and Islamic societies boast rich collections of texts and manuscripts. These provide modern historians enough source material with which to make a balanced comparison of each society's knowledge about the other, and about the world at large.[21] In this book we will examine geographic accounts, travel and diplomatic narratives, and maps, and supplement these principal sources with contextual information drawn from official histories, local gazetteers, and other kinds of literary works. Data from archaeological excavations will provide further contextual information and supplement the limitations of written sources.

Presenting a challenge to our study is the fact that few original manuscripts from this early period survive intact. In most cases, what we have to work with are copies made long after the original first appeared. As scholars well know, the original words could sometimes be distorted through successive generations of copies. The problem of copies and how to deal with them has provoked some fascinating debate, and urges us to consider the matter more seriously.[22] Here again, contextual sources will prove essential as points of cross-reference.

Geographic Accounts

This category of texts encompasses writings that convey information about another society's geography, history, customs, and trade goods, regardless of the author's purpose in writing the work. Most such accounts supply basic information about peoples and societies in an itemized fashion, organized country by country, although some authors present this information in more dynamic narrative form. The earliest of these works were written by men who had never traveled to the countries they wrote about; these writers depended instead on the secondhand reports and hearsay of others. Consequently, their accounts are full of vague and fantastic stories about *terra incognita*. As contacts increased, however, authors writing about other societies were able to include firsthand information in order to satisfy the interests of their respective governments and of the general public.

Sima Qian (circa 145–86 BCE), often considered "the Herodotus of China," was the first Chinese historian to write about western peoples. In the classic *Records of the Grand Historian* (*Shiji*), he based his descriptions of the countries of the Western Regions (*Xiyu*) on information provided to him by Zhang Qian (died 113 BCE), the envoy who first pioneered the overland Silk Route through Central Asia. Here is the first part of Sima Qian's account of the Parthian empire (*Anxi*), which flourished between 247 BCE and 224 CE in what is now Iran and Iraq:[23]

> The Parthian Empire [Anxi] is situated several thousand *li* [1 *li* = approximately ½ kilometer] west of the region of the Great Yuezhi. The people are settled on the land, cultivating the fields and growing rice and wheat. They also make wine out of grapes. They have walled cities like the people of Dayuan, the region containing several hundred cities of various sizes. The kingdom, which borders the Gui [Oxus] river, is very large, measuring several thousand *li* square. Some of the inhabitants are merchants who travel by carts or boats to neighboring countries, sometimes journeying several thousand *li*. The coins of the country are made of silver and bear the face of the king. When the king dies, the currency is immediately changed and new coins issued with the face of his successor. The people keep records by writing horizontally on strips of leather....
>
> When the Han envoys first visited the kingdom of Parthia, the king of Parthia dispatched a party of twenty thousand horsemen to meet them on the eastern border of his kingdom. The capital of the kingdom is several thousand *li* from the eastern border, and as the envoys proceeded there they passed through twenty or thirty cities inhabited by great numbers of people. When the Han envoys set out again to return to China, the king of Parthia dispatched envoys of his own to accompany them, and after the latter had visited China and reported on its great breadth and might, the king sent some of the eggs of the great birds which live in the region, and skilled tricksters of Lixuan, to the Han court as gifts.[24]

Sima Qian's history represented a breakthrough in the Chinese understanding of the far west: No longer a fantasy land of mysterious creatures and immortal spirits, the territories of the west were now real, containing societies of normal mortals complete with farms, cities, markets, currencies, kings, and even systems of writing that could be described.[25] The description of Anxi is typical of most Chinese accounts of foreign countries, specifying their geographic location, natural environment, local products, types of cities, markets, merchants, monetary system, and political and diplomatic relations with neighboring countries as well as with China. The Chinese gradually accumulated factual information about other societies that differed distinctly from the material found in the "classics" of their times, such as the *Classic of Mountains and Seas* (*Shanhai jing*), whose fantastic creatures defy empirical testing.[26] Sima Qian dismissed such texts as unreliable once actual reports about foreign places came to him from travelers like Zhang Qian.[27]

As more and more Chinese journeyed to other lands, people from other lands began to travel to China. *Records of the Grand Historian* mentions diplomatic envoys sent both by China's ruling Han dynasty (206 BCE–220 CE) and by other countries. We cannot be sure, however, how many of these envoys during this early period were official. In fact, some of the envoys who arrived in China may have actually been merchants posing as diplomats in order to obtain trading privileges with the imperial court. Nevertheless, such visitors brought with them accurate, firsthand information about their homes and neighboring countries and passed it on to the Chinese they encountered. The information would then be collected by a special Office of the Court of State Ceremonial (*Honglü si*), active even before the Tang period (618–907 CE), and compiled in the government's official histories and maps.[28]

After Sima Qian's *Records of the Grand Historian*, top-ranking historians continued writing official histories in the same format, including a section on foreign countries that was placed in the biography section of their respective works. The authors of such accounts often drew on previous manuscripts, but also included fresh information. Although many of these do not survive in their entirety, snippets have come down to us thanks to their citation in official histories or their successive duplication in other texts. One such example is a late eighth-century report on the Arabs and Muslims in the ʿAbbāsid dynasty by a Chinese man taken captive during the conflicts between the Tang and ʿAbbāsid armies in Central Asia. It is the earliest surviving detailed Chinese account of the Islamic world and sets a precedent for later Chinese writing on the region. The account circulated widely and is available to us today because it was inserted into the *Encyclopedic History of Institutions* (*Tongdian*), the most influential official history of its time.

Arabic and Persian geographic accounts provide an interesting contrast to Chinese sources from the same period because they differ both in nature and quality. Arab scholars were the first to shape Islamic literature in Arabic, the language of the Qurʾān. Soon, non-Arabs who had converted to Islam began to play an important role in developing Islamic scholarship. Early in its history, Muslim society invested heavily in the transfer of cultural knowledge, both because of its relatively late development as a society and culture and because of their incorporation of other peoples and traditions in the course of its expansion.

As it expanded, the Arabs systematically adopted a wealth of new geographic concepts, methods, and data from the Greeks, Iranians, and Indians.[29] The physical and mathematical geography (the field that calculates longitudinal and latitudinal coordinates) they acquired had its origins in ancient Greece and Rome. Greek and Roman sailors and merchants, whose long-distance trade, as we have seen, extended as far east as the Indian Ocean, brought back information about the diverse regions they encountered, including eastern Eurasia.[30] The information was then compiled into the earliest known geographies of Eurasia and North Africa.[31] This knowledge was expanded in the second century CE when Ptolemy of Alexandria, using Greek geographic data and advanced geodesy, published his two great works: the *Almagest*, an astronomical table that notes the latitude and longitude of significant places in relation to their positions in the zodiac, and the *Geography*, a treatise that describes the layout of the known world with unprecedented accuracy by means of a network of coordinates.[32]

After seizing a significant portion of the Byzantine empire and conquering the Sassanid empire of the Persians in 651, the Islamic empire-builders quickly grasped the significance of this accumulated Greco-Roman knowledge, and actively promoted its assimilation into their rapidly spreading Arabic-speaking culture through massive translation projects under the sponsorship of the first ʿAbbāsid caliphs in Baghdad. Instead of merely copying the earlier works, however, Muslim scholars developed them further by combining the more mathematical Greek traditions with the descriptive Iranian ones – the same narrative traditions that, thanks to overland trade with West Asia, had been familiar to the Chinese for centuries.[33] This synthesis of earlier geographic traditions by Muslim scholars resulted in the world's most advanced geographic and cartographic knowledge throughout the medieval period.

The needs of the burgeoning Islamic empire soon became an engine for the acquisition of fresh geographic knowledge. The reasons for continuously updating their geographic knowledge were simultaneously political, religious, and commercial. Islamic expansion prompted the ʿAbbāsids to collect practical geographic information in order to better govern their new territorial acquisitions. The requirement in the Qurʾān for Muslims to pray facing Mecca and to undertake a pilgrimage there further encouraged the acquisition of geographic knowledge.[34] Finally, Muslim merchants, who played the most active part in Indian Ocean trade during this period and who had extended their range all the way to China in the eighth century,[35] brought back new information about the lands they had seen. Fueled by the proliferation of paper (originally from China), Muslims under the ʿAbbāsids synthesized this new knowledge with the assimilated foreign traditions and produced numerous geographic and historical accounts that described various regions of the world, including China.[36] Perhaps this is why the earliest Muslim accounts of China often provide a richer portrait than Chinese accounts of the Islamic world.

As time progressed, the number and quality of firsthand geographic accounts and first person travel narratives increased in China and the Islamic world, providing geographers with greater and more reliable sources of information. The changing character of the sources illustrates the changing character of the various contacts exchanges, and phases between the two societies, which peaked during the Mongol period. The following chapters explore the change in both content and style that occurred in each society's geographic understanding of the other society over time.

We must take a critical approach when evaluating the information provided in each geographic account. It is quite likely that some of their original information was distorted in the course of its transmission from one language to another or from one manuscript to another. Even travel accounts can be less reliable as sources of historical geographical information because we cannot always be certain that the authors indeed journeyed to the places they claimed to have visited. We, therefore, will consider the following questions throughout: What geographic information can be gleaned from Arabic and Chinese narratives? What are the formats and genres of geographic and travel writing that present these bits of information? What is their status as fact or fiction, and how can we evaluate that status? What new information can we find in each period, and how can we interpret it within the context of the Sino-Islamic contacts? What are the possible conduits of new information about other societies? Finally, in what ways did increased cross-cultural understanding broaden the overall world view of these two societies and lead to further cross-cultural contact? Because space is limited, this study cannot exhaust the abundant sources available to us, nor scrutinize every fragment of information – an impossible task for any single author. Instead, this study will selectively, comparatively, and critically analyze the most important sources related to Sino-Islamic contacts for their geographic knowledge. The book's primary goals are (1) to demonstrate that certain types of collective knowledge circulated under specific circumstances of contact, and (2) to consider the historical implications of this knowledge. Due to the limitations that written sources face in the course of transmission, we will also draw on material and visual sources for evidence of the same phenomena. The most important visual source that we can use to understand the increase of geographic knowledge is maps.

Maps

This book is one of the first to make serious use of ancient maps for historical analysis, arguing that ancient maps can be seen as "texts" that encode the cultural knowledge of a society at a given time.[37] The level of familiarity of one society with another can, in a certain sense, be gauged through the visual representations it makes of that "other" land. Although more limited in their circulation than written works, ancient maps display the geographic knowledge prevailing among certain groups within a society. In many cases, maps were more epiphenomenal than written geographic accounts: They were a spinoff of the aggregated data because they incorporated developing cartographic techniques. Yet maps of foreign countries that geographers produced using newly acquired information – and even using new cartographic techniques – can reveal the degree of contact and exchange with the foreign societies that occurred during the period in which the map was produced.

Cartographers developed mapmaking techniques and learned to draw precise maps starting in the third century CE in China and in the eighth century in the Islamic world. Many maps survive in China since cartography had for centuries been essential to its administrative and military pursuits.[38] The ancient Chinese drew symbolic diagrams such as the "Yugong tu," which places China at the center of the world as the source from which enlightenment flows. However, many written sources testify that early Chinese cartographers also drew more realistic maps for practical purposes. The earliest surviving maps show that Chinese cartographers used systematic distance-measuring methods that allowed them to draw China proper at a rather precise scale by 1000 CE or earlier. Maps of the lands beyond its borders would come much later. We will see in the following chapters the process by which Chinese cartographers gradually collected new geographic and cartographic information from other societies – particularly the Islamic world – to better understand and describe the wider world, including West Asia, Africa, and Europe.

Arab and Persian cartographers drew world maps much earlier than Chinese cartographers did. An Iranian tradition from antiquity portrayed the world's land mass in the shape of a bird: China as its head; India its right wing; the North Caucasus (al-Khazar) its left wing; Mecca, Ḥijāz, Syria, Iraq, and Egypt (i.e., the heart of the Islamic world) its chest; and North Africa its tail. These bird-shaped geographic contours often appear in early Arabic geographies.[39] Although it may sound fanciful, this scheme actually demonstrates a rough knowledge of the Eurasian continent and locates the major regions in their approximate positions.

Muslim geographers and cartographers were able to create more accurate portraits of the world with more precise physical dimensions after they inherited the traditions of the Romans and Greeks. Ptolemy's *Geography*, a table of longitudinal and latitudinal coordinates, provided important raw data with which to map the world. Muslim geographers updated Ptolemy's geographic scheme with their own acquired information. Thanks to their assimilation of the Greco-Roman tradition, re-measurements of the physical locations of the major places in the world, and continuous discussions with sailors who sailed the Indian Ocean, Muslim geographers developed a sense of the coastlines between the Islamic world and China much earlier than Chinese cartographers did.[40]

Because actual navigation allows for the most continuous exposure to the shape of a coastline, an obvious source of information for land-based mapmakers was navigators' sea charts. Few original sea charts survive in China or the Islamic world, however.[41] Some of the charts used by Zheng He (1405–1433) during his famous expeditions to the Islamic world survived long enough for others to collect and compile them for public consumption two centuries later. The chart known as the "Mao Kun map" (Zheng He Hanghai tu) supplies a complete record of all the sea routes connecting China to the Islamic world that were used for actual navigation.

As is the case with geographic accounts, few original maps survive. Nevertheless it is possible to draw on copies and compilations from later periods in order to reconstruct the maps in their original form. Such is the case with the two representative world maps presented in this Introduction (see Figures 0.1 and 0.2). We will revisit these images in more detail in the following chapters in order to examine the Muslim and Chinese world views in the period of the maps' production. Fortunately, a two- to three-century gap is too short a period of time to expect additions or distortions sufficient to significantly alter the original copies. These later copies, therefore, will serve our purpose.

Archaeological Evidence

Archaeological findings constitute another source of data that will help us trace the increase in contact and mutual knowledge between China and the Islamic world. Archaeological excavations, which have grown in number since the late 1960s, provide information that may never have been available in early manuscripts. For example, textual sources rarely allow us to assess the volume of trade at a particular location the way that archaeological finds do. The archaeological evidence, therefore, helps us understand the conditions of contact that could have facilitated the transfer of knowledge between the two societies at a given period of time.

Arabic geographic and travel accounts mention ceramics as one of the most important trade goods that arrived in the Islamic world from China, and archaeological finds confirm this. Chinese ceramics excavated on the shores of the Persian Gulf and the Arabian Sea over the last four decades demonstrate that Muslims imported ceramics from China continuously between 700 and 1500.[42] Excavations at Sīrāf, begun in 1968, demonstrate that the quantity of Chinese ceramics available in this important Persian Gulf port suddenly increased in the eighth century.[43] Large-scale imports of ceramics and other desirable goods were possible via the Indian Ocean shipping routes. After all, a ship could carry many more ceramics than a caravan of camels and at a much lower cost. By the ninth century, Middle Eastern potters had begun to imitate Chinese white porcelain, although they could never fully replicate them.[44] Similar archaeological excavations in China have yielded corresponding evidence of large-scale ceramics production for export to the Islamic world. Finds in South Fujian, for example, demonstrate that this export industry contributed to the country's economic growth during the Song dynasty (960–1276).[45]

Evidence from sunken ships is now yielding important information on the commercial networks connecting China and the Islamic world. The remains of a ship's hull structure, rigging, fittings, or contents – especially its cargo – can indicate where the ship came from and in many cases, where it was headed. This in turn tells us much about patterns of communication and other details of ancient trade involving merchants from these two societies.[46] A ninth-century sunken dhow, found on the Indonesian island of Belitung between Sumatra and Borneo, may provide the earliest evidence for direct trade between China and India and points farther west, and is therefore of potentially far-reaching historical significance.[47] The discoveries of the Song period shipwreck in Quanzhou Bay (Fujian province) and the Yuan period sunken ship in Sinan, Korea, substantiate both the scale of trade in commodities such as ceramics and the descriptions of shipbuilding techniques found in written sources.[48]

Inscriptions discovered in coastal areas comprise another important archaeological source. These document population movements as well as their scale. The early Islamic cemetery in the great port city of Quanzhou, which survives to this day, bears silent witness to these Sino-Muslim contacts. Many of the cemetery's Chinese and Arabic tombstone inscriptions date to the Mongol Yuan period, when Sino-Islamic contact and exchange were at their height.[49] The evidence indicates that many of those buried there were Muslims of Arab-Persian origin, who were active in trade and other forms of cross-cultural interaction with the peoples of China, Central Asia, South Asia, and Southeast Asia.

The Growth of Geographic Knowledge in Three Phases

The present study begins in the year 750, when contact between the Islamic world and China began to flourish, and ends in 1500, when their close economic and cultural exchange was altered by the arrival of the Europeans. The long time frame of this study may remind the reader of Fernand Braudel's (1902–1986) "*la longue durée.*" In his study of the Mediterranean, Braudel explores the "structures" that shape societies and which, unlike political regimes, last for long periods of time.[50] K. N. Chaudhuri, who applied Braudel's theory to the Indian Ocean, used an even longer time frame – the eleven centuries from the rise of Islam (after 631 CE) to 1750 – to explore the unchanging structure of seaborne commerce.[51] Despite the many advantages of this approach in explaining the continuous structural features of the economy and culture in the regions, it does not address other important aspects, such as knowledge transfer, that did change as a result of the dynamic interactions between the two societies. This study, in contrast, emphasizes change over time, specifically by charting the increase in mutual geographic knowledge between the two societies, which in turn led to more contacts.

This book divides its eight-century time frame into three phases, each the subject of two parallel sections: one on the Chinese, the other on the Islamic world. Phase 1 encompasses the pre-Mongol period from 750 to 1260. Phase 2 covers the Mongol period from 1260 to 1368. Phase 3 addresses the post-Mongol era from 1368 to 1500. Each chapter combines a brief historical description of contemporary Sino-Islamic contacts, an analysis of primary sources, and a summary of the key archaeological findings. Taken together, these present a dynamic story of contact as well as the specific conditions that led to the growth of geographic knowledge during these three phases.

Chapters 1 and 2 draw on Chinese, Arabic, and Persian language sources to trace the increase in mutual geographic knowledge during the five centuries of contact between China and the Islamic world from 751 to 1260. This is the period of Tang (618–907) and Song (960–1276) dynastic rule in China and ʿAbbāsid caliphate (750–1258) rule in the Islamic world. Until the late thirteenth century, when the Song and the ʿAbbāsids fell to the Mongols, both enjoyed unprecedented economic growth as well as institutional and cultural development.[52]

As the exchange between the two societies during this period grew, so did the amount of concrete information that authors could provide in their manuscripts as to sailing routes between China and the Persian Gulf, trade goods, history, and customs. By the ninth century, Arabic accounts of China began to appear in large numbers as Arab–Persian Muslims sailed to China and established a permanent base there. For their part, the Tang and Song governments created ever larger special districts in which to house the ever growing foreign population arriving on their shores. These merchants were most likely the best sources of mutual knowledge for China and the Islamic world at that time.

Sources suggest that a new stage in Sino-Islamic contact, brought about by the increase in Chinese maritime trade, began around 1000 CE. Before that year, Arab ships had sailed all the way to China. However, sometime after 900 or 1000 CE, Chinese and Arab vessels began to meet at mid-route shipping centers instead. At the same time, diasporic communities of sojourning Muslims began to take root in South and Southeast Asia. This change contributed greatly to the overall Chinese understanding of Indian Ocean trade and their geographic understanding of the world.

Contact and exchange between China and the Islamic world reached an unprecedented scale in the thirteenth century due to the radical political changes that the Mongols brought to most of Eurasia. With their sudden rise as the continent's dominant political power in the early thirteenth century, the Mongols established a land empire larger than any that had ever existed. The resulting peace revived the overland trade routes, which had been blocked for centuries. Just as important, and often overlooked, was the Mongols' conquest of sedentary societies with naval ports, most importantly China and the Islamic world.

For the first time, China and the Islamic world were integrated politically. In 1260 the brothers Hülegü (1217–1265) and Khubilai (1215–1294, reigned 1260–1294), grandsons of Chinggis Khan, established the Mongol regimes of the Il-khanate (1256–1335) in Iran and the Yuan dynasty (1271–1368) in China, respectively. The two states remained constant allies in the disputes among the Mongol khanates, a fact that strengthened the diplomatic and commercial relations between China and Iran and encouraged scholarly exchange.

Despite their nomadic origin, the two Mongol regimes secured the ports that lay within their two states, and in so doing, took advantage of the opportunity to advance into the sea. Sugiyama Masaaki suggests that this turn to the sea began after the Mongol army met defeat by the Mamlūks at the Battle of ʿAyn Jālūt in 1260, which prevented the Mongols from conquering more land.[53] That same year, supporters in Khuriltai, jockeying for the next grand Khan of the Mongol empire, elected Khubilai, who would devote the energies of his court to advancing international contact and promoting geographic and cartographic projects. Thus, 1260 marks a convenient start date for both the Mongols' full-scale advance toward the sea, and the second phase in the development of contacts between China and the Islamic world from a maritime perspective. Chapters 3 and 4 draw on Chinese, Arabic, and Persian sources to trace the dramatic increase in mutual geographic knowledge that occurred in response to the Pax Mongolica between 1260 to 1368.

The relationship between the Islamic world and China entered a different phase after the fall of the Mongol empire in 1368. The Ming dynasty (1368–1644) governed a united China, while the Timurid dynasty (1369–1506) ruled much of Western and Central Asia, a geopolitical status not unlike that which existed before the rise of the Mongols. Relations between the two societies were often disrupted after the fall of the Mongols, yet other contacts based on the foundations of the earlier legacy continued. In the very last decades of the fourteenth and the first decades of the fifteenth century, relations between China and Central Asia deepened further thanks to the exchange of envoys between the Ming and Timurid courts. Chapter 5 deals with the final years before the arrival of the Europeans in Asia, including the most remarkable among the events that contributed to the increase of geographic knowledge during this period, the seven voyages of Zheng He (1371–1433).

In sum, this study will make use of both diachronic and synchronic comparisons to highlight the scale of contact that developed between China and the Islamic world as well as the dynamic changes in cross-cultural knowledge that took place from the mid-eighth to the fifteenth century. As we observe the gradual development of these contacts over time, it will become clear that the terms "China" and "the Islamic world" do not refer to static geographic entities. Both constantly changed, just as their political realms changed. Although China and the Islamic world once stood at opposite ends of Asia, in time, the Islamic world grew much closer to China through both land and sea routes. Let us begin our study by examining how writers in these two societies began to refine their knowledge about the farthest reaches of the known world.

1

From Imperial Encounter to Maritime Trade

Chinese Understanding of the Islamic World, 750–1260

Introduction

The first extant Chinese account about the Islamic world dates to the mid-eighth century. Du You's (735–812) description of the Arabs in his celebrated *Encyclopedic History of Institutions* (*Tongdian*) reports the most important events that occurred in the course of founding and expanding the Islamic community in West Asia during the early seventh century:

> The country is west of Persia. Others say before this a Persian Arab [Muḥammad] as if with divine aid obtained a sword and killed people. Because he summoned some of the Arabs to join him, eleven men came. Following the order of joining, they encouraged the first one to be appointed king. After this, many gradually joined him, and subsequently they destroyed Persia and defeated Byzantium and the city of India. All they encountered had no way of defeating them. Their troops numbered 420,000. Their nation has existed for 34 years [i.e., starting from 622]. Before this, when the first king [Muḥammad] died, a successor was appointed as head, and the present king is the third successor [i.e., ʿUthmān]. The king belongs to the tribe of the Arabs (Dashi).[1]

Although imprecise, this encyclopedia entry is important because it identifies a new group of people, the Arabs (*Dashi*), and identifies their location and origins somewhere west of Persia. It also identifies the Prophet Muḥammad as the founder of Islam, his growing community of followers, their rise to political power, their conquest of Persia and parts of the Byzantine empire and India, and the election-based succession process following the death of the Prophet. As following pages of this book show, this passage also reports that Muslims pray five times a day at their mosques. Their women are veiled when they go outdoors.[2] They set up the diplomatic relations with the Tang dynasty soon after the Chinese recognized their ascent as a political power. The Chinese documented this knowledge in a detailed section of an encyclopedic history little more than a century after Islam's rise, largely because of one man, Du Huan – a relative of the Chinese encyclopedia's author, Du You. Captured by the ʿAbbāsid army after they defeated the Chinese army at the Battle of Talas (in modern-day Dzhambul, Kazakhstan) in 751, Du was brought to Kūfa, the capital of the ʿAbbāsid empire, where he lived as a prisoner of war for ten years. After his release and return home to China, he recorded his experiences, which his relative used to write his encyclopedia entry. Du You's account reflects one of the most dramatic political encounters in world history, the one between the Tang and the ʿAbbāsid empire, the consequences of which would transform the political, economic, and religious landscape of Central Asia and the Indian Ocean trade networks.

After his decade living in the Islamic world, Du Huan returned to China. He traveled by ship, following the sea route that had begun to boom as a new alternative in pan-Asian travel to the overland Silk Road. This growing sea trade, which metamorphosed into a mostly peaceful commercial relationship, perhaps best illustrates the relationship between China and the Islamic world since the eighth century. Once engaged in the Indian Ocean trade, many merchants from Baghdad followed along the maritime routes until they finally arrived at the Chinese port city of Guangzhou. Many continued on, traveling into the interior to reach the Tang capital of Chang'an in order to seek business opportunities there. These Middle Eastern merchants brought merchandise like peppers and frankincense to trade with Chinese for the high-quality ceramics that were always highly prized in their home countries. Chinese welcomed foreign merchants and their wares, because the cultural and economic prosperity of China under the Tang empire (and the Song after it) generated expansive consumer demands and the wealth necessary to indulge them. Chinese contact with Muslim merchants grew, and as it grew, Chinese came to regard the Muslim homeland as the richest of all foreign countries. This accelerated Chinese understanding of Muslim society and inspired Chinese authors to seek information from the Muslim visitors they encountered in order to try to envisage the Islamic world and describe it to their readers.

This chapter draws on Chinese-language sources in order to understand the increase and character of Chinese knowledge about the Islamic world during the first five centuries of contact between the two societies (between 750 and 1260) before China fell to the Mongol rule. Sources like geographic accounts and maps will help clarify the extent of this knowledge, understand the information the Chinese appeared to seek and why, and measure the impact of contact with the Islamic world on Chinese understanding.

Early Contacts and the First Direct Accounts

Following that model of Sima Qian, whose first-century *Records of the Grand Historian* (*Shiji*) pioneered a new genre of history writing in China, historians of Chinese ruling dynasties developed principles that would govern the creation of a whole category of writing about foreign peoples and geography in imperially sanctioned histories. During the Tang dynasty, the Chinese extended their military power and cultural influence over neighboring countries. It was, according to historians, China's golden age of political strength, economic prosperity, and cultural influence. By that time, the Chinese had firmly established a China-centered "world order" over most of eastern Asia, supported by a tributary system that they used to manage relations with non-Chinese peoples. Historians of the Tang dynasty adopted earlier concepts of distinguishing Chinese and non-Chinese "barbarians" and a systematic categorization of foreign peoples who fall within or outside of the orbit of China's tributary system. They divided non-Chinese into four groups: *Dongyi* or "Eastern Barbarians," *Xirong* or "Western Barbarians," *Nanman* or "Southern Barbarians," and *Beidi* or "Northern Barbarians." Of these four groups, the one that the Chinese had to watch most closely was the *Xirong*, the people who lived beyond China's western border – in other words, the people of eastern Turkestan or further west. The Tang dynasty brought a broad part of this region into its political sphere of influence, and therefore, any changes that occurred in this region could have affected China's dominion over the region. Few events better illustrate the political importance of the western countries to Tang China and the anxiety they could stir than the rise of the Arabs and the expansion of Islamic power into the region. This event was described accurately by Du You, the most authoritative historian of the Tang dynasty.

Du You's *Encyclopedic History of Institutions* is not an official history written for the Chinese imperial court. He compiled it in order to provide a readily accessible collection of extracts from earlier literature and history to writers seeking examples of literary excellence and classical allusions. His encyclopedic concept followed an intellectual trend to categorize and organize knowledge.[3] He also responded to specialist readers: the end of the encyclopedia includes a collection of materials on border defense, as if anticipating the need for information about foreign countries.[4] Du You's section on Dashi (the Arabs or the Muslims) constitutes part of a larger section about the Western Barbarians (*Xirong*), which consists of a broad overview of the political situations in the region and specific entries about individual groups or countries. Unlike the official histories of the Tang dynasty, whose authors in the later Song dynasty wrote about events centuries after the fact,[5] Du You wrote about the people of the west as current events, utilizing contemporary accounts to construct his encyclopedia entries. His text, considered the most representative geographic account of the Tang dynasty period from a state official's perspective, provides a capsule history of Arabia, including its basic geographical features, products, and customs, as seen in the same passage on the people of Dashi:[6]

> The men of the land have large, long noses and are dark-skinned and heavily bearded, like Indians. The women are dignified and beautiful.[7] Their writing system differs from that of the Persians. They raise camels, horses, donkeys, mules, sheep, and other animals. The soil has much sand and is not suitable for cultivation. They do not have the five grains of rice, millet, beans, wheat and barnyard millet, but only eat the meat of camels, horses, and other similar animals. It was only when they had defeated Persia and Byzantium that they obtained rice and baked goods. They worship the god of Heaven.[8]

An important feature in Du You's account is that he clearly distinguishes the Arabs from the Persians, a people with whom China enjoyed limited contact for several centuries.[9] Despite some exaggeration, the passage characterizes the nomadic nature of the Arabs' lifestyle in the Arabian Desert before they began political expansion into neighboring countries. In keeping with the compilation's structure, the passage on the Arabs is preceded by a short sentence that describes the country's diplomatic relations with China: "It is said that the Arabs sent an envoy to present tribute to the Tang in the Yonghui period [650–655, probably in 655]."[10] Official histories compiled by later dynasties also show that the Muslim envoys began to come to China several times after the mid-seventh century. Some envoys provided Chinese officials with information about their country during their visits. One envoy to the Tang court in 651 (or 655) reported that thirty-six years had passed since his country was established and that changes had occurred among their political leaders, the caliphs.

Although Du You's overview contains accurate information, it also reveals how differently Chinese viewed the Islamic world. This is clear in

Du You's final paragraph, which hints about the Chinese geographic perception of the Arabs, their country, and the world beyond:

> It is also said that their king [of the country of Dashi] always sends men on ships with clothing and provisions, and they cross the sea for eight years but do not reach the western shore. In the sea is a square rock on which are trees with red branches and green leaves. On the trees are born many young children 6–7 *cun* [Approximately 15 cm (1 cun = 2.25 cm)] long. When they see people, they do not speak but all can laugh and move their hands and feet. Their heads are attached to the branches of the tree. When people pick them from trees, the [heads] come off in their hands, then dry up and turn black. The envoy took one branch and returned with it. It is now in the residence of the Arabian king.[11]

Here, "the sea" that the Arabs crossed to reach the western shore could have meant "the Western Sea" (*Xihai*), a name that often appears in early accounts beginning with Sima Qian, and which scholars regarded as a central geographic location in the western regions. The modern sea the passage indicates is vague and differs from other accounts of the same place. In Du You's passage, the Western Sea constituted the most remote place that people could reach. Later sources help identify this sea more concretely as the northwestern part of the Indian Ocean including the Persian Gulf, the Red Sea, and the Arabian Sea. The previous account by Du You about the western lands mixes fact with fantasy that includes a description of children hanging from trees. Still, Du You maintained his authority among Chinese readers because such fancy recurs in later Chinese accounts.

Du You's *Encyclopedic History of Institutions* stands out among Chinese accounts written during the Tang dynasty period because it contains realistic descriptions of foreign lands derived directly from eyewitness reports. Typical works of this genre tended to rely on less reliable secondhand information. For example, Du You allotted three times as much space to reprint a passage from the eyewitness account Du Huan, forgoing a long explanation of his relative's trip as compilers often did. He does, however, provide a brief overview:

> My relative Huan followed Go Seonji [Tang general of Goguryeo (Korean) descent; Gao Xianzhi in Chinese, died 755], the military commissioner of Zhenxi (modern Xinjiang), to go on a western expedition. In the tenth year of Tianbao (751) he reached the Western Sea. At the beginning of the Baoying reign (761) he boarded a merchant ship and returned [to China] through Guangzhou, and wrote his *Travel Record*.[12]

How fortunate that Du You received this account from such a reliable source. Du You does not explain why Du Huan traveled to the Western

Sea, but the fact that Du Huan accompanied Go Seonji on his western expedition hints that he was taken captive when the Tang general's army was defeated by the ʿAbbāsid at the Battle of Talas in 751.

At the Battle of Talas, more than a century of westward expansion by the Tang dynasty began to decline.[13] Starting in the 630s, the armies of the Tang conquered territory in present-day Xinjiang in northwestern China. Early in their reign, Tang emperors sent envoys to the lands beyond the Pamir Plateau into Central Asia. Soon western states like the country of Shi (modern Tashkent) sent envoys to the Tang capital to present tribute. Soon after, however, the armies of the Islamic caliphates rapidly spread from the Middle East. After they defeated the Sassanid empire (in modern-day Iran) in 651, Muslim armies moved into Central Asia, threatening Tang supremacy over the region. The Muslim and Tang armies then engaged in a complicated political contest for dominance over Central Asia's Silk Roads as well as other kingdoms like those ruled by the Tibetans and the Turks.[14] Then, in 751, the armies of these two expansionist powers finally collided at Talas. This is the first military encounter between China and the Islamic world verified by sources in both societies.

Chinese and Arabic sources contain conflicting information about the Battle of Talas. Chinese sources report that the Tang dynasty attacked the country of Shi with an army of 20,000.[15] The ʿAbbāsids, they say, intervened on the side of the Shi. With the Karluks rallied behind the Tang, the contest seemed evenly matched. Five days later, however, the Karluks suddenly switched sides. Having lost their key ally, the Tang armies suffered defeat. Islamic sources, however, offer a different explanation. The battle occurred, they say, because supporters of the recently overthrown Umayyad dynasty rebelled against their ʿAbbāsid conquerors in Bukhara and Sogdiana. The Tang army aided the Umayyad and their supporters. In response, the ʿAbbāsid army challenged the Tang, killing 50,000 Chinese soldiers and capturing 20,000 prisoners of war.[16]

In the long run, the battle did not affect the relationship between the two countries. According to the Tang official histories, the ʿAbbāsid caliphate continued to send envoys to the Tang court, and the Tang government asked the ʿAbbāsid to send troops to the emperor's aid when the devastating An Lushan Rebellion occurred in 755.[17] Even so, the Battle of Talas carries great significance in the history of contact between the two societies. According to an Arabic source, Chinese prisoners of war introduced the art of papermaking to the Islamic world. After the first paper mill was founded in Baghdad in 794–795, paper and the art of papermaking flourished throughout the Islamic world. Paper replaced papyrus (which is fragile) and parchment (which is expensive) as the primary medium for writing, facilitating the subsequent growth of books and libraries.[18]

No Chinese source explicitly mentions the transfer of papermaking by Chinese prisoners of war. Yet a passage in Du Huan's account suggests that such a transmission was indeed possible, because Du reports encounters with several Chinese crafts people living in the ʿAbbāsid world: "Chinese craftsmen originated the crafts of fine silk weaving, gold and silver working, and painting. Painters there [in the ʿAbbāsid society] are Fan Shu and Liu Ci from Chang'an and silk weavers are Yue Huan and Lü Li from Hedong [Taiyuan in Shanxi?]."[19] These Chinese – probably, like Du Huan, prisoners of war – contributed to the formation of an Arab stereotype that all Chinese were good at crafts. Contemporary Arabic sources, as we will see in the next chapter, regularly allude to the superiority of Chinese craftsmanship.

Returning Chinese brought information about the Islamic world home with them to China. The sections from Du Huan's account quoted in Du You's *Encyclopedic History of Institutions* include passages that provide geographic information about the Islamic world and nearby places. The surviving snippets provide a nearly complete picture of Du Huan's travel routes: from Bahanna (modern-day Fergana, Uzbekistan, a Central Asian country near Talas) along overland routes through Samarkand to the ʿAbbāsid caliphate in Iraq. Du returned to China via Sri Lanka by sea.[20] The longest and the most concrete description of the places he visited in his account of the heart of the Islamic world is the section written about the Arabs or more specifically the ʿAbbāsid caliphate. The passage reads:

> Dashi is also called Ajuluo [Akula (i.e., Kūfa, modern-day Iraq)]. The king of Dashi is called Mu-men [i.e., the Caliph Amir al-Mu'minin], and he has made this place his capital. The gentlemen and women of this place are tall and well-built. They wear fine and clean garments, and their manners are gentle and elegant. When women go outdoors, they must cover up their faces with veils. Five times a day all the people, whether humble or noble, pray to Heaven. They eat meat as a religious observance, and they consider killing animals merit-worthy. They wear silver belts decorated with silver knives. They prohibit wine and music. When they quarrel, they do not come to blows.
>
> There is also a prayer hall which holds tens of thousands. Every seven days the king attends the prayers, mounts a high seat and expounds the religious law to the people, saying: "Men's life is very hard; this is a way of Heaven that would not change. If you commit one of the following

> crimes – lewdness, kidnapping, robbery, mean actions, slander, self-gratification at the expense of others, cheating the poor and oppressing the humble – your sins are among the most heinous. Those who are killed in battle by the enemy will be reborn in Heaven; those who kill the enemy will enjoy unlimited good fortune (on Earth)."
>
> A large territory came under the king's rule, and the number of those who follow him is increasing incessantly. The law is lenient and funerals are frugal.[21]

This description clearly suggests the most important historical fact about this foreign land: The ʿAbbāsid caliphate ruled its empire according to the principles of Islam. This is one of the earliest accounts by anyone from another society reporting about the religious and political order of Islamic society. It predates the ninth and the tenth centuries when *Sharia* (Islamic principles and laws based on the Qurʾān) and the *Sunnah* (Muslim tradition, the sum of collected hadīth) was codified by Islamic scholars, the *ulama*.

His vivid description suggests the possibility that Du Huan witnessed much of what he describes in his report because the core content is quite accurate. For example, he identifies Dashi with Kūfa, which was indeed the capital of the ʿAbbāsid caliphate when he was brought to the city. Kūfa was one of the earliest urban Arab settlements, emerging during the early years of Arab expansion under the first caliphates and the Umayyad dynasty that followed. In the course of their revolt against the Umayyads in the mid-eighth century, the ʿAbbāsids took Kūfa and made it their capital in 749, two years before Du Huan's arrival. Soon afterward, in 762, the ʿAbbāsids shifted their capital to Baghdad. The prayer hall that Du Huan describes must have been the Great Mosque of Kūfa where the caliph went every Friday to lead his subjects in prayers. As one of the earliest mosques in Islam, the Great Mosque of Kūfa was constructed in the middle of the seventh century. Early accounts of the mosque include the chronicle of al-Ṭabarī, who describes its grand audience hall with marble columns and room to accommodate 60,000 people.[22] Du Huan summarizes the king's sermon, which contains some of Islam's important principles written in the Qurʾān, *Sunnah*, and *Sharia*.[23]

Du Huan's account continues:

> Within the city walls, in the villages, all of the earth's products are here. Nothing is lacking. It is the hub of the four quarters. Thousands of varieties of merchandise have been brought here in immense quantities and are sold at very low prices. Silk and embroideries, pearls and shells are piled up in the markets. Camels and horses, donkeys and mules jam the streets

> and alleys. Dwelling houses and other buildings are carved of stone-honey [earth bricks?] and resemble Chinese carriages. On each festival, the nobles are presented with glass work, porcelain, brass, bottles and jugs in enormous quantities.

Du Huan's description of the economically thriving villages in the ʿAbbāsid empire sheds light on the trade activities of the Islamic world. There, merchants sell many local products, he reports, but the merchandise brought from other places captures everyone's attention. Most of the goods that Du Huan lists, such as silk, pearls, shells, and porcelain, appear frequently in contemporary Chinese and Arabic accounts that discuss foreign trades. Glasswork was a major art commodity in the Islamic world, developed from traditions that date back to late antiquity. Glassware of different shapes and colors dating to the early Islamic period (seventh to eleventh centuries) and shards of porcelains imported from China have been excavated from local archaeological sites. Together, texts and artifacts help us to imagine the luxuries of the wealthy people living in the urban center of the Islamic world at that time.[24] Du Huan does not mention trade with China, yet leaves no doubt that China, the world's only porcelain manufacturer, exported to the Middle East by sea.

Du Huan shows a keen interest in comparing local products with those in China:

> Fine rice and baked goods are [here] as in China. Fruits include peaches and thousand-year-old dates, with roots as large as a *tou* [a measuring cup: 1.9*l*], with a beautiful flavor. Other vegetables are like other countries. Their big grapes are like chicken eggs. Two fragrant oils are expensive, one called Yeseman [Jasmin], the other Moniushi. There are two fragrant plants, one called Chasaibeng, the other Libuba.

This account and following passages about domestic animals like camels, horses, and ostriches typify Chinese writing about foreign places. In general, Du Huan keeps descriptions brief and devoid of personal feeling in accord with the traditions of this genre of Chinese writing. The passages remain rich enough in content, however, to highlight most of the key issues important to understand a foreign society. For example, the section about the Arabs ends with a brief description of their history: "Now they [the Arabs] have destroyed and swallowed forty to fifty states, all of which are subject to them. They divide their soldiers into many places to protect them, and their territory extends all the way to the Western Sea."

This passage illustrates the extent of Du Huan's knowledge about Islamic history and geography. As Du Huan correctly noticed, by the mid-eighth century, Islamic armies had conquered the Arabian Peninsula,

Iraq, and Iran, and reached Central Asia to the east and the Iberian Peninsula to the west. Under the Umayyads and ʿAbbāsids, the Arabs stationed their armies and imperial administration in major cities to manage an empire that extended all the way to "the Western Sea," which Du Huan himself visited. Judging from his itineraries, Du's Western Sea probably meant the Persian Gulf, which was the closest ocean body to Kūfa.

This early Chinese account demonstrates remarkably accurate and rich knowledge about the Islamic world. As was often the case, Chinese authors continually copied from Du You's encyclopedia, and therefore this account established the foundation for Chinese learning about the Islamic world in later periods. Later Chinese sources such as the *Imperially Reviewed Encyclopedia of the Taiping Era* (*Taiping yulan*) compiled in 984 all cite and favorably comment on Du Huan's account.[25]

The extent of Chinese knowledge about the Islamic world during this early period helps us to understand the political relationship that existed between China and the Islamic world during their initial, formative stage of contact. The ʿAbbāsid caliphate was a newly ascending power along China's western frontier. China had limited political contact with the country, with the notable exception of the Battle of Talas. The rebellion of An Lushan, which lasted from 755 to 763 and seems to have involved the ʿAbbāsid army, forced China's imperial government to withdraw its troops from Central Asia. Powerful nomadic states such as the kingdom of Tufan (modern-day Tibet) arose in Central Asia as a result.[26] This situation caused the overland routes that had been the main passageway between China and the Islamic world to decline. It also led to a gradual disappearance of non-Chinese groups like the merchant Sogdians as middlemen between Chinese and Islamic societies along the overland routes that connected them.[27] Contact between the two societies entered a new phase, however, with the success of maritime routes.[28]

Like Du Huan, who returned to China by ship, Chinese and Muslims turned increasingly to travel between China and the Islamic world by sea. As a result, maritime trade began to surpass overland trade in both volume and importance. As maritime trade flourished, Chinese geographic knowledge of the Islamic world grew to a new level.

Maritime Traffic between the Islamic World and the Tang (618–907) China and Jia Dan's Routes

Contemporary accounts and archeological sources demonstrate that maritime trade between China and West Asia dramatically increased after the

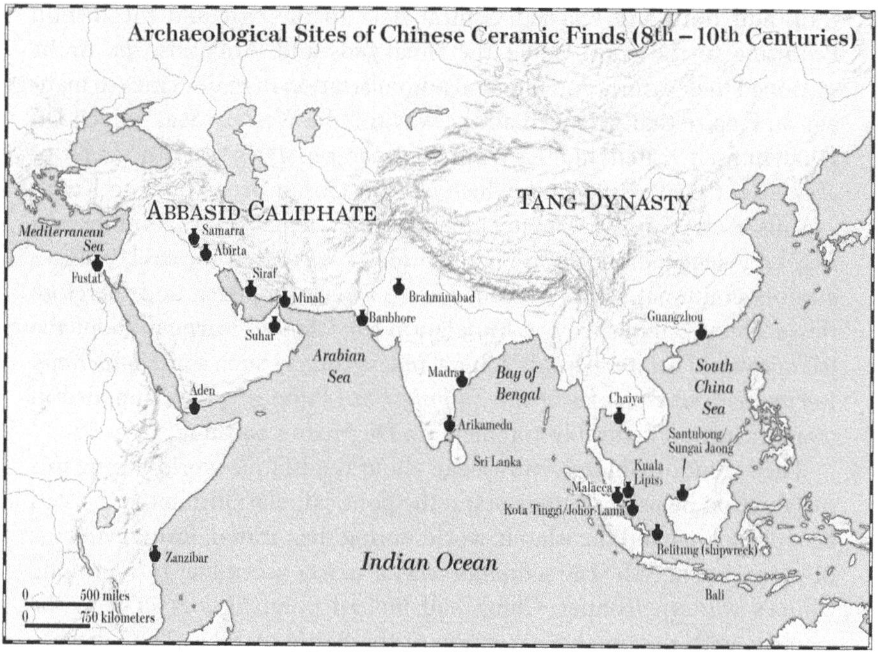

FIGURE 1.1. Archeological sites containing Chinese ceramics, dated 8th–10th centuries.

middle of the eighth century. Tang dynasty navigators inherited knowledge about other places, routes, ships, and navigation from mariners of the previous periods, and further developed this knowledge to a more advanced level. Archaeological excavations that sit along the old routes from Guangzhou to the Persian Gulf via the Indian Ocean testify to the growth in maritime contacts that occurred from the eighth century onward. Remarkably, archaeologists have found many Chinese ceramics that date to the eighth through tenth centuries – the era of the Tang and Five Dynasties – along the coastline of the Indian Ocean. If one draws a line connecting all the sites in West Asia where Tang Chinese ceramics have been found, it would connect Guangzhou with Zanzibar and go through the ports of Indonesia, Arikamedu in Madras, India; Banbhore in Pakistan; and Aden, Suhar, and Sīrāf in the Persian Gulf (see Figure 1.1).[29]

These discoveries testify to the fact that West Asia, set at the farthest western side of the Indian Ocean commercial sphere, was an important consumer of Chinese ceramics.[30]

Extant sources before 1000 CE suggest that most of the traders who shipped ceramics from China to the western Indian Ocean were

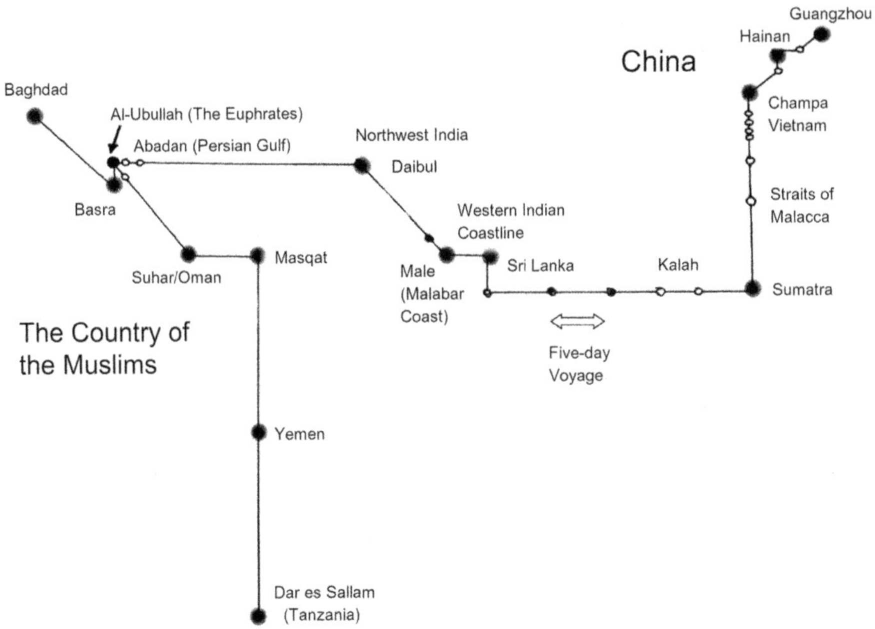

FIGURE 1.2. The route from Guangzhou to foreign countries as envisioned by Jia Dan (circa 800).

merchants from the Islamic world. As they sailed along the coast between China and the Islamic world, they probably provided information about sailing routes and trade goods with the Chinese they encountered. Only one such short account – "The Route to the Foreign Countries across the Sea from Guangzhou" (Guangzhou tong haiyi dao) compiled around 800 by Jia Dan (729–805) – survives today. Court historians included it in the geography (*dili*) section of the *New History of the Tang Dynasty*.[31]

Geography first appears as a topic of interest to Chinese scholars in *The Records of the Grand Historian* and the next official history, Ban Gu's *History of the Former Han* (*Hanshu*), includes the first monograph on administrative geography.[32] Since then, most official histories followed suit.[33] By including this section, Chinese scholars sought to give a concise yet comprehensive geography of China and its neighboring regions. Jia Dan, for example, was a prime minister and renowned geographer. According to his biography in the *New History of the Tang Dynasty*, although interested in geography since childhood, he himself never traveled to foreign countries.[34] Yet, while he was serving as a minister of the State Ceremonial (*Honglü si*), which received visitors to the imperial capital from foreign countries, he collected information in order to write geographic descriptions about various regions. One of his extant accounts, called "The Route from Guangzhou," is the earliest extant document from either China or the Islamic world that describes the maritime route between Guangzhou and the Persian Gulf.[35] The short account provides a detailed navigational itinerary for a ship starting from Guangzhou and sailing through Southeast and South Asia to the country of Dashi, the ʿAbbāsid caliphate. It gives practical guidance to sailors, providing directions and estimating the time required to travel from one port to the next until they reach the Islamic world. Jia Dan identifies these networked stopover ports by country names, although many of these countries were in fact city-states or cities that served regional regimes as their delegated ports-of-trade (see Figure 1.2).

Chinese had known about the sailing route from China to the southernmost border of southern India through Southeast Asia since the Han period (206 BCE–220 CE). Trade and later religious exchanges between China and India inspired Chinese interest in the region.[36] Jia Dan's itinerary extended beyond this, reaching the country of Tiyu (Daibul) on the northwest coast of the Indian subcontinent centered on the estuary of the Indus River. From there, travelers continued westward for another twenty days until they reached the country of Tilaluhua (Dierrarah) in the vicinity of modern-day Abadan in the Persian Gulf, which then functioned as the entry point to the heart of the ʿAbbāsid realm:

> ...[After] one more day going westward, one reaches the country of Wula (al-Ubullah), where the Fulila River (the Euphrates) of the country of Arabs [or, more inclusively, Muslims] flows southward and enters the sea. Small boats going two days upstream reach the country of Moluo (Basra), an important town in the country of the Arabs. Traveling again overland in a northwesterly direction for a thousand *li*, one reaches the city of Fuda (Baghdad), capital of the king Maomen (the Caliph Amir al-Mu'minin).[37]

Jia Dan's route, which began at Guangzhou (the most important Chinese port city at that time), utilized a series of city-ports to reach Baghdad, the capital city of the ʿAbbāsid caliphate. A few decades earlier, al-Manṣūr (the second ʿAbbāsid caliph), boasted soon after building the new capital Baghdad in 762: "Here's the Tigris, with nothing between us and China, and on it arrives all that the sea can bring. ..."[38]

Jia Dan's text clearly explains that when people go from the southeast coast of India to al-Ubullah (in Tigris delta; east of Basra), they follow the eastern coast of the sea (the western Indian Ocean); along the western coast of that sea sits the Arabian Peninsula, which belongs to the country of the Arabs. Here the continuous line from China to the Persian Gulf abruptly ends and the text introduces another route from the country of Sanlan (Bandar al-Salām in Tanzania) at the southwestern horizon of the Arab world. From there, he reports, one travels directly north for twenty days to reach the country of She (modern al-Schehr in the southern part of Yemen) and ten more days to the country of Sayiquhuajie (modern Shāriqah in the southeast Oman, or Masqat), which borders the western coast of the sea. Then, after traveling west for one more day, one can arrive at the country of Meixun (Mezoen, modern Schar in Oman?) and northwest to the country of Balihemonan (Manama in modern Bahrain?) until one reaches al-Ubullah, the final destination of the route from China. This route connected Islamized North and East Africa to the Arabian Peninsula, and helped to integrate these regions into the entire Indian Ocean system of sea travel and trade in which the Muslim merchants played a dominant role.

Jia Dan's use of route itineraries and place names demonstrate a new systematic and practical geography of the Islamic world not found in the accounts of Du You and Du Huan. Jia Dan probably compiled "The Route from Guangzhou" for governmental consumption, and he obviously based it on real knowledge that circulated among those who had personally experienced the sailing routes or who had spoken with those who had. Who were Jia Dan's informants? Jia Dan divides the Arabian Sea into two separate itineraries: (1) from the South Indian coast to al-Ubullah on the Persian Gulf and (2) from the East African coast to al-Ubullah. Al-Ubullah and Sīrāf (another Persian Gulf base for seagoing vessels departing for the Far East) acted as connecting points for the variety of overseas itineraries that existed. Jia Dan's informants for his set of itineraries must have come mostly from merchants from the Persian Gulf region who had traveled to China and India. At that time, navigators based in Middle Eastern ports-of-trade did not sail directly across the Indian Ocean from the Red Sea region, but first sailed north to the Persian Gulf, then navigated east to India's northwest coastline, and continued their voyage down India's western coast with a series of stopovers in networked ports-of-trade near India's southern tip before sailing on to China via Southeast Asia. This itinerary can be verified by the first Arabic geographic accounts that initially appear in the mid-ninth century, half a century after Jia Dan compiled his studies, and corroborate his claims (see Map 1). Desiring the luxury articles that came with them by sea, the Tang government allowed merchants from the Islamic world free access to China and even granted them self-governing districts in important ports like Guangzhou. Foreign merchants profiled these cities in their descriptions of sailing routes, as Chapter 2 shows.[39] Even though merchants from the Islamic world appear to have possessed knowledge about these sailing routes first, this Chinese account is the earliest extant source of its kind.

Jia Dan's "Route from Guangzhou" clearly illustrates how sailors transferred knowledge from the Islamic world to China and how officials recorded it. The mapping of places and itineraries in the geography section of the Tang official history shows how Chinese perceived the geography of the Islamic world at a time when their relationship was forming a new axis through the maritime routes. At an earlier stage of development, this type of descriptive geography was probably easier to both document sufficiently and circulate widely. At the same time, Chinese mapmakers worked to depict China and the world at large, including the Islamic world.

The Wider World in Surviving Chinese Maps

Jia Dan became well known for another work, the *Map of Chinese and Non-Chinese Territories in the World* (*Hainei huayi tu*). [40] Unfortunately, this allegedly global map no longer exists. In fact, no maps made of China proper or foreign regions during the first millennium survive. However, evidence does hint at what the map looked like. A passage in *The New History of the Tang* reports that the map was large, approximately nine meters in width and ten in length.[41] Considering his high position in the government and proven geographic expertise evident in "The Route from Guangzhou," Jia Dan probably produced the map on behalf of the Tang government, and there is little doubt that the map contained rich geographic information from foreign sources. Some maps that survive from the later Song period acknowledge that their creators drew from Jia Dan's world map. This is fortunate, because it means that we can use these later maps to develop a hypothetical reconstruction of the map and the Chinese image of the world during the early centuries of the Sino-Muslim relationship.

The earliest surviving map that reveals Jia Dan's unambiguous influence is the "General Survey Map of Chinese and Non-Chinese Territories from the Past through the Present" (Gujin huayi quyu zongyao tu). It was part of a wood-block printed atlas of forty-four maps entitled *Handy Geographical Maps throughout the Ages* (*Lidai dili zhizhang tu*), which dates to circa 1098–1100.[42] As the map's title shows, *The General Survey* presents the geographical, historical, and administrative sites that were important to Chinese at this time. One can only assume that the map represents the sum of geographic knowledge that existed in China at the time Jia Dan produced it. A note placed in the upper–left side of the map lists place-names of the western regions, some of which, it explains, had been conquered by Tang Taizong (reigned 626–649) and his successor Tang Gaozong (reigned 649–683) when they led China on an unprecedented campaign of political expansion to the west. The conquered sites include Kucha, Wusun, Loulan, Kashgar, Shache, and Khotan in Central Asia.[43] A separate set of annotations attached to the map provides further geographic information that served as a foundation for this map; among the hundreds of foreign place-names it lists are Bosi (Persia) and Dashi (Arabia) in West Asia.[44] It also states that the map provides only the most important names out of hundreds of the foreign places known to Jia Dan and listed on his map.

Two other maps drawn at a later time probably also based their information on Jia Dan's map. These two separate maps are engraved on opposite sides of a stone tablet inscribed in 1136. The map on the face of the stele is called *The Tracks of Yu* (*Yuji tu*); the map on the back is called *The Map of Chinese and Non-Chinese Territories* (*Huayi tu*) (see Figure 1.3).[45]

Together with the other maps in the atlas, the *Tracks of Yu* and *Map of Chinese and Non-Chinese Territories* are among the earliest surviving maps that portray all of China. Additionally, *The Tracks of Yu* is the earliest extant map to use a grid. The map's text explains that the grid served as a general measure of distance, where "[the side of] each square converts to one hundred *li*."[46] The map proves that Chinese cartographers practiced a high level of mapmaking techniques and mapped their own territory with accuracy that was unparalleled for its time. Scholars today credit the development of this grid system to Pei Xiu (224–271CE), considered "the father of geography" because he created systematic principles for drawing precise maps that Jia Dan and later Chinese geographers adopted.[47] The next prominent geographer to follow Pei Xiu's principles was Jia Dan, who valued much of drawing precisely measured maps.[48] We can, therefore, assume that Jia Dan also used a grid system for his precise mapmaking reflected in *The Tracks of Yu*.

Although *The Tracks of Yu* provides a fairly precise sketch of China's coastline all the way to Indochina and outlines its river systems,[49] it does not contain specific geographic information about foreign places. In contrast, *The Map of Chinese and Non-Chinese Territories* lists

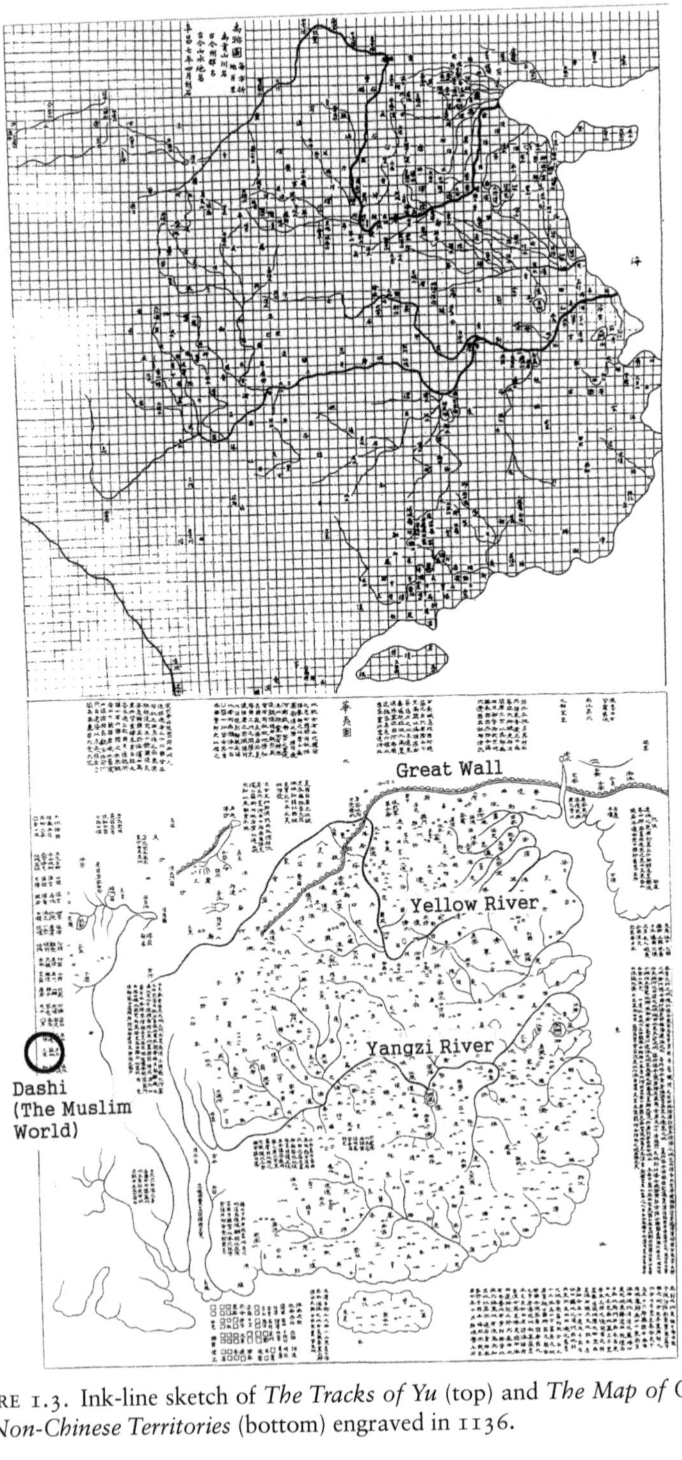

FIGURE 1.3. Ink-line sketch of *The Tracks of Yu* (top) and *The Map of Chinese and Non-Chinese Territories* (bottom) engraved in 1136.

foreign place-names on its margins.[50] Interestingly, an annotation at the bottom–right corner of the map reports that the mapmaker took the place-names for well-known foreign sites from Jia Dan's *Map of Chinese and Non-Chinese Territories in the World*. Recall a similar statement in the note on the "General Survey Map of Chinese and Non-Chinese Territories from the Past through the Present." These two notes from two different maps serve as two independent pieces of evidence that Jia Dan's *Map of Chinese and Non-Chinese Territories in the World* was both large and comprehensive, and served as the foundation for all later Chinese maps of China and foreign countries. Since a more expanded version of the *Map of Chinese and Non-Chinese Territories* was drawn during the Tang dynasty when China was outward-looking and welcomed foreigners in its territory, Jia Dan's map may have contained even more information about foreign places than the evidence reveals. We cannot be sure if his map actually contained all seven of the routes to China that he describes verbally in a surviving written source, one of which being "The Route from Guangzhou." However, sources from the Tang period show that many maps about foreign territories existed then, including a map of India brought to China by Wang Xuance (flourished seventh century) after he traveled to India as a diplomat. Unfortunately, all of these Tang maps are lost. Yet the maps that do exist, although created in a later era, reflect the geographic knowledge of Tang mapmakers like Jia Dan.

Although many people viewed stone tablet maps on the spot, most individuals probably viewed them through reproductions made by rubbings. An important Song period source called *Sea of Jade* (*Yuhai*) by Wang Yinglin (1223–96), for example, claims that the Song dynasty emperor Xiaozong (reigned 1162–89) tried to copy *The Map of Chinese and Non-Chinese Territories* onto a folding screen in his palace.[51] Although we do not know whether this map was indeed a copy of the stone original, we can assume that maps with the same title and similar contents circulated widely via reproductions.

Even though reproducing maps using ink rubbings certainly increased the circulation of maps and their knowledge, they were no match for wood-block printing. Most of the Chinese maps from the Song period are wood-block prints, many of which survived in books that circulated widely through numerous reprints. The earliest surviving wood-block printed maps are those found in the *Handy Geographical Maps throughout the Ages* of the late eleventh century.[52] No one knows how many different versions of the atlas were produced over time, but there were many, according to Song period references.[53] The atlas, along with other geographic classics, became required reading for those preparing for the civil service examinations beginning in the Song period.[54] All evidence suggests that the maps were printed many times over and circulated widely among literati, confirming that Chinese shared this kind of geographic knowledge about their country widely by this time. Some of them probably paid attention to prominent foreign countries as well, like Persia and Arabia.

Although map production lay largely in the hands of the government during the Tang and early Song dynasties, this trend changed by the eleventh and twelfth centuries, when map production became largely the domain of local elites. This led to a gradual increase in geographic knowledge about a wider range of geographic regions and distributed more broadly among different classes of people.[55] Maps were produced using newly circulated information. For example, while the map collection that apparently circulated widely among Confucian scholars limited its presentation of foreign places to the margins of its maps, two other maps made by Buddhist scholars emphasized territories outside China. The two maps, the "Map of the States in the Western Regions in the Han Dynasty" (Han xiyu zhuguo tu) and the "Map of the Five Indian States in the West" (Xitu wuyin zhi tu), were included in the *General Records of the Founders of Buddhism* (*Fozu tongji*), a chronicle of Buddhist history from 581 to 960 CE that followed the format of Chinese official histories.[56] It was written by the Song Buddhist monk and scholar Zhipan, and printed in wood-block form between 1265 and 1270 (see Figure 1.4).[57]

The "Map of the States in the Western Regions in the Han Dynasty" is a map of the western regions as the Chinese knew them during the Han period. Although simple in form, the map covers a broad scope that includes countries west of China by following the route that starts at Wuwei in Gansu and continues into Central Asia and the Middle East. It presents the most important places that Chinese envoys explored and wrote about during the Han dynasty, such as Qiuci (Kucha), Wusun, Dayuan (Ferghana, Uzbekistan), Tiaozhi, Anxi (the Parthian empire and Mesopotamia), and Daqin (the Byzantine empire). It identifies the important mountains in this region such as Congling (the Pamir Mountains), Tian Shan (the Tian Shan Mountain of today's Xinjiang), and Xihai (Western Sea; either the Persian Gulf or Mediterranean Sea). Zhipan (or the map's cartographer) drew the map based on earlier descriptions of western countries in the imperial histories of the Han dynasty.[58] Country locations are plotted with relative accuracy when compared to written geographic sources. Place-names of countries like the Parthian empire,

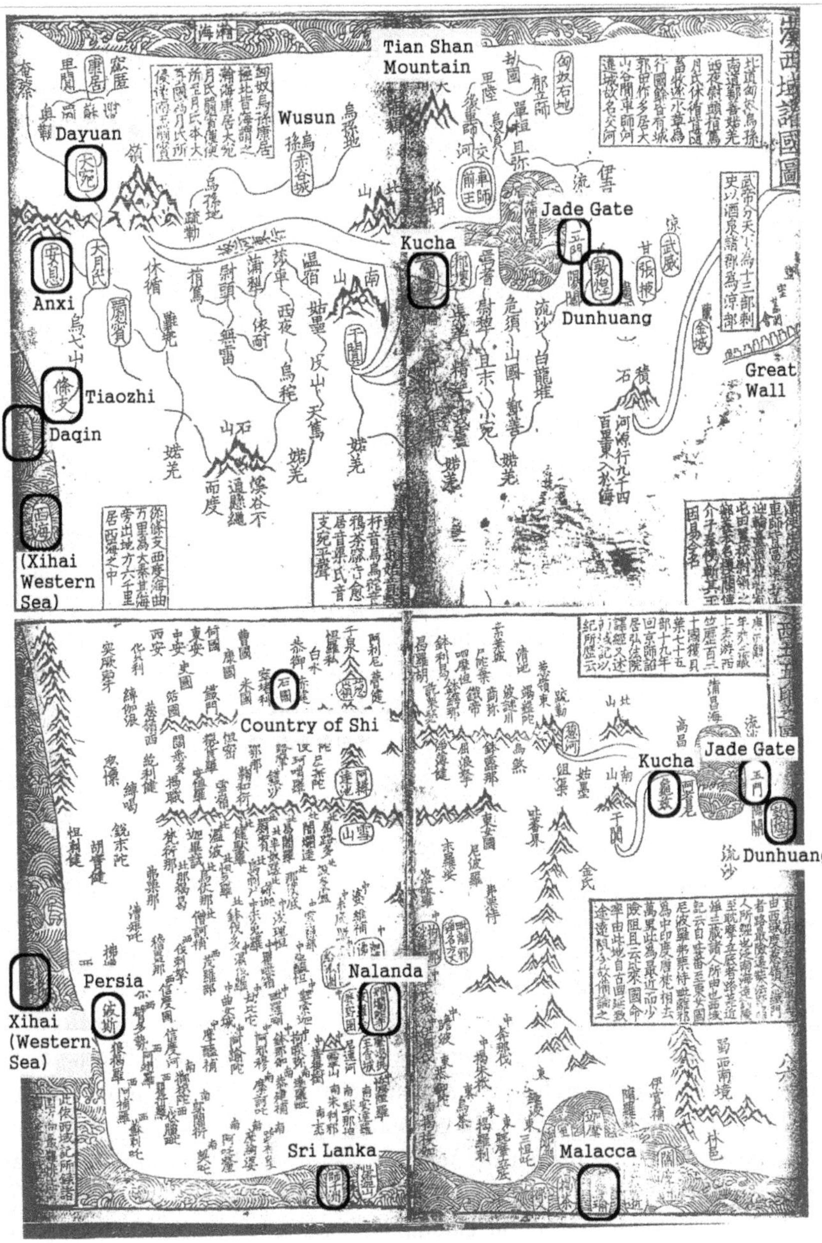

FIGURE 1.4. The "Map of the States in the Western Regions in the Han Dynasty" (top) and the "Map of the Five Indian States in the West" (bottom) from Zhipan's *General Records of the Founders of Buddhism* (circa 1270).

Note: ZGDJ/Yuan, Maps 153, 154. Originals in the National Library of China. Also see Zhipan (13th century), Fozu tongji (Yangzhou, 1991), 32:6l–7r, 9l–10r.

long since fallen from use in China, contain no information about the Islamic world contemporaneous to the time it was made. Still, this map is significant as the earliest extant map in the history of Chinese cartography to graphically portray the overland routes to all the countries of the western regions, which previously had only been described in written, rather than illustrated, form. Clearly, Buddhist mapmakers had more interest in visualizing territories beyond China than their contemporaries and predecessors did.

The other map included in Zhipan's work, the "Map of the Five Indian States in the West," betrays the Buddhist author's direct interest in the land of his religion, Tianzhu or India.[59] It maps places in Central Asia and India that the famous Tang dynasty monk Xuanzang (602/603?–664 CE) visited during his nineteen-year trip to India in the mid-seventh century. This map's outer edges are framed by well-known sites: to the east of Yumen Pass (Jade Gate), the name of a pass located to the west of Dunhuang that led into foreign lands; to the west, the Mediterranean Sea; to the south, the Indian Ocean; and to the north, Central Asia's states like Anguo or Bukhara. Text set in the upper–right corner of the map says that Xuanzang traveled to India in 629, acquired Buddhist sutras in the course of his travel through 130 countries, and returned to Chang'an in 645. When he returned, Emperor Taizong ordered Xuanzang to report what he observed and experienced during his journey in exchange for permission to translate sutras from Sanskrit into Chinese. Text located in the bottom–left corner also lists place-names based on *The Great Tang Records on the Western Regions* (*Da Tang Xiyou ji*), a narrative of Xuanzang's nineteen-year journey through Chang'an to India between 626 and 645.[60] The map remains true to the original narrative. The map shows all the holy places Xuanzang visited and where he sojourned to study Buddhism including Nalanda (Nalanda Buddhist Academy). Further explanation about Xuanzang's travel routes are shown on the map's middle–right side: "There are three routes including overland and sea routes to go to India[61] from the eastern land, that is, China." Among the 170 locations listed on the map are places in Southeast Asia like the island of Sumatra; in Central Asia, the regions of Talas and Afghanistan; in South Asia, countries like Sri Lanka, Nepal, and Pakistan; and in West Asia, places such as Iran, the Persian Gulf, and the eastern Mediterranean coast. The map bears realistic features such as a clear coastline outlining the triangular-shaped Indian subcontinent (it becomes most easily seen when the map is rotated slightly counter-clockwise). The Chinese Buddhist author probably presented the subcontinent in a rectangular form in order to illustrate the Chinese conception of a rectangular-shaped world.[62]

Although it bears realistic information about place-names and locations of India and surrounding countries, Zhipan's map still represents a Buddhist perspective. At the approximate center of the map lies the lake Anavatapta, located at the center of Jambudvīpa (*Zhanbu zhou*), the world of human beings according to Buddhism.[63] In fact, this peculiarly Buddhist worldview is presented clearly in a text supplemented by eleven maps including Zhipan's, namely Chapters 31 and 32 of *General Records of the Founders of Buddhism Buddhism*. Together, these chapters are entitled an "Account of Places and Shape of the World" (Shijie mingti zhi). Chapter 31 describes the total structure of the Buddhist universe, starting with the larger universe and ultimately focusing on the imaginary Mount Meru (*Xumi shan*) and Jambudvīpa to the south. We can also see this orientation in the "Geographic Map of the Land of China to the East" (Dong zhendan dili tu; *zhendan* is the Chinese transcription of *Chīna-sthāna*, meaning "the land of China" in Sanskrit), one of the maps in *The General Records* (see Figure 1.5).

Although the main territory portrayed in the "Geographic Map of the Land of China to the East" lies within China, it situates China at the eastern periphery of the Buddhist world's center. In this way, the map clearly differs from most other contemporary Chinese maps whose fundamental orientation places China at the center of the world. These maps demonstrate that Buddhism, a foreign religion introduced to China several centuries earlier, challenged the worldview that placed China in the center of the world.[64]

Although the "Geographic Map of the Land of China to the East" was drawn from a Buddhist perspective, its author drew China with fairly accurate contours. The author even updated foreign geographic knowledge. Arabia (Dashi), Baghdad (*Baida*),[65] and Rūm (*Lumei*: Rome/Asia Minor) do not, for example, appear on earlier maps. Yet they are described in contemporary written sources as important foreign countries with which China enjoyed trade relations. The capital city of the ʿAbbāsid dynasty, Baghdad, constituted the western terminus of Jia Dan's "Route from Guangzhou,"[66] but it was not portrayed concretely in the "Geographic Map of the Land of China to the East," probably due to limited space. These maps also project into the sea, suggesting that the author probably wished to show the maritime connections between China and foreign countries.

Another surviving map from the thirteenth century plots foreign places and provides detailed and updated information about them.

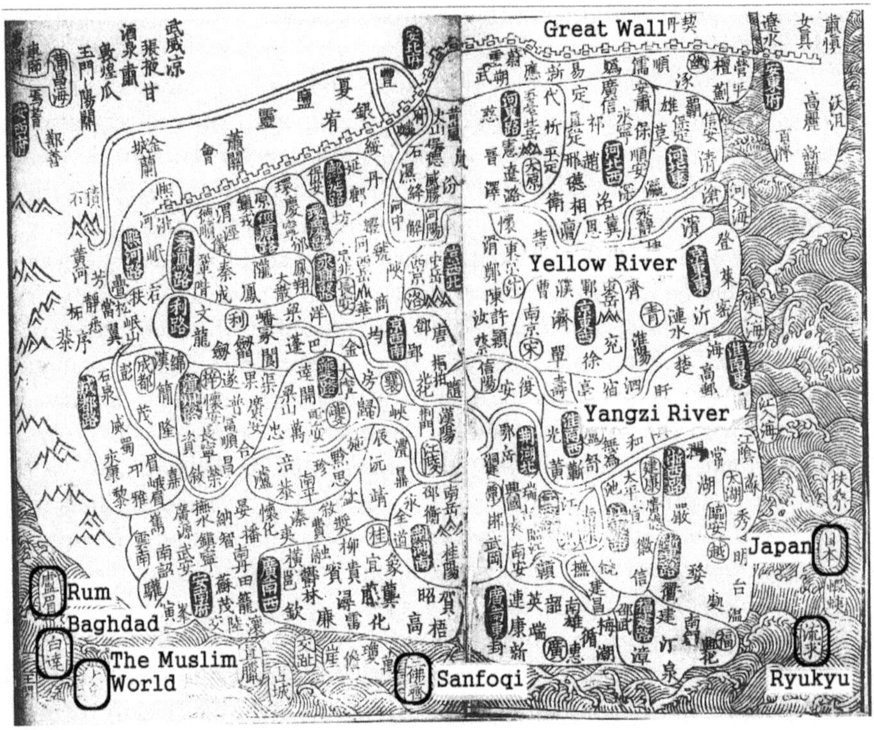

FIGURE 1.5. The "Geographic Map of the Land of China to the East" from Zhipan's *General Records of the Founders of Buddhism* (circa 1270).
Note: ZGDJ/Yuan, Map 152. Zhipan, 32:5l–6r.

Entitled the *General Map of China* (*Yu ditu*, 1265–74), this map of the imperial realm has been preserved in the Kuritoge abbey in Japan.[67] In general, the map resembles similar earlier maps with regard to its contour of the coastline all the way from Guangxi province in southern China to Indochina, and to its placement of foreign places on the sea route in round blocks. The map shows that the broadened geography depicted in Jia Dan's geographic account was not adapted to maps made in China, apparently because of limitations of space, yet the *General Map* clearly incorporated preeminent port cities whose importance in Asia's growing maritime trade was on the rise. The Chinese also participated in maritime trade more actively after the eighth century as a growing number of foreign merchants visited China. The rapid development of shipbuilding and navigation techniques helped maritime traffic to grow further, just as overland routes began to gradually decline in the face of political instabilities in Central Asia.[68] Chinese maritime contact with Korea and Japan gradually increased as well.[69] The *General Map of China* also details place-names in Korea and Japan, reflecting the expansion of Song maritime trade into these regions via new ports along China's east coast such as Ningbo.[70]

Despite the growth of China's maritime commercial activities to the east, the South China ports of Guangzhou and Quanzhou remained the most important Chinese centers of maritime trade during the Song era. A great number of foreign merchants, including many Arab and Persian Muslims, gathered in these cities. Around Guangzhou and Quanzhou one can still find the place-names of medieval South and Southeast Asia, such as Sanfoqi (the base of Srivijaya, the realm centered at Palembang in the Straits of Melaka),[71] Shepo (Java) and Zhunian (the Chola realm in South India).[72] In these cities, Muslim merchants created Islamic diasporic merchant communities in places sitting along sailing itineraries between China and the Islamic world, and set about facilitating the growth of trade between the two ends of the Indian Ocean. These Song era maps project distant unfamiliar lands as islands and randomly shaped landmasses that fill available spaces and lack coastlines that sailors needed to get there. Yet surviving geographic accounts created during the Song period – including special forms of *wenji* (individual collected works) – show that the scale of Chinese participation in maritime trade increased. At the same time, Chinese knowledge about the Islamic world grew more detailed and concrete, extending into South and Southeast Asia, West Asia, and Northeast Africa.

The Maritime Trade and the Islamic World in Maritime Literature in the Song Dynasty (960–1260)

Many types of evidence suggest that maritime contact between China and the Islamic world entered a new stage around the year 1000 CE when Chinese directly ventured into long-distance shipping trade. Both scale of sea trade and China's participation began to grow substantially. Chinese mariners and merchants, sailing on junk ships aided by new navigational breakthroughs like the mariner's compass, soon dominated sea trade in the eastern Indian Ocean.[73] As this maritime interchange grew, sea routes played an ever-increasing role in Chinese trade with the Islamic world. As trade under the Song dynasty overshadowed the Tang, governmental policies changed in response. In the early years of the Song, the government restricted access to China to the embassies of other countries that traveled to present the emperor with tribute, and limited their entry to Guangzhou.[74] This was not an anti-mercantile measure, however. In fact, commerce constituted one of the most important sources of revenue for the imperial court. The emperor used China's diplomatic system of tributary relations to control this valuable commerce, while at the same time using sea commerce to maintain relations with maritime countries that were too distant to be militarily or politically consequential to the empire.[75] During the high water period of this tribute system between 960 and 1022, fifty-six missions arrived from kingdoms in the southern seas. Of these, almost half (twenty-three) were from the Middle East. To manage sea traders, the Song government established the Office of the Superintendent of Merchant Shipping (*shibosi*) in several port cities to supervise the growing foreign trade (in contrast, the Tang court had established only a single office in Guangzhou).[76]

Even as Chinese activity overseas grew, increased foreign trade attracted more traders from the Islamic world to China, who negotiated with local merchants for valuable and exotic items such as spices, frankincense, silk, ivory, pearl, and ceramics. As John Chaffee shows, Muslim communities flourished in the ports of southeastern China from the tenth to fourteenth centuries as part of a trade diaspora that played a central role in the trade network of maritime Asia. These Muslim merchants were in fact the dominant players in pre-modern Indian Ocean trade, and succeeded so far from their homelands because they successfully formed good connections with Muslim communities that were established within host societies all over the Indian Ocean.[77] Sometimes, these merchants took advantage of the Chinese tribute system for their gain. Some Arab envoys who traveled to the Chinese capital, for example, claimed that the caliph of Baghdad had dispatched them to present tribute to the emperor, when in fact they probably were Arab merchants living in Guangzhou.[78] Islamic community and trade grew so large during this period that the Song government even provided governmental posts to Muslim Arab and Persian merchants who contributed to the promotion of trade between China and the Islamic world. During the reign of Shenzhong (1048–85) in the northern Song period (960–1126), for example, the court appointed an Arab merchant named Xinya Tuoluo from Oman to a high-ranking governmental post.[79]

As competitors with merchants from the Islamic world, Chinese traders expanded their sea trade activity beyond previous levels. In addition to ordinary merchants, many royal family members and officials invested in the sea trade for profit.[80] Archeological evidence testifies to this increased activity. A beautifully preserved shipwreck discover[illegible]ouzhu Bay in Quanzhou provides concrete evidence for the expa[illegible]le of trade in commodities from Southeast, South, and West Asi[illegible] ship sank in the late thirteenth century when Quanzhou thrives [illegible]center of maritime commerce in China. Few Chinese shipwrecks [illegible]etter preserved than this 34-meter-long craft, and therefore, it provides extremely good information on the techniques of shipbuilding.[82] The ship's interior contains twelve bulkheads that divide into thirteen different compartments; these are the watertight compartments that impressed foreign observers for the different advantages they created, such as safety from damage and the privacy they created for those on board.[83] A comparison with a similar fourteenth-century Chinese seagoing trading vessel discovered in Sinan in southwestern Korea in 1975 confirms that the Quanzhou ship fit a general pattern in the structure of large-scale Chinese seagoing vessels during this period.

Tracing what kinds of trade goods these ships carried helps us understand what items merchants sought in the Sino-Islamic sea trade's vast market. Shipwrecks are often considered as time capsules because most of the artifacts found aboard them usually come from the same period.[84] Typical commodities discovered include ceramics, coins, stone, earthen and wooden wares, and spices. Billy So's case study of the ceramic export industry in South Fujian shows significant capacity for exporting ceramics. A single firing at the largest kilns there could produce as many as 25,000 vessels, so the scale of production was enormous. Ceramics production employed a large portion of the region's inhabitants; in Dehua County, Quanzhou Prefecture in Fujian, for example, the industry employed 18.3 percent of the population.[85] In addition to durable wares like ceramics, Chinese historical sources such as official histories and local gazetteers report that many different kinds of organic commodities, like black pepper and frankincense, were stowed on merchant vessels sailing between China and South, Southeast, and West Asia. Together, evidence from archeological artifacts and historical documents shows how the Chinese maritime trade extending to the Islamic world worked during the early first millennium.

Details that explain how the Chinese accumulated experience, navigational know-how, and necessary information about maritime trades in the several centuries since Jia Dan wrote his account appear in specialized local gazetteers, which also contain updated geographic information. Two sources written in the twelfth and thirteenth centuries reveal the extent to which Chinese geographical knowledge about foreign places like the Islamic world grew. These two books are Zhou Qufei's *Notes from the Land beyond the Passes* (*Lingwai daida*) [1178] and Zhao Rugua's *Description of the Foreign Lands* (*Zhufan zhi*) [1225]. Both authors lived during the southern Song period, the second half of the Song era after northern China (including the Song's former capital, Kaifeng) was conquered by the Jurchens, an ethnic group from Manchuria, who then maintained a dynasty named Jin until their final fall to the Mongols in the early thirteenth century. Even before the Jurchen conquest, a large territory of northeastern China proper had already been occupied by the ethnic Khitans of the Liao dynasty (915–1125) until its collapse by the Jurchens. Although suffering from invasions by the northern dynasties that were ruled by different ethnic groups, the Chinese under the Song rule continued to be active in the international maritime trades, using flourishing ports in the southern and eastern coastlines. In fact, great numbers of the Chinese moved from the north to the south, corresponding with the shift of the capitals from Kaifeng to Hangzhou; likewise, the importance of China's maritime connection to foreign countries in East and Southeast Asia – and further to the west – continued to expand. The two books about China's maritime contacts were written in this context.

Zhou Qufei, the author of *Notes from the Land beyond the Passes*, was an official with a Jinshi (Metropolitan Graduate) degree. He never traveled outside of China nor worked in the Office of the Superintendent of Merchant Shipping where he would [illegible]countered trade firsthand, yet he spoke with merchants and inter[illegible]ngaged in foreign trade whom he encountered during his service [illegible]ernment official in Guangxi, a border province in southeastern C[illegible]s the title implies, Zhou sought to answer questions he received a[illegible] territories beyond southeastern China, a region of China he called [illegible]r Lingnan). Zhou Qufei's *Notes* contains 294 sections about vari[illegible]cs organized into ten chapters.[86] Most topics concern the produ[illegible] customs he observed along the border regions of Guangxi. Two ch[illegible]pters, however, deal exclusively with foreign countries, including the Islamic world.[87]

In his book, Zhou Qufei provides a substantial treatment of the countries in the Islamic world. He states in his overview of foreign countries that, "among foreign countries the richest one with many valuable goods (*baohuo*) is the country of the Muslims, the next (richest) one is the country of Java, then Srivijaya [in the Melaka Straits], and then all the other countries."[88] This corresponds to Zhou Qufei's entry for the country of Dashi in another page, which he describes as a place where the people are rich with treasures like gold and silver. Zhou devotes this section to all the countries of Dashi instead of to a single country called Dashi, as was true of Du Huan's account in the eighth century. Perhaps this is because the country Chinese called Dashi disintegrated into multiple centers following the dissolution of the ʿAbbāsid empire since the ninth and tenth centuries. The section begins: "Dashi is a collective name for several countries. There are fully a thousand and more countries, but of those of which we know the names there are only these few."[89] Zhou Qufei demonstrates a precise Chinese understanding of products and way of life in the Islamic world, although not an extensive one. He gives details for only six Muslim countries in his section of Dashi: the countries of Maliba [ma-ljię̯-b´wăt] (Mirbat in the coast of Hadramaut in modern Oman, with linkages to the west African coastline),[90] Majia [ma-ka] (Mecca), Baida [b´wâng-d´ăt] (Baghdad), Jicini [kiĕt-dz´i-ni] (Ghazni), Meilugudun [mji-luo-kuət-tuən] (Malay, Rūm, or Mulahhidun?),[91] and Wusili [miuət-się̯-ljię̯] (Egypt). All of these places appear for the first time in a Chinese geographic account except for Baghdad. They also flourished as important political and commercial centers.

These passages from Zhou's survey follow the traditional format for describing foreign countries by introducing their local products, trade goods, and cultural and religious customs. In their details, he provides a rich body of new geographic information about the Islamic world. Zhou provides new details about important Islamic religious and cultural centers. His description of Muslim worship of Heaven (Allāh) on every seventh day imitates similar Tang passages, yet it also introduces the country of Mecca as the Prophet's birthplace, where all Muslims go on pilgrimage. This pilgrimage to Mecca during the twelfth month of the Islamic calendar, called the *hajj*, marks one of the five pillars of Islam, that is, the essential religious duties that all Muslims who can afford to do so are obliged to perform at least once in their lifetime. Even after the ʿAbbāsid caliphate lost its political power over societies ruled by regional rulers, this important religious practice maintained solidarity among Muslim people living in diverse societies in West Asia, North Africa, and beyond. Interestingly, this religious practice also produced economic consequences because Muslims from diverse places gathered in Mecca, and there they not only practiced their faith together, but they also exchanged information and even goods. The number of Chinese Muslim settlers who performed the hajj during the Tang-Song period cannot be determined; however, Zhou's account suggests that some Muslims in China went to Mecca for this purpose.

The most important evidence of [illegible]dated Chinese geographic knowledge about the Islamic world [illegible]hat Chinese possessed a broader geographic understanding than [illegible]ecessary for their actual access to the region. A section lists all [illegible]s that Chinese seafarers had to pass in order to reach the Islamic [illegible] It documents how Chinese geographic knowledge about the Isla[illegible]rld fit into their perception of the entire world:[92]

> The foreign countries are largely bord[illegible] sea; each country is located in every quarter [of the known world?]. Eac[illegible]ountry has its peculiar products, and each has its trading center from which it derives its (commercial) prosperity ... [After mentioning Srivijaya, Java, Champa, Cambodia, Western India as commercial centers,] more distant [of these trading centers] is Maliba (Mirbat in Oman), the commercial center of the countries in the Islamic world, and beyond these there is Mulanpi (countries in the Mediterranean coast), the commercial center of countries in the extreme west.

The entire passage demonstrates that Chinese of the Song era divided the seas of the south and west into six major areas and, within that scheme, they had a clear idea about where the Islamic world fit into that geography, sitting on the western edge of the world surrounded by the "Eastern Sea of the Muslims" (Dong Dashi hai: Arabian Sea) and the "Western Sea of the Muslims" (Xi Dashi hai: the present Mediterranean or the Red Sea) (see Figure 1.6):

One more passage about the route to the Islamic world lies in a section of the book called "Sea Routes to the Outer non-Chinese Peoples" (Hanghai waiyi). This section documents more specific itineraries between foreign countries and the Chinese ports of Guangzhou and Quanzhou; the two port cities had the Office of the Superintendent of Merchant Shipping that took care of the foreign merchants' commercial activities. The routes in the Song source are not much different from those Jia Dan gave in the Tang dynasty. The Song account, however, gives more details about how to sail and where to transship goods:

> (Traders) coming from the country of the Dashi, after traveling south to Quilon on small vessels, transfer to big ships, and, proceeding east, reach Palembang ... A year is sufficient for all foreigners to make the round-trip voyage to China, with the exception of the Muslims who require two years....[93]

According to Zhou, the critical point of transshipment for the Sino-Islamic trade was Quilon on India's southwest coast, where seafarers transferred goods to ships that traveled either east to China or west to the

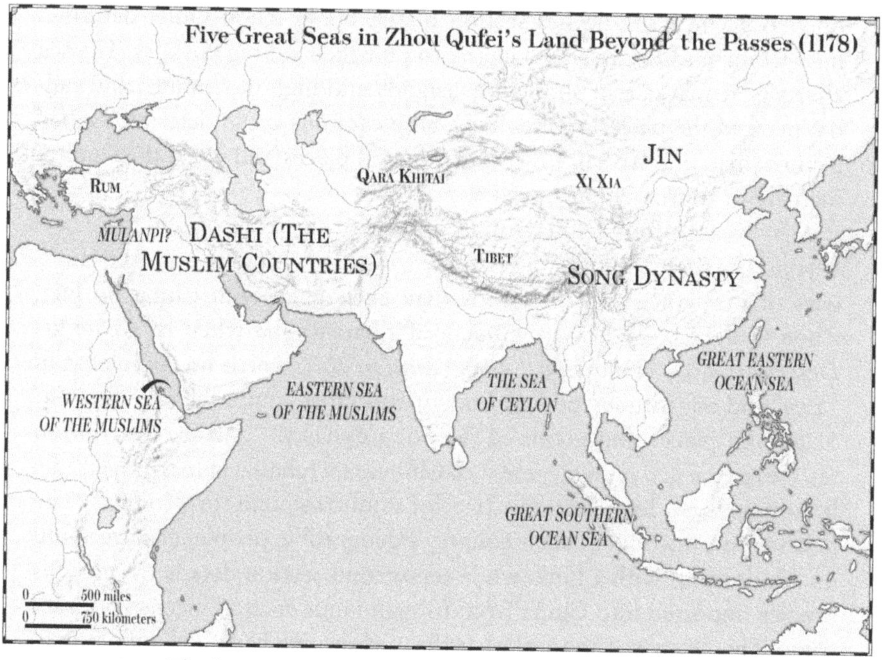

FIGURE 1.6. The five great seas described by Zhou Qufei in his *Land beyond the Passes* (1178).

Arabian Peninsula across the "Eastern Sea of the Muslims" or Arabian Sea. Because the scale of the maritime trade increased, navigators specialized in one segment of these larger seasonal networks to make the traffic/transportation more efficient. In his account, merchants could make a round-trip voyage to Quilon from China or the Middle East within one year, but it took two years to complete the full journey, due to the necessity of a seasonal South Asian layover. According to the section about Quilon in another part of the book, some Chinese merchants who wanted to sail to the Islamic world had to transfer to small ships and sail with the south monsoon for a month to get there. This section also confirms that the round-trip voyage between China and the Islamic world takes two years.[94]

There is little doubt that the Chinese merchants and sailors who sailed on big junk ships controlled most of the shipping in the eastern segment of the Indian Ocean. Their shipping activities were facilitated by their improved navigation skills based on the use of both the compass and sea charts. The Chinese had discovered lodestones as early as the fourth century BCE, although the first record of compass use aboard ship dates only to 1086.[95] In another section of the book, Zhou Qufei describes how Chinese sailors used sea charts to plot their sailing voyages. The sea charts bear marks that show large islands and high mountains, and sailors marked the places on the maps. Ship captains could determine when to turn their ships to sail toward designated places and when they had to increase or decrease their speed.[96]

Fifty years after Zhou Qufei composed his *Notes from the Land beyond the Passes*, another book appeared that surveys the trading countries of the world and the goods they exchanged with China. In fact, Zhou Qufei's book heavily influenced Zhao Rugua when he wrote his *Description of the Foreign Lands* (*Zhufan zhi*), which he completed in 1225, and constitutes the best known and most comprehensive account of foreign places and goods of the Song dynasty.[97] Zhao's *Description* testifies to the active engagement of Chinese merchants in maritime trade. It contains two long sections: one for countries, one for products. The first section introduces each country's geography, people, customs, and its relationship with China, while the second section details the various articles imported into China from foreign lands such as incense or dried fruits. This leads one to think that the author may have had a more professional interest in the book, given his comprehensive knowledge of the sea trade's structure. In the preface of the book Zhao suggests that other works of similar title and type also existed. Assumedly, the widespread distribution of wood-block-printed books encouraged an increase in the volume of publications about geography, but also improved the quality of geographical knowledge that circulated, which led to the unprecedented level of understanding evident in books printed during the Song period.

Zhao Rugua, a member of the Song imperial family, worked as the Superintendent of Merchant Shipping in Quanzhou. He enjoyed more opportunities than Zhou Qufei to speak with those who engaged directly in foreign trade. Some scholars doubt that Zhao Rugua himself collected any new information because he cites others so heavily, including Du You's *Encyclopedic History of Institutions* and Zhou Qufei's *Notes from the Land beyond the Passes*.[98] Despite his extensive borrowing, Zhao Rugua's work is important because it preserves passages that no longer survive in other works. For example, Zhao says in his preface that a *Map of Foreign Countries* (*Zhufan tu*) prompted him to compile his own geographic account, important evidence that many more maps with information about foreign countries circulated in the thirteenth century than exist today.[99]

Zhao Rugua's *Description of the Foreign Lands* begins with a long overview of the country of Dashi, meaning broadly the entire Islamic world, and pays particular attention to its social and economic situation. In his description of the main city of Dashi [probably Baghdad], Zhao reports that people live comfortable lives and possessed great stores of gold and silver, damask, and brocades – a passage that appears in most entries on Muslim countries found in the account. However, Zhao provides more original and concrete descriptions of the city and its great harbor, including a list of the country's products: pearls, ivory, rhinoceros horns, frankincense, aloes, dragon's blood (*xuejie*), opaque and transparent glass, coral, cat's-eyes, soft gold brocades, and camel hair cloth – all products of the Islamic world. Zhou Qufei also mentions most of these items, however, Zhao supersedes Zhou Qufei by providing more specific information about each of the items he inventories in the second half of his book. Zhao's book lists significantly more countries under the rubric of Dashi than Zhou Qufei and others list, a total of twenty-four countries that Zhao Rugua describes in detail in separate sections of the book. Some of these dependencies, such as the countries of Baghdad and Mecca, appear in Zhou Qufei's work, while others like Lumei (Rūm: The Roman [Byzantine] empire) and Cengba (modern-day Zanzibar in northeastern Tanzania) are new. Recall that the countries of Baghdad and Rūm appear in *The Geographic Map of the Land of China to the East* (*Dong zhendan dili tu*), a map dated to 1269. Altogether, Zhao's book provides clear evidence that trade with the Islamic world remained important to the Chinese.

Lifting much of his information from earlier and contemporaneous sources circulating at the time, Zhao Rugua reports that Muslim envoys came repeatedly to the Chinese court to present tribute after 650, and adds specific details about envoys who arrived from 966 on. The last paragraph of his section about the Islamic world introduces a story about a Muslim trader who was famous in Quanzhou and deserved special attention:

> A foreign trader by the name of Shi Nawei, a Muslim, established himself in the southern suburb of Quanzhou. Disdaining wealth, but charitable and filled with the spirit of his western home, he built a graveyard in the southwestern corner of the suburb as a final resting-place for the abandoned bodies of foreign traders. The superintendent in the Office of Merchant Shipping (*tiju shibosi*) Lin Zhiqi (1112–1176) has recorded this fact.[100]

A surviving book by a customs inspector named Lin Zhiqi confirms Zhao Rugua's report, as do more recent archeological discoveries.[101] The

Japanese scholar Kuwabara Jitsuzo makes an interesting and convincing argument that the Muslim merchant probably came from Sīrāf, because his Chinese name Shi Nawei could be a transliteration of *Sīrāfī*, meaning "of Sīrāf," as a part of an Arabic name (*nisba*) that indicates an ancestor's native place.[102] As we will see in Chapter 2, Sīrāf was one of the most important sea ports in the Persian Gulf from which many Arabs and Persians sailed to China for trade. Many Arabic accounts talk about Muslims they call Sīrāfī, such as Abū Zayd al-Ḥasan b. al-Yazīd al-Sīrāfī who compiled a lively description of China. A local gazetteer published in Quanzhou claims that Muslim tombs (or "the tombs of the Medina-men" as they were called) sat on Lingshan, the Hill of Souls, in the southeastern part of Quanzhou.[103] The discovery of Arabic tombstone inscriptions made for Muslim merchants in the southwestern district of Quanzhou provides concrete evidence for the existence of a foreign community, many of whom were merchants originally from the Islamic world.[104] Many of these inscriptions date to the Yuan dynasty period that follows the Song in China, although a few date back to the Song period, including the tomb of Shi Nawei. Interestingly, both Zhao Rugua and Lin Zhiqi offer Shi the same high praise as a generous and righteous person. This shows that Song dynasty scholars shared information as they circulated the books they wrote.

Zhao adds peculiar details to his sections about the Islamic world. This is information contained in his section about Egypt, which is not found in any other extant Chinese work:

> The country of Wusili is under the dominion of Baida [Baghdad], the 'Abbāsid caliphate] ... There is a river (in this country) of very clear and sweet water [the Nile River], and the source from whence springs this river is not known ... An old tradition says that when Shisu [Joseph], a descendant in the third generation of Puluohong [Abraham], seized the government of this country, he was afraid that the land would suffer from drought on account of there being no rain; so he chose a tract of land near the river on which he established three hundred and sixty villages, and all these villages had to grow wheat; and, so that the ensuing year the people of the whole country should be supplied with food for every day, each of these villages supplied it for one day, and thus the three hundred and sixty villages supplied enough food for a year.[105]

It is true that Egypt was ruled by the 'Abbāsid caliphate in Baghdad at the time; the caliphs continued to nominate Muslim rulers long after the caliphate as a central political power declined. With its capital Cairo, the Muslim rulers of the Fatimids and the Ayyubids successively controlled

Egypt until around 1250 when the Mamlūks, a Turco-Circassian military caste, took control. Information about the geography of regions is less susceptible to revision than political history, an example of which can be found in Zhao's descriptions of the Nile River. Intriguingly, Zhao Rugua knew about the Nile well enough to understand that its sources were a mystery.[106] This clearly suggests that encounters between Muslims and Chinese went beyond commercial transactions and reached the level cultural and intellectual exchange. As we will also see in Chapters 2 and 3, this is an important issue in Islamic geographic treatises. The story about Joseph, Abraham's great grandson who was taken to Egypt, derived precisely from the Qur'ān and the Bible; however, the story about the 360 villages mentioned by Zhao does not appear.[107] The following section about Alexandria, a country that belonged to Egypt, introduces a famous legend about a great tower built on a shore in order to protect against attacks: "On the summit of the tower was a wondrous great mirror; if war-ships of other countries made a sudden attack, the mirror detected them beforehand, and the troops were ready in time for duty."[108] The tower no doubt means the well-known Lighthouse of Alexandria, built in 280 BCE.

The accounts of Zhou Qufei and Zhao Rugua reveal that Chinese knowledge about the Islamic world had expanded in terms of the number of countries listed and the facts known about them. They do not provide a map of the coastline that linked China with the Islamic world. Yet their detailed sailing guides to the Islamic world, which included information about the products, trading goods, history, and culture of each place, helped Chinese readers to envision the actual coastline they might pass, at least in their mind's eye.

Conclusion

The mid-eighth century set foundational stages for a flourishing contact between China and the Islamic world. The first military conflict between soldiers of the ʿAbbāsid and Tang dynasties in 751 at Talas in Central Asia, an event to which both Chinese and Islamic sources testify, highlighted a set of complicated political dynamics that involved Chinese and Islamic societies, as well as other countries in Central Asia. This kind of tense political relationship did not last long, however, because the nomadic states that replaced Chinese rule in Central Asia after the An Lushan Rebellion began to block the trade routes of the Silk Road, which led to a gradual decline in overland trade. This situation stimulated the rise of sea routes as an alternative. Relations between these two societies shifted to the Indian Ocean and continued for several centuries. Ultimately, it made the Islamic world seem not so distant or unfamiliar to some Chinese, as growing numbers of Muslim merchants brought goods that Chinese wanted. The Islamic world now became accessible to Chinese, and expanded the horizons of Chinese geographic knowledge about the world.

Zhao Rugua's account of the countries in the Islamic world testifies to this increase in Chinese knowledge that occurred after 1000. The vague image of Dashi of the eighth-century Tang world became, four hundred years later, a variegated region with more than twenty identifiable countries. Chinese now understood what places in the Islamic world were important and why, where Muslim merchants gathered to trade, and where they could find specific commodities that Chinese at home desired. This change in knowledge had something to do with change in inter-Asian sea trade. Initially, Arab and Persian Muslim merchants controlled the entire Indian Ocean trade. Yet extant sources hint that after around 1000 or earlier, the Chinese began to control most of the shipping in its eastern half. The growing scale and importance of maritime trade between China and the Islamic world prompted Chinese to collect practical information about both sailing and markets, which included details about each country in the Islamic world that would affect travel or trade. Even though the Chinese geographers did not draw the full coastline between the two societies in the maps, the knowledge they did possess of these routes, and of the major Indian Ocean port cities along these routes, placed the Islamic world in an expanded geographic framework. Chinese readers could imagine a series of ports that formed a line that stretched all the way to the Islamic world. Many written sources and archaeological excavations testify that Chinese seagoing vessels began to test how far they could venture along that line, undertaking overseas voyages with greater frequency during this period. Overseas, they created greater opportunities to interact with Muslim merchants, whether in the Islamic world or in third-party markets set in ports in South and Southeast Asia, and greater opportunities to expand their knowledge of the world as a result.

This period can be characterized by an increase in Chinese knowledge about the Islamic world and the wider circulation of this information among those who were involved in the long and steadfast contact and exchange. A mutually reinforcing relationship grew between greater knowledge and greater interaction, which contributed to the period's dramatic economic growth, particularly in maritime commerce. Although the two societies did not have remarkably dynamic political and diplomatic relations, their continuous commercial contact influenced the Chinese economy as well as their culture, particularly in their worldview. Mongol rule would raise Chinese contacts with and knowledge about the Islamic world and other foreign countries to an even greater level. Before we turn to this period, however, we must turn to the Islamic sources to see how Muslims conceived of the Chinese during the same centuries of early contact.

2

The Representation of China and the World

Islamic Knowledge about China, 750–1260

Whereas the earliest Chinese accounts about the Islamic world date back to the eighth century, nothing in contemporary Arabic literature hints at Muslim knowledge about China during the same period. Through more than a century of rapid political expansion and increasing contacts with other societies, however, the Muslims dramatically expanded their geographic knowledge about the wider world, including China. The first known political contact that provided Arabs with some impression of China was the Battle of Talas in 751. Chapter 1 describes how many Chinese, including men like Du Huan, suddenly found themselves living in the Islamic world as captives of this great battle. Both Arabic and Chinese sources provide examples of Chinese who practiced some special craftsmanship there and who transferred those cultural elements in the course of their migration and resettlement; an Arabic source, for example, specifically mentions the transfer of papermaking. Other Arabic sources hint that some Chinese probably came to the Islamic heartland through various other means and maintained contact with local people there.

A famous tenth-century work of bibliographic literature entitled *Kitāb al-Fihrist* by Ibn al-Nadīm introduces an amazing episode about an interaction between a famous ninth-century Arab medical doctor named al-Razi and a medical doctor who had come from China[1]:

> A man from China came to seek me and dwelt with me for about a year. In five months of this time he learned Arabic, both spoken and written, becoming proficient in style, as well as expert and rapid in writing. When he desired to return to his country, he said to me a month in advance, "I am about to set forth and wish that you would dictate to me the sixteen books of *Galen*, so that I can write them down." I said, "Your time is short and the

> length of your stay will be sufficient for you to copy only a small part of it." Then the young man said, "I ask you to devote yourself to me for the length of my stay and to dictate to me as fast as you can. I will keep up with you in writing." I proposed to some of my students that they join in this project with me, but we did not have faith in the man, until there was a chance for comparison and he showed us everything he had written."

The ability of the Chinese scholar in this story seems exaggerated. No other evidence exists to verify the scholar's visit to Baghdad, much less his transfer of medical knowledge to China. However, the story reads in a lively way, making it difficult to refute its authenticity immediately. Passages that follow also contain more plausible information about the two kinds of Chinese scripts: seal characters and cursive characters; the Chinese scholar explains to his host that he used cursive characters only to dictate quickly. The author al-Nadīm adds that he saw these Chinese scripts "in the form of tablets, on which was stamped the image of the king."[2] What makes his story so remarkable is the fact that the author treats this event, the arrival of a Chinese scholar who travels all the way from China to Baghdad just to exchange information with Muslim scholars, quite naturally. Although the Chinese doctor's story may be exceptional in some ways, the presence of a Chinese person in the Islamic world is not. In fact, Muslims had grown familiar with China by the time this story was written. Al-Nadīm, a bookseller, owed his livelihood to the arrival of papermaking technology from China, which led to the growth of bookstores, sellers, and scribes in Baghdad.[3] When he compiled his bibliography of titles that circulated in the ʿAbbāsid empire during his time, he also collected information about other cultures from different sources, including stories about China that he heard from travelers. However, these stories about China were already circulating among the many readers who lived in the Islamic world through books based on the testimonies of merchants and other travelers. Thanks to the contributions of authors and bibliographers like al-Nadīm, knowledge about China became widespread among the people in the Islamic world, a *terra incognita* no more.

The growth of maritime travel and trade played an important role in this growth of knowledge about China. Seaborne trade already enjoyed flourishing growth by the middle of the eighth century, as Caliph al-Manṣūr made clear when he boasted that there was no obstacle between Baghdad and China. Although located at the eastern edge of the known world, China now existed as a very real place where people traveled regularly to trade. Thanks to this growing mercantile traffic, more concrete information about Chinese society began to circulate within the Islamic world as more Muslim authors wrote about them. The Islamic world produced its first surviving description of Chinese society in the mid-ninth century, about one century after a similar description of the Islamic world appeared in China. Ibn Khurradādhbih's geography (circa 870) and an anonymous record of testimonies by merchants and travelers (circa 851) introduced basic geographic and historical facts about China to the Islamic world, including a detailed coastal itinerary and an inventory of China's most important cities and products. Both books rely on information drawn from preexisting and contemporary literary sources, and reveal what Muslims knew of China when commercial contact between the two societies peaked in the ninth and tenth centuries.

Islamic geographic writing differed in one important respect from Chinese writing. Chinese geographers first depicted their own empire and only then began to consider places beyond as marginal entities, while Muslim scholars conceived of a larger world, a feature of the worldview they inherited from Greek and Persian geographers before them. Not surprisingly, Chinese cartographers only drew maps of China proper accurately, while Muslim cartographers could create world maps that plotted even distant China and its neighbors with relative accuracy. Together, the steady Islamic commercial expansion of the 'Abbāsid dynasty eastward into Asia and the continued development of Arabic writing produced a surge in the production of geographic, cartographic, and historical accounts that added to the general understanding of China in the Islamic world.

As this chapter traces the increase in Muslim knowledge about China during five centuries of contact between 750 and 1260, it will focus on the same questions as those answered in Chapter 1 about Chinese perceptions of the Islamic world. This will make a comparison between both the experiences of these two societies as well as their sources.

The Earliest Arabic Geographic Accounts about China and the Indian Ocean

By the time they began to receive concrete information about China from travelers, Muslim geographers already had established systematic frameworks to help them interpret the world's geography because they assimilated the knowledge of the societies they conquered, like the Greeks and the Persians. The earliest Arabic geography to systematically use geographic information about China relied considerably on these traditions. The major avenue for foreign knowledge like geography grew in the translation movement in which scholars rendered Greek, Persian, and Indian scientific works into Arabic.[4] The scholars of the famous Bayt al-Ḥikmah (House of Wisdom) that operated during the reign of Caliph al-Ma'mūn (reigned 813–33) actively engaged in translating many foreign academic works into Arabic. The episode about al-Razi and the Chinese medical doctor shows that Arab scholars had already translated entire books written by the ancient Greek medical doctor Galen; it was only one among many translated works in different scientific and literary fields.

Caliph al-Ma'mūn commissioned projects of physical and mathematical geography in order to create a world map that accurately depicted the shape of the world. The caliph also wished to distinguish between countries conquered by the Muslims and thus part of the Dār al-Islām (the land of Islam) and those who were not.[5] The astronomers and scholars of Caliph al-Ma'mūn benefitted especially from Ptolemy's *Geography*, which systematically synthesized the legacies of his Greco-Roman predecessors. The Greek knowledge al-Ma'mūn's scholars possessed was already five centuries out of date, however, so Muslim scholars developed it further, expanding the base of their scientific foundation by synthesizing Iranian, Indian, and Greek traditions as well as new geographical information available to them as the result of Islamic political and economic expansion.

In pursuing his precise map of the world, Caliph al-Ma'mūn commissioned a geodetic survey that would update the locations and longitudes of major cities like Baghdad and Mecca. This grand-scale survey indeed led to a more accurate world map; from this survey, al-Ma'mūn's geographers were able to calculate the earth's circumference within an error of a few hundred kilometers (off by less than 1 percent). This figure was almost as accurate as the estimate made by modern scholars and considerably better than Ptolemy who estimated the circumference with much less success.[6] Unfortunately, this map was lost, and the earliest surviving maps that bear any resemblance to it date only to 1000. Information from these innovative geographic projects survives, however, in the form of Arabic manuscripts that were produced as part of the enterprise at large. One of them, a treatise called *Shape of the Earth* (Ṣūrat al-arḍ), was written by the polymath al-Khwārizmī (died circa 850) who contributed to mathematics, astronomy, and geography as one of al-Ma'mūn's scholars.[7] This is the earliest surviving geographic account of the Islamic world and the first Arabic account to use the term *al- Ṣīn* to refer to China.

Shape of the Earth provides longitudinal and latitudinal positioning of the known world using coordinate tables (*Zīj*). Al-Khwārizmī arranged the information according to a system that divides the inhabited world into seven horizontal strips or bands parallel to the equator called climates (*iqlim*). This system essentially bases itself on one introduced by Marinus and Ptolemy; however, al-Khwārizmī built on the Greco-Roman foundation by incorporating ideas that had spread along with the rise of Islam. For example, while the Greco-Roman system introduced more than twenty climates, al-Khwārizmī's *Shape of the Earth,* and later works influenced by it, draw from Persian sources and presents seven climates. As for geographic content, Ptolemy's longitudinal and latitudinal table locates Serica (Sērikē, China) east of Central Asia, thereby emphasizing northern China and overlooking southern China.[8] Since the most important Muslim trade ports were located in Southern China, al-Khwārizmī provides a fuller description of southern China, adding three port cities including Khantu, probably Yangzhou, a city that hosted many Muslim merchants.[9]

The first Muslim geographers of the ʿAbbāsid empire supplemented their Greek theoretical frameworks for geographical understanding of the world by incorporating the methods of the Persians and Indians. Persian sources (including Sogdian geographical knowledge) provided descriptions of the world including China based on extensive overland contacts with China. Once the Arabs overthrew the Sassanid dynasty, many Persians converted to Islam because of social and economic benefits. Once converted, the rich literary traditions of the Persians were absorbed into the multiethnic Muslim tradition. *The Book of Routes and Realms* (*Kitāb al-Masālik wa-ʾl-mamālik*), written by a Persian Muslim, Ibn Khurradādhbih (died 912), departs from earlier physical and mathematical geographic treatises which gave longitudinal and latitudinal coordinates but little else. Instead, Ibn Khurradādhbih offered the first descriptive geography in Arabic. The first detailed reports of China and the Indian Ocean trade also appear here.

Ibn Khurradādhbih served as the Director of Posts and Intelligence during the reign of Caliph al-Muʿtamid (869–92). This situation enabled him to collect rich sources – probably Greek and Persian records and travel reports – to compose his *Book of Routes and Realms.*[10] The book systematically describes the earth's geography and provides detailed studies of the seven climate zones, the seventh of which is located in China.[11] Ibn Khurradādhbih's short history of ancient kings who descended from Ifrīdūn, a Persian version of Noah in the Old Testament, includes a king of China with the name Baghbūr, a Persian noun meaning "son of heaven."[12]

Chinese emperors traditionally called themselves the Son of Heaven, where heaven refers to the universe that interferes with earthly rule. This type of information, clearly gleaned from earlier sources, often appears in this new generation of Islamic accounts. However, as the title suggests, *The Book of Routes and Realms* provides more practical information about administrative divisions and cities, stations located on the roads leading from Baghdad to various destinations, important trade ports and routes, and the tax assessments of different regions. The information was intended primarily to help the ʿAbbāsid rulers who inherited the administrative and economic system of the Persian Sassanid empire. Interestingly, one of the book's most detailed accounts charts the "sea route to China [the East]," a special section that Ibn Khurradādhbih devotes to tracing the routes that extended through known non-Islamic territory.[13] Clearly, his geography benefitted enormously from his position in government.

Unlike the rest of his book, which breaks overland routes into separate regions distinguished by individual introductions, Ibn Khurradādhbih's section on maritime routes devotes itself to tracing one long continuous route from the Islamic world to China. His focused interest in local products and trade goods reflects the frequency and importance of long-distance direct trade with China that existed in the author's world. The route begins in Basra, a flourishing port in the Persian Gulf close to Baghdad. It continues through the ports of Oman and Aden on the Arabian coast, crosses the Arabian Sea to the Indian coast and Ceylon, passes through the Strait of Malacca to Malaysia, Cambodia, and extends all the way to the harbor of Khānfū, present-day Guangzhou (see his route in Map 1).[14] Interest in commerce is so keen that Ibn Khurradādhbih frequently interrupts his sailing instructions with anecdotes about native products and commercial goods:

> From al-Ṣanf to Lūqīn [present-day Hanoi in Vietnam],[15] which is the first port of/in China, is 100 *farsaḥ* [about 600 km/345 miles][16] by land and sea. Lūkīn has Chinese stones [jade?], Chinese silk, Chinese porcelains of good quality, and rice. From Lūkīn to Khānfū [present-day Guangzhou], which is the largest port (in China), is four days' journey by sea and 20 days' journey by land. Khānfū has all kinds of fruits, vegetables, wheat, barley, rice, and sugarcane. From Khānfū to Khānjū [present-day Quanzhou] is eight days' journey. Khānjū has products like those in Khānfū. From Khānjū to Qānṭū [present-day Yangzhou] is 20 days' journey, and Qānṭū has products like those of Khānfū and Khānjū.
>
> Each of these ports in China has a large river into which the ships sail, and in which the tide ebbs and flows. One can see geese, ducks, and chickens in the river of Qānṭū. The length of the country of China along the coast

> from Armābīl to its furthest regions is two months' journey. China has three hundred populous cities, ninety of which are famous. The boundary of China runs from the sea [in the south] to Tibet and the country of the Turks and to India in the west.[17]

This basic guide provided information to those who wanted to sail to China's major four ports: Hanoi, Guangzhou, Quanzhou, and Yangzhou. Lūkīn, or Hanoi, the capital of modern-day Vietnam, was under Chinese rule during Ibn Khurradādhbih's times. The other three cities were all major foreign trading ports during the Tang period. Although the author listed Khānjū خانجو among these ports, the name most likely was a copyist's mistake, confusing it for the name Jānjū جانجو or Quanzhou.[18] Qānṭū, probably today's Yangzhou, marked the final port China along the eastern maritime route (which, in fact, ran north once it rounded the coast of Southeast China).[19] Ibn Khurradādhbih estimated China's total number of cities at 300, a figure often used by later writers.

Unlike similar itineraries, Ibn Khurradādhbih's maritime route continues beyond China, to a mountainous region east of China called al-Shīlā, meaning Silla, a dynasty in Korea that ruled from 503 to 935 CE. This marks the eastern endpoint of the known world for Muslims.[20] Ibn Khurradādhbih reports that many Muslims settled in al-Shīlā because it is "rich in gold" and the land is "beautiful." His description reflects true features of the Korean peninsula, which has many mountains, a mild climate, and fertile soil. Many gold objects, such as crowns and earrings, were among the many discoveries archeologists made in excavations of the Silla royal tombs in its capital Kyungju. It is not difficult to assume that many West Asian merchants based in China traveled to Silla, which had close relations with the Tang empire.

Not all of the geographer's reports are as accurate as his account of the remote Korean kingdom in the east. Ibn Khurradādhbih also describes the legendary lands of *al-Wāqwāq*. It, too, lies east of China, he alleges, and possesses gold in such quantity that "dog-leashes and monkey-collars are made with it."[21] Unlike al-Shīlā, however, there have been many debates over what is *al-Wāqwāq* in Ibn Khurradādhbih's book. Once Ibn Khurradādhbih introduced it, Islamic geographers continued to reproduce it, and many added further exaggerations like the fantastic illustration of trees that bear fruit that look like a woman's head and shout "wāqwāq" when they ripen. This story, which continuously recurs in later Muslim accounts,[22] is reminiscent of the Chinese account by Du You, examined in Chapter 1, which claims there is a tree on the western sea – in other words, at the edge of the known world for Chinese – and on that tree children hang. By comparing the Islamic and Chinese cases, patterns emerge in both groups in the way in which they make sense of places at the edge of their known world. Gradually, more realistic information begins to replace fantastic tales, transforming distant places from *terra incognita* to *terra cognita*, although full knowledge remains elusive because they are so far away. Stories about country in the east with bountiful gold – whether a very real al-Shīlā or a mythical Wāqwāq – continued to pique people's interest into the thirteenth century and beyond. After all, Marco Polo similarly describes Jipangu (Japan) as a country rich with gold, an idea that greatly interested Christopher Columbus.

All the pieces of information that Ibn Khurradādhbih provides in *Book of Routes and Realms* are central to the work of understanding Muslim geographic knowledge about China because they circulated widely in the Islamic world and became standard passages in the maps and essays that later scholars produced about China. Much of that influence rests on the regard that later generations of Islamic intellectuals paid him as a pioneer and authority in the literature of descriptive world geography, in a similar way that Sima Qian's *Records of the Grand Historians* served as a model for all following Chinese geographic writings about foreign lands. Some scholars consider Ibn Khurradādhbih the father of Arabic geographic literature. Later geographers wrote similar geographic works, often with generic titles like the *Book of Routes and Realms*.[23] This kind of influence on later works is found in another Muslim geographical classic that, along with Ibn Khurradādhbih, constitute the two earliest major sources to provide information about China. *Accounts of China and India* (*Akhbār al-Ṣīn wa-l-Hind*) provides the first extant account of China based on the detailed testimony of those who had visited China, and became another source from which Muslim writers drew their impressions of the country in the Far East.

Compiled in 851, *Accounts of China and India* appeared only a few years after the first edition of Ibn Khurradādhbih's account. In contrast to the *Book of Routes and Realms*, the author's identity remains unknown. Earlier scholars thought merchant Sulaymān had penned the book, but scholars like George Hourani point out that an anonymous author more likely compiled the testimony of Sulaymān and other informants; the main informants were merchants and sailors who traveled to China to trade.[24] Ibn al-Nadīm did not enter the book into his famous bibliography *Kitāb al-Fihrist*; however, the several copies that have survived shed light on why the book circulated widely among Muslims, especially for those interested in India and China. Unlike Ibn Khurradādhbih's formal and systematic format, the author of *Accounts of China and India* mainly focuses on China and India and is filled with much richer geographic and historical information about China compared to Ibn Khurradādhbih's account. The book provides the sum of practical information available about geographic locations, trading goods, and local culture that Muslim traders needed to succeed in the Sino-Islamic trade through the Indian Ocean. Interestingly, the author regards China and India with equal importance, even though India lies halfway between the Islamic world and China and lies much closer to the Islamic world. Clearly, China carries great weight in the Islamic world by the time this book was written in the ninth century.

Other surviving contemporary Arabic accounts written in a more casual style also testify to the brisk activities of Muslim merchants who played active roles in the Indian Ocean trade reaching China. *The Book of the Wonders of India* (*ʿAjāʾib al-Hind*; circa tenth century) and the famous Sinbad the Sailor story in *One Thousand and One Nights* (also known as *Arabian Nights*, circa tenth century) contain many episodes about Muslims and Jews who sailed from Baghdad to China and gained huge wealth by trading a great quantity of silks and porcelains that they brought with them from China.[25] These short stories reflect the trade networks that linked together Baghdad, China, and the Indian Ocean around the tenth century, the goods they traded like musk, silk, and porcelain, and the potential for enormous wealth that these merchants could gain by venturing forth on perilous sea voyages. These isolated episodes do not supply any concrete geographical information about how to travel to those lands, although the merchants in these tales clearly could not have sailed into the vast Indian Ocean and reached China without good information and navigational techniques like those found in *Book of Routes and Realms* and *Accounts of China and India*.

The first part of the original version of *Accounts of China and India* was lost. The extant portion of the manuscript begins with a description of one of the seven seas, a traditional division of Indian Ocean popular in West Asia at that time. It continues to illustrate the rest of the seas eastward, and lists the Sea of China as the Indian Ocean's seventh sea. From this fact, it seems safe to assume that the original manuscript provided a complete, systematic explanation of all the seven seas that lay between the Islamic world and China. The theoretical geographic explanation of the sea prefaces a complete description of routes and sailing information that spans from the Persian Gulf to Guangzhou. The route essentially conforms to those described by Ibn Khurradādhbih and his Chinese contemporary Jia Dan, suggesting that all three authors used the sum of knowledge in circulation at that time (See Map 1).

The extant content of *Accounts of China and India* has survived to the present because, thankfully, another geographer copied it for his collection. This should not be surprising; after all, demand for the book was high and so the book circulated widely. In 916, Abū Zayd al-Ḥasan b. al-Yazīd al-Sīrāfī copied *Accounts of China and India* in full and preserved the anonymous account as the first volume of his collected work entitled *The Chain of the Histories* (*Silsilat al-tawārīkh*).[26] Little is known about the compiler Abū Zayd except for the little information he provided in his own preface.[27] Part of his name, al-Sīrāfī, indicates that he came from Sīrāf, like the Muslim merchant in China named Shi Nawei discussed in Chapter 1. From Sīrāf, merchants of Iraq – that is, the central and southern Tigris and Euphrates river valleys – embarked for China.[28] Abū Zayd also gathered information, which he found trustworthy and closely matched what he had learned about the sea trade, directly from merchants and compiled it into the second volume of his *Accounts of China and India*.[29]

After describing the geographical conditions of the Indian Ocean, the first volume of Abū Zayd's compilation, *The Accounts of China and India*, comes back to the Persian Gulf where "Chinese ships (al-Sufun al-Ṣīnīyah)" began their journey to China.[30] The second volume provides a description of the structure of these "Chinese ships," which actually fit the characteristics of dhows, the indigenous boats that Arabs, Persians, and Indians used to sail in the Indian Ocean: "And this stitched wood does not exist except on the ships of Sīrāf especially, and the ships of Syria and Rūm (The Roman [Byzantine] empire) are nailed, rather than stitched."[31]

Dhows were made from planks that were sewn together. A ninth-century Arab or Indian shipwreck found off the coast of the Indonesian island of Belitung proves to be just such a dhow.[32] It has planks joined by stitching, with no sign of the wooden dowels or iron fastenings used in Chinese ships of the time.[33] Abū Zayd's use of the term "Chinese ships" must refer to Arab ships sailing to China rather than ships of Chinese design. Analyses of a number of sewn boats of the Indian Ocean suggest that the same single web pattern were used throughout the Indian Ocean.[34]

We cannot be sure about the ship's provenance. Yet many heavy Chinese ceramics and silver ingots and lead coins help us to assume that the ship departed from a port in China before it sank off Indonesia. The cast ingots had all been manufactured in a government mint in China and used to collect and transfer revenue from the government salt monopoly and in trade.[35] The cargoes' places of origin include China, Indonesia, India, and the Persian Gulf; the ship probably operated as one of many ships plying regional ports.[36] Some of the total 2,212 Chinese ceramics contained in the sunken ship were probably destined for ports in the Islamic world and brokered by Middle Eastern merchants. If so, the excavated ship perfectly matches the one documented by Abū Zayd. Most of the Chinese ceramics that filled the surviving cargo came from Changsha, whose kilns had manufactured primarily for export since the early ninth century.[37] This type of Chinese ceramic was also found in Sīrāf itself, whose excavations since the 1960s produced sufficient evidence to corroborate the dramatic increase in Chinese ceramics export at the beginning of the ninth century.[38]

The "Chinese" ships in Abū Zayd's account took on their cargo in Sīrāf, one of the ports of the Persian Gulf that flourished during the early centuries of Islamic society. The city also played an important role as a transit port in the Islamic world, since some goods shipped at Sīrāf came from Basra, Oman, and other places.[39] After passing through ports in the Persian Gulf such as Masqat (in the province of Oman) the ships reached India. Moving on, the ships then stopped at many islands in Southeast Asia along the way where merchants obtained local products such as amber, coconut, shells, pearls, and gold. Here, the ships had to negotiate headwinds, whirlpools, and rough waves. Several months after sailing from Sīrāf the ships finally reached their destination in Guangzhou:

> "When the ship crossed the gates (of China) and entered the inlet, it reached fresh water where it dropped anchor in the country of China. This is called Khānfū (Guangzhou), a city. The rest of China has fresh water from rivers and valleys, garrison and marketplaces in every district."[40]

Once anchored in Guangzhou, the ships then had to undertake several steps with Chinese customs in order to win permission to trade:

> When the merchants entered China by sea, the Chinese took their goods, put them into warehouses, and guaranteed responsibility up to six months until the last merchant [of the trading fleet] has arrived. Then they take a third of each commodity, and surrender the rest to the merchants. The ruler takes what he needs on the basis of the maximum price, pays it quickly, and does not treat [the visitors] unjustly.[41]

The procedures for merchants to enter China to trade appear both systematic and fair. Merchants from the Islamic world had to sojourn in Guangzhou for a long time. Although Abū Zayd does not mention this, it is important to know that traders had to wait for the monsoon winds to change before they could sail back to West Asia. Many had to stay in the city for more than a year due to fires, plundering, and damage to their ships during the voyage. The merchant Sulaymān, one of Abū Zayd's informants for the first volume, reports that the Muslim population in Guangzhou was so large that Muslim judges protected the interests of the Muslim merchants:

> The merchant Sulaymān relates that in Guangzhou, which is the meeting place of the merchants, the Chinese ruler placed a Muslim to serve as the judicial authority over the Muslims who traveled to this region with the goal of [reaching] the kingdom of China. On holy days he led the Muslims in prayer, delivered a *khuṭba* sermon, and prayed for the ruler [i.e., caliph] of the Muslims. The Iraqi merchants in no way challenge his authority over matters in his rulings and his righteous conduct according to the book of God [the Qurʾān] – exalted is He – according to the judgments of Islam.[42]

The acting ruler mentioned in the *khuṭba* refers to the fact that the Muslims of Guangzhou remained legally under the caliph's authority at least in matters concerning the Muslim community. The model for leading religious rituals on festival days followed the norm practiced throughout the Islamic world. *The Tang Code* sanctioned this status quo because it stipulates that all disputes among foreigners should accord with the laws of their own society, as long as both plaintiffs and defendants came from the same country; if they did not, then their dispute fell under Chinese law instead.[43]

The Muslim merchants who sojourned six months or longer in Guangzhou learned much about the region from its locals. One section of *Accounts of China and India* lists export commodities such as "gold, silver, pearls, brocade and silk, all these stuffs in great abundance" on the Chinese side, and imports of "ivory, frankincense, cast copper [bronze?], sea shells, which are the back skins of the tortoise" on the Muslim side. The narrator also mentions that "the Chinese have an excellent kind of cohesive green clay (al-ghaḍār) with which they make cups as fine as phials in which the light of water is seen, although it is of clay."[44] Clearly, this is porcelain.

Accounts of China and India also offers many descriptions of Chinese cultural practices arranged in no specific topical or chronological order. These include mourning customs, silk dresses, and the script and writing system. The book often compares Chinese religious and social customs such as idol, star, and ancestral worship and ethical teaching (which may indicate Buddhism, Confucianism, and other popular religious practices) with those in India. In the Muslim merchants' eyes, China was "more beautiful," "more populated," and "better governed" than India.[45]

Equal and universal justice in legal dealings throughout China features prominently in the travel account. A small bell suspended above each local ruler's head embodied this system of equal right to fair treatment, as any person in China could ring the bell to demand that his case be heard.[46] China indeed had this kind of court appeal system by means of a drum set outside the city gates.[47] Muslim sources first reported this use of a bell, although the bell described in *Accounts of China and India* could well be a fictional elaboration. The procedure of tort redress was actually a Sassanid institution that was later adopted by Muslims.[48] This example may show how the Muslims projected their own customs onto their understanding of other societies.

Like other Muslim characterizations of Chinese people, the second volume of Abū Zayd's compilation characterizes the Chinese as good craftsmen. Abū Zayd describes Chinese as "the cleverest people on earth: they have extraordinary skill in plastic and other arts, so that no other nation can be compared with them in any kind of workmanship."[49] This general Muslim perception of the Chinese took shape early; in his literary work, *The Table Talk* (*Majlis al-uns*), al-Tawḥīdī (died 1023) quoted earlier Arabic prose pioneer Ibn al-Muqaffaʿ's (died 757), who viewed the Chinese as "[m]asters of furniture and crafts."[50] Recall, too, Du Huan's account of Chinese craftsmen in Baghdad. As we will see throughout this book, this characterization of the Chinese people persisted for centuries.

The most notable part of Abū Zayd's second volume provides a comprehensive report about the Muslim merchants trading in China. For example, he relates a story about Ibn Wahab, who was from the Tribe of Quraysh (the same tribe as that of the Prophet Muḥammad). Ibn Wahab left his home city of Basra and traveled to Sīrāf, and from there embarked on a pleasure trip to China. After arriving at the port of Guangzhou, he traveled for two more months to the Tang capital Khumdān to see the emperor. Khumdān appears in other contemporary and later Arabic geographic accounts, and no doubt refers to Chang'an, the Tang dynasty's cosmopolitan capital. Contemporary Chinese sources include collections of stories and poems that testify to the Iranian and Central Asian merchants in the city and the strong cultural influence of their flourishing activities on the lives of Chinese including foreign fashions, music, and foods.[51] Ibn Wahab arrived in Chang'an sometime in the 870s and, claiming that he came from the family of the Prophet Muḥammad, he petitioned to meet the Tang emperor. After a long and careful investigation among Muslim merchants in Guangzhou, the emperor finally granted him an audience. Ibn Wahab spoke with the emperor through interpreters about the history of the Arabs and all various nations. His report that the Chinese emperor esteemed the king of Iraq as the world's most supreme ruler and ranked himself second is difficult to credit, but we can imagine the claim appealed to Abū Zayd.[52] Abū Zayd also says that he directly asked Ibn Wahab many questions about Chang'an and quotes Ibn Wahab's brief description of the city:

> He mentioned the size of the city and its great number of inhabitants, and that it is divided into two districts, separated by a long and broad street. The emperor, his minister, guards, the supreme judge, the eunuchs of the emperor, and all their retinue are on the right-hand [of the city] which is towards the east. They do not mix with any of the common people. There are no markets [in this part]. [gap in text.] It has rivers flowing along their streets lined with trees and spacious houses. In the left-hand part [of the city], which is towards the west, there are subjects and merchants, stores and markets; and when the day rises you see the stewards of the emperor and his retinue, pages of his house and the pages of the generals, and their agents enter, either riding or walking, into that part of the city that contains the markets and merchants [in order] to obtain their services and needs. Thereafter they depart and no one of them returns to this part [of the city] until the next day.[53]

Anyone familiar with the Tang capital Chang'an will be surprised that Ibn Wahab mentions the Western Market in "the part towards the west" but does not give any details about the bustling foreign quarter that crowded with many non-Chinese residents including Persian- and Arabic-speaking merchants. Chinese documents and archeological artifacts together confirm that the western portion of Chang'an had many religious temples of foreign religions including Zoroastrianism, Nestorian Christianity, and Islam.[54] Chinese people enjoyed easy access to the foreign quarter, and went there for wine and foreign foods and to enjoy the music and dancing of foreign ladies.[55]

How many Muslim merchants came to China to trade? Abū Zayd provides a clue by describing a major revolt that erupted in 877 CE (264 AH [Anno Hegirae: Islamic calendar]) and broke China up into small and warring principalities. The rebellion's date corresponds to an actual crisis that seriously weakened the once mighty Tang dynasty, called the Huang Chao Rebellion (875–884). Attracting millions of impoverished followers, Huang Chao plundered and burned several cities throughout China including the empire's largest, Chang'an and Louyang, in 880. Although Abū Zayd misidentifies the leader ("Bābshuā" cannot correspond to

Chinese name Huang Chao [died 884]), his details about the political situation in China and the course of the revolt match Chinese accounts.[56] Abū Zayd gives a concise yet lively narration of the rebellion's events, which plagued China for nine years and played a decisive role in weakening the Tang empire:

> He [Huang Chao] targeted Guangzhou [Khānfu], among the cities in China, which was the town the Arab merchants headed for. Between Guangzhou and the sea is a journey of many consecutive days, and the city is located in a great valley near fresh water. Its citizens kept him [Huang Chao] at bay, and therefore he besieged them for a long period, this being in the year 264 (AH; 877 CE), until he conquered the city and put its inhabitants to the sword. Those who are experienced with the affairs (of China) related [to me] that in addition to the Chinese he killed one hundred and twenty thousand people – Muslims, Christians, Jews, and Zoroastrians who had sought refuge in the city.[57]

This account reveals the large number of foreigners including Muslims who lived in China under Tang rule. The number of non-Chinese killed in the rebellion was correct, Abū Zayd maintains, because the Chinese government kept an accurate census of the population.[58] After their siege of Guangzhou the rebels moved on to conquer many other cities until they finally occupied the capital Chang'an.

According to Abū Zayd, the rebellion struck a heavy blow to Muslim trade in Guangzhou and caused a decline in the commercial activities of Muslim merchants. Another contemporary Arabic account adds an important fact about the rebellion's drastic effect on the whole system of inter-Asian maritime traffic and trade: Whereas vessels from the Islamic world had once sailed the entire distance between the Persian Gulf and China, after the rebellion they began to meet the Chinese halfway in Kalāh on the Malay Peninsula in Southeast Asia. The author of this Arabic account is the celebrated writer al-Masʿūdī (896–956), who extensively mined Abū Zayd's information about China and India to write his celebrated encyclopedic work *The Meadows of Gold and Mines of Gems* (*Murūj al-dhahab wa-maʿādin al-jawhar*). A single event of political turmoil in a Chinese city probably did not solely cause this change in Muslim behavior; structural changes such as the decline in direct Sino-Islamic trade usually occur in response to contemporary political and economic changes in the maritime commercial sphere as a whole.

Whatever the case, by the late ninth century, Sino-Islamic sea trade with China via Southeast Asia came to be the norm, and operated out of Southeast Asian ports like Srivijaya, a kingdom on Sumatra that Chinese accounts, such as those by Zhou Qufei and Zhao Rugua, called Sanfoqi. This new form of networked trade, depicted in Zhou Qufei's account, relied on traders and seafarers specialized in one segment of the Sino-Islamic route, making it less likely that individual merchants made the entire sea passage from Sīrāf to Guangzhou. This is also confirmed in contemporary Middle Eastern sources, most notably the Geniza records that were originally held in a Jewish depository in old Cairo (Fustat), the terminus of the Red Sea connection to the Indian Ocean trade that gradually surpassed the Persian Gulf connection.[59] The consequences of this shift in the sea trade system was disproportionate; although Chinese knowledge about the Indian Ocean increased thanks to their expanded involvement as middlemen into Southeast Asia, Middle Eastern knowledge appears to have declined.[60] Both al-Masʿūdī and Abū Zayd share the same opinion about what caused this decline. This is no surprise if we consider the fact that al-Masʿūdī reveals that he met Abū Zayd in Sīrāf and probably exchanged notes with him.[61] Many of the same passages in Abū Zayd's two volumes (including those just mentioned) also appear in al-Masʿūdī's book, a good example of one way in which geographic knowledge transferred between individual authors.

Whereas Abū Zayd focuses exclusively on India and China, al-Masʿūdī, both a historian and geographer, presents China in the context of the entire world known to him in his *Meadows of Gold and Mines of Gems*. Born in Baghdad in 896 and well traveled throughout both the ʿAbbāsid empire and India during his lifetime, al-Masʿūdī acquired a variety of sources that he used to compile his encyclopedic historical and geographical masterpiece. Al-Masʿūdī claims he visited China, yet he actually depended very much on previous accounts to write his section on China and what he learned from contemporaries like Abū Zayd.[62] The eighty-five sources that he lists at the beginning of his book include Ibn Khurradādhbih's *Book of Routes and Realms*. Like Ibn Khurradādhbih, he states that China was one of the seven ancient nations that existed before Islam and claims that its people descended from Noah. In contrast, al-Masʿūdī supplies richer and more detailed description than Ibn Khurradādhbih does, providing detailed geographical facts and a genealogy of the imperial family (which is unreliable, however, because it provides names that are difficult to trace in contemporary Chinese sources).

Al-Masʿūdī supplies much theoretical information about world geography in *Meadows of Gold and Mines of Gems*, which derives from earlier Greek works that he studied in Baghdad and Damascus. It begins with traditional Greek theories about the shape of the earth and the division of

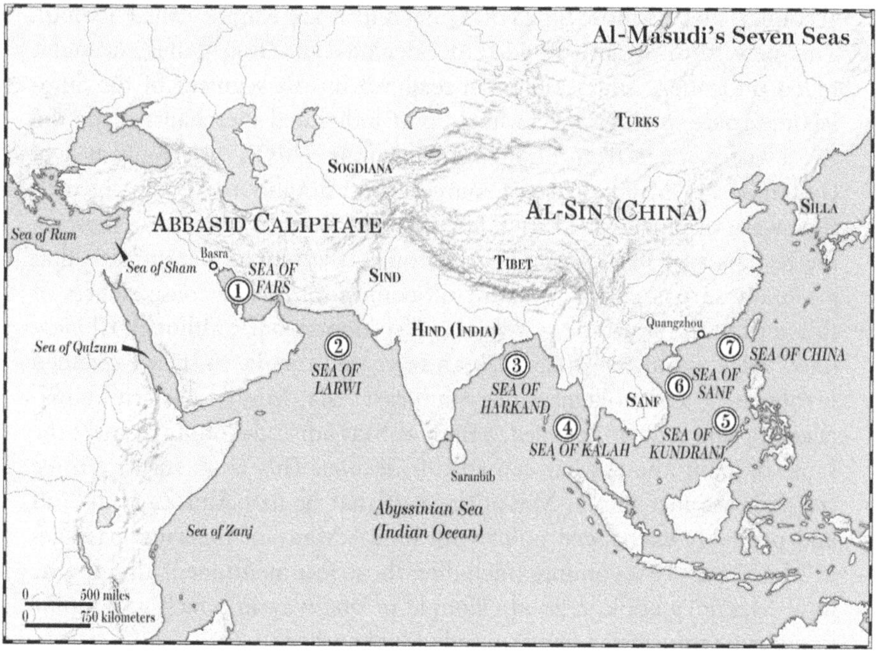

FIGURE 2.1. The seven seas described by al-Masʿūdī in his *Meadows of Gold and Mines of Gems* (circa 947).

the lands and seas.[63] A general account of the seas based on Greek tradition ends with the "Abyssinian Sea," that is, the Indian Ocean. Al-Masʿūdī portrays the Indian Ocean as one mass of water comprising seven connected seas. Each of these seas has its own name and features; the seventh of these lying at the easternmost end is the Sea of China.[64] This complete description of the Indian Ocean's seven seas supplements the missing part of the extant manuscript for the original volume of *Accounts of China and India* in 851 (Figure 2.1).[65]

This concept of sea division is similar to the Chinese division of five great seas in Zhou Qufei's *Land beyond the Passes* examined in Chapter 1, although the actual divisions and standards differ from each other. Whatever form it took, systemized information about sea divisions was crucial to geographers who sought to understand the shape of the world, and they were able to receive information about the seas from those who actually sailed in the vast ocean to reach their destinations. Muslim geographers always began their accounts with the descriptions of seas and islands, and they often updated these discussions based on new information from contemporary sailors of the Indian Ocean. Al-Masʿūdī also provided new geographical information about the coastline of the known world in his time, which can also be found in Abū Zayd's account:

> In the Sea of Rūm [the Mediterranean] near the island of ʾIqrīṭish [Crete], planks of ships of Indian teak, which were perforated and stitched together with fibers of the coconut tree, were found. They were of ships that had been wrecked and tossed about by the waves from the waters of the seas. This [type of ship] exists only in the Abyssinian sea [the Indian Ocean] because all of the ships of the Sea of Rūm and the west [emending ʿArab to gharb] are nailed, while the ships of the Abyssinian sea are not fastened with iron nails, because the sea water dissolves the iron, so the nails become thin and weak in the sea. So people [of the Abyssinian sea] used stitching with fibers instead of the nails, and [the ships are] coated with grease and lime. This proves, and God knows better, the connection of the seas, and that the sea near China and the country of Sīlā [Korea] goes all round the country of the Turks, and reaches the sea of the west [the Mediterranean?] through some straits of the encircling ocean.[66]

This discovery near Crete of the planks of a boat from the Indian Ocean surprised geographers of the tenth century, who correctly knew that the Indian Ocean was not linked to the Mediterranean. This could only explain how the individual planks flowed into the Mediterranean, al-Masʿūdī concludes. The seas did not connect to each other until the Suez Canal was constructed in the late nineteenth century. Yet, as we now know, Abū Zayd and al-Masʿūdī's suggested route is unimaginable because small dhow planks could never have floated all the way from the Sea of China to the Pacific Ocean, through the straight of the Bering Sea and into the Arctic Ocean, down Norwegian Sea near Skandinavia, and then through the Strait of Gibraltar at Spain in order to finally enter the Mediterranean Sea. Could the dhow ships have been carried overland to Egypt? Did shipbuilders in the Mediterranan Sea build ships without using nails, consciously or unconsciously imitating dhows? We may never know the story, but we can understand from the passage how Abū Zayd and al-Masʿūdī understood the geography of the world during their time.

Muslim geographers often describe the division of land and sea in narrative form, yet it is difficult to understand without considering their discussions about the world's physical geography, and maps that present geographic knowledge in visual form. Several different geographic schools and individual geographers coexisted and produced cartographic works from the tenth century onward. The most influential of these schools was the Balkhī School, named after al-Balkhī (died 934?), but there were also other geographic accounts and maps that portray the world and China

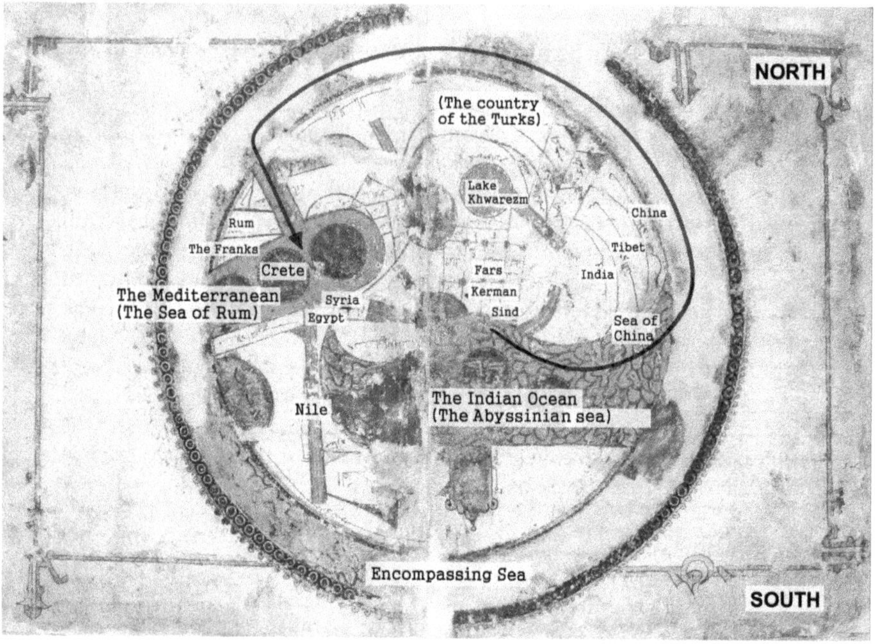

FIGURE 2.2. Al-Iṣṭakhrī's world map from his *Kitāb al-Masālik wa-'l-mamālik* (tenth century), copy of 1193. The original map placed the south on top; the map is reversed here for clarity (top). By permission of the Leiden University (MS. Leiden, Rijksuniversiteit, Or. 3101, pp. 4–5).
Note: *HC2:1*, Plate 7.

in independent ways based on a cartographer's personal experience in distant lands and other cultural influences. The earliest extant map that shows the relation of these seas, dated 1193, is attributed to a geographer of the Balkhī School named al-Iṣṭakhrī (died 961).[67] For example, the black arrow shows the route that Abū Zayd and al-Masʿūdī thought the planks of the dhow took from the Sea of China around the Northern Eurasian continent to the Mediterranean (see Figure 2.2).

The map helps us to understand Abū Zayd and al-Masʿūdī's idea in light of contemporaneous visual conception of the world that Muslim geographers shared at that time. The development of cartography in the Islamic world differs from that of China in that they attempted to show the entire world including Asia, Europe, and Africa. This fact stems partly from the legacy of the Greek geographic tradition and partly from the legacy of extensive contacts that the people in West Asia made with societies both to the east and west, which placed them strategically in the middle of the trading routes that connected these two parts of the world.

China and the World in Surviving Maps and Geographic Works in the Late ʿAbbāsid Period (circa 934–1260)

The authors of the earliest extant Arabic maps, al-Iṣṭakhrī (died circa 961), Ibn Ḥawqal (died circa 990), and al-Muqaddasī (died after 988) represent a new trend in geographic writing often dubbed the "Classical" or Balkhī School style, named for the earlier geographer al-Balkhī (died 934?) who influenced them.[68] They produced many geographic works in the free academic atmosphere that flourished during the reign of the Buyid Rulers of the ʿAbbāsid dynasty (although, to be clear, these scholars received no special sponsorship from the government). These cartographers classified the world systematically by political region. For the first time, they employed geographic boundaries to differentiate one country from another.

Living in the mid-tenth century, this new generation of geographers witnessed the gradual breakup of the Islamic world into separate political entities that acknowledged the religious, but not the political, authority of the caliph in Baghdad. We have seen in Chapter 1 that twelfth-century Chinese writers such as Zhou Qufei understood this simultaneous division of the Islamic world into different polities and cohesion as a region bound by shared religious and cultural traditions. Although contemporaries like al-Masʿūdī continued to show a broad interest in the world including China, the Balkhī School of geographers focused their agenda on the task of giving a full and detailed account of the Islamic regions, which they believed were most important and about which they received reliable information. Although the Balkhī scholars did not write about the non-Islamic world extensively, their works suggest a basic interest in the world and understanding of it. They mapped the entire known world, including China, before they composed regional geographic treatises and maps comparing different parts of the Islamic world.

Some contemporaries continued to follow much earlier traditional methods of geography that portrayed the world as a landmass in the shape of a bird with China as its head. For example, the tenth-century writer Ibn al-Faqīh (flourished 902) says:

> The image of the world consists of five parts: the head, two wings, breast, and tail of a bird. The world's head is China. Behind China is [a place] people called Wakwak. Behind this [country called] Wakwak are people whom no one except God counts [as one of his creatures]. The right wing is India, and behind India is the sea; behind this sea there are no creatures at all. The left wing represents Khazar [of the Caspian], and behind Khazar are two nations each of which is called Manshak and Māshak. Behind

> Manshak and Māshak are Gog and Magog, both of which are nations whom only God knows. The breast of the world represents Mecca, Hijaz [the western shore of the Arabian Peninsula], Syria, Iraq, and Egypt. The tail represents the land from dhāt al-Ḥumām [the frontier of Egypt] to the Maghreb [Northwest Africa]. The tail is the worst part of the bird.[69]

Ibn al-Faqīh, a writer of Persian origin, received his influence from the descriptive geographic tradition that began with Ibn Khurradādhbih. Instead of locating the world's places physically and in a dry form of narrative, Ibn al-Faqīh incorporated many legends and other forms of folklore to explain the geographic features of the different regions he studied, including China. This approach shaped his geographic study, *A Book of the Lands* (*Kitāb al-Buldān*), a type of book popular at that time.[70] His book marked the peak of an era in which Arabic geographic writing evolved into a form of *belle lettres* (*adab*) that attracted a broad readership. At the same time, other geographers including members of the Balkhī School maintained their scientific taste and sought to advance geography beyond this folkloristic method in order to create a more accurate geography of the world.[71]

In fact, the Balkhī School maps (see Figure 2.2) became a prototype for most maps made by later Muslim geographers.[72] A ring representing the "Encompassing Sea" surrounds the known world. The map is oriented along a north–south axis, and the south placed at the top in accord with the convention of Muslim geographers. Africa occupies much of the Southern Hemisphere, and the continent stretches eastward into the band of oceans that Islamic geographers thought encircled the world, with the southern part of the continent being *terra incognita*.[73] The Arabian Peninsula with Mecca is located at the center of the map. China is located at the eastern edge of the Northern Hemisphere and its coastline in the south lies close to the eastern coast of Africa. Although rough, this is a quite accurate representation of Eurasia and the northern part of Africa as Muslim geographers knew them at that time.

Later Muslim geographers like al-Masʿūdī testify to the world map that the scholars under Caliph al-Maʾmūn created in the early ninth century.[74] Unfortunately, the map no longer exists. Because the lost map was drawn based on new methods of astronomical measuring and mathematical calculations that were based on the Ptolemaic geographic tradition, it probably focused on presenting places in their accurate longitudinal and latitudinal positions. In addition, it most likely incorporated new theories proposed by al-Maʾmūn's scholars that challenged Ptolemy's works, including al-Khwārizmī's conclusion that the Indian Ocean was not an inland sea (as Ptolemy claimed) but connected to the Pacific Ocean.[75] This feature can be clearly seen in the earliest extant Islamic maps, in other words, the Balkhī School maps, in which the Indian Ocean links with the Encompassing Sea that surrounds the known world. Recall that Abū Zayd and al-Masʿūdī's theory about the dhow planks was based on this up-to-date geographic knowledge. Except for this new feature, other features of the Balkhī School maps resemble reconstructions of Ptolemy's longitudinal and latitudinal coordinates.[76] All this evidence suggests that the earlier maps based on the Ptolemaic tradition under ʿAbbāsid sponsorship continued to influence later geographic and cartographic works such as those made by the Balkhī School.

Despite their reliance on precedent, the Balkhī School geographers of the tenth and eleventh centuries certainly incorporated new features and updated information in their geographic and cartographic works. Breaking from the tradition that simply arrayed place-names according to the longitudinal and latitudinal coordinates, Balkhī School cartographers created the first maps to portray physical features such as mountains and rivers, a feature that would influence later maps. Although they did not draw their maps from firsthand observation, these geographers reported that they consulted travelers, sailors, and sea captains about the geographic features of distant regions and seas that they plotted and described. For example, al-Muqaddasī, a Balkhī School geographer who set the methodological foundation for the development of Islamic geography, says:

> Thus I became acquainted with men of standing who were born and bred there – shipmasters, cargo masters, coastguards, commercial agents, and merchants – and I considered them among the most discerning people with regard to this sea and its anchorages, its winds, and its islands. I questioned them about it, about the conditions on it, and about its limits. I also noticed navigation instructions in their possession, which they study together carefully and on which they rely completely, proceeding according to what is in them. From these sources I took copious notes of essential information, after I had studied them and evaluated them; and this I compared with the maps I have referred to ... I omit anything on which there is disagreement, and include only that on which there is complete accord.[77]

This episode shows how the geographers tapped new information circulating among merchants and travelers in order to update the geographic and cartographic works they published for a broader readership. As a member of the Balkhī School who concerned himself more with the Islamic lands than the wider world, al-Muqaddasī did not include China in his detailed regional maps. However, he does give the Sea of China, which earlier writers identified as the seventh sea to the east, a prominent role in his portrait of the Indian Ocean.[78] Although it was outside the Islamic world, China lay within the Muslim geographer's realm of knowledge about the world.

Although the Balkhī School maps exerted the greatest influence on later mapmaking, we should pay attention to the several other types of world mapping that developed independently of Greek geographic traditions. A sketch map drawn by al-Bīrūnī (973–1048) exemplifies just such a map, and exerted considerable influence on some important geographers. His map shows a different distribution of space that more closely matches modern-day representations (see Figure 2.3).

The relative locations of places in Asia, including China, bear similarity to sites plotted in the Balkhī School maps, yet al-Bīrūnī's sketch of the world bears considerable differences. An open oceanic expanse in the Southern Hemisphere that corresponds to the Indian Ocean replaces traditional *terra incognita* at the southern part of Africa in the Balkhī School maps. The Indian Ocean is therefore connected to the Atlantic Ocean under the southern tip of Africa (which is depicted as a rectangular, not triangular, shape).

Al-Bīrūnī was born in 973 in Khwarazm in Central Asia, which at the time sat at the eastern end of the Islamic world, although still far from the Islamic cultural center Baghdad. He was perhaps best known as a polymath; his skill in diverse fields like astronomy, mathematics, geography, and multiple languages (including Persian and Turkish) were well known. With this unusual intellectual talent, al-Bīrūnī amassed earlier geographic works in order to create a synthesis of all known theories of world geography from Greek, Persian, and Indian traditions, including ideas about longitudes and latitudes. He was familiar with Indian traditions of mathematic geographical measuring, such as the Indian coordinate table called the *Zīj* book that determined geographical positioning independently of the Greeks.[79] Together, the multiple perspectives of different schools and the knowledge he synthesized helped him to utilize new ideas about how to sketch the world map that presents new theories about the distribution of land and sea.

However, many of al-Bīrīnī's new ideas and information came to him through the journeys he personally made, especially to Asia. Although al-Bīrūnī did not travel as far as China, he gleaned much new information about places like China when he worked in the court of Maḥmūd of Ghazna in Northwest India. He knew enough about China to become the first Arabic author to distinguish between Khitā' (the Khitan Liao

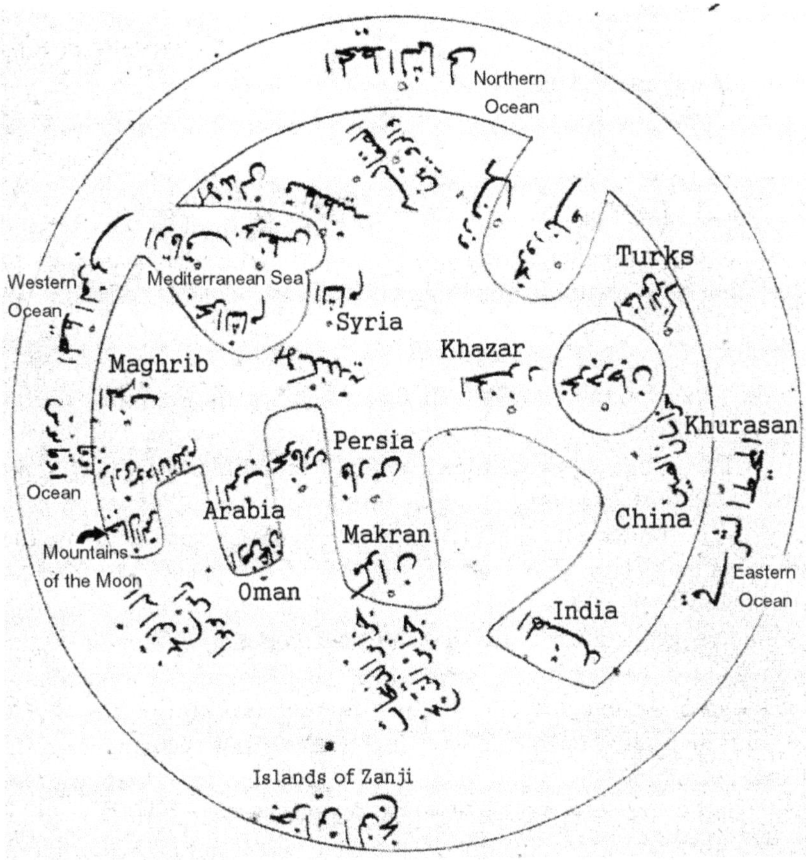

FIGURE 2.3. Al-Bīrūnī's sketch of the distribution of land and sea from his *Book of Instruction in the Elements of the Art of Astrology* (1029). The original map placed the south on top. By permission of the British Library, London (MS. Or. 8349, fol. 58a).

empire; Qitāy), which controlled the northern part of China proper, al-Ṣīn (the Song dynasty), which was confined to China's central and southern regions, and the Tangut Xixia to the west. The study provided the most significant update to Muslim knowledge about China's political division since the early tenth century. Al-Bīrūnī himself mentions in his writing that he received his information from the emissary of Khitai (*rasūl qitāy*; the Khitans), which his contemporary, the Persian geographer Abū Sa'īd Gardīzī (1049–1062), also recorded for the year 1026.[80] Although the overland silk routes after the ninth century were no longer flourishing, scattered sources like these show that occasional contacts between societies in northern China, Central Asia, and India did exist. Although the sketch map by al-Bīrūnī portrays only China (al-Ṣīn) and not the Khitai in northern China,[81] it does identify the lands of the Turks and Khurasan, places close to China by way of the overland routes.

Other types of maps from this period show how the people of the Near East gained greater knowledge about China through the overland connections. Kāshgharī's eleventh-century encyclopedic dictionary of Turkish language, for example, places Turkic Central Asia at the center of the map.[82] Obviously, the geographic knowledge of the world portrayed in the map circulated to the broad readership that had access to his dictionary.[83] This round Turkish map differs significantly from the contemporaneous Balkhī School maps because it does not show the coastline for any of Afro-Eurasia, or draw clear spatial relationship between regions. Yet, as Andreas Kaplony argues, Kāshgharī's small illustrative map records geographic data using unique visual language signs distinguished by color and shape. For example, the map usually marks the Turkish tribes with a yellow dot. Interestingly, the use of color-coding on the map in a language dictionary calls to mind the color-coding common to the language maps often found on the cover or back page of modern-day dictionaries. Although Kāshgharī, an educated Turkish nobleman, was Muslim and relied on methods of his Arabic-Islamic geographer forebears, he omitted Mecca and Medina.[84] Its form may seem simplistic, yet Kāshgharī's map adds new geographic knowledge that Turkish authors gained through overland contact between his country and northern China. He resembles al-Bīrūnī in that he reveals new knowledge about the political division that tore China into northern and southern halves during this period. Yet Kāshgharī used different terms, Chīn [China] and Māchīn [greater China], that would often appear in later Persian works.[85] Perhaps Kāshgharī learned about a political division of China when he undertook his alleged journey to the northeastern part of Eurasia, which may have included northern China; or perhaps this information was common among those who traveled along the overland routes of Central Asia.[86]

In an eleventh-century book entitled *The Book of Curiosities of the Sciences and Marvels for the Eyes* (*Kitāb Gharā'ib al-funūn wa-mulaḥ al-ʿuyūn*), a unique map illustrates the Silk Road extending across Central Asia without connecting to China.[87] This map probably reflects the decline in overland trade between the Islamic world and China in the tenth and eleventh centuries. However, as the information in al-Bīrīnī's account and the Kāshgharī map indicate, some partial overland contact between the Islamic world and China appears likely.

Some contemporary treatises written by Persian authors who utilized earlier Persian sources as well as Arabic geographic accounts also provide unique geographic information gained through several century-long overland connections. The earliest version of a Persian work by an anonymous author, entitled *The Regions of the World* (*Ḥudūd al-ʿĀlam*, 982), describes the entire world as it was known to Muslims in the tenth century.[88] It also distinguishes China as one of the world's countries. Most of the book derives from earlier lost Sogdian and Persian geographical treatises including al-Jayhānī. In describing cities and customs in China, the book calls China *Chinistan*, signaling the earlier influence of Sanskrit and Indian from the east on the Persian work. Similar to *The Regions of the World* is a work by another contemporaneous Persian geographer Abū Saʿīd Gardīzī, which would also influence later descriptions of China. The two works, along with other medieval Persian and Arabic texts, are important because they contain descriptions of various towns of China taken from a lost text that dates back to the second half of the eighth century. For example, Kashgar and Kucha, the towns in Eastern Turkestan that were occupied by various political forces including Chinese, Tibetans, Uighurs, and Muslims at the time of the Battle of Talas, were described as still belonging to China.[89]

A later twelfth-century Arabic work by the Iranian author Marwazī shares features that are similar to other Arabic-influenced Persian works, and moreover, supplies much greater detail in its account of China. It reflects previously divulged information about the division of China into northern and southern territories as seen in al-Bīrīnī's works. China "is divided into three categories," Marwazī explains, "namely al-Ṣīn, Qitāy, called by common people Khitai, and Uyghur," of which the greatest is the region and kingdom of al-Ṣīn. Marwazī also mentions the same source that al-Bīrūnī probably used to gather his new data about China; that is, the envoys of the northern China Khitan emperor to the court of Sultan Maḥmūd (died 1027), conqueror of India. In addition to recycled information, however, Marwazī's book contains much more detailed and accurate information about China than did earlier accounts. These include, for example, the Chinese zodiac and Chinese port cities like Guangzhou, where administrative and international trading systems were recorded in precise details.[90] Considering that this account provided detailed procedures and tax instructions for foreign ships that entered China (information that Marwazī's Chinese contemporaries carefully recorded), it seems likely that the Persian geographer gained additional information through channels created by limited connections between the overland and sea routes at the time. In any case, these unique pieces of geographic information produced in the eastern Islamic sphere, Iran, and northern India hint at one noticeable trend: The Muslim geographers who enjoyed closer access to Asia received better updates on China more swiftly than those who lived in the western Islamic world since the eleventh century. This trend grew soon after the Mongol conquest directly connected China with Iran in the thirteenth century.

The variety of maps and geographic treatises written in Arabic, Persian, and Turkish clearly shows a process of variation in Islamic geographic knowledge about the world based on different traditions and sources. It accompanied the diversification of the Islamic world through its expansion into Asia and interaction with its different peoples from the tenth century on. Regional Muslim writers interpreted the geography of the world, including China, in various ways by incorporating new information into their particular geographic treatises and maps in addition to expanded experiences and travels. Studies of geographic treatises in the eastern and western Islamic world over time show that core knowledge developed in different regions was mutually transferred, thereby helping the overall acceleration of geographic knowledge throughout the Islamic world. Ideas circulated throughout the Islamic world thanks to the interactions of scholars who moved freely to different political realms in search of royal patronage for their academic pursuits. It is not always easy to trace the channels of such influence; however, we can assume that new information gradually mixed with older local bodies of knowledge to create a new synthesis that in turn circulated through other regions.

One of the most important sets of cartography and geographic writing that reflect this accumulation and expansion of knowledge was made in mid-twelfth century Sicily, a Christian kingdom with a large Muslim population.[91] There, al-Idrīsī (flourished 1154) created a set comprised of a large, flat map of the world cast from silver (now unfortunately lost), paper maps, and the geographical treatise entitled *The Pleasure of He who Longs to Cross the Horizons* (*Nuzhat al-mushtāq fī ikhtirāq al-āfāq*), also called *The Book of Roger*.[92] Al-Idrīsī's compilation synthesized earlier works of geography from multiple sources, including physical and mathematical geographic theories about the shape of the earth in the Greek and Persian traditions, earlier Muslim geographical writings, and earlier Arabic maps (including those of the Balkhī School). This comprehensive world geography not only optimized earlier works but also added new information that became available to him due to his privileged sponsorship by the king of Sicily.

It would be impossible to discuss al-Idrīsī's celebrated works without acknowledging the role played by his sponsor, Roger II, the Christian king of Sicily (reigned 1130–54). Seized by Christians at the turn of the twelfth century, Sicily became a meeting ground for Christian and Muslim civilizations in the midst of conflict brought on by the Crusades in the Middle East. Unlike other European Christian monarchs of his day, Roger studied under Greek and Arab tutors who fed his intellectual curiosity and scientific interest, which included world geography. Roger hosted scholars from many regions, including al-Idrīsī from Morocco, who became one of the most celebrated Muslim scholars who worked in his court. Al-Idrīsī's patron charged him with an intellectually phenomenal task: Collect and evaluate all available geographical knowledge – from both books and firsthand observation – and organize it into an accurate and meaningful representation of the world.[93] His purpose was partly practical – to show off his political glory as well as better understand the true conditions of his kingdom. Yet Roger's interest in geography also sounds like an expression of the kind of scientific curiosity just beginning to awaken in Christian Europe. Eventually, this would replace older standards of geography, whose approach to making world maps was symbolic, fanciful, and myth-based rather than scientific. In this new spirit, the Christian king sought the Moroccan geographer to summarize all contemporary knowledge about the known physical world.[94]

Each section of *The Book of Roger* opens with a general description of the region under study and then lists principal cities, followed by detailed accounts of each city (including the distances between cities, a common feature of earlier geographic accounts). In his preface, al-Idrīsī sums up Muslim understanding about the shape of the world: The earth is a round globe covered with water and surrounded by air, and all creatures remain stable on the earth's surface thanks to gravity. These are all scientific ideas inherited from Greek scholars like Ptolemy and Muslim scholars who adopted and developed Greek geographic knowledge.[95] From here, Al-Idrīsī then describes the seven seas, including the Sea of China that begins from the east above the equator at thirteen degree and then passes along the equator to the west.[96] The flat silver map (almost eighty inches in diameter and more than 300 pounds in weight) that preceded the treatise could have illustrated the shape of the world as they imagined it.[97] Although it is lost, the accompanying maps survive and they provide glimpses into the kind of geographic content the silver map contained. They include a circular world map like that of al-Iṣṭakhrī (see Figure 0.1 for the original map and Figure 2.4 for the reconstructed sketch with English transcription) and seventy sectional maps that, when put together, form a world map that is similar to the round map. These are the first extant world maps that drew most of Eurasia and North Africa with detail and accuracy.

The seventy sectional maps present the known world using the longitudinal and latitudinal location system first created by the Greek geographers. These seventy maps together represent the seven climates of the habitable world (arbitrary divisions that circle the globe in parallel east-west bands from the Arctic to the Equator), and divide longitudinally into ten sections. When the first Arab geographer al-Khwārizmī created his maps in the eighth century, he adopted the Greek system directly, including the longitudinal-latitudinal coordinate table and the climate system with slight modifications. Numerous Muslim scholars in turn adopted al-Khwārizmī's climate system, including al-Idrīsī, who used the seven climatic bands and ten sub-sections to create a rough means for plotting longitudinal and latitudinal location. Each sectional map, therefore, represents a region of the world that readers could identify by placing it into context with other sectional maps. Al-Idrīsī inserted detailed material into each individual sectional map, which his geographical treatise supplemented with detailed descriptions of each region's society, culture, products, and goods. The northwestern part of the collected sectional maps (three climatic and two sectional bands) roughly corresponds to China.[98]

Al-Idrīsī's greatest achievement shows Europe with a precise coastline and provides accurate information about Europe's interior. He provides less precise information about Asia and China because he drew primarily on earlier sources like Ibn Khurradādhbih, Abū Zayd, and al-Mas'ūdī.[99] Like the Balkhī School and al-Bīrūnī maps, al-Idrīsī placed Central Asia north of China, which is roughly correct, and follows the Greek tradition of locating the legendary places of Gog and Magog northeast of China.[100] After comparing al-Idrīsī's maps with contemporary Chinese maps, Japanese scholar Ohji Toshiaki provided the interesting hypothesis that al-Idrīsī used a Chinese map to draw the country's coastline because their coastlines are similar. It is true that Roger II's court was crowded with scholars from many different societies. Some modern historians even claim that a few of these scholars probably came from China.[101] However, the contour of China's coastline in al-Idrīsī's map also bears similarity to the earlier Balkhī School maps, which undermines

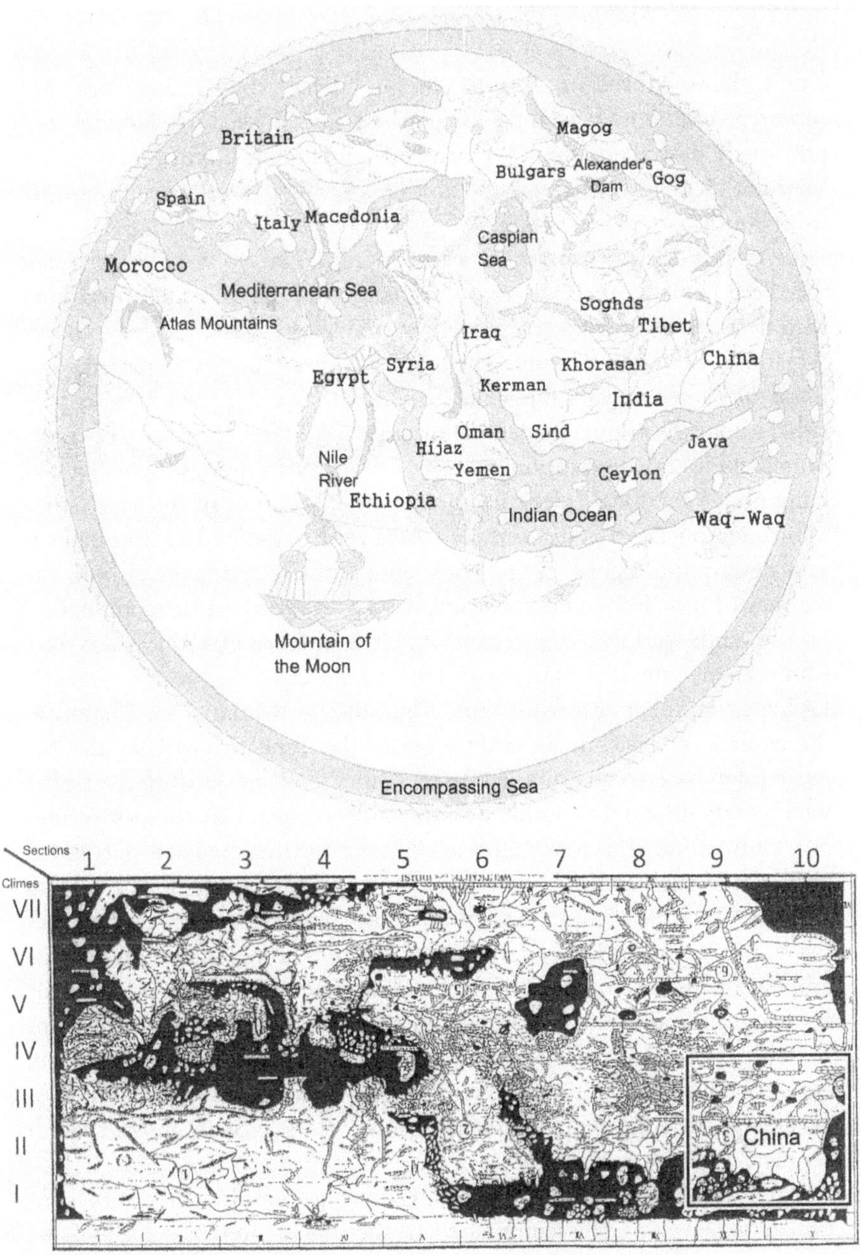

FIGURE 2.4. Al-Idrīsī's map of the world with place-names (top), and the sectional maps put together (redrawn based on a reconstruction by Miller) (bottom), from his *Pleasure of He Who Longs to Cross the Horizons* (1154). The original maps placed the south on top.

Note: The map is redrawn based on an earlier reconstruction of al-Idrīsī's maps by Konrad Miller. Miller, vol. 4, 160.

Ohji's claim. Moreover, al-Idrīsī's maps portray only those cities that earlier generations of Islamic geographers like Ibn Khurradādhbih had previously described but never mapped – including Lūkīn (modern-day Vietnam), Khānqū (Guangzhou), and Jānkū (Quanzhou) on the coastline from Southeast Asia to China.[102]

In fact, al-Idrīsī's geographic compendium *The Book of Roger* filled the three climatic and two sectional bands that he allocated for China with derivative knowledge obtained by analyzing the Islamic geographers previously cited. For example, the tenth section of the first climate in *The Book of Roger* repeats the same accounts that earlier works also provided about the Chinese ruler, major cities, and the importance of trade. This includes his description of the court appeals system in which a bell hung above the local ruler's head, a clear elaboration of the same story found in Abū Zayd's *Accounts of China and India*, and recapitulates it as a description of justice that took on a Chinese character in both the manner of monarchy and government.[103] At the core of the compilation (in the tenth section of the second climate), al-Idrīsī introduces the river Khumdān as one of the largest and most famous of the world's rivers.[104] Earlier geographers used the name Khumdān as the name for Chang'an, the capital of the Chinese empire under the Tang dynasty, so al-Idrīsī must refer here to the Yellow River, China's second-longest river near which early imperial cities like Chang'an developed. Clearly, al-Idrīsī did not know about the new Chinese capital cities that existed during his own period such as Kaifeng and Luoyang, capitals of the northern Song dynasty (960–1127) and the southern Song dynasty (1127–1276) respectively. Because al-Idrīsī predominantly used previous Muslim knowledge and hardly any original material, he did not need Chinese informants for his geographical works. The assumption that there were Chinese maps or scholars at Roger II's court in Sicily, therefore, sounds far-fetched. However, his compilation provides a good demonstration of the geographic knowledge available to Muslim scholars in Sicily in the twelfth century.

After al-Idrīsī's masterful work, Islamic geographic literature continued to develop. This culminated in the production of a place-name dictionary that remained the most authoritative geographical dictionary in the Islamic world for centuries – the *Geographical Dictionary* (*Muʿjam al-buldān*, circa 1224) by Yāqūt ibn ʿAbd Allāh al-Ḥamawī (died 626/1229).[105] Alphabetically arranged, this dictionary bases each entry on historical and sociological data accumulated from many earlier literary and scientific works.[106] By devoting considerable space to

China, Yāqūt helped to formalize and broadly circulate Muslim knowledge about China among intellectuals seeking to enhance their knowledge of the world.

Yāqūt's entry on China follows his usual format: He cites the historical or mythological origin of the place-name, plots the kingdom's physical location, and then provides historical notes and anecdotes. Following this pattern, Yāqūt begins by analyzing the meaning of al-Ṣīn, repeating the old legend that the Chinese are descendants of Noah's son Yaphet, information he would have found in Ibn Khurradādhbih's earliest surviving work. Then he determines China's location at the longitude 164 °30′. Yet, in addition to this derivative information, he adds new knowledge. For example, he describes the division of northern China (the Khitan Liao) and southern China (the Song dynasty) – an historical fact that Muslim geographers acknowledged since the tenth century, including al-Bīrūnī, Kashgari, and Marwazī. He also incorporates anecdotal information about Muslims who traveled to China for trade and in doing so received the sobriquet *al-Ṣīnī*, "one who had been to China."

Although Yāqūt relies on prior sources for all his information, he considers these secondhand accounts as less than reliable. He argues that none of his contemporaries actually ever visited China because it was too distant from their own land, even for those merchants who traveled only as far as the Muslim communities of Southeast Asia. His information confirms earlier accounts by Abū Zayd and al-Masʿūdī that Muslim traders no longer traveled to China as they had in the eighth and ninth centuries (due to Huang Chao rebellion from 875 to 884) and confined their sea trade with China to Southeast Asia. This may be correct for the maritime routes (or according to what Yāqūt knew), but it is certainly incorrect with regard to the land routes that experienced dramatic political changes beginning in the early thirteenth century. By the time of Yāqūt's death in 1229, the charismatic Mongol leader Chinggis Khan had already conquered parts of north China with the help of Muslim merchants (among others) in Central Asia and transferred myriad Muslims to Mongolia and northern China.

The period of the United Mongol empire (1206–1260), although not examined thoroughly in this book, was crucial for the Chinese-Muslim contacts along the land routes between the Qarakhanids and China. The Qara Khitai (Western Liao) empire in Central Asia, which was founded by a Khitan Liao descendent who fled from the Jurchen conquest of their homeland in North China, also played a crucial role in maintaining contacts between China and the Islamic world during this period.[107]

Finally, we should not overlook an important Persian geographical work written by Muḥammad ibn Najīb Bākran in 1244. His *Jahān-nāmah* (World Book) illustrates the Iranians' updated understanding of China through new contact channels from the land and sea at that time. First, it pointed out the sea ways briefly, mentioning that, "from Kholzum (red sea) to China there are 200 places (or stations)."[108] Although earlier Arabic accounts describe routes between the Persian Gulf and China, this Persian work presents new routes that connect China and the Red Sea. It also provides a general description about China similar to those found in earlier geographic works like Ibn Khurradādhbih's, namely that China is a very big state that has 300 large and affluent villages and cities. Yet it adds additional information about China being divided into "Chīn (China)" and "Māchīn (greater China)": "[O]ne part, which is safe and affluent, is called Absolute China or Exterior China, and the other part, which is located in the east, is called Interior China or Machīn."[109] More importantly, although the world map is not extant, the written text contains a vivid description of the world in which China and countries related to it are clearly distinguished. Judging by the written description, the lost map might well have been the oldest Islamic grid map, 130 years older than the first extant grid map drawn by Ḥamd Allāh Mustawfī in the fourteenth century; these maps will be discussed further in Chapter 4.

Preceding the Mongol conquest of a significant part of the Islamic world by 1260, knowledge about China that had accumulated during the previous centuries of flourishing contact continued to expand in different parts of the Islamic world at different times. It was a small yet important part of overall Islamic understanding of *terra cognita*; an understanding that was the most accurate and comprehensive in the world at that time.

Conclusion

The political and commercial expansion of the Islamic world during the ʿAbbāsid dynasty prompted the development of the field of geography beyond the inherited Greek, Iranian, and Indian traditions. Based on earlier world geographic theories, the ʿAbbāsid geographers situated the Islamic world at the center of the known world. To this, they incorporated fresh contemporary information unknown to their Greek predecessors, illustrated by the clear inclusion of detailed information about China at the eastern edge of their known world. The merchants and sailors who frequently sailed in the Indian Ocean to China during the ninth and tenth centuries returned to their West Asian homelands with valuable goods and abundant information about the societies in which they visited and often settled for long periods of time. Their stories about the exotic goods and cultures of eastern Asian societies found their way not only into nonfiction literature, but also into fantastic fables about Indian Ocean sailors like Sinbad the Seaman and stories that took place in China in *One Thousand and One Nights*. Muslim merchants and sailors also gave more substantial, detailed, and accurate information about China, its society, and its trade routes to professional writers like Ibn Khurradādhbih, Abu Zayd, and al-Masʿūdī who collected, systematically arranged, and published this information for general readers during the ninth and tenth centuries. Thanks to its flourishing contact with China, largely through the dhow ships that sailed directly between the port cities of Arabia and China, Islamic geographical knowledge about the known world grew, transforming China from *terra incognita* to *terra cognita*. This early description provided a crucial foundation for later works that further expanded that knowledge.

A close comparison of Muslim accounts from different periods shows that much information about China was transmitted directly from earlier to later generations, as can be seen in the case of Ibn Khurradādhbih's contribution to the geographical achievements of the two great Arabic geographers: al-Idrīsī in the twelfth century and Yāqūt in the thirteenth century. In the process of recycling earlier information, scholars of twelfth- and thirteenth-century China and the Islamic world show different approaches to perpetuating a phenomenon of accretion. Whereas Zhao Rugua borrowed massively from Zhou Qufei while adding considerable new information, Yāqūt, by comparison, adds little new information. He claims that a change in the sea transportation system that began in the late ninth century led to the decrease in merchant travel from the Islamic world to China.

The event that affected this change finds testimony both in Chinese and Arabic sources. At the turn of the ninth and tenth centuries, Muslims gradually began to settle in South and Southeast Asia and establish permanent diasporic communities there. With few exceptions, Muslims no longer sailed all the way from the Persian Gulf to Chinese ports; instead, they conducted trade far from China through middlemen merchants who sailed between South and Southeast Asia and China through the eastern Indian Ocean. This shift in the structure of transportation probably decreased the amount of information merchants from the Islamic world could obtain about the country through maritime connections. From the tenth century onward, in fact, Middle Eastern knowledge about the entire Indian Ocean realm grew largely derivative. Interestingly, some Muslim writers who enjoyed closer connections to China through overland routes provided updated information about China, such as the empire's division into north and south. As information aggregated and circulated, geographers developed more diversified and comprehensive images of the world and China by incorporating new information into their geographic treatises and by drawing maps in creative ways. Even after the breakup of the ʿAbbāsid empire and the Islamic world fragmented into multiple regional powers, Muslim scholars continued to share both an academic tradition and a body of common knowledge through constant travel and exchange.

All this accumulated geographic knowledge created the foundation for the two great syntheses by al-Idrīsī and Yāqūt. Al-Idrīsī created the most sophisticated world map of his time, which clearly shows China at the eastern edge of the world and delineates itscoastline, connecting China to the Islamic world. This map would exert a lasting influence on the Islamic world for centuries to come. The basic framework for al-Idrīsī's map came from earlier Islamic geographic works that were, in turn, based on Greek and possibly Iranian traditions. However, Muslim cartographers like al-Idrīsī updated these earlier theories with newly acquired facts. Departing from the Greek theory that the Indian Ocean is a closed sea, Islamic world maps began to portray the Indian Ocean as an open sea connected to the Pacific Ocean. These maps retained many inaccuracies, of course. Like the Balkhī School's diagrammatic world maps, al-Idrīsī's map of Africa stretches so far eastward that it occupied most of the Southern Hemisphere. Nevertheless, his Ptolemaic framework contains accuracy to resemble modern maps.

In Chapter 3, we will return to China to consider the intriguing possibility that these Muslim maps probably influenced Chinese cartographers as well during the Mongol Period, when many Muslim scholars transmitted Islamic scholarship to the Mongol court in China. This led to the first production of a Chinese map that includes a fairly accurate coastline of the Arabian Peninsula, Africa, and Europe.

3

Interpreting the Mongol World

Chinese Understanding of the Islamic World, 1260–1368

In the middle of the fourteenth century, Wang Dayuan from China wrote an account about his travels through the Indian Ocean in which he allegedly sailed as far as West Asia and the East African coast. The author, who probably had a classical Chinese literary education, modeled himself after the great historian Sima Qian to create a narrative based on both extensive travel and information collected from firsthand interviews. In contrast to his Venetian contemporary Marco Polo, whose story about travel to China between 1271 and 1298 was initially rejected by his fellows, Wang Dayuan enjoyed acceptance – even sensation – among Chinese, with a preface by the famous Chinese writer Wu Jian and citations in local gazetteers. Wang was not the first Chinese to visit West Asia, bring back information about it, and report on it. Travelers like Du Huan had already undertaken these tasks centuries before, as Chapter 1 shows. However, Wang Dayuan traveled west freely in order to satisfy his curiosity; Du went there forcibly as a prisoner of war. A change in environment resulted in a growing interconnection between China, West Asia, and the East African coast commercially and culturally and reached its prime by the time Wang Dayuan set forth on his journey in 1328. This great expansion of maritime contacts and pan-Asian commercial networks (evident in Wang's travelogue) resulted from the great political change that swept through Eurasia during his era – the establishment of the Mongol empire – that also reopened the overland routes and enlarged the scale of Eurasian contact.

Between the thirteenth and fourteenth centuries, all of China became a part of the Mongol empire, the largest continuous land empire that ever existed. Mongol rule over all of China lasted barely one century, yet during this short time it provided Chinese with unprecedented opportunities to establish contacts with people living in the distant western regions of Asia, including Muslims. At the same time, their successful expansion into West Asia, and particularly the establishment of a Mongol regime in Iran during the middle of the thirteenth century, prompted many Muslims to travel to China by both land and sea. This movement of people, bringing with them commodities and ideas from their homelands, brought about the direct transfer of information and knowledge from Mongol-ruled Iran to Mongols living in China and to Chinese themselves. The consequences of this two-way pan-Asian traffic are quite clear. For the first time, Chinese cartographers began to draw fairly accurate representations of Arabian, African, and European coastlines based on Muslim maps. They began to depict the sea route to Hormuz, the most important port in the Persian Gulf during the Mongol era. Before Wang Dayuan, another Chinese named Yang Shu also followed the Asian coastline directly to Hormuz in the Persian Gulf and contributed first-hand to the explosion in Chinese knowledge about West Asia and the greater Islamic world. These travelers' ventures to West Asia reflect only part of the thriving contact that the people of the Mongol period witnessed. Thanks to this expanded contact, a greater number of Muslims, both from the Islamic world and the developing Muslim communities in South and Southeast Asia, migrated to China and settled there, establishing Muslim communities.

This chapter examines Chinese language sources in order to determine the extent of cross-cultural contact between China and the Islamic world between 1260 and 1368 and its impact on the dramatic expansion of Chinese knowledge about the Islamic world due to the unparalleled scale of contacts during the Mongol era. It will explore how the Mongols contributed to the acquisition of this new knowledge about the Islamic world, thanks in part to the cosmopolitan atmosphere that they developed during their one-century rule over China. It is clear that Chinese expanded their geographic knowledge by taking advantage of their increased contact with foreigners, including Muslims. This raises the following questions: What kind of legacy did earlier Chinese leave for Chinese and Mongols during this period? What was the type of knowledge that first appeared during this period, and how does it differ from that of the previous period? What events precipitated specific knowledge acquisitions and who was involved? How did the Mongols facilitate the transfer of ideas in these instances of increased contact? And finally, how reliable were the sources?

Expanded Chinese Knowledge about the Islamic World through the Mongol Conquest of China and Iran

When the Mongols began to sweep across northern Eurasia, China was divided into two kingdoms: The Jin dynasty that ruled northern China under the Jurchens (1115–1234),[1] and the southern Song dynasty that ruled southern China (1127–1276). Because of geographic limitations, they each used different channels to receive new information about the Islamic world. The Chinese of the southern Song already had a clear sense of the coastal route to the Islamic world due to their engagement in maritime trade with foreign countries. For example, Zhao Rugua's early thirteenth-century geography, *Description of the Foreign Lands*, provided Chinese with unprecedented information about foreign countries that they could reach by sea. In contrast, geographers living under the Jurchen-Jin dynasty in northern China were exposed to new information about overland routes to West Asia when the Mongols began to reclaim these routes in the course of their conquests, and the dynasty began to interact with the ascendant empire.

The Mongols were herding nomads who historically lived on the Eurasian steppe, moving to different pastoral lands in pursuit of new grass for their herds. In the course of their movements, they contended with other nomadic tribes and the Chinese. This pattern continued over many centuries, until Chinggis Khan unified the Mongols in 1206 and the conquests began, and did not end until Mongol rule stretched all the way to Hungary from the Pacific. The conquerors moved relatively swiftly: the Qara Khitai empire in 1218, the Khwārazm Shāh dynasty in 1231, North China in 1234, Russia in 1240, Baghdad in 1258, and South China in 1276. The Mongol conquests of Eurasia helped to revitalize diplomatic contacts between China and the Islamic world through overland routes that had been hindered by political conflicts since in the mid-eighth century. Yet the conquests did even more than that: They resulted in the political unification of two societies by joining Islamized Central and West Asia to China. When Chinese living under Jurchen-Jin rule in northern China submitted to Mongol rule after it destroyed the dynasty in 1234, they quickly became directly engaged with the western reaches of the Islamic world because the Mongols recruited them into their armies and sent them westward. The reports of those who traveled to these western regions helped Chinese back home quickly understand changes in the political landscape that were taking place around them and update their general knowledge about the geography and societies of the Islamic world.[2]

One surviving account from this period, *The Record of an Embassy to the Regions in the West* (*Xishi ji*) [1263], describes the most important political event in the Islamic world at that time; namely, the fall of Baghdad to the Mongols and the establishment of a new Mongol regime, the Il-khanate in Iran. The book's author, Liu Yu (flourished 1260s), recorded what the Chinese envoy Chang De (flourished 1260s) saw and heard during his journey to see Mongol Khan Möngke's brother Hülegü (died 1265) just as Hülegü's armies conquered Iran.[3] Liu divided the general's account of his journey into two parts. The first part is an itinerary of his trip to Iran. Chang De departed from Khara Khorum in 1259 and traveled along the overland Silk Road through the Central Asian regions of Bishbalik, Talas, Samarkand, and Qilier (probably near Mazanderan) where his journey ended on April 28, 1259. The first part of Liu Yu's account of Chang De's travel itinerary probably derived from firsthand information because it includes the distances and times required to travel between places. Liu's dull description of each country, including geographic location, natural environment, and local products leave us to only imagine the likely astonishment that the Chinese in general must have felt as he passed through the vast and exotic landscapes that existed outside China.

The second part of Liu Yu's account includes details about the fall of Baghdad and descriptions of countries in the Islamic world that were conquered by the Mongol armies. Unlike the first part of the book, this part was probably based solely on secondhand testimony. By the time Chang De arrived in Iran, Hülegü's campaign had already ended. The fourteen months that Chang De spent in Iran after leaving Khara Khorum did not allow the envoy enough time to travel so widely. Still, his description of the fall of Baghdad is quite vivid:

> In the year of Dingsi (1258) [Hülegü's Mongol army] conquered the kingdom of Baoda (Baghdad). It stretches 2000 *li* from north to south. The king is called Helifa (Caliph). The city (the capital) was divided into a western and an eastern part. A large river [the Tigris River] ran within the city. The western city had no walls, but the eastern one was fortified by walls built of large bricks. The upper part of the walls was splendidly constructed.
>
> When the imperial army [of Hülegü] arrived beneath the walls of the city, they initiated battle, and defeated over 400,000 soldiers in gaining victory. [At first] the western city was taken and the army massacred all of the population. Then they pursued besieging the eastern city and conquered it after six days, and those who were killed were several hundred thousand. The Helifa (Caliph) tried to flee in a river boat [through the river], but he was captured.[4]

Contemporaneous accounts such as that of Marco Polo confirm the last days of the Abbasid caliphate.[5] Liu's passage on Baghdad continues with fairly accurate information about the caliphate:

> With regard to its society and population, the kingdom [of Caliph at that time] stood in the lead of the western regions ... This kingdom had existed for around the six hundred years under forty rulers, and fell during the time of the (last) Caliph ... Local people say that Baghdad was the patriarch of all the Hu people (people of the western regions) and therefore all of them were subject to it.[6]

Here, Chang De provides specific, contemporary information. He realizes, for example, that the Abbasid caliphate retained symbolic authority over the decentralized Islamic world until it fell to the Mongols.[7]

His brief descriptions of different parts of the Islamic world, such as Mecca (Tianfang), Egypt, Fulang (Franks), and Shiraz, focus on regional products and customs. The most notable one describes the Shiraz region of southwestern Iran:

> The kingdom of Shiraz produces pearls. The name of the ruler is Aosi Atabei [Atabeg: Common title for a Turkish governor of a province in Mesopotamia from the twelfth century]. To the country's southwest is located a sea (the Persian Gulf), and pearl fishing flourishes. They use a leather bag. In order not to bother their hands [in order to have their hands free], they attach a rope to their loins, and thus they glide down to the sea. Take pearl-oysters along with sand and mud, and put them in the bag. When they encountered sea monsters [insects?], they squirt vinegar against them and drive them away. When they filled the bag up with oysters, they pull the rope so that the men above in the boat hoist them up. Sometimes some pearl-fishers die (in the sea).[8]

In the thirteenth century, after flourishing several centuries as a capital under Arab and Iranian Muslim rule beginning in 693 CE, Turkish governors (atabegs) who had become independent of the ʿAbbāsid dynasty began to govern the region as the dynasty's power declined. Some atabegs cooperated with and even joined Mongol armies in their conquest of the Persian region.[9] Possibly, Chang De acquired some of his information about the territories west of Iran from Shiraz men that he encountered in Mongol barracks. Chang De's description of pearl fishing serves as one of the earliest information available today about pearl fishing in the Persian Gulf, along with contemporary Arabic geographers like al-Masʿūdī and al-Idrīsī.[10] The practice would have been well-known at places that Chang De visited like Shiraz, not to mention other places in West Asia.

Liu Yu's *Record* concludes by stating that updated information from the Mongol expedition allowed Chinese to learn about many of the changes that had taken place over the years in western countries, a region that Chinese had known since Zhang Qian's expedition there in the second century BCE.[11] Liu Yu's account has survived to the present by virtue of its insertion into significant literary collections by contemporaneous Chinese authors such as Wang Yun (1227–1304).[12] Were there similar Chinese accounts of the Islamic world and the Mongol's world-changing westward expansion and geographic information about its countries?

A similar account of Hülegü's expedition into the countries of western Asia can be found in the biography of a Chinese general who fought for the Mongols, Guo Kan (1217–1277); it appears in the official history of the Yuan dynasty, which the Mongols formed to rule China.[13] The account clearly reflects a wider dissemination of information about the Islamic world into China through different sources. Many Mongolian and Chinese soldiers participated in this successful westward expedition, so it is not surprising that some of them chose to write about the Islamic world they saw firsthand. The two generals (Guo Kan and Guo Ziyi) produced accounts that bear many similarities, but the differences are worth noting.[14]

According to the Yuan official history, Guo Kan actively engaged in Mongol campaigns of conquest against more than 300 cities in West Asia, and pursued one of the Caliph's generals, named Zhou-da-er, whom he had been ordered to kill.[15] Considering the fact that the Ming dynasty editors of *The History of the Yuan* omitted much information about the dynasty's expanded contacts and relations with other countries in their rushed compilation process, this surviving information offers particular value. The Ming court historians were hardly interested in shining a light on the Islamic world and its peoples. In fact, they sought to bring into relief the meritorious deeds of General Guo Ziyi (697–781), a Han Chinese hero and descendant of the famous Tang dynasty. In doing so, they coincidentally produced a narrative valuable to understanding how the Mongol conquests in western Asia laid the foundation for further contact between China and the Islamic world.

The Mongol conquests of West Asia under Hülegü soon led to cross-cultural migration between Chinese and Islamic worlds. At about the same time as his conquest of the ʿAbbāsid empire, Hülegü created the Il-khanate in the Islamic heartland, whose territory comprised modern-day Iran, Iraq, Turkmenistan, Azerbaijan, Georgia, Armenia, and a large part of Anatolia. In other words, the core of the Islamic world became a part of the Mongol empire and integrated with Mongolia and Mongol-ruled northern China where the Grand Khan of the Yeke Mongol Ulus (the Great Mongol empire) resided.[16] This newly opened overland connection between China and the Islamic world through the largely Islamized societies of Central Asia allowed large numbers of Iranian Muslims to migrate from Central Asia to Mongolia and China.[17] No doubt this migration led to increasing contacts between Muslims and Chinese living in northern China, leading some Muslims to become active collaborators with Mongol rulers.

Yet it was Khubilai's enthronement as the fifth Grand Khan of the Mongol empire in 1260, and Hülegü's acknowledgment of his brother's position, that facilitated full-scale exchanges of commodities, people, and information between Mongol-run China and Iran. Khubilai, brother to both Hülegü and the reigning Khan Möngke, hoped to conquer southern China and therefore, he challenged his younger brother Arigh Böke (died 1266), whose camp lay on the Mongolian steppe. Upon Möngke's death in 1259, Khubilai enthroned himself as both Khan of the Mongol empire and Emperor of China. Arigh Böke and his supporters opposed Khubilai, but Hülegü sided with Khubliai and recognized him as Grand Khan, settling the matter.[18] Twelve years later, in 1271, he named his Chinese dynasty the Yuan.

After Khubilai's victory, the solidarity of the khanates of the Mongol empire weakened and as political conflict erupted among rival Mongol khanates, the security of the reopened overland routes connecting China and the Islamic world again fell into peril. Nonetheless, the relationship between the two Mongol regimes in China and the Islamic world remained secure, and this set stronger foundations for continuous exchanges by developing a direct route between the two societies, this time interacting more by sea than by land. After all, China and the Islamic world had already communicated across the maritime routes for centuries.[19] Nevertheless, how did the Mongols, who had absolutely no experience with maritime travel, come to utilize the waterways?

Here, we should remember that the Mongols' speedy and successful conquest of such a vast portion of Eurasia was thanks to their special ability to embrace and utilize the expertise of conquered populations in order to facilitate further expansion. They adapted to Chinese political realities, for example, when the Khan proclaimed the Yuan dynasty and thereby asserted his legitimate succession to previous Chinese dynasties. Despite their nomadic origin on the steppe, the Mongols achieved victory over the navy of the southern Song dynasty ruling over southern China by quickly adopting Chinese naval techniques and strategies. Their defeat of the southern Song in 1276 granted the Mongols full maritime access to the Islamic world through the international seaports in South China like Quanzhou. This marked a significant turning point in the history of Mongol rule in China.[20]

After destroying the southern Song and uniting all of China, the Yuan dynasty received support from both Chinese and Muslims, including Pu Shougeng (flourished thirteenth century) who held extensive power over China's sea trade. Pu served the Song government as a superintendent in the Office of Merchant Shipping in Quan[illegible] where he played a decisive role in the Yuan victory over the So[illegible] after he defected from the Song to the Yuan.[21] Pu Shougeng wa[illegible]endent of Muslims who came to China for trade and settled ther[illegible]rname "Pu" is a Chinese transcription of the Arabic word *Abū*[illegible] means "father of."[22] Pu Shougeng and other influential Muslim[illegible]nese families in Quanzhou supported the Mongols in order to pr[illegible]eir family interests, including their investment in maritime trad[illegible] result, these maritime people found themselves in an advantage[illegible] position, serving a regime that considered the sea as an important means to maintain contact with the Il-khanate, their closest political ally. An expedition sent to Java between 1292 and 1293, and the dispatch of envoys to Southeast and South Asian states, can both be understood as an effort by the Yuan court to maximize maritime contact that had already flourished under their southern Song predecessors.[24] As a result, maritime contact and exchange grew beyond its previous levels.

The increased inter-Asian contact on both land and sea, which was facilitated by the two Mongol regimes in Iran and China, saw new groups of middlemen contributing to the exchange of geographic knowledge between the societies. Mongol nomads served as mediators for cultural transmission and exchange between the two societies, as Thomas Allsen argues in a series of studies of exchanges that took place between the Yuan dynasty and the Il-khanate.[25] When early campaigns began to sweep across Central and West Asia, the Mongols recruited Muslim soldiers, artisans, and merchants into their fold.[26] Allsen provides a vivid picture of the wide transference of silk and gold brocade from Central Asia to China, as well as their skilled craftsmen, who were mostly Muslim textile workers. The Mongol ruling elite made extensive use of these textiles as a kind of benchmark measuring military success, which encouraged consumption.[27]

Mongol rulers appointed Muslims and other non-Chinese foreigners (*semuren* in Chinese) to important government positions traditionally held by the Chinese.[28] Muslims who worked alongside the Mongols and the Chinese often served as financial administrators, governors, and tax collectors, which caused some ill-feeling amidst the Chinese. Negative images of Muslims began to take form as they were portrayed as avaricious, aggressive, and miserly. Among those Muslims that Chinese writers regarded with abhorrence was Aḥmad, who wielded great power as a minister in the Yuan government. He was assassinated by his opponents in 1282. This negative stereotype was not universal, however. Other Muslim officials received Chinese praise for their work. Among these was the first governor of Yunnan province during Khubilai Khan's reign, Sayyid ʿAjall Shams al-Dīn (1211–1279), whose dedicated work for economic and cultural development in Yunnan earned him a great reputation.[29]

The Yuan court did not confine its appointment of Muslims to political and commercial spheres. Muslim officials during the Yuan period also exerted a profound influence on the government's academy, an institution of great prestige and political importance that traditionally remained under the control of Chinese officials. However, the Mongol government created special offices for Muslims, like the Islamic Imperial Academy (*Huihui Guozijian*) and the Islamic Astronomical Bureau and Observatory (*Huihui Sitiantai*), an indication of the important role that Muslims played in the Yuan academic system. Chinese usually referred to Muslims as the "Huihui" instead of *Dashi* as Chinese documents had done during the Mongol period.[30] Scholars attending these Muslim institutes at the Mongol court, according to Chinese sources, conducted their discourse in the "Huihui" or "Muslim" language, which in most cases meant Persian.[31] We can assume, then, that Persian-speaking Muslim officials from Central Asia and Iran introduced Islamic culture to their Chinese peers as they worked together in the Mongol court. Undoubtedly, their intellectual activities contributed to the further increase of Chinese academic knowledge about the Islamic world. Concrete examples exist. For example, one of these recruited Muslims, Jamāl al-Dīn (*Zhamaluding*, flourished at the end of the thirteenth century), became the first director of the Islamic Astronomical Bureau, which had been established in Shangdu in 1271 in order to operate as a parallel institution to the traditional Chinese Astronomical Bureau.[32] Jamāl al-Dīn soon became the supervisor of the Palace Library (*xing mishujianshi*), where he supervised both astronomical bureaus as subordinates.[33] Both the official Chinese court history of the Yuan and a work called *The Account of the Palace Library* (*Mishujian zhi*) document his achievements in the fields of astronomy and geography.[34]

Jamāl al-Dīn contributed to Chinese astronomy with his 10,000-year calendar (*Wannian li*), essentially a Chinese translation of the Islamic planetary tables that modified Ptolemy's *Almagest*. Although the court distributed it as an official calendar only for a short while, the calendar probably influenced the Huihui calendar (*Huihui li*) that Chinese officials came to use along with the official Chinese *Shoushi* calendar (*Shoushi li*).[35] The astronomy section in the *History of the Yuan Dynasty* states that Jamāl al-Dīn provided Khubilai Khan with seven astronomical instruments in 1267. This included an astrolabe and a colored terrestrial globe with grids, which probably represented the longitudinal and latitudinal coordinate system that Islamic cartographers used.[36] It is also possible that Jamāl al-Dīn brought Islamic maps to China or acquired them in China from other Muslims. Most of these maps no longer exist, nor do many other Chinese maps of the western regions from the Mongol period. This does not prevent an examination of geographic knowledge, but it does call for new approaches. Historians can extract valuable data from maps that were drawn in later periods based on earlier maps like the lost works of the Yuan period. This is critical to understanding geographical knowledge during the Yuan era because only one original Yuan-era map of the world still exists.

The Expanded Chinese Knowledge about the Islamic World Reflected in Extant Maps

The Yuan-era map, originally a part of *The Encyclopaedia of Yuan Dynasty Institutions* (*Yuan Jingshi dadian*, circa1330), survived by virtue of its insertion into a Qing period compilation, Wei Yuan's *Illustrated Treatise on the Sea Kingdoms* (*Haiguo tuzhi*, 1842) (see Figure 3.1).[37]

This Yuan map deviates considerably from earlier Chinese maps, both with regard to its techniques and to its geographic contents. First, the orientation of the map differs. Although the mapmakers placed the Chinese characters for each of the four directions at corresponding corners of the map, they placed the south on top of the page. In this case, Islamic geographic thinking influenced Chinese cartography. No earlier surviving Chinese map contains such an orientation. Grids may also reflect a second Islamic influence in Chinese geography. Similar grids appear on the Song map called *The Tracks of Yu*, which was carved on the backside of the stone tablet *Map of China and the Non-Chinese Countries* in 1136. As we have seen in Chapter 1, its grids serve as a general measure of distance in which each square converts to 100 *li*. In contrast, the grid

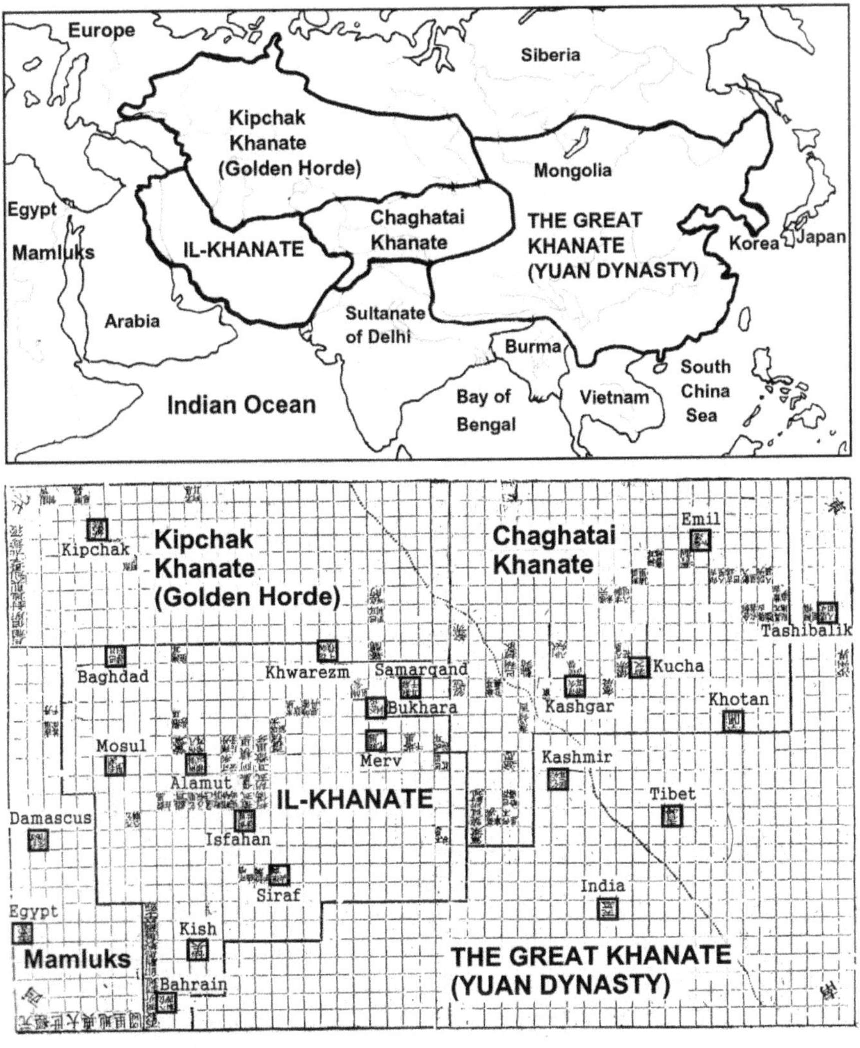

FIGURE 3.1. Four Khanates of the Mongol empire (top); a geographical map from *The Encyclopedia of Yuan Dynasty Institutions* (*Yuan Jingshi dadian*, circa1330), in Wei Yuan's *Illustrated Treatise on the Sea Kingdoms* (*Haiguo tuzhi*, 1842). The original map placed the south on top; this map is reversed here for clarity (bottom).

Note: Wei Yuan, Haiguo tuzhi (Taibei, 1967), 219–220. Bretschneider compared the place names with those in an appendix entitled "Sibei di (the countries of the north-west [of China Proper])", which is at the end of the geography section of the Yuanshi (YS 63:1567–1574). They correspond with each other, although there are some differences. For details of the place-names, see Bretschneider, vol. 2, 18–136.

on the Yuan map probably serves as a system for locating specific points in a two-dimensional projection of the terrestrial sphere. Although the map's x-y axes bear no numerical markers, each place has been assigned to a single square, suggesting the axes function as precise longitudinal and latitudinal coordinates. As Chapter 2 showed, this two-dimensional projection of the terrestrial sphere predominated in Islamic mapmaking. Most likely, Chinese geographers of the Mongol period were exposed to the technique through Islamic geographical works that they acquired. Such a coordinate system probably resembles the grids of the colored terrestrial globe that Jamāl al-Dīn provided in 1267 to Khubilai Khan.[38] In fact, the earliest use of a map grid employing both longitudinal and latitudinal coordinates appears in thirteenth and fourteenth-century Persian works, which includes a map that resembles the Yuan map. Chapter 4 will further compare the two maps to analyze the possible transfer of the geographic information and cartographic techniques between China and the Il-khanate during the Mongol period. First, it is important to understand what new geographic knowledge this map contains.

The Yuan map displays the place-names of regions far to China's west – in all, fifty-five sites in Central Asia and another fifty in West Asia, all the way to the Mediterranean. This includes sites like Damascus, Kish, Alamut, and Isfahan that are not found in surviving Chinese maps of earlier periods. The Qing dynasty editor Wei Yuan mentions only his addition of four place-names to the southeastern side of the map that he originally took from the *Yongle Encyclopaedia* (*Yongle dadian*) [1408].[39] Wei Yuan probably kept the entire map intact except for these minor changes. The overall geographic content of the map clearly differs from previous geographic information about overland routes between Mongolia and West Asia because it depicts a complete, two-dimensional image of the world in Central and West Asia. At the time of the map's composition, most of this world had been conquered by the Mongols and incorporated into one of four khanates: the Yuan dynasty, the Golden Horde, the Chagatai khanate, and the Il-khanate. The map shows these four subdivisions of the Mongol empire and, in one small area on the left-bottom side, the Mamlūk domain, which resisted a Mongol invasion in 1260. Most of the places on the map are quite accurately located, showing that the cartographer had precise knowledge of the geographic space he observed. The Yuan government was clearly aware of this expanded geographic knowledge before the publication of *The Encyclopedia of Yuan Dynasty Institutions* in 1331, yet it is obviously earlier, most likely during Khubilai's reign (reigned1260–1294). In the short text that annotates the Yuan map in his *Illustrated Treatise*, Wei Yuan cites the *Yongle Encyclopaedia* as his source yet fails to explain how its creators drew their map. In the same text, however, he also mentions the compilation of *The Treatise on the Great Unified Realm of the Great Yuan* (*Dayuan da yitong zhi*), the Yuan dynasty's greatest geographical project, which was ordered by Khubilai Khan and completed in 1303. Wei Yuan's acknowledgment strongly indicates a connection between the project and the map. The historical context also reinforces this.

After conquering southern China in 1276, Khubilai became the head of an empire that stretched all the way from Hungary to the Pacific. Although his actual authority covered mainly China, Mongolia, and Tibet, we can easily surmise that he ultimately intended to bring the entire world under his dominance. If so, geographic information about his realm was vital to his political ambitions. Khubilai's desire for such knowledge was satisfied by Jamāl al-Dīn in 1286 when he petitioned the khan to sponsor the production of a unified geographic treatise that would cover all the lands that the Mongols had conquered. Khubilai ordered the Palace Library to collect geographic gazetteers and maps from every region of his empire in order to compile his great treatise.[40] Completed in 1303, the *Treatise on the Great Unified Realm of the Great Yuan* contained 600 books and 1,300 chapters, with emendations and additions. Although it does not survive today except for its introduction, we can assume from references to it that the treatise originally included extensive descriptions of foreign countries.

The compilation of maps deserves more attention with respect to this project. The following memorial, submitted by Jamāl al-Dīn to Khubilai in 1286, discusses the court's interest in drawing a new and larger world map to accompany the *Treatise*:

> The entire land of China was very small in the past. The geographic books of the Khitai (Chinese) had only forty to fifty types. Now all of the land from the place of sunrise to sunset has become our territory. And therefore, do we not need a more detailed map? How can we understand distant places? The Islamic maps are at our hands. And therefore, could we combine them [with the Chinese maps] to draw a [world] map?"[41]

This passage, reported in *The Account of the Palace Library*, plainly states that the scale of geographic understanding about China and the world under the Mongol emperor and his staff exceeded that of previous Chinese courts. Its speaker embraces the entire world and implies that the world the Chinese knew in previous times had been a much smaller world. In order to satisfy this need for increased geographic knowledge,

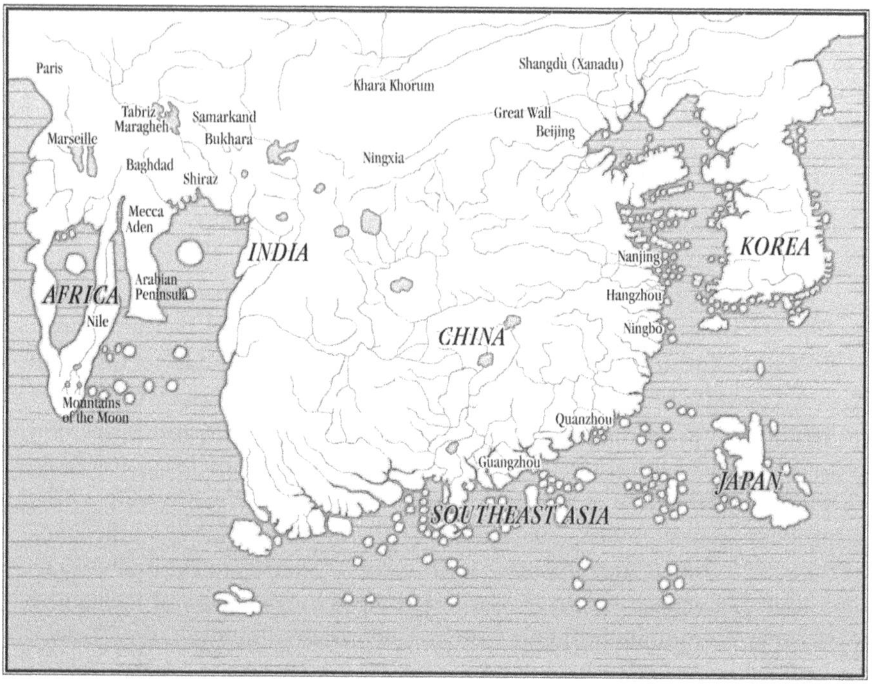

FIGURE 3.2. *The Kangnido* (1402) with place-names (see also Figure 0.2 for the original picture).

the Mongol court could draw on both Islamic maps, which Jamāl al-Dīn and other Muslims acquired from the Islamic world, and also existing Chinese maps.

Despite the possibility that scholars used Islamic geographic works to compile *The Treatise on the Great Unified Realm of the Great Yuan*, no Yuan dynasty maps survive even as later copies, with the exception of the grid map previously examined. We can reconstruct what other Mongol period maps might have been like by examining surviving maps from later periods that based their information on Mongol period maps. The most useful map of this kind is *The Map of Integrated Regions and Terrains and of Historical Countries and Capitals* (*Honil gangli yeokdae gukdo jido*), hereafter referred to as its short name, the *Kangnido*. Drawn in Korea in 1402, it survives thanks to a copy dated 1470 (see Figure 3.2)[42]:

The authors of this map combined data from different maps to compose its various parts. In his afterword located at the bottom of the map, one of the map's authors, Gwon Geun, reports that he and his fellow

Korean mapmakers used two Chinese maps that a Korean envoy named Kim Sahyung brought home with him from China in 1399: Li Zemin's *Map of the Resounding Teaching (of the Khan) Prevailing All Over the World* (*Shengjiao guangbei tu*) and Qing Jun's *Map of Integrated Regions and Terrains* (*Hunyi jiangli tu*).[43] Scholars assume that the Korean authors used Li Zemin's *Map of the Resounding Teaching* to draw the western part of the world because another extant Ming period map, *The Broad Terrestrial Map* (*Guangyu tu*), used Li Zemin's map to create its partial drawings of Africa.

An analysis of the *Kangnido* helps to reconstruct the Mongol worldview of West Asia, Africa, and Europe as it existed around 1300. Looking at its cartographic contours, the map shows West Asia, Europe, and Africa together for the first time in the East Asian cartographic tradition. The proportions of these regions in relation to China are distorted; China and Korea loom large while the Arabian Peninsula, Africa, and Europe appear small. Although not drawn to scale, the shapes of these landmasses were drawn with surprising precision. For the first time in history (on an extant map), Africa appears in the form of a triangle. The Chinese cartographers who drew this could only have consulted Islamic maps. However, no extant Islamic map provides precisely the same content provided in the western section of the *Kangnido*, leaving a mystery that will have to be solved later when new evidence appears. Perhaps this content derived from the firsthand observations of some Muslims who sailed around the African horn[44]; after all, some argue that the Chinese sailed around the horn of Africa before the Portuguese, although no extant archaeological, documentary, or inscription evidence supports this assertion.[45] One plausible hypothesis based on existing evidence is that Chinese cartographers modified the contour of Africa in the course of combining both Chinese and Islamic maps. The explanation for Africa's elongated curve to the east in Arabic world maps such as those by the Balkhī School and al-Idrīsī could be a simple one: It was necessary in order to fit the continent into the round frame of Muslim world maps. However, Chinese maps were traditionally drawn in a rectangular frame because Chinese cosmology viewed the earth's shape as a quadrangle under a spherical sky.[46] Therefore, when Chinese cartographers incorporated Africa into their rectangular frame, they had to stretch it back vertically while still maintaining its pointed bottom as depicted in Arabic maps, thus making it look like an upright inverted triangle.

The detailed, colored illustrations of the African continent in the *Kangnido* provide clear evidence that the mapmakers drew on the earlier

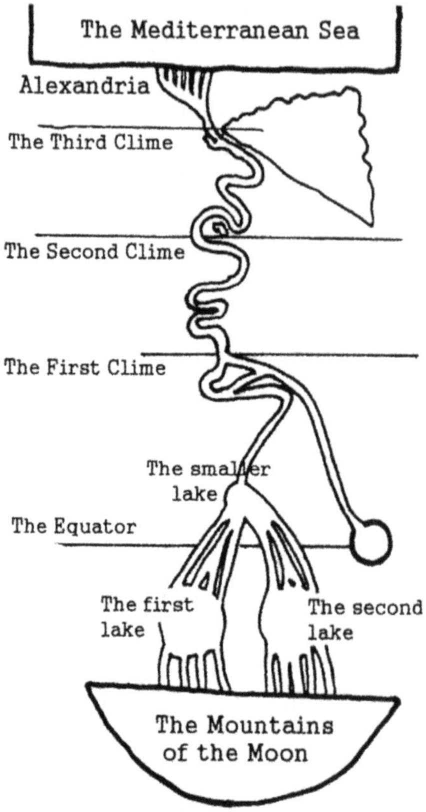

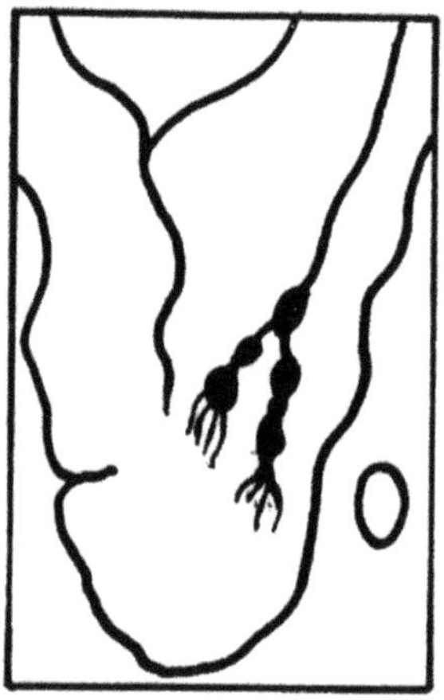

FIGURE 3.3. Comparing depictions of the Mountains of the Moon. Al-Khwārizmī's picture of the Nile (left); a depiction in al-Idrīsī's world map (top, right); and a depiction in the *Kangnido* (bottom, right).

Islamic maps for their information. In addition to the Sahara Desert and the Pharos lighthouse of Alexandria, the map shows the three sources of the Nile River called the Mountains of the Moon in almost identical fashion to Islamic geographic works that date back to al-Khwārizmī (died around 850) (see Figure 3.3).[47]

The Mediterranean Sea in the *Kangnido* is also quite precise. The map appears to portray the body of water as a lake instead of a sea, but on closer examination it becomes clear that a later copyist mistakenly painted over the Straits of Gibraltar with the color for land, erasing the Mediterranean's channel to the Atlantic.

In addition to its fairly accurate contours, the *Kangnido* provides detailed content. It demonstrates knowledge about 100 European and thirty-five African and West Asian place-names. For example, the city of Marseille in modern-day France appears on the European part.[48] African and West Asian place-names include Samarkand and Bukhara in modern-day Uzbekistan, Maragheh/Marāgha in modern-day Iran, Tripoli in modern-day Libya, Baghdad, Mecca, Aden, and Shiraz in modern-day Iran.[49]

Even though the *Kangnido* portrays entire Eurasia, it misses one significant piece of information: It does not clearly depict a clear coastline for South and Southeast Asia. This is not unusual; earlier Chinese and Islamic maps similarly fail to draw accurate coastlines beyond the cartographer's homeland. In general, earlier Chinese maps drew places in Southeast and South Asia as islands surrounded by a large sea, whereas the Islamic maps followed the model of al-Idrīsī and simply did not present accurate coastlines for these regions. The Chinese and Korean authors who created their maps from a combination of several different maps (including one of China and another of West Asia, Africa, and Europe) neglected to fill in the area in-between.

Still, literary sources make clear that many Mongols and Chinese during the Mongol period were familiar with the sea routes that connected China and the Islamic world. The Mongol government in China possessed sea charts that they acquired from Muslim sailors. A passage in *The Account of the Palace Library* dated February 1287 says that "Muslims who sail on the seas of Fujian Province (*Fujian dao*) possess *la nama* (*Rāh-nāma*, literally 'the book of routes' in Persian) that shows the sea route in their language [meaning Persian]. They brought it to those who came from the Secretariat (*zhongshu xing*) to submit."[50]

The "Map of the World Regions" (Guanglun jiangli tu) that was included to a Ming dynasty work whose preface was written in 1452, yet which was originally drawn in 1360, draws several lines in the sea that look like sea routes.[51] It also provides concise long-distance navigation guidance in blocks near the most important ports on the coast. A block near Quanzhou along with a line that extends toward the west says, "Riding the wind from Quanzhou, one can reach Java in sixty days, Malabar in 128 days, and Hormuz in around 200 days" (see Figure 3.4).

Hormuz (an island near the modern-day Strait of Hormuz) was one of the small states in the Persian Gulf that became a vassal of the Il-khanate and paid tax (*kharāj*) in order to keep a high degree of autonomy.[52] Sīrāf, once the most important port in the Persian Gulf for trade with China during the Tang period, gradually declined. In its place arose Qais (*Kīsh* in Persian) and Hormuz, two islands that competed with each other for trade supremacy. Hormuz gradually replaced Qais as the Gulf's main

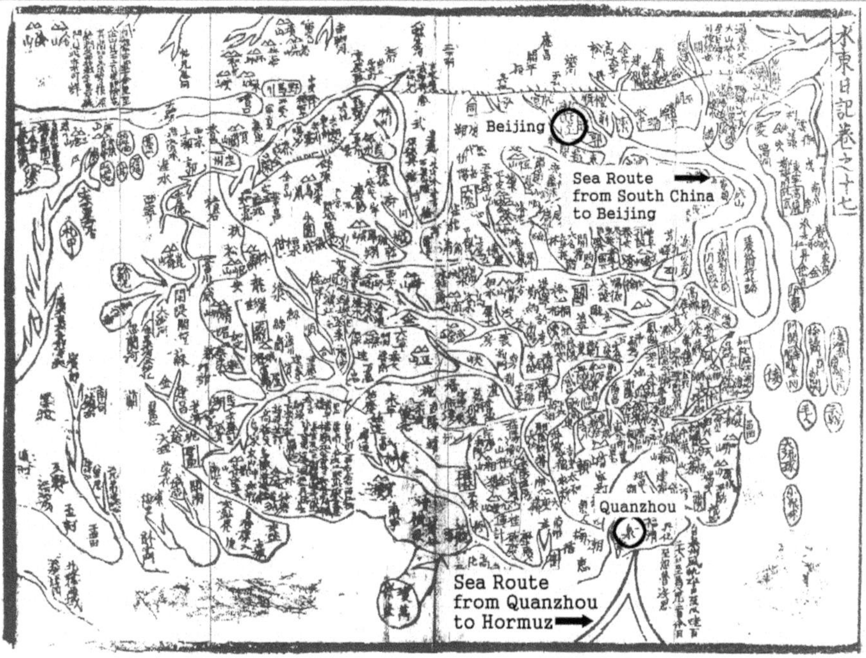

FIGURE 3.4. "Map of the World's Regions" (1360) from Ye Sheng's (1420–1474) *Diary from East of the River* (*Shuidong riji*). Preserved in the Library of Congress.

port in the thirteenth century, and flourished for more than two centuries as a focal point for Indian Ocean trading networks and the most important cosmopolitan commercial center in the Persian Gulf. From Hormuz, merchants transshipped goods from India and China to the Islamic world.[53] As we will see, most Yuan period Chinese geographic accounts of western countries mention and even describe Hormuz (whose name they transcribe in various ways), an indication that contemporary geographers utilized up-to-date information about West Asia and its maritime connections instead of recycling earlier information. The route shown on the map suggests that maritime routes were frequently traveled; contemporary Islamic sources discussed in the next section support this claim.

Another block of text indicates a route that leads from South China to the Yuan capital Dadu (or Daidu; modern-day Beijing) by way of the Shandong Peninsula. Traders began to use this route as an ordinary sea shipping (*haiyun*) route beginning only in the Yuan dynasty.[54] This route connected to Zhigu, the port at Tianjin, and to Dadu through "Jishui tan," facilitated by a lock canal built by Khubilai.[55] The two blocks of text about navigation testify to the maritime route that connected the Yuan capital with the Persian Gulf under the Il-khanate during the Mongol period. Many envoys from the Yuan court and the Il-khanate, as well as merchants and travelers from other Muslim countries and Europe, traveled along sea routes. This map confirms the active interest that Mongol and Chinese geographers paid to maritime trade, and documents their accurate knowledge about the maritime routes leading to the Islamic world.

As we saw at the beginning of this chapter, the reopening of the land route between China and West Asia by the Mongol conquest expanded overland contacts between China and the Islamic world. Yet, the maritime realm should not be neglected, because Sino-Islamic maritime contacts also peaked during the Mongol period, thanks to the expansion of routes and commercial connections in the Indian Ocean. The overland routes remained not entirely safe due to wars among the feuding khanates of the Mongol empire; the maritime routes suffered fewer obstacles by comparison. Many policies facilitating maritime trade and expeditions to Southeast and South Asia enacted by Mongol rulers in China demonstrate to the importance of the maritime routes to the ties between the Yuan dynasty in China and the Il-khanate in Iran and further west.[56] Written and archaeological evidence testify explicitly to the booming maritime contact during the Mongol period. That vivid traffic was an important gateway for the exchange of commodities and knowledge between China and the Islamic world.

Expanded Chinese Knowledge about the Islamic World through Increased Maritime Contacts

Muslims spread throughout China during the Mongol era. Chinese had long interacted with Muslims, especially with merchants who mainly lived in Chinese port cities like Guangzhou and Yangzhou. Under Mongol rule, however, the number of Muslim residents increased dramatically because many Muslims had migrated to China as army recruits during the Mongol conquests. Also, Muslim traders had been providing financial support to Mongol rulers since early Mongol campaigns. The most important category of these Muslim merchants who cooperated with the Mongols was the *ortagh*, a name that originated from the Turkish word "*ortoq*," meaning "colleagues."[57] Persian sources about the Muslim *ortaghs* who worked for the fourth Grand Khan Möngke describe many episodes that testify to activities of these Muslim merchants in China before 1260.[58] As the Mongol empire expanded south, many of these Muslims migrated southward and settled largely in commercial centers of port cities like Quanzhou and Hangzhou in southern China, increasing Muslim populations there.

With the defeat of the southern Song, the Mongols won control over China's sea routes, encouraging Muslim merchants there to continue collaborating with the Yuan court by engaging in international maritime trade. The *ortagh* merchants exemplify this trend, given the important role they began to play in government-sponsored maritime trade. The process was simple: The Mongol court would ask these merchants to purchase certain commodities by prepaying for them, then the merchants would acquire the goods and bring them to the court, sometimes through a governmental office like the Branch Quanzhou Prefecture Office (*xing Quanfu si*). In return, they received an interest in the trade[59] through an instrument that resembles present-day limited partnerships.[60] Some of the commodities that *ortagh* merchants purchased (such as pearls, ivory, and slaves) arrived through maritime trade.[61] No doubt the *ortagh* and other foreign merchants who engaged in maritime trade based their operations in Quanzhou, the most important seaport connecting China with foreign countries during the Mongol era. Muslim merchants took advantage of not only their Mongol ties but also their extensive ties to diasporic Muslim communities that inhabited all the major seaports in the Indian Ocean and the expanded trading world it offered them.[62]

As all Mongol period accounts about Quanzhou testify, the previously small port city reached its heyday as one of the world's biggest international seaports during the thirteenth and fourteenth centuries. Evidence indicates that Muslim families who settled in Quanzhou during the Yuan period arrived from both northern overland and southern maritime routes. Arabic funerary inscriptions in Quanzhou provide the most concrete evidence of the large-scale presence and activities of the Muslims who migrated to China from various places in the Islamic world. A Muslim trader named Shi Nawei from Sīrāf built the first of these Muslim graveyards in the southwestern corner of the city's suburb during the Song period (960–1276), which places the community in Quanzhou long before the arrival of the Mongols. Nonetheless, the fact that the number of tombstones increased markedly during the Yuan period suggests a time of prosperity for the Muslim communities in the city. Most of the tombstones with clear Yuan-era dates indicate names of West Asian origin, including Qazvin and Tabriz in Iran, Bukhara and Herat in Central Asia.[63] It is highly likely that many of the Muslims who claim *nisba* (a part of an Arabic name that indicates one's ancestral home) in West and Central Asia actually came from diasporic Muslim communities in South Asia; Southeast Asian Muslims probably adopted *nisba* as well. Although they had long lived outside the Islamic heartland, they maintained political and, more importantly, commercial connections with the Islamic world, and used their in-between position to develop international trade networks between West Asia and China. The scale of the Muslim community in China undoubtedly spanned a much larger part of the empire than simply Quanzhou, but the evidence clearly identifies the city as the central hub of a vast network of Muslim international trade and community.

Some newly found inscriptions in Quanzhou help us to identify influential local Muslim families, other than the Pu family that became famous because of the thirteenth-century Muslim official Pu Shougeng. The tombstone for Amīr Sayyid Toghān Shāh from Bukhara provides concrete evidence of a Muslim family that, according to the official history of the Yuan dynasty, migrated to China as a consequence of Chinggis Khan's westward expedition and settled in Quanzhou.[64] In addition to his tombstone, the official history of the Yuan dynasty contains his biography, which identifies him as *Huihui* or Muslim and a descendant of *Peyghāmbar*, a Persian word for the Prophet (Muḥammad). Another Quanzhou tombstone for Ding Jiezhai from the Yuan era (1327) states that family migrated to China at the end of the southern Song dynasty and settled in Quanzhou to conduct maritime trade, a claim supported by the family's extant genealogical records. Genealogy of the current Ding family living near the southern gate of Quanzhou states that their ancestor Ding Jiezhai later became a government minister in Yunnan.[65] In fact, ancestor Ding was none other than the famous Yuan minister Sayyid ʿAjall Shams al-Dīn (Saidianchi Shansiding: 1211–1279), who indeed ruled Yunnan as governor during Khubilai's rule. Most of the Hui people with family name Ding who live near the southern gate of Quanzhou's old city claim to be his descendants.

These Muslims living in Quanzhou, many of whom held governmental positions during the Yuan dynasty, worked with the Yuan government to facilitate and control the city's trade activities. One of the systems that the Yuan government established for that purpose was the Governmental Ship (*guanben chuan*) system, created in 1285 to monopolize foreign trade and prohibit private maritime trade activities. Soon, the government abolished the Governmental Ship system and allowed private trade, only to revive the system in 1298 by establishing the Bureau for the Procurement of Necessities (*zhiyong yuan*), which encouraged both governmental and private maritime trade activities at the same time.[66]

Muslims as well as Chinese participated in the international trade that the Yuan government supported. A well-documented case of state engagement in maritime trade and its connection to Chinese relations with the Il-khanate recalls the voyages of a Chinese merchant named Yang Shu. He sailed to Hormuz in the Persian Gulf on a government ship while escorting envoys from the Il-khanate back to their homeland. Yang Shu came from the Yang family in Ganpu (Zhejiang province), who were originally from the region of Min (in present-day southern Fujian) and had engaged in high positions of maritime trade for several generations.[67] Even at the age of nineteen, his experience in navigation and trade won the young Yang selection by the Mongol government to sail to West Asia.[68] His epitaph describes his two voyages:

> ... In 1301, when he was nineteen, the Bureau for the Procurement of Necessities (*zhiyong yuan*) sent him to sail on a Governmental Ship. Reaching the Western Ocean (*Xiyang*), he met the envoys Na Huai and others whom "qinwang" Ghazan dispatched to the capital [of China: Beijing], and finally boarded [their ship] and came back [to China]. When Na Huai's tribute mission ended, he asked Yang to escort them to return to the West. A prime minister (*chengxiang*) Hala hasun·da lahan (Qarqusun tarqan) followed that request and proposed to give Yang "zhongxian xiaowei," and "haiyun fu qianhu" to accompany him and make him adorn a golden-tablet (paiza?).
>
> In 1304 he departed the capital, and reached the destination called Hormuz in 1307. During this task, Yang traveled in the midst of long winds and big waves over the course of five years. On the whole, all of the ships, foods, and utensils came from him, and he did not trouble officials [in the Zhiyong Yuan]. For the most part, Yang used his private money to trade local products – white horses, black dogs, amber, wine, and a kind of foreign salt to present [to the government], the manager of governmental affairs Chana and others received him in audience to the emperor's chamber (*Chenqing zhan*) and [he] left.[69]

Yang Shu sailed to the Western Ocean on his first voyage (1301–1304) and met with the envoys of Ghazan, who became the seventh ruler of the Il-khanate (1271–1304). The second voyage (1304–1307) names his destination in Iran as Hormuz, which was also the final destination of the maritime route drawn in the "Map of the World's Regions" (Guanglun jiangli tu). Persian sources as well as Marco Polo's travel account recall the exchange of envoys between the Yuan dynasty and the Il-khanate (see

Chapter 4). One of these exchanges resulted in Na Huai's visit to China in which Yang Shu played an important role.[70]

Yang Shu's account of his first voyage to the Western Ocean demonstrates a Yuan period geographic concept that divided the Indian Ocean and the China Sea into the Eastern Ocean and the Western Ocean for the first time in Chinese history, a division that later geographers gradually adopted to refer to a world divided into east and west. This systemic geographical division first appears in *The Record of the Southern Sea* (*Nanhai zhi*, 1304), edited by Chen Dazhen.[71] *The Record of the Southern Sea* divides countries in the western regions between the Eastern Ocean and the Western Ocean.[72]

In this scheme, the Eastern Ocean and Western Ocean are divided along the west coast of Kalimantan and the Strait of Sunda; thus, the Western Ocean that encompasses the Indian Ocean starts at the west coast of Kalimantan. *The Record of the Southern Sea* first defines the "small" Western Ocean, which spans from western Java to Sumatra and Malacca, and secondly the "large" Western Ocean that extends further west across the Indian Ocean. It then defines the small Eastern Ocean that stretches from northern Kalimantan to the islands of the Philippines and the large Eastern Ocean from the Strait of Sunda to the islands of Sulawesi, Timor, and Molucca via Java and southeastern Kalimantan.

Compilers of *The Record of the Southern Sea* drew from a mix of new and old sources to create the place-names they used to describe the Islamic world. Some countries such as Baghdad, Ghazni, Wuba (Mirbat), and Mojia (Mecca) in the Arabian Peninsula, and Wusili (Egypt; *Misr* in Arabic) in Africa appear in the earlier Song-era *Description of the Foreign Lands* by Zhao Rugua. Some parts of the book use Chinese characters with pronunciations that were similar, yet slightly different, from earlier accounts. For example, Mecca was presented as *Majia* [*ma-ka*] in accounts by Du Huan and Zhao Rugua but as *Mojia* [*mək-?*] in *The Record of the Southern Sea*. These new transcriptions indicate that the author did not borrow all of his information entirely from earlier works. New names such as Kuolifusi (Hormuz), Wengman (Oman) and Yada (Aden??) irrefutably demonstrate expanded Chinese geographic knowledge of the Islamic world during the Mongol period.

The Chinese needed geographic information about these distant societies because of their commercial networks in the Indian Ocean. As a local gazetteer from Guangzhou, *The Record of the Southern Sea* documents the prosperity of the port city and its foreign trade, and therefore provides a key primary source on Chinese contacts during the Mongol period.[73]

Like Zhou Qufei's *Land beyond the Passes* and Zhao Rugua's *Description of the Foreign Lands*, the *Record* describes local products, foreign trade, and foreign countries based on information that the authors acquired from others. For example, the section on trade goods (*bohuo*) begins:

> The Yuan dynasty covers the ends of the four seas [all over the world] where the sun and the moon rise and set, and no one dares not to bring tribute, kowtow, and call themselves vassals. Therefore the strangeness of seas and mountains, and humans and beasts, and the diversity of pearls and rhinoceroses are always stored in the internal [governmental] storages ... the [dynasty's] wealth in precious goods is now twice that written in previous gazetteers. Now I listed the countries, the names of which we know, as an attachment after the section of bohuo (trade goods).

Indeed, the number of the foreign countries listed in the *Record* is twice that found in Zhao Rugua's *Description of the Foreign Lands*, written during the southern Song dynasty (1127–1276), numbering 143, about twenty of them from the Islamic world. The narrative does not provide a detailed description of each country as earlier accounts like Zhao Rugua's do, yet the different purposes of the books probably explains this omission. The authors of the book intended it to be an official gazetteer that included topics specific to Guangzhou.

The Record of the Southern Sea, however, contains much new and interesting information. For example, the book describes pirate farms in Quanzhou and Guangzhou called Lemon (Limu). Lemon (the origin of the English word stems from the Persian "līmū" or the Arabic "laimun") was an important source of Vitamin C for sailors on long-distance voyages. Because Chinese sailors ate lemons, they did not suffer from scurvy like European sailors who were deficient in the vitamin.[74] The fact that this kind of medical information had become common knowledge by the Mongol era suggests that this necessary wisdom circulated among Chinese because they received information about it from other merchants and sailors through their frequent adventures in the sailing trade.

However important these gazetteers are to historians as indicators of the increased trade and geographic awareness that occurred under the Yuan dynasty, they lack the sure reliability of firsthand sources. Fortunately, we have an important firsthand account produced during the period. Although less well-known than either the European Marco Polo or the Muslim Ibn Baṭṭūṭa (see Chapter 4), Wang Dayuan (1311–1350) deserves attention for his *Shortened Account of the Non-Chinese Island Peoples* (*Daoyi zhilüe*), in which he wrote about the various places in Southeast Asia, South Asia and even West Asia, and northeastern Africa – places that he claimed to have visited in the 1330s. His account is significant because, while most of his fellow travel writers of the day moved from the west to the east, Wang went in the opposite direction.

The best firsthand sources for Wang Dayuan's account include two prefaces by Wang Dayuan's contemporaries, Zhang Zhu and Wu Jian, written around 1350, and the postscript to his *Shortened Account* by Wang himself.[75] According to Wu Jian's preface, Wang originally wrote his book as a supplement to a local gazetteer about Quanzhou called *A Continuation of the History and Topography of Quanzhou* (*Qingyuan xuzhi*). A later Ming dynasty local gazetteer for the Fujian area, *Book of Min (Minshu)* introduces *An Account of the Non-Chinese Island Peoples* (*Daoyi zhi*) as a part of *A Continuation of the History and Topography of Quanzhou* (*Qingyuan xuzhi*), edited by Wu Jian[76]; little doubt this is Wang Dayuan's account that Wu Jian included to his gazetteer. Later, Wang Dayuan published his book as a separate work. Both prefaces deplored the fact that previous Chinese histories and sources had failed to address foreign countries at length and declared their wish to widen Chinese knowledge about the outside world. They portray Wang Dayuan as a very open-minded Chinese who possessed an unusual drive to travel around the world since he was a child, a desire he later fulfilled. It is not surprising that Wang Dayuan's international long-distance travels met with a favorable reception by Chinese intellectuals living in "cosmopolitan" Quanzhou. Zhang Zhu's preface begins with Zou Yan's (circa 340–260 BCE) ancient theory of the nine great continents, which views the world as comprising multiple geographic centers.[77] In the open international atmosphere of seaport Quanzhou, where local Chinese regularly interacted with many foreigners, some of them probably recalled diverse geographic ideas originating in ancient periods in order to break from the authoritative Chinese-centered worldview.[78]

In his postscript, Wang Dayuan claims that he visited all the foreign places he describes.[79] He provides no further information about himself. Wu Jian says that Wang modeled himself on the great historian Sima Qian, so it seems that he had obtained a classical education.[80] Compared with Marco Polo's lengthy travelogue, Wang Dayuan's account is much shorter and gives little detail about his itinerary. Some western scholars, including Philip Snow and Roderich Ptak, doubt that Wang traveled as far as the Red Sea, the Mediterranean, or the East African Coast, thus proposing debates about authenticity that resemble recent controversy over Marco Polo's travelogue.[81] Could Wang have traveled as far as the western end of the Indian Ocean realm? He claims that he wrote about things that he witnessed and not about what he simply heard from others. Of course, we cannot rely simply on this one claim; nor does this rule out the possibility of travel. We should note that earlier and later works of Chinese travel literature, like the extant version of Du Huan's account, follow the standard Chinese format for describing a foreign country that Sima Qian first established in his *Records of the Grand Historians*. Contemporary sources also testify that dynamic merchant activities had already created strong maritime networks spanning southern China and the Persian Gulf in the fourteenth century. Therefore, it would not have been that difficult for Wang Dayuan or his reliable informants to reach Islamic regions if they simply accompanied Chinese, Indian, Arab, or Persian merchants who sailed between West Asia and China. More importantly, his account contains a high proportion of updated and accurate information, including a much larger inventory of foreign countries than earlier Chinese accounts, a series of ninety-nine sections containing a total of 220 place-names. The Ming period account, *Book of Min*, also confirms that the Yuan period *Account of the Non-Chinese Island Peoples* documents approximately 100 countries, most of which were located in the western Indian Ocean and all interacting with Fujian for trade.[82]

Wang Dayuan left Quanzhou sometime before 1330. He passed through Southeast Asia and then sailed to South Asia. Given that Wang devotes more than ninety percent of his book to these two regions, scholars agree that he witnessed them firsthand. He devotes a mere ten percent of the book to countries in the Middle East and East Africa, only eight places in all. Wang does not describe his route to the west, nor does he describe his itinerary for any region, although a reconstruction of a possible sailing route from South India to West Asia can be created based on the list of places that he claimed to have visited (see Map 3).

Wang Dayuan presents details about the Islamic world that differ in veracity; some are more reliable, some less so. Wang follows a similar pattern for each of the book's sections. After plotting the relative location of the place under discussion, he inventories its important geographic features, social customs, and trading goods. In the section about Mecca (*Tiantang*, meaning the heavenly house), he reports that Mecca lies in the middle of a sandy desert and its temperature is warm. He hints that one could travel from Yunnan in Southwest China to the Islamic world by either land or sea. In addition to descriptions of various native products from different regions such as horses, ambergris, and coral, Wang Dayuan devotes much space to various specialty goods used in trading.

These include import and export goods such as cloves, nutmeg, blue satin, musk, pepper, silver, iron pots, frankincense, incense, Yunnan gold foil, white silver, lead, ivory, iron vessels, and cinnamon. Most of the book's sections also mention trade goods from China, such as Suzhou and Hangzhou colored satins and blue-and-white porcelain.

The archaeological evidence to verify the production of blue-and-white porcelains is plentiful, enough to justify its own research topic. Many excavations of old Chinese kilns in places like Jingdezhen prove that Chinese began to produce large volumes of blue-and-white porcelain specifically for export under Mongol sponsorship. Blue-and-white porcelain, which differs from pre-Mongol Chinese ceramics such as Longquan celadon, appealed to the Muslim tastes and echoes the colors that they often chose in Islamic architecture.[83] The Mongols and their Muslim collaborators most likely informed Chinese potters of the colors, shapes, and decorative motifs that they believed would appeal to potential customers in West Asia.[84] Experts in porcelains argue that China imported the special good-quality oxidized cobalt that its producers used to create the blue glaze on blue-and-white porcelains from Iran because it was not available in China. Most of the cobalt that came to China by way of the maritime trade ended its journey at Jingdezhen. Once produced, Chinese merchants exported the blue-and-whites to Iran using the reverse route. Chinese blue-and-white porcelain remained a favorite import in the Islamic world from the Mongol period on, a fact verified by excavations in West Asia. Thirty-eight among the 12,000 porcelains exhibited in Topkap Sarai Museum in Istanbul bear the unmistakable marks of Yuan dynasty blue-and-white porcelains.[85]

In the section on Hormuz,[86] Wang Dayuan reports on the horse trade and the transshipping of horses. Merchants probably transported horses to Quilon or other nearby ports along India's southwestern coast.[87] His book's section on Quilon refers to this trade: "[Sometimes these merchant vessels] arrive late [due to] the direction of winds – [i.e.], after the departure of the horse ships [from Hormuz] – and cannot take on a full cargo."[88] The information in the sections about Hormuz and Quilon overlap, indicating frequent overseas trade and strong commercial networking between the two cities. Merchants often carried pepper westward to Hormuz from its production sites in South and Southeast Asia; it brought them great profit because local demand was insatiable, despite the high volumes they carried.[89]

While the information in his *Shortened Account* is generally concise, Wang Dayuan's descriptions are both concrete and interesting. His description of shipbuilding technology in the section about Hormuz appears to have come from direct experience. The description reads: "They build ships in this country to transport horses. Their sides are [made] of planks, and they use neither nails nor mortar (to join them), but coconut fiber. Each ship has two or three decks with a wooden shed. To make headway against leaking, the sailors take turns, day and night, at bailing out the water, without any intermission."

This is the earliest surviving Chinese description of dhows. Wang's description of shipbuilding without nails resembles an Arabic account by Abu Zayd written in the ninth century (see Chapter 2).

Although Wang Dayuan left only short reports about these regions, his claim to have visited all of them is intriguing. His account, one of the most revealing sources of information about Sino-Islamic maritime contacts written during the fourteenth century, was reprinted many times during later periods. The original Yuan editions were lost during the turmoil of the transition between Yuan and Ming dynasties; however, several versions of *The Shortened Account of the Non-Chinese Island Peoples* were reprinted during the Ming period. We can assume that Wang Dayuan's account, or accounts with similar titles and contents, circulated widely throughout China for some time because contemporary and later writings refer to it frequently. Wang Dayuan's writings probably influenced Zheng He's voyage to the Islamic world during the early years of the Ming dynasty, as we will see in Chapter 5.

While Wang Dayuan added to Chinese knowledge about the Islamic world by traveling there, many Chinese had the opportunity to observe Muslim communities within China because, unlike the previous period when the Muslims mainly lived in international port cities like Guangzhou, Muslim communities spread all over China during the Yuan era.[90] Several accounts by Chinese intellectuals who took different stances on Mongol rule in China also wrote about the country's Muslims from divergent perspectives. Zheng Sixiao (1241–1318), who resisted Mongol rule and disdained the Mongols to his death, also showed hostility and antagonism toward Muslims and their cultural behaviors. In one clear exaggeration, Zheng tells the story about a frenzied Muslim who committed suicide after being called by Allah near a minaret.[91] In contrast, some of Zheng's contemporary intellectuals wrote more objective accounts about the life and culture of the Muslims they observed. For example, Zhou Mi (1232–1298), who chose neither to resist nor collaborate with the Mongols, wrote more objective and factual accounts of the funeral ceremonies and calendar used by those living in Hangzhou's Muslim communities.[92]

There were even Chinese literati who show a highly positive view toward the Muslims with whom they interacted. One of them was Wu Jian of Sanshan (present-day Fuzhou), who wrote a preface for Wang's *Shortened Account*, in which he demonstrated his open-mindedness toward countries outside China. Wu Jian's pro-Muslim attitude is best seen in his stele of 1350, placed in front of a Muslim mosque during the Yuan period. It provides the most detailed introduction to Islamic religion and society found in Chinese accounts, and acts as a summary of Chinese knowledge about the Islamic world. Because it is remarkably comprehensive and accurate, its entire contents deserve a careful look. The original text in the stele has worn down, but luckily a group of Muslims re-carved it onto an extant Arabic inscription entitled "Re-erection of the Stele to Qingjing Mosque" in 1507:

> More than 10,000 li west beyond the Yumen Gate [in Gansu province] is located the country of the Arabs,[93] who are called the Tajiks today. It is bounded on the north by Partia and Tiaozhi, on the east by Turfan and Gaochang, on the south by Yunnan and Annan, and on the west by the sea. This country covers a large plain, measuring thousands of li in width and length. It never ended overland contacts with China through overland transportation. The houses and gardens, ditches and drains, fields and cattle, distribution and range are very different from those in the Yangzi River and Huai River. The cold and hot weather are harmonious, and people and things are flourishing. They plant all kinds of grains, grapes and all kinds of fruits. The people never treat killing lightly and love the good in their customs. They write from side to side; their writing is divided into three styles: the seal character, the regular square style of script, and the cursive hand. They compose classics, history, poetry, essays, history, geomancy, astronomy, medicine and music. They show expertness in all these branches of knowledge. Their manufactures, textiles, and carved utensils are also sophisticated.[94]

Because Muslims who resided in Chinese cities carved their tombstone inscriptions in Arabic, Chinese living close could have learned the specific writing styles through close observation. Yet the author would probably not have gained information about the Islamic writing system's division into three styles (most likely different styles of Arabic calligraphy like Kufic and Thuluth) or details about Muslim cultural practices and academic expertise without detailed discussions with well-versed Muslim leaders or intellectuals.

Some phrases that hint at religious faith such as "the populace loved the good and never treated killing lightly" appeared in Du Huan's account in the eighth century (see Chapter 1). Yet Wu Jian's passage provides much more detail about the origin of Islam and the Muslim religious faith than that found in Du Huan's account:

> In the beginning, the king of Medina, *Peyghāmbar* Muḥammad, was born and possessed by holy spirits. He governed with virtue, and his subjects subjugated all of the countries in the western region, and all of the people called Muḥammad the sage. *Peyghāmbar* was like the Chinese word for "prophet," and in general [it] is an honorary title. His religion considers that everything originates from Heaven. Heaven is incomparable; therefore, there is no image for Heaven for the most devoted. Every year there is one month of fasting when one changes clothes and bathes oneself, and moves to a quiet place to live in. They prostrate [themselves] toward the west to worship Heaven every day and cleanse [their] heart, and recite scripture [the Qur'ān]. The scripture was handed down by the Heavenly being. It consists of 30 volumes, 134 chapters, or 6,666 sections, all of which contain profound and subtle ideas. The doctrine is deep and sophisticated, and it models on being just and unselfish and straightening mind and cultivating virtue. Their duty is to go on pilgrimage, educate people, and save the miserable from danger. They have to repent for self-reform, deal with themselves properly and others modestly, be mindful of their own conduct at home and abroad, and not to permit [themselves] to go astray to the least degree. Up to now it has been over 800 years [since the rise of this religion], and the country and people firmly adhere to the faith, so that even when living in foreign lands they transmit the faith to their descendants, and the generations of their descendants have never strayed from it.[95]

Some information differs from fact, such as the Qur'ān having 134 chapters rather than its actual 114 chapters, yet descriptions of Muḥammad and the pilgrimage are accurate. Wu Jian must have received his information directly from Muslims.

Wu Jian's passage on Islam also relates a Chinese Muslim legend about Sahaba Sa'd b. Abī Waqqās, Muhammad's relative and allegedly the first Muslim to reach Guangzhou by sea during the Sui dynasty (581–618), and who erected the city's Huai Sheng Si mosque. The account focuses mainly on another mosque founded in the South City of Quanzhou by Najīb Mujīr al-Dīn, who came to Quanzhou during the Song dynasty on board a trading ship that sailed from Sīrāf. The mosque had fallen into disrepair for some time, yet after petitions from Muslims in Quanzhou, a new official in Quanzhou's Minhai (Fujian) District permitted its restoration:

> He governed with integrity, and people and officials admired and obeyed him. Shaykh al-Islām Burhān al-Dīn[96] ordered Sharīf al-Dīn Ḥāṭib[97] to lead the followers in lodging a lawsuit, whereupon, the law official made a thorough investigation of the case and appointed Darughaqi [governor by the

> Mongol court] of Gaochang Xie Yuli to the post of Zhengyi [a civil official] so that he could properly restore the above-mentioned old property [mosque]. The populace was greatly satisfied with that.[98]

As we will see in Chapter 4, the Muslim traveler Ibn Baṭṭūṭa reports that when he visited Quanzhou, he met two people whose names were previously mentioned – Shaikh al-Islan Burhan al-Din and Sharīf al-Din Hatib, two of the city's most influential Muslim leaders. The following passage shows that Wu Jian enjoyed close relationships with Muslims and supported Muslim communities in Quanzhou:

> I have once heard the elders say that when the people of the Dashi (Arabs/Muslims) first began to enter China, their customs and education were greatly different from other countries. Consulting all the gazetteers like *[Record of an] Embassy to the Regions in the West* (*Xishi*) and *[Shortened Account of the] Non-Chinese Island Peoples* (*Daoyi*) confirmed that assertion. Therefore, I have the following to say ... When I once compiled *The Annals of Qingyuan* (Quanzhou), I wrote this event down. Now I inscribe this full account of the restoration again on a piece of stone so that it everyone can see that a good religion in general spreads far and wide and there is no place that it does reach.[99]

The inscription continues to list more people related to the resurrection of the stele, including several Chinese literati who helped the Muslims in Quanzhou maintain their communities. We can assume from Wu Jian's credits for the existing accounts such as *Embassy to the Regions in the West* (possibly by Liu Yu) and *Non-Chinese Island Peoples* (possibly by Wang Dayuan) that these books circulated widely among both Chinese and Muslims literati.

As the number of foreign Muslims living in China during the Mongol era increased dramatically, Chinese encountered many kinds of Muslims and discovered that their views varied greatly. Regardless of the wide differences in perspective, all of these authors possessed a degree of recognition and awareness of Muslims and their cultures, as well as geographic information about their home societies, and this knowledge expanded and became firmly established in the thirteenth and fourteenth centuries.

Conclusion

The thirteenth and fourteenth centuries witnessed a dramatic advancement in both the quality and quantity of Chinese understanding about the Islamic world. This acquisition of knowledge intertwined with the period's genuinely international atmosphere and the dynamic cross-cultural contacts that flourished during this century. The Mongols initiated this explosion of knowledge when they created a transcontinental empire that politically integrated China to the eastern part of the Islamic world for the first time. The states that the Mongols in 1260 imposed on China and Iran – the Yuan and the Il-khanate – maintained close political ties, and, although the period was short, allowed an unprecedented quantity and variety of commodities, people, and information to flow between them. After defeating the southern Song and becoming both the de facto emperor of China and the *de jure* ruler of the Mongol empire, Khubilai sought to dominate his empire politically and economically – and grew zealous to secure geographic knowledge about the world.

Starting in the 1280s, under Khubilai, the Muslim scholar Jamāl al-Dīn compiled a world geographic account using Muslim maps to depict distant places. Few world maps from the period survive, yet later maps such as the *Kangnido*, drawn in Korea in 1402, help us reconstruct the Chinese geographers' understanding of fairly accurate contours of the Arabian Peninsula, Africa, and Europe. The map jams the Indian subcontinent between China and the Islamic world, depicts Southeast Asian countries as small islands, and omits a complete coastline between China and the Islamic world. A surviving Mongol period map, however, depicts the sailing route from Quanzhou to the Persian Gulf in visual form. These maps circulated in China and, through them, Chinese expanded their knowledge about the Islamic world by acquiring more concrete geographic information about West Asia, Africa, and Europe.

Although the Mongol opening of the overland route brought Muslims to China, the sea trade at Quanzhou created the most important venue for international trade and cross-cultural connection between China and the Islamic world during the Mongol period. The Yuan government enjoyed full access to the maritime route that had already flourished for centuries before them, which became the most important passageway to the Il-khanate. Inheriting the maritime trade that Chinese had developed under the previous Tang and Song dynasties, the Mongols took international sea trade to a whole new level. The Mongol rulers in China understood the importance of maritime trade to financing the government and actively worked with Muslims and Chinese who engaged in the trade. Contemporary Chinese sources demonstrate that navigation and trade on the frequently used Indian Ocean route reached a high level of development under Mongol rule. Chinese sources written during the earlier Tang and Song periods also describe sailing routes to the Islamic world, but accounts about Chinese who traveled to the West – such as Yang Shu and Wang Dayuan – appear during the Mongol period; other Chinese travelers like them provide more reliable information about these routes and China's connections to the Islamic world and the world at large.

The prosperity of Muslim communities in China and their role in trade contributed to Chinese knowledge of the Islamic world. Among the many Muslim inscriptions in Quanzhou lies Wu Jian's stele of 1350. The Chinese scholar Wu Jian, who also wrote a preface for Wang Dayuan's travel account and who enjoyed a close relationship with Quanzhou's Muslim community, dedicated the inscription to the renovation of a Muslim mosque in the city of Quanzhou. Not only does it provide a succinct description of Muslim geography and history, but it also displays the open attitude that some Chinese held toward Muslims and Muslim communities. The stele mentions contemporaneous Chinese works that provide information about the Islamic world, an indication that updated knowledge circulated during the period.

In sum, Chinese learning about the Islamic world grew more dynamic, extensive, and flexible compared to that of the earlier period. The cosmopolitan atmosphere that flourished during the Mongol period inspired Chinese to broaden their horizons and their knowledge about the wider world. Many Chinese, like other foreign retainers including Muslims, were active in fields as varied as politics, academics, and trade during the period. As we will see in Chapter 4, sources in the Islamic world show a similar increase in knowledge about China during the same period.

4

Beyond Marco Polo

Islamic Knowledge about China, 1260–1368

Now that we have considered Chinese travelers like Wang Dayuan, a Chinese globetrotter of the Mongol era who has been compared to Marco Polo, it is time to consider Wang's counterpart in the Islamic world, the Moroccan Ibn Baṭṭūṭa (1304–1368). Although his fame far surpasses that of Wang Dayuan, and continues to grow, it is not yet so great as that of his European counterpart Marco Polo. Yet historians recognize his significance as an adventurer who covered 120,000 km (75,000 miles) – three times as far as Marco Polo – and as a source of information about the world in the thirteenth century. Although historians continue to debate whether he actually traveled to China, Ibn Baṭṭūṭa remains one of the most cited authors of Mongol period literature, along with Marco Polo. His travelogue provides valuable information to historians of cross-cultural contact, including very detailed descriptions of Chinese ships. Beginning with his pilgrimage to Mecca, Ibn Baṭṭūṭa's curiosity inspired him to continue. In the end, he claimed to have traveled to more places than perhaps anyone else in history until that point, including non-Muslim regions in Asia such as China.

Perhaps Ibn Baṭṭūṭa's adventures struck his fellow Muslims as less sensational than Polo or Wang Dayuan did to their societies because he was among countless people who went to China from West Asia. By the time he set forth on his adventures, Muslims had already been traveling to China for many centuries, including the maritime routes that connected China and the Islamic world. Ibn Baṭṭūṭa's travelogue confirms what Chapter 3 showed: During the Mongol era, a greater number of Muslims traveled to China using a more systemized set of trade networks that connected eastern and western Eurasia through the Indian Ocean. Largely divided between Mongol-ruled Iran and Mongol-free parts of the Islamic world, the open sea continued to link a more fragmented Islamic world with China through intermediary bases in South and Southeast Asia, thanks to the large number of Muslim communities that had already been long established there, and that maintained political and economic relationships with Islamic regimes in the Muslim heartland of West Asia and Northeastern Africa. Expanded contacts between China and the Islamic world during the Mongol period provided an unparalleled opportunity for Muslims from diverse regions to learn about China, while they also allowed Chinese to learn more about the Islamic world. Ibn Baṭṭūṭa testifies to this expansion and intensification of connection between two worlds and the expanded collective knowledge about China and the wider world that Muslims gained from this contact. The Moroccan traveler's tale is confirmed by the more abundant sources available for the Mongol era that vividly illustrate the flow of people, goods, and ideas on the rise all over his known world.

The most important period in the history of Muslim knowledge about China occurred during the Mongol Il-khanate (1260–1335). During this era, even the state, which maintained direct political and diplomatic relations with kingdoms far to the east like the Mongol-run Yuan dynasty, engaged with China at all levels of society. Whereas Muslim scholars like Jamāl al-Dīn traveled from Iran to Yuan China and contributed to the production of the first world map there, a Mongol minister and diplomat who traveled from China provided historians in Iran with substantial documentation they could use to enhance China's place in their unprecedented world history project. Because his name Bolad (Boluo) sounds similar to Marco Polo, some scholars eager to demonstrate Polo's presence in Chinese sources have proposed the intriguing yet problematic hypothesis that Bolad and the world famous traveler are one and the same. With each arrival of ministers and diplomats from other Mongol states, new materials and new information arrived in Iran, providing opportunities for Muslim scholars to expand the horizons of Muslim knowledge about world geography. Rashīd al-Dīn (1247–1318), for example, created the first systematic chronicle of societies in the "known" world, the *Compendium of Chronicles*, based largely on source materials brought from other societies, including those brought to him by Bolad from China. This is the most representative source of the quantum leap that occured in Muslim knowledge about China during this period. Even geographers in Islamic countries further west that escaped Mongol rule, like Mamlūk-ruled Egypt and Syria, also expanded Muslim knowledge about China. Much of this new geographic information about China was the by-product of scholarly connections with the Il-khanate and commercial connections with China.

This chapter uses Arabic- and Persian-language sources to reconstruct contacts between China and the Islamic world during the Mongol period from 1260 to 1368. These materials reveal a level of Muslim knowledge about the known world that far surpasses anything Europeans like Marco Polo provided, supplying abundant information about people and riches of societies even as far-flung as China. The Mongol order in Asia created an environment in which an unprecedented amount of new, more reliable geographic information and cartographic technology flowed more freely and widely than ever, both within Mongol states and beyond.

Expanded Geographic Knowledge about China under the Mongol-Ruled Il-Khanate (1260–1335)

Before the Mongol invasion, the Arab-dominated Islamic world had already experienced non-Arab rule by regimes like the Iranian Buyids (945–1055) and the Turkish Seljuks (1055–1194). These non-Arab ruling elites ultimately converted to Islam, and paid lip service to the caliph in Baghdad even as they remained politically autonomous. In doing so, they began to integrate into a culturally united, if politically fragmented, Islamic world. The Mongol's sudden rise in northeastern Asia after 1206 and their continuous raids on the Islamic Middle East in the years that followed produced substantial changes. In 1218, they destroyed the Qara Khitai (1141–1218) in Central Asia, which, after its rulers came from China, had existed for nearly a century, ruling over a mostly Muslim population. In 1231 they destroyed the Khwārazm Shāh dynasty that had flourished as an Iranian Muslim kingdom in Central Asia and Iran for nearly two centuries. In 1258 Mongol armies destroyed Baghdad, still the cultural center of the Islamic world, and brought the ʿAbbāsid caliphate to an end. The major events related to the Mongol conquest to West Asia were witnessed by the Chinese generals who joined the Mongol armies. In its place, Hülegü (Khubilai's brother and the commander of the Mongol army's western expedition) established a non-Muslim government to govern conquered portions of the Islamic world that now formed a major part of the Mongol empire, which he called the Il-khanate.[1] The fall of Baghdad to the Mongol infidel stunned Muslims everywhere, and motivated Muslim historians to write histories of this transformative event.[2] Soon after the great city's fall, the Persian chronicler ʿAṭā Malik Juwaynī (died 1283 CE) completed his *History of the World Conqueror* (namely, Chinggis Khan) in 1260.[3] Having served the Mongols in Baghdad and traveled to Mongolia, Juwaynī could draw on a wide range of sources close to him in order to amass a large quantity of information about the Mongol expeditions to Central and West Asia.[4] As a Mongol government servant, he did not describe the chilling moments during the sack of Baghdad when Mongol soldiers killed the last ʿAbbāsid caliph because he found it hard to explain to his Muslim readers. Instead, he concluded his history with a description of the Mongol conquest of the assasins, which he represented as a victory of Sunni orthodoxy over Shīʿa Ismāʿīlīs. Juwaynī was only one of many Muslims who decided to serve the Mongol overlords of their newly created Il-khanate and contributed to the settling of Mongol rule over the Islamic heartland.

The Mongol dominion over the Islamic world fell far short of complete, however. While Hülegü's campaign did not cease with the conquest of Baghdad and the annihilation of powerful and longstanding dynasties in Iran and West Asia, he proceeded south to Mamlūk Egypt. This time, however, Hülegü met defeat at the historic Battle of ʿAyn Jālūt in Palestine in 1260. Mongol expansion into the Islamic world virtually ended. Thereafter, the region divided into two halves: 1) The eastern half where the non-Muslim Mongols ruled over Iran and Mesopotamia, and 2) the western half, including Egypt and Syria, under the Muslim Mamlūks.[5] The division of the Islamic world into Mongol and non-Mongol halves creates an opportunity to do a comparative analysis between the two subregions in order to understand by which channels and contacts Muslims actually learned more about China.

The Mongol-ruled Il-khanate in Iran enjoyed a close relationship with the Mongol government in Yuan China, the closest political relationship that China and any part of the Islamic world ever had. The Yuan dynasty's added status as the suzerain state over the entire Mongol empire made this relationship crucial to the Il-khanate. As a consequence, official exchanges regularly moved between the two courts. In fact, more than political relations held this relationship together. Hülegü's descendent actually held an economic interest in China. During his reign over the Il-khanate, the khan's brother had a small number of households in China as part of the typical allotment of lands and peoples bestowed to Mongolian princes all over the empire after Chinggis Khan's death. As a precaution, Hülegü assigned agents in China to take care of his economic assets, and even dispatched diplomats to oversee his interest.[6] Continued exchanges of diplomats, scholars, and even brides further deepened this political relationship.

The position of the Mongol-ruling families in the Il-khanate resembled that of the Yuan elite in China, described in the Chapter 3. Despite the initial destruction of Baghdad and the caliphate, the new Mongol overlords in Iran encouraged Muslim culture and scholarship. Indeed, it did not take long before the Mongol elite converted to Islam. This conversion during the reign of the Il-khanate's seventh ruler, Ghazan (reigned 1295–1304), led to an active adoption of the home cultures. [7] Even before they converted to Islam, Mongol rulers in the Islamic world patronized Muslim scholars who studied the arts and sciences in both Persian and Arabic. In one case, the court sponsored the establishment of the Maragheh observatory in 1259. Its founder Naṣīr al-Dīn Ṭūsī (1201–1274), who based Maragheh on a previous observatory and older library resources, submitted his allegiance to Hülegü when Hülegü's army conquered the Shīʿa Ismāʿīlī fortress of Alamut in 1256. Ṭūsī served the Mongols as many other Muslims, such as Juwaynī, did at that time. Ṭūsī received permission and patronage from Hülegü to embark on his project for the observatory because the khan credited Ṭūsī's advice for the Mongols' military success in West Asia.[8] In the observatory, the largest of its time, scholars gathered from all over the Mongol realm, including China, to work on a new set of astronomical tables, *Zīj-i Īlkhānī*, based on observation of the Earth's rotation that improved the Ptolemaic system of the universe. The *Zīj-i Īlkhānī* contains an accurate description of the Chinese calendar, which proves that scholars from China were closely involved in its production. Beyond the Mongol realm, Ṭūsī's enterprise eventually influenced the Copernican model in Europe.[9]

Like Ṭūsī, most Muslim scholars in the Il-khanate wrote their scientific, historical, and geographic works not only in Arabic but also in Persian, the primary language of learning in Iran during the Il-khanate era.[10] New Persian, different from the Old Persian of the Achaemenids (559–330 BCE) and the Middle Persian (or Pahlavi) of the Sassanids, absorbed Arabic vocabulary beginning in the ninth century, and gradually replaced Arabic, which had been the main language of learning in Iran under the Khwārazm Shāh dynasty.[11] Arabic continued to play an important role in the emerging new literature, of course, because scholars continued to consult Arabic works and maintained contacts with scholars in the Arabic-speaking world beyond the frontiers of Mongol rule. Thus, the Muslim literature of world geography in both the Il-khanate and the Arabic-speaking world at large continued the earlier Muslim geographic tradition, creating continuity in the evolution of Islamic knowledge about China.

This growth of geographic knowledge during the Mongol period contained two components: Regular updates based on newly acquired information, and new geographic information and cartographic techniques that re-shaped representations of China in geographic works. Extant manuscripts of the maps that circulated widely during the Mongol period show that many Muslim cartographers continued to copy earlier maps, especially those created in the styles of the Balkhī School and al-Idrīsī.[12] This created a mass of reproductions that varied little throughout the thirteenth and fourteenth centuries. At the same time, other mapmakers produced innovations that added new elements in both form and content to Muslim cartography even as they continued to build on earlier cartographic traditions.

The earliest example of scholars who wrote geographic accounts under Mongol patronage, the famous Iranian geographer and cosmographer Zakariyā' b. Muḥammad al-Qazwīnī (1203–1283), exemplifies this innovative trend in geography and cartography in the Islamic world. Born into a family that settled in Qazvīn in Persia, al-Qazwīnī served politically in several localities throughout the Il-khanate, including Persia, Baghdad, Mesopotamia, and Syria. After his retirement, he wrote his two monumental works, one geographical and the other cosmographical. His geographical dictionary, entitled *Monuments of the Lands* (*Athar al-bilad*), drew heavily on Yāqūt's *Geographical Dictionary*, written earlier in the century. Al-Qazwīnī innovatively rearranged Yāqūt's rubrics from seven climates to the letters of the alphabet.[13] Nonetheless, the work borrows heavily from Yāqūt. Most importantly, however, al-Qazwīnī 's *Geographical Dictionary* provides clear evidence that Arabic geographic traditions continued to influence academic circles in the Islamic world under Mongol-rule profoundly.

A map sketch of the world found in al-Qazwīnī's famous *Marvels of Things Created and Miraculous Aspects of Things Existing* (*ʿAjā'ib al-makhlūqāt wa-gharā'ib al-mawjūdāt*) also reveals the continued influence of the earlier Arabic geographic tradition in the lands of the Islamic world under Mongol rule.[14] Witten in Arabic, this treatise has unique significance as the first Muslim cosmography. While it concentrates mainly on supra-terrestrial matters like angels, the second part of al-Qazwīnī's book describes the division of the earth into seven climates and charts the world's known seas and rivers. His description of China contains no new information and simply describes the country as a large territory with many people and resources. Yet the attached sketch showing the distribution of land and water in the world is noteworthy because of its unique portrayal of China and Africa (see Figure 4.1).

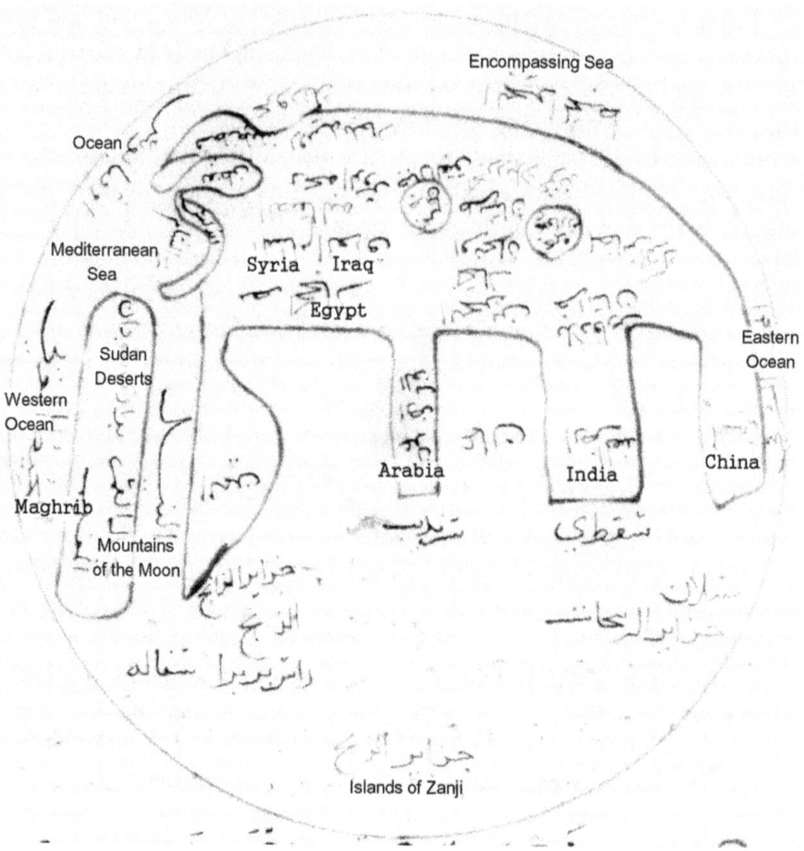

FIGURE 4.1. Al-Qazwīnī 's sketch of the distribution of land and sea from his *Marvels of Things Created and Miraculous Aspects of Things Existing* (*'Ajā'ib al-makhlūqāt wa-gharā'ib al-mawjūdāt*, late thirteenth century). The original map placed the south on top. By permission of the Bodleian Library, Oxford (MS. Pococke 350, fol. 73v).
Note: The manuscript is dated 1539.

This sketch map by al-Qazwīnī was obviously influenced by that of al-Bīrūnī from the eleventh century. The two maps differ, however. Al-Qazwīnī's map portrays China as a major subcontinent at the eastern edge of the northern hemisphere; that is, as an important and large region as big as India and the Arabian world. It continues to depict Africa as a continent in shape but cleaves Africa into two halves divided by the Nile River.[15] In fact, al-Bīrūnī was the first geographer who argued that the Indian Ocean must be connected to the Atlantic through waters that ran south of the Mountains of the Moon, the legendary sources of the Nile. It is likely that al-Qazwīnī, who was influenced by al-Bīrūnī when drawing this sketch, applied al-Bīrūnī's theory faithfully. This trend was imitated by many later cartographers in various ways.

What new sources did al-Qazwīnī use to write his geographic studies including the sketch map? The scholar dedicated *Marvels of Things Created* to the governor of Baghdad, Juwaynī, who authored *History of the World-Conqueror*, a chronicle of Chinggis Khan. Thus, al-Qazwīnī perhaps wrote his studies in an academic circle patronized by Juwaynī. The Baghdad governor's *History* provides important information about the political developments surrounding the Mongol conquest in Persia and elsewhere.[16] Al-Qazwīnī probably received some information or ideas about China from his patron, who had access to up-to-date information about eastern Asia. Juwaynī learned about the Mongols in the course of serving them, in addition to gaining knowledge about the Qara-Khitai in Central Asia and the Uighurs further east. The scholarly governor probably continued to amass more information about the wider world and this influenced other scholars in the Il-khanate like al-Qazwīnī.

The accumulation of knowledge among Muslim scholars culminated in a work that was written at the apogee of Mongol dominion over Eurasia and deeply influenced Muslim thinking about the world. The *Compendium of Chronicles*, written first in Persian and immediately translated into Arabic, was compiled in 1308 by Rashīd al-Dīn (1247–1318), the son of a Jewish apothecary family who converted to Islam during his early adolescence. He rose to prominence in the court of the seventh Il-khanate ruler Ghazan Khan, and eventually served as prime minister where he became well known for his many economic reforms.[17] Perhaps in gratitude, Ghazan Khan gave Rashīd al-Dīn a special commission to write this monumental work. This work initiated a new genre of writing in Muslim scholarship, one that covers the historical developments of the world's diverse societies in unified fashion and chronological order.[18] Rashīd al-Dīn originally sought to write a history of the Il-khanate in order to commemorate the origins, history and achievements of the Mongols. However, Ghazan died just before the book's completion and his successor Öljeitü (reigned 1304–1316) took over sponsorship of the project and broadened its scope to embrace a history of the entire world. Rashīd al-Dīn makes this point clear in his introduction, directly quoting Öljeitü:

> Until now no one at any time has made a history that contains the stories and histories of all inhabitants of the climes of the world and the various

> classes and groups of humans, there is no book in this realm that informs about all countries and regions, and no one has delved into the history of the ancient kings. In these days, when, thank God, all corners of the earth are under our control and that of Chinggis Khan's illustrious family, and philosophers, astronomers, scholars, and historians of all religions and nations – Cathay [Khatāy (Khitai), North China], Māchīn [South China], India, Kashmir, Tibet, Uyghur [Eastern Turkistan or today Xinjiang], and other nations of Turks, Arabs, and Franks – are gathered in droves at our glorious court, each and every one of them possesses copies of the histories, stories, and beliefs of their own people, and they are well informed of some of them.[19]

The ruler's comment echoes a similar suggestion that Jamāl al-Dīn, a Muslim official in the Yuan court, made to the Mongol ruler Khubilai that they make a world-scale geographic work. The Mongol empire broke up into four regional regimes after the death of the fourth grand Khan Möngke (reigned 1251–1259), leaving the Il-khanate to govern only the Islamic world centering on Iran. Yet this passage shows that Öljeitü still felt a strong connection to other Mongol regimes, and envisioned a unified empire in which the Mongols ruled over China, India, the Islamic world, and Europe. Likewise, in reality, despite some conspicuous political conflicts among grandsons of Chinggis Khan, the Mongol empire maintained unity to a certain degree after the establishment of the four khanates.[20]

As the title indicates, Rashīd al-Dīn's *Compendium of Chronicles* is mainly a historical work that combines the chronicles of Mongol and other rulers. Yet, according to the author's preface, the original manuscript contained, or was at least intended to contain, a third volume of world geography entitled *The Routes of the Realms* along with maps of the world entitled *The Map of the Climates*.[21] No such volume or any relevant manuscript survives, raising doubts about whether the author actually wrote the volume of world geography in question.[22] The inclusion of the world geographic section in the table of contents, however, clearly shows that the author and his sponsors were interested in the topic.

Some basic geographic information survives in the extant history volumes of the *Compendium of Chronicles*. Although somewhat spotty, the work's geographic information shifts from the previously dominant Islamic-centered view of the world to a new perspective centered on the Mongols. Moreover, the author drew on a much wider range of sources to write about the world's countries by acquiring reliable sources in many different languages directly from the region in question. This led to a particularly significant advance in Muslim knowledge about China as Rashīd al-Dīn integrated China into the history and geography of the world with considerable accuracy. In his drafts, the Yuan dynasty in China figured large as the suzerain kingdom of the Mongol empire. This attention to China partially reflects the interest of Rashīd al-Dīn's sponsor, Ghazan Khan, who actively developed diplomatic relations with the Yuan dynasty in China.

Rashīd al-Dīn's descriptions of China in the *Compendium of Chronicles* fall mainly in the complete manuscripts of Volume One, *The History of Ghazan,* while some fragmentary manuscripts about the genealogies of Chinese emperors can be found in Volume Two. Scholars have divided Volume One into two parts: Part One describes the genealogy of the Mongol tribes and Part Two provides a major history of the Mongols that proceeds in chronological order from the ancestors of Chinggis Khan to his successors. In addition to the mainstream chronicles of the Mongols, Part Two divides into shorter periods of approximately a decade in which the author relates events that occurred in non-Mongol regions. In this way, the book presents a systematic history of the entire known world, which for Rashīd al-Dīn and his Mongol benefactors encompassed all of Eurasia and North Africa. China first appears in the book as an important region that had always fostered close political relations with the Mongols and then later reappears after its conquest by the Mongols as a major section of their world empire.[23]

The first geographic feature in China to receive sustained treatment by Islamic geographers was the Great Wall. Said to have been first linked together during the Qin dynasty (221–207 BCE), the wall was built to prevent invasions by northern nomads.[24] Most of the wall that exists today was built in the fifteenth century, long after the ancient walls eroded. Before the fifteenth century, documentation usually refers to the repair of earlier sections of the wall under the northern dynasties, occurring before the Yuan period. Even before Ming emperors built their stronger and more elaborate Great Wall along their northern border, maps depicted the various sections as a continuous wall. This includes the Song dynasty *Map of Chinese and Non-Chinese Territories* that contains a detailed explanation of the history and changing geographical scope of the Great Wall over time (see Figure 1.3). This shows a trend in which earlier major historical events continued to influence people's understanding of important symbolic monuments. The story about the Great Wall probably also inspired Western writers to envision the construct in their own cultural context. For example, earlier Muslim geographers like Ibn Khurradādhbih and al-Idrīsī mention a fictitious wall that they believed Alexander the Great built in Gog and Magog, a legendary place that Muslim geographers and cartographers located somewhere in the north of China. Interestingly, Rashīd al-Dīn still associates the wall of China with the wall of Alexander, and even adds a portion of the Qurʾānic account of Gog and Magog. Nonetheless, the *Compendium of Chronicles* presents the wall as a genuine geographic location and examines China's history of conflicts with northern nomadic peoples as part of the wall's context:

> Since the people of Cathay [Khitai; North China] were next to these people and their territory and camping grounds, in every epoch the Cathaians killed many of the tribes who practiced nomadism in Cathaian territory, while the tribes in turn raided and plundered the Cathaian realm. Because the rulers of Cathay were constantly vexed by Mongol nomads, they took every precaution against them, like constructing a wall like Alexander's Dam between Cathay and the tribes.[25]

Here, Rashīd al-Dīn incorporates new information from a reliable source, while respecting the earlier, legendary Islamic geographic tradition.

Rashīd al-Dīn placed his first full entry for China in a larger description of "the history that is known of Chinggis Khan's contemporaries, the monarchs and khagans of Cathay [Khitai], China, the Kerayit, the Naimān, the Mongols, the Uyghur, Turkistan, Kiral-Bashghurd, Qipchaq, Ūrūs [Rūs], Circassia, Ās [the Alans], Transoxiana, and the caliphs and sultans of Iran, Anatolia, Syria, Egypt, & c." who ruled from 1155 to 1166.[26] During this period, the author explains, China comprised three different polities: Cathay (Khitai, that is, the former Liao), Chīn (the Jin), and Māchīn (the southern Song). Earlier Turkish and Persian accounts had already used this division, yet Rashīd al-Dīn demonstrates a greater familiarity with the topic. His discussion of the basic political history of the changing dynasties during the Song period exemplifies his knowledge well, when he correctly explains the advance of the northern nomads (first the Khitans, then the Jurchens) who forced the Song regime to retreat to south China, Rashīd al-Dīn's Māchīn, where they established a new state called *Namsūn* – in other words, *Nan Song* (the southern Song). The *Compendium of Chronicles* is the first history written in the Islamic world to give accurate names and reign dates for the Chinese emperors. For example, Rashīd al-Dīn states that the first southern Song emperor *Kāuzūn* (Gaozong) ruled for forty years, relatively close to the actual number, thirty-six (reigned 1127–1162).

Rashīd al-Dīn's description of China grows more detailed when he arrives at the period of history that follows the Mongol conquest of North China in 1234 and more detailed still for the reign of fourth Grand

Khan Khubilai. From this time on, all of China becomes a central player in Rashīd al-Dīn's chronicle of the world's nations.[27] Here he describes the country's geography:

> The province of Cathay [Khitai] is an extremely vast and broad realm, and it is as thickly inhabited as possible. Trustworthy sources report that in the entire inhabited quarter of the globe the habitation and population that are there are to be found nowhere else. There is a gulf, not very large, that extends inland from the ocean from the southeast along the borders and coast that separate Manzī and Goryeo [Korea]. It comes into Cathay to within [twenty]-four leagues of Khanbaligh [Khanbalik; Daidu; present-day Beijing], and one can go that far by boat. Because of the nearness of the sea it rains a lot. Part of the country has a warm climate, and part has a cold climate.[28]

As we see from this passage, Rashīd al-Dī[illegible]ls part of China *Manzī*, another term for southern China used b[illegible]inese. These terms referring to different parts of China also ap[illegible]Marco Polo's account, an indication that updated geographic te[illegible]e Islamic world circulated throughout Eurasia during the thi[illegible]and fourteenth centuries.[29] Korea, a neighboring country to the [illegible]as called Silla (57 BCE–935 CE) in earlier and some contemporary [illegible]abic and Persian accounts, but it appears here with the updated dynastic name of Goryeo (918–1392). So is the case of Marco Polo's account, which describes Goryeo (*Kawlī*) as one of the four regions that submitted to Khubilai Khan after he defeated his uncle Nayan.[30] Goryeo became a puppet kingdom under Mongol rule in 1270 after the Khan crushed its navy in their last act of resistance.

The continuing passage below briefly surveys the geographic attractions that led Khubilai Khan to build his new capital Daidu (Dadu, meaning "great capital") immediately adjacent to the previous capital, Zhongdu (meaning "middle capital"), also called Khanbaliq ("great residence of the Khan"):[31]

> In his time Chinggis Khan conquered most of this realm, and then during Ögödei Khan's reign the rest was taken. Chinggis Khan and his sons had no capital in Cathay, as has been mentioned in every history; however, since Möngke Khan gave that realm to Khubilai Khan, who, with his far-sighted view, could see what an extremely flourishing land it was and what important countries and realms neighbored it, he chose it as his capital. He designated as his winter residence the city of Khanbaligh, which is called Jūngdū [Zhongdu] in Cathaian [Chinese language] and had been an imperial capital. It had been chosen as a site in ancient times by astrologers and philosophers under a highly favorable ascendant, and it was always considered to be very auspicious and lucky. Since Chinggis Khan had destroyed it,

> Khubilai Khan wanted to rebuild it, so for his own fame and reputation he built another city next to it. That city was named Daidū [Dadu].[32]

This passage celebrates Khubilai's move from Xanadu (Shangdu, which would remain as the Yuan summer capital) to Daidu, ancestor to modern-day Beijing. Contemporary Chinese sources confirm this historical fact. With this move, the center of Mongol rule over China settled in China rather than Mongolia, and provid[illegible]bolic moment in which the Mongols legitimated their succession [illegible]er Chinese dynasties.

Rashīd al-Dīn also describes the cana[illegible]hubilai rebuilt in order to connect the two capitals Khanbaligh ([illegible]hongdu) and Daidu with the cities of coastal South China:

> Khanbaligh and Daidu have a huge river t[illegible]es from the north, where summer pastures are located, from Chan[illegible]ere are other rivers too, and outside the city a very large lake has bee[illegible]structed that is like a small sea. A dam has been made on it so that boats [illegible]n be launched in it for pleasure cruises. The water of this river used to flow through another place and empty into the gulf that juts inland from the sea near Khanbaligh. Because the gulf in that vicinity was narrow and boats could not get through, cargos were mounted on animals and brought to Khanbaligh.
>
> The architects and wise men of Cathay determined and reported that it was possible for boats to come to Khanbaligh from most provinces of Cathay as well as from the capital of Māchīn, the city of Khingsai [Hangzhou], Zaitūn [Quanzhou], and other places. The Khan ordered a large canal cut, and the water of the aforementioned river, as well as that of another river that flows ulam-ulam [uninterruptedly] from the Qara Muran [Yellow River] and others into the cities and provinces, was diverted into the canal. From Khanbaligh to Khingsai and Zaitūn, which is the port to Hindustan and the capital of Māchīn, is a forty-day journey by boat. Many dams have been built on this river to provide water to the provinces. When a boat reaches those dams, it and its cargo, no matter how large, are lifted by winch and crane and replaced in the water on the other side of the dam. The canal is more than thirty yards wide.[33]

The first Grand Canal, which connects the Yangzi River valley to China's northern capitals and major cities in the vicinity of present-day Beijing, was built during the Sui dynasty (581–618) and immediately functioned as an important transportation route. Khubilai rebuilt the Grand Canal between Hangzhou and the new imperial capital in Beijing, and promoted the waterway as a strategic means of transporting food and other goods from southern Chinese port cities like Quanzhou and Hangzhou directly to "Jishui tan," the artificial lake that Khubilai built in Beijing. Ultimately, this man-made river transportation connected to sea as well. Marco

Polo describes a grand canal with the same route between Hangzhou and Beijing as does another contemporaneous Muslim traveler from the west, Ibn Baṭṭūṭa, whom we will meet again later in this chapter. More interestingly, these sources written in similar periods all use the same place-names for the major cities such as Khanbaliq (Beijing), Khingsai (Hangzhou), and Zaitūn (Quanzhou).

Rashīd al-Dīn's *Chronicles* provides meticulous details about topics that might have been boring to general readers eager to read about exciting action but which provide important historical information about Islamic understanding of China. For example, the book provides detailed information about the administrative divisions and bureaucratic systems of Yuan China. Given its generally high levels of accuracy and detail, these passages sound very much like a Chinese official record of the period. Rashīd al-Dīn lists the country's twelve biggest cities (*sheng*), providing new Muslim knowledge about important cities like Namgīng (Nanjing), Yangjū (Yangzhou), Khingsai (Hangzhou), Fūjū (Fuzhou), and Lūkīnfū (Lūqīn, Hanoi in modern-day Vietnam). *Sheng*, originally meaning government departments in the Han period, began referring to provinces from the Yuan period after the government established Branch Secretariats (*Xing zhongshu sheng*) as territorial administrations.[34] Rashīd al-Dīn's understanding of *sheng* as a provincial capital city, therefore, is not quite accurate, although some of the particular details about the cities are both updated and precise. The order of cities' ranks, from the largest capital *gīng* [*jing* in Chinese] to the tiniest village *shūn* [*cun* in Chinese], and the ranks of the ministers and government officials from the first grand counselor *chingsangs* (*chengxiang*) to the director of a section in a ministry or a branch secretariat *lanjūn* (*langzhong*) in the *Chronicles* corresponds exactly to those used in Chinese sources. Among the governmental offices that Rashīd al-Dīn lists are *Senvīsha* (*Quanfu si*) in Quanzhou "where all envoys, merchants, and comers and goers report. It also deals with *yarlighs* [decree, order, law] and *paizas* [tokens to use a post horse]."[35] This confirms that Quanzhou took charge of basic administrative tasks relating to maritime contacts and thus played an important role in the governmental system of trade and diplomacy. Contemporaneous Chinese sources verify that the Yuan government closely checked the commercial activities of the foreign merchants living in Quanzhou.[36]

Political systems and geographic features are not the only topics that figure in the *Compendium of Chronicles*. Rashīd al-Dīn paints vivid portraits of people who played important roles in Yuan China, including some remarkable anecdotes about them. Among those are several of the officials whom Khubilai assigned to important positions at his court, like the Muslim Prime Minister Aḥmad, whose assassination in 1282 Rashīd al-Dīn describes and Chinese sources corroborate. Here, the *Chronicles* provides some telling differences between Islamic and Chinese accounts; Rashīd al-Dīn portrays Aḥmad as a skillful financial expert whereas Chinese documents vilify him as a bad and avaricious person.[37]

Such detailed inventories and stories raise the question: From what sources did Rashīd al-Dīn obtain his rich and accurate information? The author's information about the reigns of Ögödei and Möngke derived from Juwaynī's *History of World Conqueror,* written in the mid-thirteenth century, an account whose narrative overlaps considerably with that of the *Compendium of Chronicles*.[38] However, Juwaynī completed his book in 1260, and Rashīd al-Dīn had to collect data to cover the years that followed. He must have obtained this data from newly-acquired Chinese sources through some indirect set of scholarly exchanges because, unlike Juwaynī, Rashīd al-Dīn did not travel to Mongolia or China. His most likely intermediary was Bolad Chingsang (*Boluo Chengxiang*), a Mongol aristocrat who served Khubilai Khan as an official in the Yuan court and whom the khan later dispatched to the Il-khanate as a political advisor. Rashīd al-Dīn was able to write about China accurately by relying on a reliable source, Bolad Chingsang. Although his name sounds similar to that of Marco Polo, Bolad cannot be credibly identified with Polo because he appears in both Chinese and Persian sources as an envoy of Khubilai Khan who arrived in the Il-khanate in 1285. He served the two Mongol rulers as an advisor in China and Iran and brought a large quantity of scholarly materials from China to Iran, sources that Rashīd al-Dīn acknowledges as a major source of his information.[39]

Later Rashīd al-Dīn also published the history of China under the commission of Öljeitü as a supplement to the *Compendium of Chronicles*, and, in this project, Rashīd al-Dīn was assisted by other scholars from China. This volume includes portraits of almost all of the Chinese emperors who appear in official Chinese documents, beginning with the legendary first emperor Ban Gu, in chronological order. These are the first illustrations in the Islamic world that portray Chinese people appearing in identifiably Chinese styles, which leads one to conclude that the artist must have seen Chinese pen-and-ink sketches.[40]

As for the source of these scholarly exchanges, writings in various languages including Syriac bear witness to the exchange of envoys and commodities between the Il-khanate and Yuan dynasty China, in which Bolad Chingsang constituted only one of many agents. One famous intermediary between China and Iran – and even Europe – is Rabban Bar Sauma (circa 1220–1294). A Nestorian monk of Mongol origin, he traveled with a student named Rabban Markos, from Xanadu (Shangdu) to the Il-khanate along the overland routes of Asia. They first aimed at Jerusalem for the sake of religious pilgrimage, but military unrest prevented them from reaching their original destination; instead, they traveled to Baghdad where they lived for many years. In time, Rabban Markos even rose to selection as the Nestorian Patriarch of Baghdad, Mar Yaballaha III (1245–1317). As patriarch, he recommended his teacher to lead a mission to Europe as Mongol ambassador. There, the elderly monk met with many of Europe's monarchs, as well as the Pope, in a failed attempt to arrange a Franco-Mongol alliance. In his later years, Rabban Bar Sauma documented his lifetime of travel, which provides a valuable insight into the kinds of journeys that moved from the east to the west in an era of relatively frequent cross-cultural contact.[41]

Before Rabban Markos became patriarch, Baghdad's previous patriarch attempted to dispatch Rabban Bar Sauma and Rabban Markos back to China as messengers, yet failed because military conflict again hindered their access.[42] This suggests that, although overland routes continued to provide passage to facilitate diplomatic relations among the four Mongol khanates, they ceased to function as well as they had before the thirteenth century, and that the sea now provided the primary means of long-distance travel between China and West Asia. Marco Polo describes his return trip from China to the west in about 1292, when he accompanied a Mongol princess named Kökejin from China to Iran where she would become consort to Ghazan Khan. Contemporaneous Chinese and Persian sources both prove that the story about the princess's marriage is true. An internal administrative document in Chinese also verifies the names of the three Mongol envoys that Polo claims led the mission to Iran. Since no other source gives the same three names, historians who believe Polo's version of events find this fact compelling evidence of his accuracy.[43]

The Il-khanates also sent envoys to the Yuan capital, using the sea routes. The history of Waṣṣāf claims that Il-khanate envoys sailed to China around 1297, bringing with them gifts of costly garments and jewels for the Tīmūr Khan (probably the second emperor of the Yuan, Temür Öljeitü, reigned 1294–1307) and other commodities to trade there before they returned to the Il-khanate, carrying many gifts presented by the Mongol emperor in China:[44]

> Fakhru al-Dīn laid in a supply of necessaries for his voyage by ships and junks, and laded them with his own merchandise and immense jewels and pearls, and other commodities suited to Tīmūr Khan's country, belonging to his friends and relations, and to Shaikh al-Islām Jamāl al-Dīn. He was accompanied on the voyage by an army of expert archers, Turkish and Persian .... The ambassadors remained four years in China and were dismissed with honor, and a daughter of one of the nobles was bestowed upon Fakhru al-Dīn. A friendly reply was written to Ghazan Khan, and presents were sent in return, together with some valuable silk stuff, which had fallen to the share of Hülegü Khan, but had remained in China since the time of Möngke Khan. An ambassador took charge of them on a separate junk, and he was commissioned to deliver expressions of friendship and regard....

We have seen in Chapter 3 that, between 1301 and 1304, the Chinese envoy Yang Shu also met with Il-khanate envoys dispatched by Ghazan Khan of the Il-khanate to Temür Khan of the Yuan dynasty and sailed back to China with them. These maritime diplomatic exchanges that continued between the two countries of Mongol power clearly provided extensive opportunities for further transfer of goods and information during the lifetime of Rashīd al-Dīn and other scholars of the Il-khanate.

Clearly the *Compendium of Chronicles* provided a path-breaking account that satisfied the ambition of the Il-khanate ruler Öljeitü and his subordinates; it confirmed the legitimacy of the Mongol world empire and provided new knowledge about the empire's central asset, China. A document written in Rashīd al-Dīn's own hand explains that the historian originally planned to reproduce and circulate many copies of the *Chronicles* in both Persian and Arabic but, before he could do so, political rivals successfully accused him of poisoning Öljeitü Khan and the court executed him. Four complete manuscripts, written in Persian, survive; a few fragments in Arabic show that someone indeed translated the work into Arabic.

Despite Rashīd al-Dīn's sudden fall, Rashīd al-Dīn's works and other forms of updated geographic information brought by intermediaries from Yuan China had begun to influence new generations of geographers in Iran. This most likely includes a world map that was drawn during the Il-khanate era and inserted into the *Treasury of Tabriz* (*Safineh-yi Tabrīz*), an encyclopedia completed by an anonymous author in 1321–1323 and only recently discovered in Iran. This map, which depicts only the northern hemisphere of the known world, distinctively outlines the coastlines of major regions like China, the Arabian Peninsula, and Africa. The author cleaves Africa into two halves, following the fashion of al-Qazwīnī of the thirteenth century. However, his way of division is unique, situating the Mountain of the Moon (the source of the Nile) in the eastern half of the continent. In fact, the cartographer combined several different features found on different types of earlier Muslim maps in order to create this map. For example, it divides the northern hemisphere into different climate lines that run parallel from south to north, in ways similar to works by al-Idrīsī and Yāqūt. It also includes the Mediterranean Sea and the upper part of Indian Ocean, following the style of the Balkhī School maps. Despite this borrowing from earlier works, the map also contains updates that only appear notable during the Mongol period. For instance, it shows place-names in Eurasia that were more famous during the Mongol period such as Khara Khorum and Tabrīz. The map divides China into two, into Chīn and Māchīn, a distinction that earlier Persian and Turkish writers like Rashīd al-Dīn had also applied but which had yet to clearly appear on early Arabic maps. The anonymous Il-khanate cartographer who drew this map probably combined earlier and contemporaneous geographic information in order to create his unique design.[45]

Another work of Persian geography that shows signs of new geographic knowledge received through contact between the Il-khanate and the Yuan dynasty is *The Hearts' Bliss* (*Nuzhat al-Qulūb*) by Ḥamd Allāh Mustawfī al-Qazwīnī (circa 1281–1349). Born in Qazwin in Iran, the same home as the geographer Zakariyā' b. Muḥammad al-Qazwīnī, Ḥamd Allāh Mustawfī wrote his *Hearts' Bliss* in 1340, a couple of decades after the completion of Rashīd al-Dīn's *Compendium of Chronicles*. The elder statesman appointed Ḥamd Allāh Mustawfī as the financial director of his hometown and probably inspired him to pursue historical studies.[46] *The Hearts' Bliss* differs from Rashīd al-Dīn's *Chronicles* and resembles earlier Islamic geographic works in its return to an emphasis on explaining each geographic region rather than putting them into historical context as the *Chronicles* did. It is possible that *The Hearts' Bliss* resembles the third volume of the *Compendium of Chronicles*, entitled "World Geography," which could have followed a convention found in earlier Islamic geographic treatises, although no evidence exists unless the missing part of Rashīd al-Dīn's work is found. The work lacks the richness and dynamism found in the extant part of the *Chronicles*. However, it still contains distinctive updates that are useful to understanding changes in Muslim knowledge about China.

For example, *The Hearts' Bliss* provides the first surviving grid maps in the Islamic world, on both the map of the world and on the regional map of the Iranian-Turkestan area that supplement the text. Previous geographic works in Arabic had located places by means of precise longitudinal and latitudinal positions in a system devised by Ptolemy and transmitted into Islamic geography by al-Khwārizmī. However, Ḥamd Allāh Mustawfī's maps demonstrate a novel grid system in which longitudinal and latitudinal lines form a grid of one-degree squares in which only one location is plotted, thus identifying each site on the map with a specific set of coordinates (see Figure 4.2). Some scholars argue that the grid concept was probably transmitted from China to the Islamic world for use in architectural planning.[47] Joseph Needham suggests in his *Science and Civilisation in China* that Ḥamd Allāh Mustawfī, who was in contact with China, probably drew the idea for his grid map from the Chinese map in *The Encyclopedia of Yuan Dynasty Institutions*. Indeed, Needham calls this style of grid map "Mongol style." [48] Although Muslims in Iran might have adopted grids as a new visual form in the art of drawing maps, the concept and function of their new grid system drew on conventional concepts of longitude and latitude coordinates that already existed in the Islamic geographic tradition. As demonstrated in Chapter 3, evidence in Chinese sources reveals the presence of scholars in the Yuan court like Jamāl al-Dīn, who used Islamic geographic tools in his mapmaking and geographical works in China. It seems more likely, then, that Jamāl al-Dīn took the grids as a new and popular system of longitudinal and latitudinal coordinates in the Islamic world and adapted them to world maps made in Yuan China. We have textual evidence, as mentioned briefly at the end of Chapter 2, that proves the existence of earlier Muslim cartography that used the longitudinal and latitudinal coordinates to precisely locate places. Muḥammad ibn Najīb Bākran's *World Book* (*Jahān-nāmah*) describes his lost map, drawn 130 years before Ḥamd Allāh Mustawfī, in which, "by means of longitude and latitude the location of each city can be determined."[49] Considering all these pieces of evidence, we can be convinced that Ḥamd Allāh Mustawfī's grid system was hardly influenced by Chinese grid system; in fact, the direction of influence appears to be vice-versa.

A direct comparison of the two contemporaneous maps made in Iran and China hints at possible connections between them (Figure 4.2).

Because of their similarities regarding geographic content and cartographic techniques, Unno Kazutaka argues that Chinese geographical mapping in *The Encyclopedia* drew directly from the works of Ḥamd Allāh Mustawfī, an argument that directly challenges that of Needham.[50] However, other than eleven place-names, including Baghdad and Kashgar, which appear on both maps, most place-names

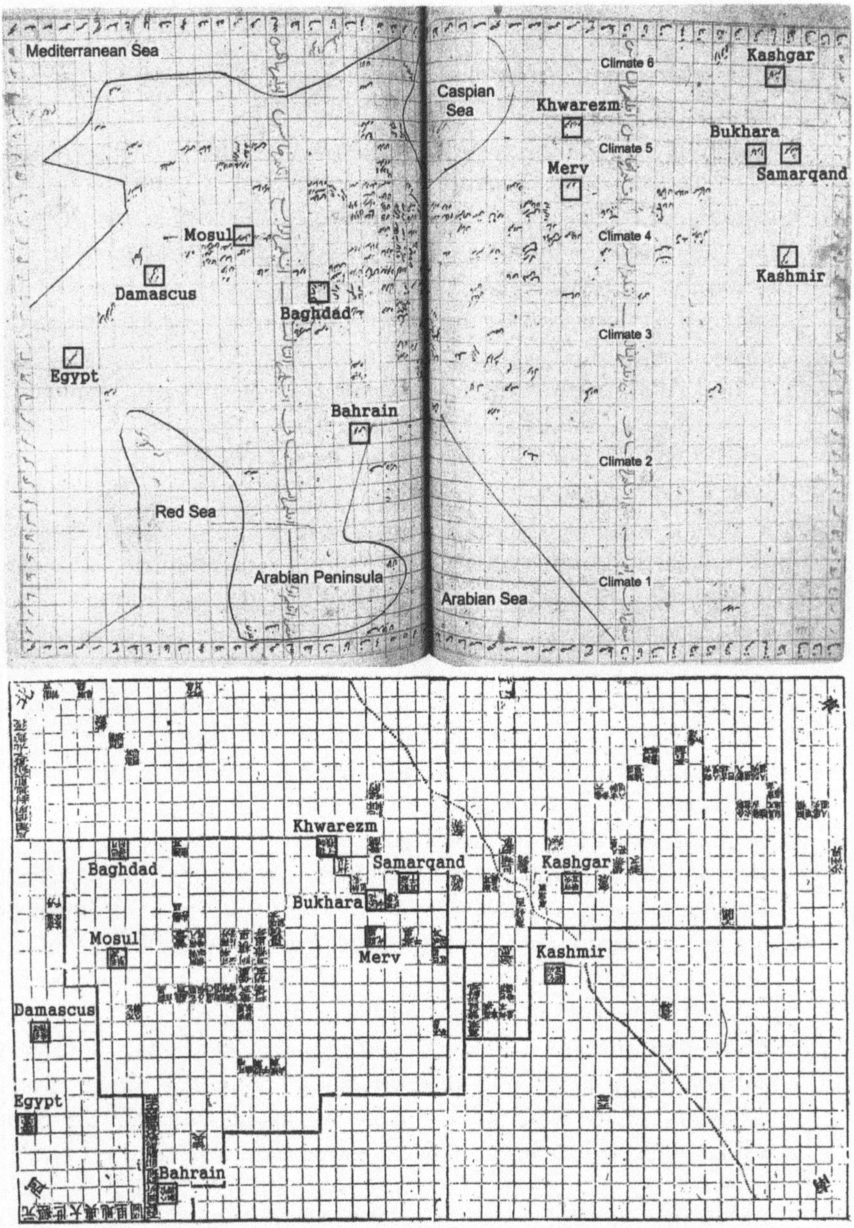

FIGURE 4.2. Comparison of Ḥamd Allāh Mustawfī al-Qazwīnī's map of the Iranian-Turkestan area from his *Hearts' Bliss* (*Nuzhat al-Qulūb*; circa 1330, MS., British Library) (top) and the geographical map from *The Encyclopedia of Yuan Dynasty Institutions* (circa 1330) (bottom). The original maps placed the south on top. By permission of the British Library, London (MS. Add. 16736, fols. 143b-144a).

Note: I added some place-names in English. For all of the place-names on the map, see Miller, vol. 5, Taf. 85.

do not match on the two maps, a fact that does not support Unno's argument. Furthermore, Ḥamd Allāh Mustawfī's maps date only as far back as the fourteenth century, creating a time gap that renders such a direct transfer unlikely. Although it is difficult to trace the lines of knowledge transmission, the simultaneous existence of similar maps in Yuan China and the Il-khanate Iran still hints strongly at some kind of information exchange between geographers in both societies and the transfer of the new coordinate system from Iran to China during the Mongol period.

Ḥamd Allāh Mustawfī's world map also uses a grid, although it does not display longitude and latitude, neither does the Chinese geographical map in *The Encyclopedia of Yuan Dynasty Institutions* (see Figure 4.3).

The map resembles the earlier sketch of land and sea that al-Qazwīnī drew in the thirteenth century, including its separation of Africa into two peninsulas. His division of Africa that situates the Mountain of the Moon (the source of the Nile) in the eastern half of the continent and the Maghreb (i.e., Northeast Africa) in the western half resembles the earlier anonymous map in *Treasury of Tabriz*. At the same time, Ḥamd Allāh Mustawfī portrays the Eurasian and African landmasses more realistically, and not simply as a diagram with fixed geographic shapes. Clearly, Ḥamd Allāh Mustawfī attempted to represent the world in a new way, rather than simply borrow earlier ideas.

Ḥamd Allāh Mustawfī's map also differs significantly from the sketch maps of al-Qazwīnī and the *Treasury of Tabriz* map in its depiction of China. In fact, he does not present the country clearly at all. He confuses China (Arabic name *al-Ṣīn*) with several places in Central Asia. Despite the fuzzy representation of China on this map, his written survey of foreign countries provides a fuller and more complex description of China's geographic features. Ḥamd Allāh Mustawfī consulted earlier Arabic geographers like Ibn Khurdādhbih in researching his treatise; however, he also adds unprecedented information about countries based on Persian sources. For example, he divides China politically into Chīn, Khitāy, and Māchīn – the same divisions that Rashīd al-Dīn used in his *Compendium of Chronicles*.

Ḥamd Allāh Mustawfī sets himself apart from his predecessors by dividing foreign countries into two categories: Those that have close relation with the Il-khanate and those that were situated far from the Islamic world and were not built by Mongol governors. Curiously, he places all three regions of China in the second category. Ḥamd Allāh Mustawfī's

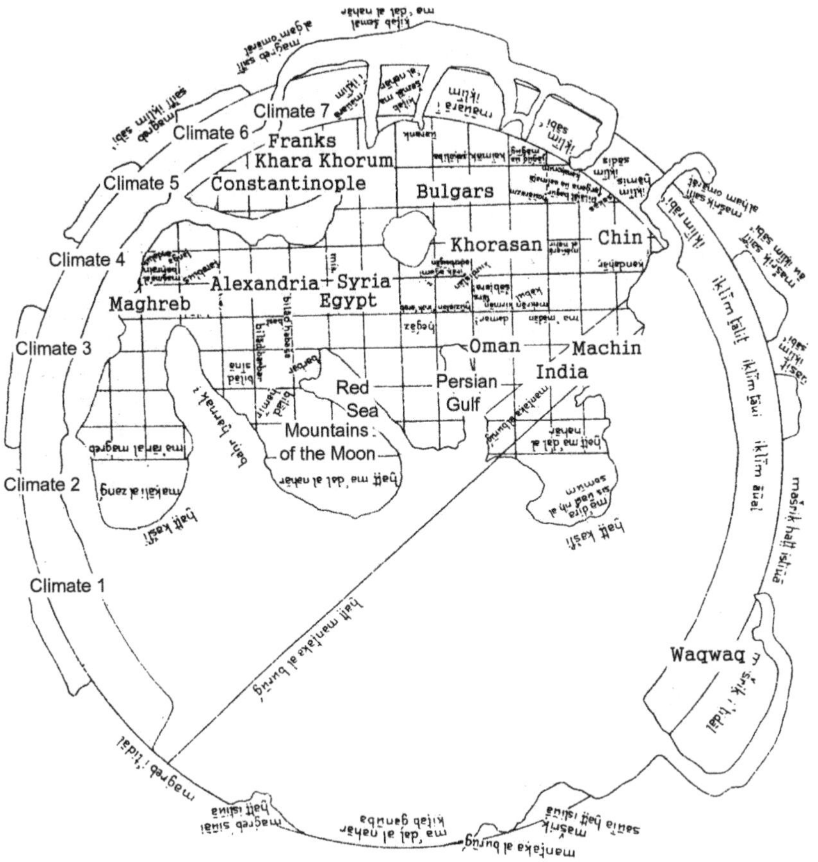

FIGURE 4.3. Ḥamd Allāh Mustawfī's world map (circa 1330). The original map placed the south on top.
Note: *HC2:1*, 150.

account of China contains both old and new information. For example, in his description about Chīn [North China formerly under Jurchen rule], he accurately says that the Mongols designated this land as Manzī at that time. The claims in this passage – that the majority of the population worshiped idols, that all arts and crafts had reached perfection, and that numerous great cities flourished throughout the land – mostly constitute the recycling of earlier accounts of China and present the same stereotypes of China and the Chinese that appear in earlier Muslim accounts. Interestingly, Marco Polo makes similar points in his account of China.[51]

That said, Ḥamd Allāh Mustawfī's plausible longitudinal and latitudinal figures distinguish his geography from previous generations of Islamic geographers. This is evident in the passage about the capital of Chīn at 125 °/ 22 °.[52] Interestingly, the treatise also follows the traditional system of grouping the world into seven different climes, locating the broad wide kingdom of Chīn stretching over the second, third, and fourth climes. Ḥamd Allāh Mustawfī applied the same method in developing his sections on Khitāy and Māchīn:

> Khitāy [Khitai (Cathay), North China formerly under Khitan rule]. This is a great kingdom of the Fourth and Fifth Climes. Its capital is Khān Bālīgh [Khanbaligh] in the Fifth Clime, whose longitude is 124 °, and latitude 37 °. This is a mighty city, and it was called originally Changdū; and Qubilāy Khān built another city outside the same. Of other great towns and well-known districts are the following: Nanking [Nanjing], where a great river runs through the city, Tabaksīk [?], Qalʿah Shīkāt [?], and Almaskū [?]. Further, and besides there are many others.[53]

His description of Khitāy's capital Khān Bālīgh, built by Khubilai Khan, certainly utilizes updated information, most likely from Rashīd al-Dīn's work. The same applies to his description of Māchīn:

> Māchīn [the part of South China that was under southern Song rule]. A great and extensive kingdom which the Mongols know as Nankiyās. It is of the First and Second Climes, and its capital is the city of Khansāy [Hangzhou], which some call Siyāhān. They say that in all the habitable world there is no greater city than this, or at any rate that in the regions of the east there is no larger town. There is a lake in the midst of the city, six leagues in circumference, and the houses of the town stand round its borders....[54]

Ḥamd Allāh Mustawfī's image of Māchīn as a great and extensive kingdom and its Mongol name Nankiyās match the account of Rashīd al-Dīn. His description of its capital Khansāy as the largest city in the world with a large lake in the middle and a great population echoes the account by Marco Polo, who stated that "it is without doubt the finest and most splendid city in the world."[55] He continues describing Khansāy's warm climate and abundant sugarcane and rice crop production, the city's great population that extends upwards of 10,000, and its political situation in which a few Muslims hold power over the many non-Muslim Chinese.

These sources show that Muslims living in the Il-khanate in Iran made quite significant advancements in the development of geography and cartography of the world during the Mongol period, and greatly improved their understanding of China. What did their counterparts living outside Mongol domains know?

Knowledge of China in Mamlūk Syria and Egypt

Several compilations of geographic accounts and maps appeared during the Mongol era in the westernmost reaches of the Islamic world, beyond the pale of Mongol rule. Most of these were encyclopedic works that drew from earlier geographic treatises. From these, however, it is possible to discern new information about China, much of which originated in the Il-khanate-rule to the east.

The geographic compendium entitled *Survey of the Lands* (*Taqwīm al-buldān*, circa 1321) by Abū al-Fidā᾽ (died1331), the prince of Syria, constitutes the most important of these updates in the Islamic world beyond Mongol rule. This descriptive geographic work contains physical and mathematical data in tabular form and supersedes earlier Arabic geographic accounts. The brief geographic description of China corresponds to the China envisioned in the Arabic world maps that are part of the Balkhī School tradition. Abū al-Fidā᾽ himself explicitly cites outdated sources such as al-Bīrūnī in his description of major places in China and beyond; that is, Khānqū (read Khānfū by omitting one dot, modern-day Guangzhou), Khānjū, Yanjū (Yangzhou), Zaitūn (Quanzhou), Khansā (Hangzhou, here confused with Guangzhou), Sīllā (an outdated name for the Goryeo dynasty in Korea under Mongol rule), Jamkūt, Khājū, and Sūkjū (Suzhou).[56] Khansā, Yanjū, and Zaitūn correspond to the names that appear in contemporaneous Persian works like Rashīd al-Dīn's *Compendium of Chronicles*. At the same time, Abū al-Fidā᾽ reports that a certain voyager from China told him about Hangzhou and Quanzhou, two important port cities during the Mongol period. However, *Survey of the Lands* fails to match the accuracy and systemic thoroughness of the Persian geographies, despite evidence of updated knowledge that Abū al-Fidā᾽ apparently acquired from his contemporaries.

The works of another contemporary Arab geographer and cartographer named Shams al-Dīn Dimashqī (died1327), who worked in Mamlūk-ruled Egypt, displays some knowledge about China that the author probably borrowed from Persian geographic works. Dimashqī divides China into outer China and inner China, the latter of which he calls *Ṣīn al-Ṣīn*, literally "China of China."[57] Ṣīn al-Ṣīn probably refers to Māchīn, the Persian name for southern China under the southern Song dynasty that quickly came into widespread use.[58] His geographic account, *The Choice of the Age, on the Marvels of Land and Sea* (*Nukhbat al-dahr fī 'ajā'ib al-barr wa-'l- baḥr*), repeats the recurring stereotypes about Chinese in Arabic literature, namely, that the Chinese are descendents of Noah and excel at industry and painting. Dimashqī also incorporates less reliable information, like his description of a hairy people with round eyes, sharp and protruding teeth, a tail, claws, and short fingers who live beyond China.[59]

Many Arabic works used the term "Ṣīn al-Ṣīn" during the Mongol period. For example, it appears on a fourteenth-century map attached to the geographic work *Ways of Perception Concerning the Most Populous [Civilized] Provinces* (*Masālik al-abṣār fi mamālik al-amṣār*). The geography was written by Ibn Faḍlallāh al-'Umarī (died 1349), a distinguished administrator and author who was active in Cairo and Damascus under Mamlūk rule.[60] He claims that the map is a copy of the world map made for Caliph al-Ma'mūn (reigned 813–833); al-Mas'ūdī also mentioned this map earlier (see Figure 4.4).

The map's landmass contours, including the plausible – though inaccurate – longitudinal and latitudinal lines, roughly resemble reconstructions of al-Khwārizmī's geographic table, which was directly influenced by Ptolemy's geographic treatise. Thus, it is possible that the map in *Ways of Perception* descended from maps made by the scholarly community under Caliph al-Ma'mūn's patronage, which included al-Khwārizmī.[61] With regard to the map's contents, however, the name Ṣīn al-Ṣīn on the northern hemisphere's eastern edge of Ibn Faḍlallāh al-'Umarī's map does not appear in al-Khwārizmī's geographic table that merely documents al-Ṣīn. The presentation of both al-Ṣīn and Ṣīn al-Ṣīn (Chīn and Māchīn in Persian) suggests that Ibn Faḍlallāh al-'Umarī updated al-Khwārizmī's geography using available contemporary information, in the same way that al-Khwārizmī updated Ptolemy's treatise in order to write his own.[62]

The illustration of Africa marks another distinctive feature of Ibn Faḍlallāh al-'Umarī's map. Although the map presents Africa as flat at the bottom and diffuse where it meets the edges of the globe, it does not stretch all the way to the east as it does in the maps by the Balkhī School and al-Idrīsī. The possible source of this adaptation is intriguing, because Ibn Faḍlallāh al-'Umarī hints in his narrative that Muslims attempted to discover the actual contour of Africa through exploration. He reports

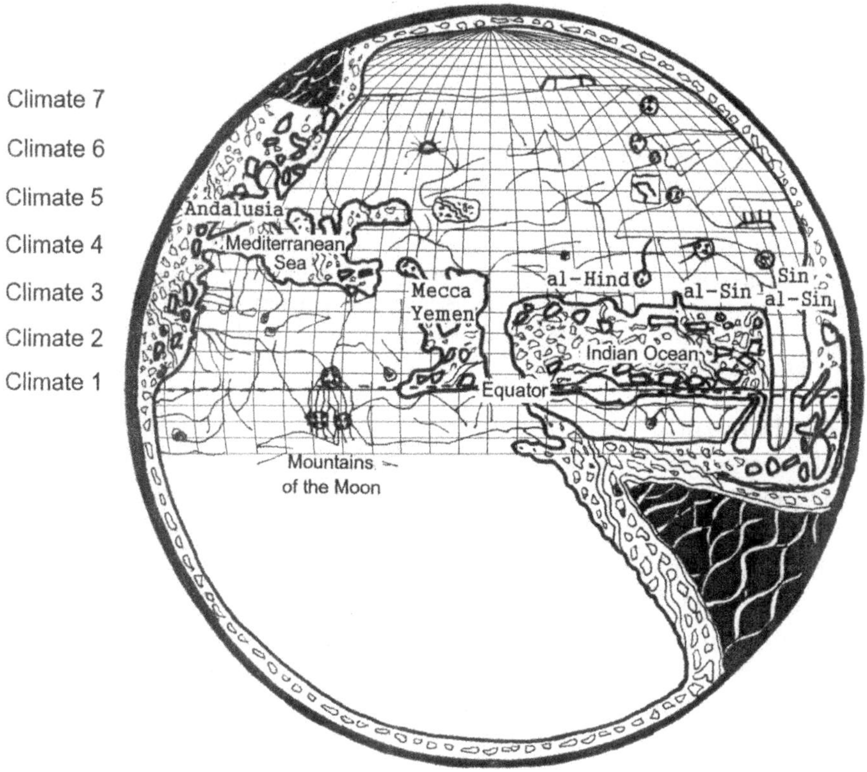

FIGURE 4.4. The world map of Caliph al-Maʾmūn from Ibn Faḍlallāh al-ʿUmarī's (1301–1349) *Ways of Perception Concerning the Most Populous [Civilized] Provinces* (*Masālik al-abṣār fi mamālik al-amṣār*), redrawn after the original. The original map places the south on top.
Note: Fuat Sezgin, Science and Technology in Islam (Frankfurt am Main, 2004), 12.

that the Sultan of Mali dispatched fleets to sail around the continent, although he does not say exactly when:

> Ibn Amīr Ḥājib said: I asked the Sultan Mūsah how the kingdom fell to him. He said, "we are a dynasty and pass down the rule among us, and he [the former king], who was before me, did not believe that it was not possible to know the end of the Encompassing Sea. He wanted to know this and was fascinated by it, so he prepared two hundred ships, equipped with people, and the like number, equipped with gold, water and supplies that would be sufficient for years. He said to the travelers [in the ships]: do not return until you arrive at the end [of the ocean], or until you have used up your food and water. They sailed out, and their absence lasted, with none

> of them returning, then a single ship of them returned. We interrogated the captain about their case and their news, and he replied: 'Know, O Sultan, that we navigated for a long time until [when we reached] in the open sea, valley appeared with a strong current, when I was the last one of the ships. Those ships sailed ahead of us, and when they arrived at that place, they did not return and reappear, and we did not know what had happened to them. I myself retreated from this place and did not enter that valley.' He (Ibn Amīr Ḥājib) continued: He was reprimanded. He said: "After that, this sultan equipped two thousand ships, a thousand for himself and men he took as company, and a thousand for provisions and water. Then he made me his deputy and sailed out to the Encompassing Sea with his company. And this was the last time he was seen and all of those who were with him; and the rule fell to me alone."[63]

Ibn Faḍlallāh al-ʿUmarī's report about the ruler of Mali resembles Herodotus's story about the Phoenicians.[64] Very likely, Ibn Faḍlallāh al-ʿUmarī referred to a similar legend about failing to sail south along the west coast of Africa. We have seen in Chapter 3 that the first geographers to depict the correct triangular shape of Africa were Chinese working sometime during the latter part of the Yuan dynasty.[65] No Islamic maps before this time display a triangular Africa. However, if the Muslims who conducted the most vigorous activities in this region did not know the shape of Africa, how could Chinese cartographers draw the continent so exactly? Some other small pieces of evidence show that credit goes to North African merchants who sailed as far as the southern tip of Africa.[66] The best evidence, however, still comes from the series of Portuguese fleets that first successfully explored the West African coast during the fifteenth century and reached the southern tip of Africa in 1488, marking a turning point in world history. In order to achieve this feat, the Portuguese heavily utilized the geographic knowledge and navigational experiences that Muslim mariners had accumulated for centuries.

Before the Portuguese, Muslims in North, West, and East Africa sailed far and wide throughout the Indian Ocean through their main access channels in the Mediterranean Sea, the Red Sea and the Persian Gulf. The maritime connection during the Mongol period greatly expanded the commercial activities of merchants all over the Islamic world. With the help of these transportation networks, Muslim merchants and sailors played a major role in facilitating the transfer of information as well as commodities between China and the Islamic world during the thirteenth and fourteenth centuries. All of the Islamic world, both inside and outside the Mongol domain, fell within the radius of Indian Ocean exchange, connecting them ultimately with China. In response, powerful government and private merchant interests established midpoint shipping centers in South Asia in order to advance the extent of their trade further east.

Muslim Trade Networks and China as Reflected in the Travelogue of Ibn Baṭṭūṭa

Painstaking analyses of scattered written and archaeological sources have begun to provide us with concrete and complex pictures of the systematic commercial networks involving Muslims, Chinese, and other peoples that spanned the Indian Ocean from West Asia to China. In order to maintain such vast networks, Muslim traders depended on transshipping centers that they had built and maintained all over South and Southeast Asia since earlier centuries.[67] Some of them also formed organizations that linked merchants across commercial networks, either independently or with the backing of local regimes. The history of Waṣṣāf testifies that some influential local rulers, such as Jamāl al-Dīn Ibrāhīm b. Muḥammad al-Ṭībī in Qais (Kīsh), made great profits by conducting their own independent trade with trading partners in India and China. The rulers of the Persian Gulf regimes like Qais and Hormuz competed with each other in their attempts to dominate the transit trade to southern India; for instance, al-Ṭībī, the king of Qais, conquered Hormuz for a short time.[68] Waṣṣāf states that the prosperity of the Islamic world derived from the merchandise it imported from India and the Far East and that the merchants of Qais controlled those operating in the latter. Elizabeth Lambourn's study of Muslim urban networks between Yemen and South India based on newly available Yemeni court documents provides substantive evidence of political and commercial networking among the Muslim residents of South Asia and their continued ties to Middle Eastern "home" ports in places like Yemen.[69] This document lists stipends that the Rasulid Sultan in Yemen awarded Islamic judges and clerics of Muslim communities in India who acknowledged his political authority in religious rituals like the sermon given at Friday prayers (*khuṭba*). This evidence suggests that Muslim communities in India maintained political and economic allegiances that helped to foster long-distance trade relations over the long run.

When we consider these examples, we learn that long-distance traders from the Islamic world did not encounter uncrossable boundaries, even though their region was not politically unified in the same way as

China. Many Arab and Persian Muslim merchants developed international trade networks by developing trading hubs along sailing routes, fostering Muslim communities in coastal India and Southeast Asia. This situation is reflected in earlier sources, yet more concrete examples can be found in sources from this period. Other examples include a special group of merchants in Egypt and Syria called the Kārimī who conducted trade in the Red Sea and the Mediterranean under limited Mamlūk sponsorship. Some Arabic sources, including Ibn Khazar, hint that Kārimī merchants also engaged in maritime trade between India and China, acting as intermediaries on behalf of interests in Mamlūk Egypt, South Arabia, and East Africa on one side of the exchange and India and China on the other, through a series of agents.[70] Several merchants secured a foothold in India and then worked systematically to create branch outposts along the routes. Well-structured networks and a convenient form of transportation allowed the Kārimī merchants to sail to China frequently. The Kārimī merchants were not the only traders engaged in the Indian Ocean trade, of course; they competed and cooperated with a large number of Arab-Persian merchants from Hormuz, Jewish and Armenian merchants, and South and Southeast Asian merchants, some of whom had close connections to the Muslim merchants in China called *ortagh*. More examples include a huge Indian Ocean network of a Sufi order Kāzarūnīya that was involved in long-distance trade to a considerable degree. Their organized activities in coastal towns to protect sea travelers in their perilous journeys based on their religious virtue – providing accommodation and money transfer service – were vividly reported by the famous fourteenth-century Muslim traveler Ibn Baṭṭūṭa (1304–1368) in his travel account.[71] Although not a merchant, Ibn Baṭṭūṭa traveled along with merchants in his journey reaching China and provides the most detailed description of the Islamic trade networks that connected China to the Islamic world across the Indian Ocean.

Ibn Baṭṭūṭa originally entitled his account *The Gift to Those Eager to Observe the Wonders of Cities and Marvels of Journeys* (*Tuḥfat al-nuẓẓār fī gharāʾib al-amṣār wa-ʿajāʾib al-asfār*), but the most people know the work as *The Travels of Ibn Batuta* or *Rihlatu Ibn Battūah* (*riḥla* literally means "journey" in Arabic). Born into a family of Muslim legal scholars in Tangiers, Morocco in 1304, Ibn Baṭṭūṭa received the kind of literary and scholastic education that was typical among the upper classes of Muslim society. In 1325 he set forth on the pilgrimage to Mecca, or *ḥajj*, one of the Five Pillars of Islam. The medieval Arabic genre of pilgrimage travel, or *riḥla*, had already taken shape by Ibn Baṭṭūṭa's time. Ibn Jubayr's *riḥla* about his hajj in 1183 defined the genre. However, the scope and content of Ibn Baṭṭūṭa's journey transcended the typical hajj because he traveled 75,000 miles, across present-day southern Europe, Africa, the Middle East, and Asia, including China, for twenty-two years (from 1325 to 1347).

The boom in trade that catalyzed the flow of people, commodities, and ideas across the Indian Ocean during the Mongol period facilitated Ibn Baṭṭūṭa's adventures. This provided him with an unprecedented repository of eyewitness information that superseded all previous geographical writing. It is true that Ibn Juzayy, who recorded and edited Ibn Baṭṭūṭa's narrative, incorporated many literary embellishments and stories of marvels drawn from other *riḥla* literature and premodern travelogues. He also borrowed from earlier works; one-seventh of his whole text (in particular, details about Syria and Arabia) came from the work of Ibn Jubayr.[72] Even so, Ibn Baṭṭūṭa provided a great deal of new data about the world to Islamic geographers in the fourteenth century.

The passage that describes Ibn Baṭṭūṭa's journey through China distinguishes the book among works of Muslim geography and travel, yet many scholars view this section with the same skepticism they have applied to Marco Polo and Wang Dayuan. Ross Dunn argues persuasively that, when we allow for the timing of the monsoon, Ibn Baṭṭūṭa's entire tour of China must have been jammed into the summer and early autumn of 1346. A few months would have been sufficient time for him to stay in Quanzhou and even travel to Guangzhou, but a journey to Beijing would have been impossible and must be constructed from hearsay.[73] Ibn Baṭṭūṭa's account of China also includes much second-hand information that contemporary Chinese sources can confirm. Whether Ibn Baṭṭūṭa actually traveled to China matters less to this book than how his account added to Islamic knowledge of China.

In this light, a reconstruction of Ibn Baṭṭūṭa's possible itinerary to China based on his description will help shed light on what Muslims to the west learned about travel to China. His trip to China began at the Dehli Sultanate of northern India when its sultan, Muḥammad Ibn Tughluq, ordered him to travel with a diplomatic mission to China.[74] Ibn Baṭṭūṭa and the embassy first traveled to the key international ports of Southwest India, Calicut and Quilon. Then they sailed east to Southeast Asia through the Strait of Malacca, where they presumably stopped at the ports of Vietnam before sailing on to Quanzhou, which Ibn Baṭṭūṭa made his base while in China. During his stay in China, he made a round trip journey to Guangzhou via river. Ibn Baṭṭūṭa also claims that he traveled to Fuzhou and Hangzhou (we do not know if by land or sea), and from Hangzhou to Beijing along the Grand Canal. This final segment of the trip Dunn finds most unlikely (see Map 2 for Ibn Baṭṭūṭa's itinerary).

Ibn Baṭṭūṭa tells a lengthy tale about his trip from India to China via Southeast Asia, embellishing it with many lively episodes about shipwrecks on India's southwestern coast and details about years spent on the islands of South Asia. He also provides his readers with an in-depth description of travel to China by ship including the ships' construction technology:

> The Chinese method of building ships is that they construct two walls of timber, and join them with very thick planks fastened, both in breadth and length, by huge nails the length of which is three cubits [dhirāʿ: one dhirāʿ is about 0.65m]. When the two walls are firmly joined together by these planks, they built on top of them the bottom flooring of the vessel, and launch them into the sea to complete the construction [of the ship].[75]

Ibn Baṭṭūṭa's description of watertight bulkheads and separate compartments matches the structure of a thirteenth-century Chinese ship discovered in Quanzhou and a fourteenth-century Chinese ship found in Sinan in southwest Korea.[76] Like the Quanzhou ship, the Sinan ship has seven bulkheads that divide the ship into eight compartments.[77] Joseph Needham argues that the bulkheads prevent the ship from sinking because any water that penetrated the hull would fill only one of the ship's compartments.[78] Marco Polo provides the best explanation of the ship's advantages:[79]

> Some of the ships, that is the bigger ones, have also thirteen bulkheads or partitions made of stout planks dovetailed into one another. This is useful in case the ship's hull should chance to be damaged in some place by striking on a reef or being rammed by a whale in search of food – a not infrequent occurrence, for if a whale happens to pass near the ship while she is sailing at night and churning the water to foam, he may infer from the white gleam in the water that there is food for him there and so charge full tilt against the ship and ram her, often breaching the hull at some point. In that event the water coming through the breach will run into the bilge, which is never permanently occupied. The sailors promptly find out where the breach is.

Despite Polo's accuracy about the ship's outward appearance, scholars claim that Polo's account exaggerates the purpose of the bulkheads, which technological analyses suggest were actually used only for structural reasons.[80] Ibn Baṭṭūṭa describes another one of the bulkheads' advantages based on his personal experience:

> They build four decks for the vessel, and it has cabins, suites and rooms for merchants. Such a suite has rooms and a latrine, and there is a key for its occupant to lock it, and he can take along with him slave-girls and wives. Possibly a man will live in his suite without other people on board knowing of him until they meet when they arrive at some towns .... There was an agent of the junk called Sulaymān al-Ṣafadī al-Shāmī with whom I was acquainted. I said to him: 'I want a suite that no one can come to because of the slave girls, for it is my habit never to travel without them.' He replied to me: 'The merchants from China have hired the suites for the outward and return journey. But my son-in-law has a suite which I can give you, but it has no latrine ...'[81]

Ships with bulkheads had private cabins, and Ibn Baṭṭūṭa wanted such a compartment.

Chinese ships like these were built in port cities like Quanzhou or Guangzhou. Curiously, Ibn Baṭṭūṭa calls Guangzhou *Ṣin Kalān*, which literally means "Great China," and also Ṣīn al-Ṣīn. Geographers like Dimashqī used the term Ṣīn al-Ṣīn more broadly, referring to South China as a whole. Ibn Baṭṭūṭa describes Guangzhou's Muslim community. All administration and lawsuits were handled by a Muslim judge and a group of elders, a practice also reported on by observers in ninth-century accounts like *The Accounts of China and India*. By Ibn Baṭṭūṭa's time, however, Muslim communities distributed more widely across China, and Quanzhou possessed the country's largest Muslim population. Guangzhou and Quanzhou, the biggest international sea ports in China, were the first Chinese ports that Ibn Baṭṭūṭa visited in China. Here, he reported, one could find the only places where people produced the Chinese ceramics that exported all over the known world – to India, Maghreb, and even his hometown in Morocco. In fact, however, Chinese ceramics were typically produced in other places and then sent to these cities for export.[82] Ibn Baṭṭūṭa also claims that while in the city of Fuzhou he encountered another Moroccan named Bushuri, someone whom Ibn Baṭṭūṭa had already met in India, and who came to China hoping to become a rich merchant there. This illustrates the kinds of connections that Muslims from different countries formed throughout the Islamic world. It is also possible, however, that Ibn Baṭṭūṭa or his editor Ibn Juzayy fabricated or exaggerated this episode of accidental encounter in order to create a more compelling narrative for readers. Whatever the case, this passage hints that such chance of encounters were possible among Muslims who traveled across the Indian Ocean realm.

In some passages, Ibn Baṭṭūṭa simply repeats information that already exists in earlier Arabic accounts, like the stereotype of Chinese as clever with crafts and painting. Ibn Baṭṭūṭa embellishes this stereotype with interesting but implausible anecdotes. When he and his companions arrived at the imperial palace in Beijing, for example, the Yuan emperor ordered court painters to create their portraits on paper and hang them on the walls. Ibn Baṭṭūṭa explains that this was a Chinese custom intended to keep a record of foreigners in case they later made trouble, yet no surviving Chinese documents corroborate this claim.[83]

Many other passages, like Ibn Baṭṭūṭa's description of the advantages of paper money in China, however, provide new information not found in earlier Muslim sources. The Chinese began to use paper money for the first time in world history beginning in the ninth century, and the Mongols continued the practice, using notes in tandem with coins. Marco Polo repeatedly refers to the use of paper money as a cultural facet of Chinese society. No doubt some part of Ibn Baṭṭūṭa's account was both up-to-date and reliable. In the mid-fourteenth century, however, the Yuan rulers issued too much paper money in order to solve their financial difficulties, compounding problems that contributed to the fall of its regime.[84] Interestingly, the Il-khanate also introduced paper money, but the Mongols and Persians there similarly failed to use it efficiently.[85]

Ibn Baṭṭūṭa's descriptions of Quanzhou (Zaitūn) are the most informative. Here, in this great international port city, he allegedly first stepped onto Chinese soil:

> When we had crossed the sea, the first city at which we arrived was the city of Zaitūn. There are no olives in it, nor anywhere in the whole of China and India, but it is [just] a name given to it. It is a huge and magnificent city in which clothes of damask and satin are manufactured. The clothes are known by attribution to it and preferred the clothes of Khansā (Hangzhou) and Khān Bāliq (Khanbalik; Beijing). Its [Zaitūn's] harbor is among the biggest of the world, or the biggest; I have seen in it about a hundred big junks and, as for little ones, their number cannot be counted. It is a great inlet of the sea which penetrates into the land to mingle with the great river.[86]

While in a Muslim quarter in Quanzhou, Ibn Baṭṭūṭa met Muslim leaders, including religious leaders like Shaikh Burhan al-Din of Kazarun and Muslim merchants such as Sharaf al-Din of Tabriz. Dunn admits that he finds the traveler's claims about meeting other Muslims credible because he clearly did not know Chinese. Additionally, the names of both Burhan al-Din and Sharaf al-Din match names on the list of Muslim community leaders that were carved into a Chinese inscription of 1350, an indication that Ibn Baṭṭūṭa did not make these names up.[87]

From Quanzhou, Ibn Baṭṭūṭa continued his northward journey by river. In the next city Qanjanfū (Fuzhou), he meets local Muslim shaikhs and merchants. One of these merchants was the Muslim *qadi* from Morocco whom Ibn Baṭṭūṭa previously met in India. Next, he traveled to the city of al-Khansā (Hangzhou), which he claims was the biggest city that he had ever seen, a claim that corresponds to contemporary Persian and Arabic descriptions of Mongol–era China as well as those of Marco Polo. There, he saw large Muslim communities and a canal "which runs from the big river and on it small boats bring to the city supplies of food and stones for burning [coals]," namely the Grand Canal.[88] Ibn Baṭṭūṭa purports to have journeyed along the Grand Canal in order to reach his final destination, the region of Khitai in northern China. Such a claim supports Rashīd al-Dīn's description of a waterway connecting the Yuan capitals in Northern China to the sea ports of South China. So there are many geographical facts about China that contemporaneous Persian, Arabic, and Chinese sources confirm. Ibn Baṭṭūṭa's account also indicates the importance of international maritime trade to Mongol rulers. Actually, the most reliable information in the section about North China comes from descriptions of the capital Khanbalik and a discussion about the title of khan that contemporaneous Arabic and Persian sources also provide. The episodes about military conflicts in the capital and the death of the khan are unconvincing because the last Mongol emperor Toghun Temür died in 1370, whereas Ibn Baṭṭūṭa claims that he went to China around 1347. This is obviously an addition that the editor Ibn Juzayy made after he received updated information; however, it is still noteworthy that Ibn Juzayy received this additional information from other reliable sources at that time. As the narrative progresses, Ibn Baṭṭūṭa journeys home through Java and India before he reaches his home in the Maghreb of Morocco.

In *The Account of China and India,* compiled in 851, the first Muslim writers strove to provide guidance to Arab traders who ventured eastward. Since then, Muslim writers occasionally added new information to the body of Muslim knowledge, most of it acquired indirectly. Ibn Baṭṭūṭa's *Riḥla* to China during the Mongol period is significant because it was the product of new opportunities to travel directly to China using the extensive connections throughout different societies during the thirteenth and fourteenth centuries. Muslim readers gained a more reliable, updated picture of China as a result. Judging by the surviving manuscripts, Ibn

Baṭṭūṭa attracted a steady readership over the centuries, at least in the western parts of the Islamic world.[89] A great Islamic historian named Ibn Khaldūn (died 1406) refers to Ibn Baṭṭūṭa's return to Maghreb after twenty years abroad and repeats the skepticism that met the astonishing stories he narrated at the court of the sultan Abū ʻIān. Ibn Khaldūn himself preferred to take a critical stance toward any information that could be exaggerated; for example, he was probably critical of the incredible stories about miracles in India.[90] Nonetheles, this episode testifies to the circulation of Ibn Baṭṭūṭa's stories among Muslim intellectuals. Therefore, fresh information about China, both old and new, circulated among merchants and other travelers who moved between the Islamic world and China during the Mongol period. Yet obviously, Ibn Baṭṭūṭa's stories startled his contemporary Muslims less than Marco Polo's stories startled his European contemporaries, perhaps because the inhabitants of the Islamic world knew so much more about Asia and the world at large.

Conclusion

The Mongol period marked a breakthrough in Islamic learning about China, as it did in Chinese learning about the Islamic world. As part of the larger Mongol empire, the government of the Il-khanate enjoyed close relations and direct exchanges with the Yuan dynasty, a situation that contributed to the expansion of Islamic knowledge about China. For the first time, Muslims could update information about China with relative speed. Emissaries between the Yuan and Il-khanate courts such as Bolad helped to make this possible as they provided detailed, up-to-date information to Muslim scholars wishing to write about the history and geography of China. These exchanges led to the compilation of Rashīd al-Dīn's *Compendium of Chronicles*, sponsored by the Il-khanate's Mongol rulers, which provided more substantial descriptions of China than any earlier accounts written in the Islamic world. An earlier tradition of Islamic historical and geographic literature influenced these new studies, but this new generation expanded scholarship in significant ways. The *Compendium of Chronicles* uniquely combines history and geography in an integrative way, and its scope reaches far more extensively than earlier Muslim works. It surveys the history of different regions chronologically and synchronically, providing readers with an integrated view of the world, its different regions, and their dynamic development. In this world, China is far from a *terra incognita*. No longer simply a foreign place to which only a few interested merchants traveled for trade, China becomes more fully formed and integrated into the Mongol-centered world to which Iran also belonged. Although contemporaries in China produced the first world map in the Chinese cartographic tradition, those in the Il-khanate produced this "genuine" world history.

It was not only Rashīd al-Dīn's *Compendium of Chronicles* but also other geographic works produced in the Il-khanate that demonstrate the circulation of extensive up-to-date information about the broader world facilitated by the Mongol empire's connections. Much updated geographic knowledge about China such as details about important cities like Khara Khorum, Beijing, Yangzhou, Hangzhou, and Quanzhou found their way into contemporaneous Persian studies during the reign of the Il-khanate, as well as Arabic geographic works in the non-Mongol ruled parts of the Islamic world that lay further west. The Islamic world did not witness the kind of breakthrough in cartographic knowledge about China that their contemporary Chinese counterparts did with respect to the Islamic world; however, they did continue to make improvements to geographic content and cartographic technique. Both contemporary Chinese and Muslim cartographers assigned precise locations to some of the world's major places under Mongol rule.

Not all of the sources are traceable like Rashīd al-Dīn's *Chronicles*, yet it seems plausible that increased contacts encouraged updates in geographic knowledge. Muslim merchants and travelers who traveled between China and the Islamic world provided new information about China to Islamic writers. Despite the lack of political unity that prevailed in China, Muslim merchants in the Islamic world took advantage of the open sea to develop international trade networks that spanned the Indian Ocean, creating merchant communities along the sea routes through India and Southeast Asia. The gradual Islamization of large parts of South and Southeast Asia and the growing prosperity of Muslim communities in China under Mongol rule encouraged a large number of Muslims to travel to China. Ibn Baṭṭūṭa describes a possible direct journey that Muslims could take to travel from South and Southeast Asia to Chinese port cities and on to the Yuan capital in Beijing via waterways from the sea to rivers to the Grand Canal. All along the way, Muslim travelers could sojourn in Muslim communities where they could receive the resources and information necessary for them to continue their travels. Ibn Baṭṭūṭa's account thus hints at the dynamic interactions between Muslims who settled in China and those who plied their ways as itinerants following the coastline between China and the Islamic world. Yet inscriptions in Muslim mosques and Muslim cemeteries in places like Quanzhou add further verification.

How did the fall of the Mongols affect geographic learning in China and the Islamic world? Chapter 5, the final chapter, will turn to the development of mutual geographic knowledge of China and the Islamic world in the changed context of the post-Mongol period.

5

Legacy from Half the Globe before 1492

Chinese Understanding of the Islamic World and Islamic Knowledge about China, 1368–1500

The end of Mongol rule in China and Iran led to a multipolar Eurasia. After overthrowing the Mongol Yuan dynasty, Han Chinese created the Ming dynasty, which included China proper, Gansu, Yunnan, and Manchuria. The Islamic world divided among different kingdoms: The Chaghadaid Moghuls in Central Asia and the Golden Horde formed from remnants of the Mongol empire whereas the Mamluks, the Ottomans, and most notably Timur rose to power on their own. Timur (reigned circa 1370–1405), was known to Europeans as Tamerlane, a man of Turkish-Mongol origin who sought to conquer Eurasia by virtue of his claims to Mongol ancestry, his appeal to Islam, and his personal charisma. A significant part of the old Islamic empire fell under his control.[1] This changed political atmosphere limited the contacts the two societies once enjoyed through diplomacy and trade. However, the legacy of the earlier period was strong, and the geographic and cartographic knowledge that had accumulated in both societies continued to spread. This circulation culminated in such academic projects as the making of Eurasian and African maps in China and a summary of al-Idrīsī's geographic works in Ibn Khaldūn's great history of the world.

In addition, the Zheng He (1371–1435) voyages to West Asia and East African Coast, unprecedented official ventures that were also based on the earlier legacy of maritime exchanges, contributed to the further increase of Chinese knowledge about foreign countries, particularly the Islamic Middle East. Ma Huan, a Muslim interpreter who accompanied Zheng He's fourth and seventh voyages, recalled in his preface to the mission's famed chronicle that he had read an earlier account about foreign countries, which was related to Wang Dayuan's

A Shortened Account of the Non-Chinese Island Peoples that we examined in Chapter 3:

> I once looked at [a book called] *An Account of the Non-Chinese Island Peoples*, which recorded variations of season and of climate, and differences in topography and in peoples. I was surprised and said 'How can there be such dissimilarities in the world?' In the eleventh year of the Yongle [period], The Grand Exemplar The Cultured Emperor issued an imperial order that the principal envoy the grand eunuch Zheng He should take general command of the treasure-ships and go to the various foreign countries in the Western Ocean to read out the imperial commands and to bestow rewards. I too was sent in a subordinate capacity as a translator of foreign documents ... I passed through the various countries, with their [different] seasons, climates, topography, and peoples; and I saw [these countries] with my own eyes and I walked [through them] in person. After that I knew that the statements in *the Non-Chinese Island Peoples* were no fabrications, and that even greater wonders existed.[2]

In the same way that Marco Polo's travel account inspired voyages in search of Asia by Henry the Navigator and Christopher Columbus, accounts by earlier authors like Wang Dayuan inspired Zheng He's grand voyages. In turn, Zheng He's voyages greatly impressed the Europeans who heard rumors about them through Muslim intermediaries.[3]

As China conducted its grand expeditions toward the western Indian Ocean, the Islamic world continued to struggle with political division. Rivalries formed among the several empires that competed with the Timurid dynasty for supremacy, and city-states took sides in these conflicts by joining with coalitions of larger states. The period also witnessed the ascent of a new Islamic power in Eurasia, the Ottoman empire (1299–1922), which, unlike its Muslim neighbors to the east, was less familiar with earlier Muslim scholarly traditions, including geographic heritage. The Ottomans were preoccupied with territorial expansion into Europe during its early history, but after 1500 began to compete with the Portuguese, their main political rival, for dominion over the expanding trading market in the Indian Ocean.[4] In the midst of this change, Muslims connected to the Indian Ocean commercial sphere continued to seek new advances in geographic knowledge about the world, indebted as they were to earlier Chinese and Muslim geographers. Among this advance was the navigational treatise written by Ibn Mājid (circa 1421–1500?). Given his fame and the importance of his treatise, some have mistakenly credited Ibn Mājid with guiding Vasco da Gama from Malindi (in modern-day Kenya) to India. Ibn Mājid's actual achievement in world history, however, bears no less significance than this erroneous claim. Indeed, he created a navigational treatise that owes much of its knowledge to a popular genre that drew on the rich experiences of Muslim seafarers on the Indian Ocean, summarizing geographic knowledge accumulated throughout the past. Thanks to Ibn Mājid, it is possible to understand the state of Muslim geographic knowledge about the Indian Ocean that circulated in Asia in the years that followed the Mongol fall and which eventually flowed into Europe, encouraging Europeans to seek Asia directly.

This final chapter draws on both Chinese- and Muslim-language sources to explore contacts between China and the Islamic world from 1368, when the Yuan dynasty fell, to the eve of European expansion in the late fifteenth century. Geographers during this period were strongly influenced by the legacy of the previous period's achievements, yet also laid an important foundation for the generation to come. During this important period, Asia grew more interconnected and gradually opened to Europeans seeking the wider world. The Portuguese began to undertake serious adventures in search of direct routes to Asia by way of the African coast beginning in the early fifteenth century, using relatively advanced geography obtained from works of the Islamic world and the Byzantine empire. This enterprise marks an important turning point in world history, one in which the agents of this advance depended on the knowledge they obtained from more knowledgeable societies in Asia. We will focus on the following questions: How did the new political context that emerged after the fall of the Mongols affect the exchange and growth of Chinese and Muslim learning about the other society? What was the Mongol legacy and what immediate changes did it bring to China and the Islamic world? How much new and reliable information did Chinese and Muslim societies add to what they had previously known? When we compare both Chinese and Muslim learning of the other society and the wider world in this period, what kind of similarities and differences can we find in the trends of the two societies? Finally, what changes did this updated knowledge bring to the two societies, as well as to world history?

Political Changes, Foreign Relations, and Geographic Knowledge of the World during the Early Ming Dynasty

The Yuan dynasty in China came to an end in 1368 when Han Chinese rebelled against their foreign Mongol rulers. One of the rebel leaders, Zhu Yuanzhang (1328–1398), established the Ming dynasty and moved the Chinese capital to Nanjing in Jiangsu province, where he was born.

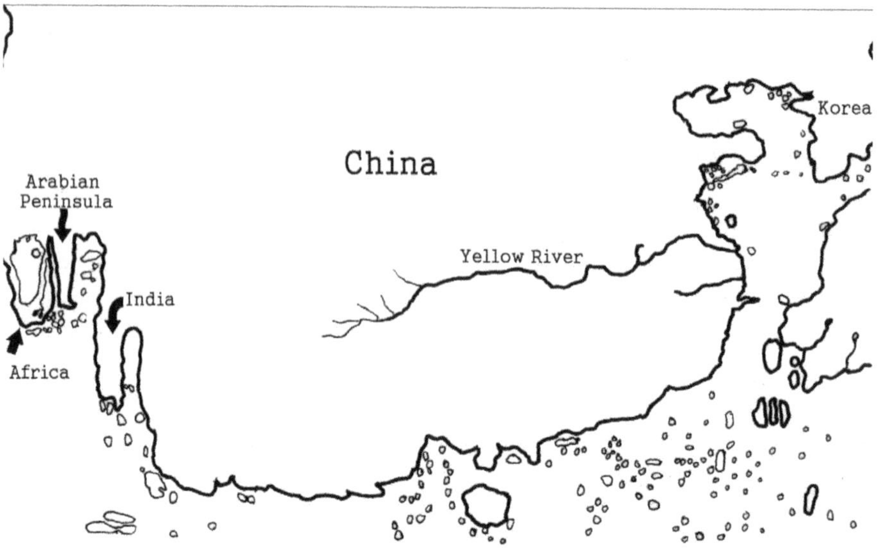

FIGURE 5.1. *The Comprehensive Map of the Great Ming Empire* (*Daming hunyi tu*, 14–15th centuries), redrawn after the original. 386 × 456 cm.
Note: The map was preserved in the imperial archives of the Forbidden City and is now in the Number One Archive in Beijing, which often exhibits the map in public. No one has yet published a full-scale analysis of the map.

Although claiming to repudiate the foreign influences that the Chinese had incorporated during Mongol rule, the Ming dynasty's self-conscious Han leaders assimilated much from their Yuan predecessors.[5] The Yuan left as its legacy intellectual and scientific achievements, and presented its Ming successors with updated political, administrative, social, and economic systems. Thus, the Ming dynasty could not ignore the expanded geographic knowledge that had flowed into China during the previous dynasty's reign; the broad foreign connections that were part of the Mongol legacy in China continued to function for some time. Works like *The Comprehensive Map of the Great Ming Empire* (*Daming hunyi tu*) testify to the extent of geographic information about the world including West Asia, Africa, and Europe that circulated throughout China during the Ming period (see Figure 5.1).

The Comprehensive Map of the Great Ming Empire shows entire Afro-Eurasia. The map bears no marks to identify either the cartographer or the year in which it was made. Only the use of certain place-names allow us to date the map to between 1389 and 1391 because they were no longer used in the later period.[6] Although the author remains unknown, it is highly likely that the Ming government commissioned it since the map was clearly intended to illustrate administrative divisions and because it was preserved in the imperial archives of the Forbidden City. The appearance of Manchu writing inside red labels, which replaced the original Chinese script, probably result from modifications made by officials of the later Qing dynasty (1644–1911), who instituted the use of Manchu in court documents after their Manchu leaders overthrew the Ming dynasty and seized its archives. Manchu language scholars transliterated the map's Manchu place-names and realized that they nearly match the place-names written in Chinese script on the Korean map drawn in 1402 based on Mongol-period Chinese maps, the *Kangnido*.[7] Here is an example of a Ming-era map that directly borrowed geographic information from Mongol-period maps.

Although it borrows from previous maps, the *Comprehensive Map of the Great Ming Empire* does not entirely imitate them. For example, the proportion of Euro-Africa relative to the rest of the world in the *Comprehensive Map* is smaller than that found on the Korean *Kangnido*. Still, *The Comprehensive Map* retains the coastlines of West Asia and Africa shown on the latter map. Yet it even shows a protruding Indian continent that the *Kangnido* does not, making the coastline more complete.

The Broad Terrestrial Map (*Guang yutu*), a geographic compilation of both maps and texts compiled by Luo Hongxian in 1541, provides another piece of evidence that the Ming inherited its geographic view of the world from its Mongol predecessors. Two connected maps of foreign countries in the compilation, the "Map of Foreign Lands in Southeast Sea" (Dongnan haiyi tu) and the "Map of Foreign Lands in Southwest Sea" (Xinan haiyi tu), fill in most but not yet all of the Indian Ocean coastline (see Figure 5.2).

This map does not show the Arabian Peninsula, unlike *The Map of Integrated Regions and Terrains* and *The Comprehensive Map of the Great Ming Empire*, because the upper part of the map was cut off. The African coastline, however, appears in the same triangular shape as it does on Mongol period maps. In creating his maps of the southeastern and southwestern seas, Luo Hongxian clearly indicated that he used a Mongol-period map by Zhu Siben, which is now lost. Zhu's map may have been Luo's source for his representation of places like Europe and Africa that were so common to Yuan world maps. Given the evidence that Ming maps borrowed from their Yuan predecessors, it is possible to infer the scope of Yuan geography and cartography through the surviving

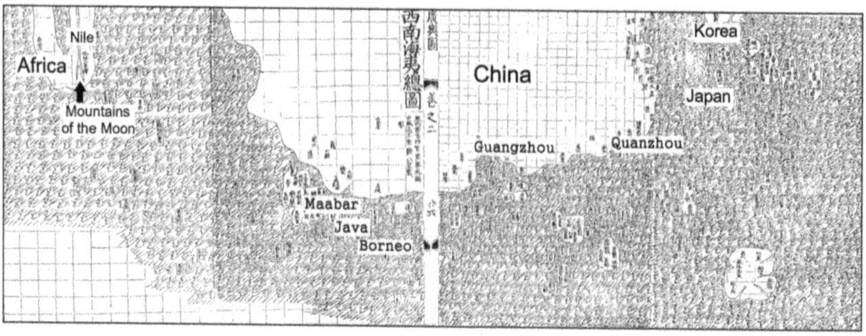

FIGURE 5.2. The "Map of Foreign Lands in Southeast Sea" (Dongnan haiyi tu) (right) and the "Map of Foreign Lands in Southwest Sea" (Xinan haiyi tu) (left) from Luo Hongxian's *Broad Terrestrial Map* (*Guang yutu*, 1541).
Note: Luo Hongxian, *Guang yutu* (Taibei, 1969), 386–389.

Ming-period maps. The lost Yuan maps of Li Zemin and Zhu Siben that Ming geographers once consulted had circulated throughout Chinese society during Mongol rule, mostly among literati.[8] Both Li and Zhu privately produced their maps, although there is little doubt that they benefitted from the increased circulation of knowledge about western Afro-Eurasia that Muslim scholars brought to the Yuan court, evidence of which can be found in Yuan government-sponsored geographic works. People of the Ming dynasty, those in both government and ordinary society, inherited this knowledge. Examples like *The Comprehensive Map* and the two charts in *The Broad Terrestrial Map* show that Chinese cartographers would continue the Mongol practice of mapping the known world, and not return immediately to the pre-Mongol tradition where cartographers drew only China and assigned its neighbors to a list of names that ran alongside the map's four boundaries. In these ways, the early Ming maps mark a genuine advance in traditional Chinese cartographic knowledge carried over from the Yuan period.

Both of these early Ming maps also depict many islands and ports. Clearly, the cartographers wished to emphasize the importance of China's sea connection. This raises questions about the reliability of these maps, however. Do the maps actually indicate a flourishing maritime traffic that continued from the Yuan into the Ming eras? Or do they simply reflect realities that vanished with Mongol rule? Although the maps in *The Broad Terrestrial Map* depict the southern coastline of Africa, its presentation of South and South Asia is problematic, depicting the Maabar coast of India as an island. The maps also contain information about legendary places, such as the country of the hairy people and the country of the small people, as well as other place names that are difficult to identify. This provides a hint that Luo Hongxian and other Ming geographers may not have acquired new empirical information about maritime routes in their times.

In fact, unlike its Yuan predecessors, the Ming court promulgated policies that limited foreign contacts among Chinese subjects. The fall of Mongol rule across Eurasia resurrected obstacles to overland travel between China and the Islamic world, and it encouraged a new rivalry between the new powers in China and the Islamic world, the Ming and the Timurid empires. A similar drawback occurred in Chinese maritime connections to the Islamic world. Soon after it came to power, the Ming emperor tried to control trade with foreign countries by banning private commercial activities that had been relatively open under the Yuan. The government issued bans (*haijin*) on all private sea travel in 1371 and on trade relations with foreign countries in 1381.[9] Allegedly, the emperor instituted these policies in response to the increasing problem of Chinese and Japanese pirates.[10] Trade with Southeast Asia continued, however, both as an illegal activity and under the auspices of a state monopoly, so the maritime commercial networks that flourished during the previous dynasty's rule continued to survive.[11] Nonetheless, the new government policy dealt a deadly blow to the direct maritime connections that China once enjoyed with West Asia and Northeastern Africa under previous dynasties. The Ming-period account *Book of Min*, testifies to a decreased scale of Chinese maritime trade with countries in the western Indian Ocean realm. The author reports that most of the goods from these western countries were not able to make it to China, but were rerouted instead to the Philippines.[12]

After the first Ming emperor prohibited private maritime trade, the early emperors who succeeded him remained preoccupied with China's northern border, seeking an effective response to continuous invasions by the Mongols in their futile attempt to reconquer China after Ming armies pushed them back into Mongolia. These political and military troubles exacerbated setbacks in China's foreign relations with the Islamic world, in particular the new regime of Timur. After the collapse of the Il-khanate, Timur laid claim to the line of succession to the Mongol khans through his marriage to a descendent of Chinggis Khan. Under the mantle of restoring the Mongol khanate, he reunited Central Asia, Iran, Iraq, and Syria under his rule. Throughout his reign, Timur never established harmonious relations with China. Apparently the new Ming approach to foreign relations was partly to blame. In the Ming empire's early days, the first emperor repelled invading armies at the borders, dispatched diplomatic envoys to prevent further attacks, and attempted to recreate the Sino-centric world order that existed before Mongol rule. To this end, he dispatched an embassy of 1,500 Chinese led by three envoys to Samarkand to visit Timur. When they arrived, the envoys handed the king a letter that clearly treated him as an ordinary vassal of the Chinese court. Timur grew enraged and detained the embassy. After conquering a large part of the Islamic world, Timur set out to conquer China in 1404. Although he may have harbored a religious motivation to convert Chinese to Islam, Timur's ultimate goal remained the resurrection of the Mongol empire in Eurasia, including China. Naturally, his armies posed the biggest potential threat to China from the outside world, which held the government's attention to its northern borders.

A change of course came, however, with the rise of the third emperor, Yongle (reigned 1402–24). He himself fought against the Mongols many times, even repelling Timur's armies when they threatened China's western borders, so he understood the potential dangers of advances by the Mongols in the northern steppe and by Muslim rulers in Central and West Asia.[13] Only the death of Timur in 1405, while he was on his way to China, ultimately prevented war. Because Yongle understood the Ming empire's predicament in Central and Northern Asia, he addressed this precarious political situation in the most dynamic and practical way in order to reverse Ming China's political weakness. He adopted a new approach that set him apart from his predecessors and changed the course of China's relations with its neighbors, not only by land, but by sea as well. This affected the history of Chinese knowledge about the outside world as well, in important ways.

Emperor Yongle dispatched many envoys to foreign countries both east and west in order to establish diplomatic relations but also to obtain political intelligence about his neighbors. He sent envoys to both Timur and his Islamic rivals in Central Asia, hoping to maintain political balance in that region. In one famous example, Yongle dispatched Chen Cheng (1365–1457) to Samarkand in response to a request from Timur's successor, who preferred to consider Ming China a source of profit, not an object of hostility.[14] Undertaken between 1413 and 1415, Chen's mission successfully established border defense and developed harmonious and practical relations with the countries of Central Asia. After his return, he wrote a memoir of his travels entitled *Record of Routes to the Western Regions* (*Xiyu xingcheng ji*) and a geographic explanation of the western regions entitled *Account of Foreign Countries in the Western*

Regions (*Xiyu fanguo zhi*). His geography provides fascinating details about the state of Central Asian societies during the fifteenth century, like his description of Samarkand, an estimate of its size, and a sketch of life in the flourishing markets crowded by foreign merchants there.[15] Unfortunately, Chen Cheng's success appears to only have helped preserve harmonious relations until the late fifteenth century when Ming policies toward its northwestern borders took an aggressive turn.[16]

Emperor Yongle's most conspicuous diplomatic endeavor – in terms of the scale, purpose, and significance of the enterprise; its success in projecting political power into the Islamic world; and its consequence for the history of Chinese knowledge about the Islamic world – occurred not on land but on sea. This was the series of voyages aboard the Ming treasure fleets to the Western Ocean under the admiral Zheng He, an event described as Zheng He's "descent to the Western Ocean (*Xia Xiyang*)."[17] The emperor sought to assert China's power with foreign countries as far away as West Asia and the East African Coast, hoping to reestablish the traditional tribute system of Chinese diplomatic relations with states all along the Indian Ocean's rim.

Chinese Learning about the Islamic World that Resulted from the Seven Voyages of Zheng He from 1405 to 1433

The Chinese naval expeditions initiated by Emperor Yongle, which lasted from 1405 to 1433, marked a significant page in Chinese – and world – history. Several hundreds of large vessels sailed from China to the Indian Ocean, completing a total of seven journeys; archaeological, documentary, and inscription sources reveal that four of Zheng He's voyages traveled as far as the Arabian Peninsula and East Africa.[18] It may seem surprising that the emperor dispatched fleets of such grand scale at a time when the first emperor's ban on ocean travel was still in effect.[19] The court would have perceived no inconsistency here: The ban pertained to private travel and trade, and Zheng He's fleets sailed under the auspices of a governmental enterprise. It appears that the emperor wished to relax restrictions to some degree; during his reign, Yongle took initial steps to resurrect government offices that once supervised and assisted maritime trade such as the Office of the Superintendent of Merchant Shipping (*shibosi*). However, commercial trade constituted only one facet of Zheng He's mission. Primarily, the Ming court sought to rebuild China's commercial networks as an integral part of the state's tribute-based diplomatic order, as well as show off the power of their new empire.[20]

In order to carry out such grand maritime projects, the Ming government needed experienced sailors, advanced navigation techniques, shipbuilding technology, and information about sea routes and foreign countries including those in the Islamic world. To this end, the government made practical use of resources and knowledge it inherited from the previous dynasty. Descendents of Muslim merchants who had been the most actively engaged in the Indian Ocean sea trade during the previous century also participated in the projects.[21] The most representative figure among them was the chief commander Zheng He himself, a descendant of immigrants from Bukhara (in today's Uzbekistan) who settled in Yunnan province in Southwest China during the Mongol period.[22]

In fact, Muslims who engaged in foreign trade in Fujian, Guangdong, and Yunnan suffered from Chinese political unrest during the Yuan-Ming transition, and many of them fled to Southeast Asia in response. Although this political change accelerated the development of Muslim communities in Southeast Asia, it diminished the scale of Chinese maritime trade activities in the port cities of southeast China. This led to a gap between demand and supply in the import market that the Ming government tried to restrain within the parameters of their limited tribute trade system.[23] As a consequence, many Chinese merchants who inherited their fathers' professions continued private trade illegally, and in doing so, they maintained their trade ties with Muslim merchants in Southeast Asia.

The first three voyages of Zheng He in 1405, 1407, and 1408 sailed through Southeast Asia to Calicut on India's western coast. Along the way, the fleets anchored in each port to negotiate treaties with local rulers who agreed to pay tribute to China. The emperor ordered the next voyage to travel further west, and so in 1412 the fourth voyage sailed to Hormuz, the most important seaport in the Persian Gulf, a place visited by many foreign travelers since Mongol times including the Chinese merchant Yang Shu. Timur attempted to conquer Hormuz during his Middle East campaigns without success. The rulers of Hormuz, in response, sought to maintain their independence by promoting international commerce and creating a welcoming environment for foreign traders in order to earn sufficient revenues to pay the land tax (*kharāj*) they owed to the Türkmen dynasty of Aq Quyunlu, a fierce rival of the Timurides who protected them.[24] In preparation for this voyage to the heart of the Islamic world, Zheng He actively recruited Muslims who were familiar with the Indian Ocean trade networks to serve as translators and navigators.[25]

Shipbuilding techniques that Chinese developed during earlier periods allowed them to build a fleet of several hundred vessels. Both written and archaeological evidence shows that a large number of big Chinese junks measuring 100 feet (thirty meters) dominated the maritime route between South Asia and China during the Song and Yuan dynasties that preceded the Ming. Similar sources from the Ming period also verify the manufacture of a large number of sea-going vessels in the shipbuilding yards of coastal cities. The largest of these shipyards, which produced many of the ships used in the Zheng He expeditions, was located in the suburbs of the Ming capital, Nanjing.[26] Excavations there produced the dockyard and some ship parts that provide archaeological evidence for the launch of ships via canals to the sea.

Debate continues over the size of the largest vessels called treasure ships (*baochuan*). Many scholars have taken the figures reported in written sources literally to claim that the ships measured as long as 120 meters (400 feet). Those who are familiar with shipbuilding technologies, however, argue that these scholars misunderstood a traditional measuring unit and ignored contemporaneous shipbuilding technology. Modern shipbuilding experts add that it would be impossible nowadays to build a wooden vessel of 120 meters long. Those who continue to believe that the ships measured 120 meters long also point to an immense rudder found in the Nanjing shipyard in 1957 to defend their argument: A ship with so large a rudder, they argue, must also have been big. Using known ratios of rudder to ship sizes, they calculate the rudder's size to measure as large as the original estimates for the treasure ships. However, experts in the history of shipbuilding technology like Yang You and Yamagata Kinya point out that the ratio scholars have used to support this claim applies only to riverboats, not to ocean-going vessels that have relatively large rudders in order to help stabilize the ship's balance. These skeptics also point to recent failed efforts to build such a ship, implying that if it was impossible for people to build a 120 meter-long wooden vessel today, even using the modern-day technology, it would have been impossible during the Ming.[27] Considering technological limitations in shipbuilding at that time, it is more likely that the largest treasure ship measured an estimated sixty to seventy meters (200–230 feet) long. This size may seem disappointing, but in fact, a wooden vessel of this length would still have been a remarkable feat in light of the shipbuilding technology of the period. A ship sixty to seventy meters long would still dwarf Columbus's *Santa Maria*, which measured merely twenty-four meters. Even at this size, no other country could build ships of comparable scale.[28]

So the voyages across the Indian Ocean to West Asia and the East African coast still demonstrate China's impressively high level of shipbuilding and nautical knowledge at the turn of the fifteenth century. The Ming shipbuilders and navigators did not receive this wisdom in a sudden flash of inspiration; instead, they learned from their predecessors who knew the location of important countries in the Indian Ocean, their geographic features, the cultures of their inhabitants, how to sail there using the seasonal monsoons, and how to build more than thirty-meter long seagoing vessels. Thus, when the Ming emperor formed a special government commission to create a fleet of unprecedented size and complexity to sail to the westernmost shores of the Indian Ocean, his chances for success were assured. The enterprise could look to a well-developed body of accumulated knowledge about the topography, societies, and sailing routes of the Indian Ocean, and utilize shipbuilding and navigation technology, thanks to centuries of maritime contact between Chinese and the world.

With the exception of a few written sailing guides inserted into early literary works, like the Song dynasty's *Notes from the Land beyond the Passes*, no actual sea chart from the period before the Ming dynasty survives. We are fortunate, therefore, to have an extant sea chart that helps us understand the possible routes that Zheng He's fleet took from China through the Indian Ocean to West Asia and the East African coast. The sea chart, most likely derived from actual sea charts used by the Zheng He voyagers, was inserted into a Ming-era military book entitled *The Treatise of Military Preparation* (*Wubei zhi*) by the book's compiler Mao Yuanyi in 1621. The sea chart tracing Zheng He's sea route comprises forty individual maps, including eight maps for West Asia and the East African coast, and provides a linear route that connects China to the countries in the Islamic world. The following illustration shows the whole map (see Figure 5.3).[29]

The final section provides the first extant Chinese map that details the Indian Ocean region. At first glance the map does not appear to give a precise shape to the coastline, unlike some earlier maps like *The Comprehensive Map of the Great Ming Empire* that were drawn based on maps from the Islamic world. The sequence of the routes seems incorrect because places in East Africa, like Malindi, appear before those in South Asia, like Calicut. The main method of charting routes does not rely on a linear coastline but instead plots precise compass directions (*zhenlu*), explained along the dotted lines that connect major seaports and other landmarks. The map shows the route across the Indian Ocean that links South Asia and the Arabian Peninsula, each of which stretches horizontally across the upper and lower parts of the map.

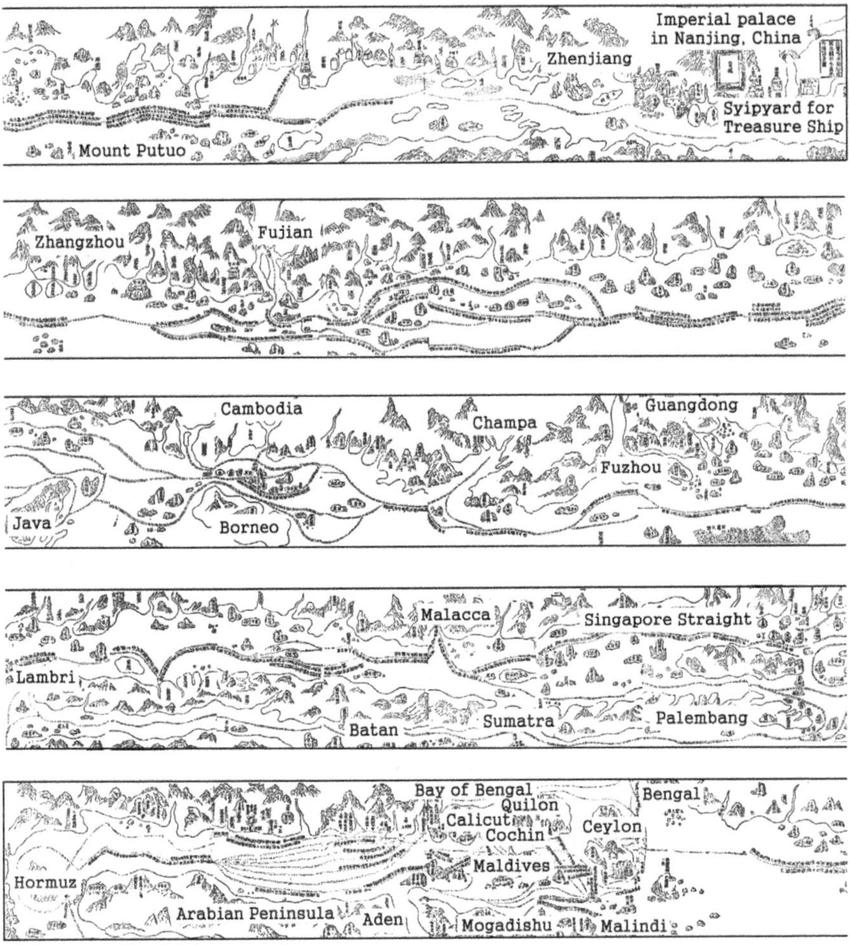

FIGURE 5.3. Reconstructed sea charts of Zheng He's maritime route in Mao Yuanyi, *The Treatise of Military Preparation* (*Wubei zhi*) (circa 1621).

The Arabian Peninsula appears elongated, not all that different from the form typically presented on Mongol-period maps. The South Asian subcontinent protrudes into the Indian Ocean in the same way as *The Comprehensive Map of the Great Ming Empire*. Zheng He's navigators possessed a reasonably accurate understanding of the coastline that they passed along the way, although they were probably more familiar with sailing directions between the landfalls than with the overall shape and balance of continents presented in world maps like *The Comprehensive Map*. The southernmost part of the East African coast that appears on the map is Malindi, which sits on the coast of modern-day Kenya. The map suggests that the Chinese did not sail to the southern tip of Africa, because the chart's East African coastline does not extend that far. The surviving Zheng He sea chart gives not only precise sailing directions by compass, but also the locations of islands and reefs, the depths of different parts of the sea, and other miscellaneous information necessary for successful navigation. The mariner's compass had been used by Chinese sailors since the Song period or earlier, but no earlier surviving account provides such detailed compass sailing guides as the Zheng He chart. All of this suggests that the map was based on the actual maps that Zheng He's crew used – both those that they inherited from previous generations of seafarers and those that they updated based on more recent sailing experiences.

The Zheng He sea chart suggests a possible transfer of Arabic navigational technique to Chinese sailors. Although the main method of navigation between China and South Asia required a mariner's compass to travel between landmarks such as coastal peaks, the map indicates instead that navigators traversed the Indian Ocean using both a compass and the measurement of star altitudes to plot a ship's latitudinal position, a technique Chinese called "suoxing shu."[30] This way of navigation resembled the method navigators traditionally used to sail the Indian Ocean, as seen in a contemporaneous Arabic treatise by Ibn Mājid. This method required the use of a *kamāl*, which Chinese called a "suoxing ban" – an instrument consisting of twelve square wooden boards that navigators used to measure latitude and originally developed by Muslim navigators.[31] Placing the board's base line parallel to the horizon, navigators adjusted a string attached to the board's center until the board's upper line overlapped with the star. Once accomplished, navigators could measure the length of the string to estimate the height of the star from which they calculated the ship's latitude.[32]

Along the sailing routes of West Asia and the East African coast, the cartographers of the Zheng He charts annotated each port city they identified with the heights of certain stars such as the polar star and Ursa Minor (Little Dipper), in addition to compass directions. The final page of the Persian Gulf maps in Mao Yuanyi's chart centers on Hormuz, and is followed by four different star charts (*guoyang qianxing tu*) with specific explanations for sailing to certain destinations. Two of these charts were about Hormuz (see Figure 5.4).

The chart on the first page describes the passage from Calicut to Hormuz, while the fourth page directs the return voyage from Hormuz to

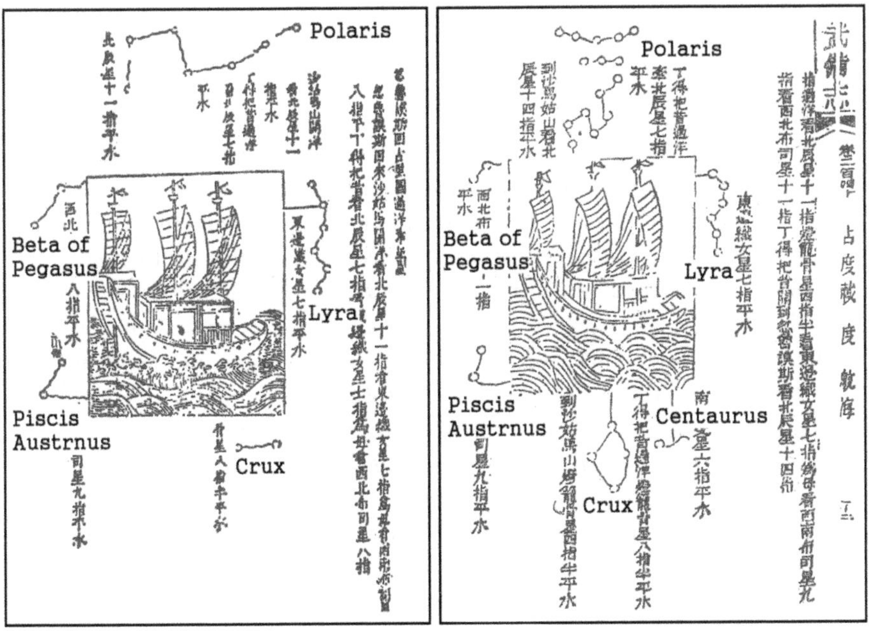

FIGURE 5.4. Star charts from the Zheng He sea charts in *The Treatise of Military Preparation.* The first page (right) and the fourth page (left).

Calicut. Both pages contain pictures of several unlabelled constellations. The constellation on the upper side of the fourth page appears to be Ursa Minor. These pictures were probably drawn to aid visual understanding, as a supplement to the star altitudes that were critical to navigation.

Chinese most likely learned this method of navigation during the Yuan dynasty, when Chinese and Muslims frequently sailed between China and the Islamic world and Muslims regularly submitted their sea charts to the Yuan government. Chinese mariners of the Ming inherited these navigation methods from their Yuan-era forebears.

One of Zheng He's sailors, Fei Xin, a veteran of the third (1409–1411), fourth (1413–1415), and seventh voyages (1430–1433), also wrote his own account, entitled *The Overall Survey of the Star Raft* (*Xingcha shenglan*). His preface mentions the existence of an imperial world map that illustrated the foreign countries bordering the southern and western seas:[33]

> Admirable [indeed]: the imperial map covers a vast terrain and the great Ming dynasty is tied to [the course of] Heaven. Truly, [in terms of splendor it] surpasses [the times of] Tang and Yu and the [period of the] three

> dynasties. [This also] made it possible [for me] to find out [more on] the maritime regions and the territories of the southern barbarians – whether [their] customs are beautiful or bad, and whether [their] mountains and streams are dangerous or easy [to cross]....

Fei's *Survey of the Star Raft* describes not only the foreign countries that he personally visited, but those he had heard about from others as well. It divided Fei's narrative into two parts: firsthand and secondhand accounts. The veteran sailor can describe only one Muslim country using firsthand experiences: Hormuz, the ultimate destination of Zheng He's fourth, fifth, sixth, and seventh voyages. To describe countries of the Islamic world like Aden, Dhofar, and Mecca in the Arabian Peninsula and Mogadishu, Giumbo, and Barawa in Somalia, Fei resorts to secondhand information. Many of his country profiles seem to repeat information given in older Chinese narratives, like his description of trading commodities such as porcelains decorated in blue and white which Wang Dayuan described. Unlike Wang Dayuan, who mentions porcelain as an important trading item only occasionally in his travel memoir, Fei Xin refers to it in each section of his book that relates to the Islamic world. Both historical and archaeological evidence confirm the continued large-scale production and export of blue-and-white porcelains to the Islamic world during the Ming dynasty through Southeast Asian intermediaries. Ceramics experts argue, however, that the persistence of the sea ban policy and the consequent decline of open maritime trade undermined the quality of Ming blue-and-white porcelains. It gradually deteriorated as manufacturers shifted their production of blue-and-white porcelains to sites near Hanoi.[34]

Another account of the Zheng He voyages, the *Overall Survey of the Ocean's Shores* written by a Muslim crewmember named Ma Huan, provides more vivid detail about the countries of the Islamic world. Ma Huan was a Muslim Chinese who joined the fourth voyage to Hormuz as a translator. The voyage gave him the opportunity to fulfill his hajj to Mecca.

Ma Huan's account of Mecca includes a description of the Kaʿbah, Islam's holiest site and the primary object of Muslim pilgrimage, which exceeds any previous Chinese account:

> If you travel on from here for a journey of more than half a day, you reach the Heavenly Hall mosque [the Sacred Mosque]; the foreign name for this Hall is *Kai-a-bai* [*al-Kaʿbah*]. All around it on the outside [there] is a wall; this wall has four hundred and sixty-six gates, on both sides of which are pillars all made of white jade-stone; of these pillars there are all together four hundred and sixty-seven – along the front ninety-nine, along the back

> one-hundred and one, along the left-hand side one hundred and thirty-two, and along the right-hand side one hundred and thirty-five....
>
> Every year on the tenth day of the twelfth moon all the foreign Muslims – in extreme cases making a long journey of one or two years – come to worship inside the Hall. Everyone cuts off a piece of the hemp-silk covering to take it as a memento and reflects it when he leaves. When it has been completely cut away, the king covers over [the Hall] again with another covering woven in advance; this happens again and again, year after year, without intermission....
>
> Inside the wall [of the mosque], at the four corners, four towers are built; at every service of worship they ascend these towers to call for prayer [*adhan*]. On both sides, left and right, are the halls where all the patriarchs have preached their doctrine; these, too, are built with layers of stone, and are decorated elegantly.[35]

As the fifth pillar of Islam, the hajj takes place during the first ten days of the month of *Dhul-Hijjah*, the twelfth month of the Islamic calendar. Although Ma Huan does not give a full description of the essential rites performed during the hajj, this discussion of the annual covering of the Ka'bah by Mecca's ruler is fairly accurate.

The gathering of Muslims from all over Euro-Africa in Mecca for the hajj created an unusual opportunity to exchange goods and ideas. Both faith and trade appear to have interested Ma Huan during his voyage aboard the treasure fleet; his *Overall Survey* devotes as much attention to the import-export trade of individual countries as it does to religious customs. For example, after explaining that frankincense was grown in Jufar at the southern edge of the Arabian Peninsula, Ma lists an inventory of the tributary gifts the local king submitted to Zheng He, an act of trade as well as diplomatic ritual from Sino-centric point of view:

> When the treasure-ships of China arrived there, after the reading of the imperial will and the conferment of presents was finished, the king ordered chiefs everywhere to issue instructions to the people of the country and they all took such things as frankincense, dragon's blood, aloes, myrrh, benzoin, liquid storax, and *mubiezi* [gac], and came to barter them for hemp-silk, porcelain ware, and other such articles....
>
> On the day when the imperial envoy was returning, the king of this country also ordered his men to take frankincense, camels [camels' furs], and other such things, to accompany the treasure-ships in order to present tribute to our court.[36]

Sources in Arabic confirm that Chinese junks led by a Chinese commander-in-chief (most likely a detachment of Zheng He's main fleet) traded in Aden.[37] The passage from the section about Mecca also shows that among the items that Zheng He's fleets brought home to China from abroad were unusual animals such as ostriches. The section about the country of Aden talks about animals such as zebras and lions, for example. The most sensational animal was the giraffe:

> The *qilin* [giraffe] has two fore-feet which are around nine *chi* high (3 meters; 9.8 feet); the two hind-feet are about six *chi* high (2 meters; 6.5 feet); the head is carried on a long neck which is one *zhang* six *chi* long (5 meters; 16.4 feet); since the front part is tall and the hind part low, men cannot ride it; on its head it has two short fleshy horns, beside the ears; it has the tail of an ox and the body of a deer; the hoof has three digits; it has a flat mouth; and it eats unhusked rice, beans, and flour-cakes....[38]

The veritable records of Ming Taizu report in their entry for 1415 that "the country of Malin [Malindi] and other foreign countries submitted giraffes (*qilin*), heavenly horses, and divine deer, and the emperor came out to the gate of Fengtian, and civil and military officials bowed to congratulate and praise it."[39] The name "qilin" refers to an imaginary unicorn-like animal in ancient Chinese literature thought to bring good fortune. Chinese spectators must have been filled with excitement the first time they saw the animal whose Somali name (*Kilin*) sounded so similar to the name of the legendary qilin of Chinese antiquity.

Ma Huan's section on Hormuz (Zheng He's final destination) portrays the port as the most flourishing commercial center in the region: "Foreign ships from every place and foreign merchants traveling by land all come to this country to attend the market and trade; hence the people of the country are all rich."[40]

Many geographic accounts and maps of the Mongol period portray Hormuz as a trading center that all foreign merchants and travelers visited. Even after the Mongols' fall, Hormuz suffered little interruption in maritime trade, and continued to flourish.[41]

Ma Huan's account leaves little doubt that the Zheng He expeditions provided Chinese with a remarkable opportunity to increase their knowledge about the Islamic world and to confirm ancient accounts that once seemed unbelievable. Ma Huan obtained eyewitness confirmation of Wang Dayuan's reports about the local variations in factors like climate, season, topography, and culture that he encountered in the various countries he visited. Ma explains:

> So I collected notes about the appearance of the people in each country, about the variations of the local customs, about the differences in the

> natural products, and about the boundary-limits. I arranged [my notes] in order to make a book, which I have entitled *The Overall Survey of the Ocean's Shores*. It enables an interested reader in a brief glance to learn all the important facts about the various foreign countries; and in particular he will see how the civilizing-influence of the Emperor has spread to an extent which could not be matched during formal dynasties.... It was in truth a wonderful opportunity [such as occurs only once] in a thousand years.[42]

The countries listed as part of the Islamic world, where "the kings and the people all profess the Muslim religion" and "speak the *A-la-bi* (Arabic) language," number only four, far fewer than those mentioned in earlier geographic accounts. However, Ma Huan intended only to discuss the most important places that the Zheng He expeditions visited, rather than to provide a world geography. He informs readers how to reach these four Islamic countries departing from Calicut on the southwestern coast of India.[43] The routes of the Zheng He expeditions overlap with the sea lanes that both Muslim and Chinese merchants, mariners, and other travelers had used since the Tang dynasty to sail between China and the Islamic world. Similarly, the missions benefitted from a variety of information including shipbuilding and navigational technologies that developed during the flourishing era of maritime international trade on the Indian Ocean under the auspices of the Song and Yuan governments. In turn, sailors aboard these voyages compiled their own accounts that both confirmed and expanded these earlier writings and maps. Emperor Yongle succeeded in displaying Ming political power as far as the shores of West Asia and the East African coast and in securing Ming influence over local rulers around the Indian Ocean rim by establishing tribute relationships with them.

The grand historic voyages completely ceased within ten years of the death of Emperor Yongle, its main proponent.[44] Opponents to the expeditions even destroyed relevant documents in order to deny the emperor's successors the information they would need in order to resurrect the voyages. As a result, only a few sources, including those examined in this chapter, survive. The Chinese court seems to have grown indifferent to maintaining active contact with the countries of West Asia. In one example, it ignored a formal request by the ruler of Hormuz to receive a Chinese envoy. Interest declined to such an extent that, by the end of the fifteenth century, provincial administrations began to assume the burden of dealing with their foreign neighbors.[45] In less than a century after the voyages of Zheng He, Chinese maritime activities that once flourished across the Indian Ocean languished, and Chinese knowledge about the Islamic world and other foreign countries correspondingly slowed. How did these changes in China affect the Islamic world?

Political Changes and a Synthesis of Muslim Knowledge of China Immediately Following the Mongol Period

The fall of the Mongol regime in Il-khanate Iran brought many changes to the Islamic Middle East. Following the Mongol rulers' conversion to Islam during Ghazan's reign (1295–1304), many conflicts among different Sunni and Shia sects arose. Soon after the death of Abū Saʿīd (reigned 1317–35), Öljeitü's son and the ninth and the final ruler of the Il-khanate, the dynasty broke up into different local regimes.[46] The actual fall of the Il-khanate, however, occurred when Timur conquered Iran in 1353, fifteen years before the fall of the Yuan dynasty in China.

Because Timur maintained a hostile attitude toward China and contact between the two societies decreased, Muslims in the early days of post-Mongol Iran had fewer opportunities to gain new information about China. Still, the period experienced a wider circulation of Muslim geographic knowledge about the world including China thanks to the scholarly use of preexisting geographic works. Despite the political upheavals that followed the Mongol collapse, academic and cultural development continued, as many extant works testify. Timur became one of its most important supporters. Like his Mongol predecessors, he brought numerous technicians and scholars to the capital of his empire, Samarkand, as part of his plan to transform the city into a prosperous center of learning. One of these recruits, whom Timur was delighted to meet after an attack on Syria, was Ibn Khaldūn (1332–1406), the great historian from Spain who pursued his studies in Mamluk Egypt.[47]

Ibn Khaldūn, who was in his seventies when he met Timur, possessed great knowledge that he set forth in his celebrated work, *The Introduction* (*Muqaddimah*, 1375). *The Introduction* stands as a masterpiece of historical and sociological philosophy, yet it holds great value as a summary of Muslim geographic knowledge at the time it was written. Ibn Khaldūn regarded al-Masʿūdī, the tenth century writer who wrote his geographic and historical compendium of the entire known world, as a model historian.[48] In fact, Ibn Khaldūn resembles al-Masʿūdī because he similarly organized *The Introduction* into sections according to subject fields like geography. Whereas previous geographic studies explained cultural and temperamental difference by referring to stereotypes, Ibn

Khaldūn hypothesized that different temperatures and foods affected inhabitants of different climates. He portrays the Chinese as inhabitants of the temperate climates – specifically, the third, fourth, and fifth of the seven climes – a part of the world where inhabitants possess sciences, crafts, and foods. The Chinese shared this temperate zone with the Arabs, Byzantines, Persians, Israelites, Greeks, and Indians, people about whom the Arabs possessed historical information.

Ibn Khaldūn's geographic knowledge was hardly consistent. At another section he describes China physically as the country furthest from the core of the Islamic world yet places it in the first and second climes, which, according to his theory, situates China outside the temperate zones. One reason for his misunderstanding may lie in the fact that he not only synthesized some of the accumulated geographic and historical information at his disposal but also consulted outdated al-Idrīsī's *Book of Roger* to construct his assumptions about China's physical geography. In fact, the geography section of Ibn Khaldūn's *Introduction* provides a neat summary of each of the seven climes and ten sections that appear in *The Book of Roger*. This summary serves to provide narrative detail to his attached world map, which is a copy of al-Idrīsī's world map.[49] Like al-Idrīsī, Ibn Khaldūn places China in the ninth and tenth sections extending to the Encompassing Sea that lies in both the first and second climes and sits at the eastern edge of the world. He also identifies Guangzhou as the country's center; this is outdated information because Guangzhou was surpassed by Quanzhou, which rose as the biggest international port city in southern China in the Song-Yuan period.[50]

Although Ibn Khaldūn relies primarily on al-Idrīsī's twelfth-century geographic knowledge, up-to-date information about the world occasionally appears. Ibn Khaldūn mentions no updated Persian sources from the Mongol years; however, he does refer to Ibn Baṭṭūṭa, if only to raise the problems he perceives in the adventurer's incredible stories of travel to the East.

Moreover, *The Introduction* begins its geographic summary with information about an event that occurred sometime during the author's lifetime or just before it, long after al-Idrīsī compiled *The Book of Roger*, and which bears some relevance to the history of Sino-Muslim contact. Ibn Khaldūn explains this recent event – the European conquest of the indigenous inhabitants of the Canary Islands – as follows:

> We learned that ships of the Europeans passed by them [the Eternal Islands: the Canaries] in the middle of this century, fought with them [their inhabitants], plundered them, captured them, and sold some of the captives along

> the most distant Moroccan coast where they came into the service of the ruler. When they had learned Arabic language, they gave information about conditions on their island... [51]

The passage clearly refers to the decimation of Canary Islanders as Europeans initiated slave-raiding enterprises on their island homes in the fifteenth century.[52] It accompanied Portugal's expansion into the Canary Islands between 1402 and 1496. It was also here on these islands that Christopher Columbus heard about the possibility of sailing west to reach Asia. Ibn Khaldūn continues:

> The location of these islands can be discovered only by chance and not by an intentional navigation towards them. For travel of ships in the sea depends on the winds, the knowledge of the directions the winds blow from and where they lead when [the ships] pass in the straight course from the lands that lie along the path of this wind. When the direction of the wind changes and it is known where it will lead along the straight course, the sail is set for it, and the ship is carried by it according to nautical norms received by the mariners and sailors who are in charge of sea voyages. The countries situated on the two sides of the Mediterranean and on its two shores are all written on a chart (*ṣaḥīfah*) which shows all the facts regarding them and regarding their positions along the coast of the sea in the proper order; and the directions of the winds and their different paths are [likewise] depicted [along with the countries] on the chart. This [chart] is called the "compass (lit. *qumbāṣ*, which is the rose of rhumb lines appearing on the European chart)," and the sailors rely on this [compass] in their voyages.[53]

The passage documents navigation methods using winds and compass with rhumb lines to sail on the ocean. Here Ibn Khaldūn mainly discusses sailing in the Mediterranean, yet this navigation method was most commonly used by Muslim navigators in the Indian Ocean. Works like this display a continued interest by Islamic writers about world events generally, focusing specifically on the trends of European voyages at that time, but displaying less interest in China.

Although Ibn Khaldūn's geographic section did not add much new information about China, some of his Muslim contemporaries traveled to China and brought back firsthand reports with novel information about their experiences there. The most famous of these accounts comes from the embassy of Sultan Maḥmūd and Ghiyāth al-Dīn Naqqāsh (flourished 1419–22), who were dispatched by Mirza Shahrukh (reigned 1404–47), Timur's son and the ruler of the Timurid dynasty to the court of Yongle, emperor of the Ming dynasty. Leaving their capital Herat in 1419, the embassy reached Samarkand in 1420 and joined Chinese envoys that returned to Beijing. There, they stayed for five months in the emporer's court before returning home in 1421. One of the envoys, Ghiyāth al-Dīn Naqqāsh, kept detailed reports about what he observed during his travels between Herat and Beijing, mentioning specific dates for some important events.

The account provides Ghiyāth al-Dīn Naqqāsh's detailed observations about China, which he called Cathay: its religious landscape characterized by many Buddhist temples, its people's customs, the governmental courier service consisting of many postal stations that provided the embassy with comfortable lodging and food throughout their travels, the grandeur of the emperor's palace, and the well-organized governmental and administrative systems of China. Ghiyāth al-Dīn Naqqāsh reports that more than 100,000 foreigners from different countries assembled in the emperor's court, thus confirming Yongle's success in expanding his authority into new regions. This had been the impetus behind his active foreign policies including the Zheng He voyages. Earlier authors, such as Ibn Baṭṭūṭa, specifically mention the well-organized postal relay system that connected the eastern and western sides of the vast Mongol empire and the convenient hostel service that served it in every post. Although the Ming dynasty probably developed an enhanced version of the Yuan system based on the earlier dynasty's legacy, it worked more systematically within China, with more limited connections to western countries.

Ghiyāth al-Dīn Naqqāsh's records were considered trustworthy by Ḥāfiẓ-i Abrū (died 1430), an eminent Persian scholar of Shahrukh's court, who incorporated the summary of the narratives into his chronicle. This account, therefore, provides a good example about how Muslim writers updated geographic information about China by incorporating travel accounts and other forms of testimony. Ḥāfiẓ-i Abrū is also famous for his world map with grids. Although it depicts major continents and seas in a blurry way, the map presents the country of Japan (al-Yāban) near the country of China (al-Ṣīn) for the first time in Islamic maps. Like earlier maps of al-Bīrūnī style, it does not present Africa stretching eastward into the encircling ocean. Its grid system may have been influenced by earlier ones such as those of Ḥamd Allāh Mustawfī, yet Ḥāfiẓ-i Abrū's grid system is unique in that it puts the grids outside the circular world map.

Other Muslim writers, contemporaries of Ibn Khaldūn and Ḥāfiẓ-i Abrū, wrote about sailing the Indian Ocean, the main arena of Muslim seafaring activities. The Persian historian ʿAbd al-Razzāq al-Samarqandī (1413–1482) testifies to the flourishing international seaport of Hormuz and its merchant visitors from many different places including China in his book, *The Rise of the Two Auspicious Constellations and the Confluence of the Two Oceans* (*Maṭlaʿ-i Saʿdayn wa-Majmaʿ-i Baḥrayn*):

> Hormuz, which is also called Jarūn, is a port located in the center of the sea, and which does not have any parallel over the surface of the globe. The merchants of seven climates, of Egypt, of Syria, of the countries of Rūm, of Azerbaijan, of Arabian Iraq, of Persian Iraq, of provinces of Fārs, of Khorāsān, of Transoxiana, of the kingdom of Dasht-i-Kapchak (the desert of Kipchak), of habitual regions with the Kalmaks, of the total kingdoms of Chīn and Māchīn [China], of the village of Khanbalik, all sail out for the port [Hormuz]. The people of the coast of the Ocean arrive there from the countries of Chīn, Java, Bengal, Ceylon; cities of Zirbad, Tenasserim, Socotra, Schahrinou; islands of Dīwah-Mahal (Maldive), regions of Malabar, Abyssinia, Zanzibar; ports of Bidjanagar, Kalbargah, Gujarat, Cambay; coast of regions of Arabia that extends to Aden, Jidda, Yanbu. They all bring precious and rare items that the sun, the moon, and rains contribute to embellish, and which can be transported by sea. The voyagers flood there from all of the world, and by exchanging their merchandise that they bring there, they can, without efforts and long searching, procure all of the things that they want. The business transaction is based on money or exchanging.[54]

ʿAbd al-Razzak still presents China according to Mongol-era designations – dividing the country into the kingdoms of Chīn and Māchīn and highlighting the "village" of Khanbalik. Most likely he received this information during his visit to Hormuz as the ambassador-at-large for the Timurid ruler Shah Rukh (1377–1447).[55] As we have seen in earlier pages, the local rulers of Persian Gulf seaports supported international trade and welcomed Chinese ships, including the fleets of Zheng He. Muslim maritime activities in the Indian Ocean continued to flourish after the Mongol period, and Muslim mercantile communities continued to expand into East Africa, India, and Southeast Asia. Trade contacts with China persisted as well, albeit through limited private (often illegal) connections, and at a scale that had decidedly diminished. The production of navigational treatises by Muslim authors peaked during this period due to an accumulation of navigational knowledge in the Islamic world and the widespread adoption there of navigational technology like the mariner's compass. The authors themselves were mostly sailors, as was the most renowned – Ibn Mājid, who himself sailed in the Indian Ocean.

Muslim Navigation before the Coming of the Portuguese to the Indian Ocean

As we have seen in previous chapters, Arab-Persian Muslims played the dominant role in maritime trade in the Indian Ocean from the eighth century on. In the course of their activities, they accumulated knowledge about how to sail to China using the monsoon winds and other navigational techniques. Unfortunately, no sea chart or direct instruction that these sailors might have used survives.[56] However, extant geographic accounts provide general descriptions of sailing routes and their navigational directions that the authors learned from sailors. *The Book of the Wonders of India* (*'Ajā'ib al-Hind*), compiled around 1000 CE, narrates many stories about Arab voyages on the Indian Ocean and hints at navigational facts outside the use of a mariner's compass, which Chinese innovators were only just beginning to use and Muslim sailors had not yet adopted.[57]

Muslim navigation indeed advanced further after they adopted the mariner's compass from the Chinese and combined it with their own astronomical methods of navigating the sea. Similarly, the Chinese integrated Muslims methods, as was the case with Zheng He's crews who also combined Chinese and Muslim methods, perhaps the result of hiring local Muslim sailors. Here the culmination of centuries of accumulated experience, moving from generation to generation, advanced Muslim sailing techniques to an unprecedented level of sophistication by the fifteenth century, and spread quickly to other seafaring cultures, including those of the Mediterranean.

This evolution is evident in the pilot guides that some renowned navigators began to publish as a guide to locating the *Qibla* or direction of prayer to Mecca. Most of these published works of navigation were also intended to be used as technical manuals rather than geographic accounts, although in this context they refer to theories and information about world geography in order to explain their systems of navigation. As seen in previous chapters, earlier Islamic geographies and travel accounts often describe the shapes and conditions of the seas and the most popular routes to sail them, particularly on the Indian Ocean. However, their descriptions were less technical probably because the informants (mostly merchants and travelers) and authors were less interested in nautical affairs. For example, Ibn Baṭṭūṭa gives some plausible details about Chinese seagoing vessels but writes little about sailing methods.[58] Authors wrote this navigational literature in order to provide practicing seamen and their seafaring colleagues with up-to-date manuals.[59] This results in content that emphasizes practical and sometimes extremely technical details about actual sailing. Among the several published navigational authors before 1500, the most renowned and influential was Aḥmad b. Mājid al-Sa'dī (flourished 1462–1498), an Arab navigator and geographer often called Ibn Mājid. His fame, which has outshined his contemporaries, arose less from his legacy as a geographer and more because some scholars identified him as the navigator who guided Vasco da Gama from Africa to India.[60]

Ibn Mājid was born in 1421 in Dhofar (in present-day Oman), one of the ports on the Arabian Peninsula that Zheng He's fleets visited, and there he grew up in a family famous for seafaring. His nearly forty works on the art of navigation include a long verse called *The Gathering of the Summarizing Concerning the First Principles of the Knowledge of the Seas* (*Ḥāwiyat al-ikhtiṣār fī uṣūl ʿilm al-biḥār*) [1462] and a guide entitled *The Book of Profitable Things Concerning the First Principles and Rules of Navigation* (*Kitāb al-fawāʾid fī uṣūl ʿilm al-baḥr wa-l-qawāʿid*) [1490].[61] The two books constitute a complete encyclopedia of Islamic navigational science. Ibn Mājid drew on his own experiences, the accumulated family knowledge that he received from his father and grandfather, and generations of know-how provided by sailors of the Indian Ocean's seafaring communities.

The Gathering of the Summarizing Concerning the First Principles of the Knowledge of the Seas, Ibn Mājid's poetical work, is the earliest dated work that discusses longitudinal and latitudinal measurements for the ports of the Indian Ocean.[62] Better known for its rich and more up-to-date information, *The Book of Profitable Things Concerning the First Principles and Rules of Navigation* offers an encyclopedic treatise about navigation that thoroughly explains all the details that professional pilots of Ibn Mājid's day had to know. It provides meticulous instructions on how to sail the Indian Ocean using twenty-eight lunar mansions and star positions, compass rhumbs lines (i.e., *qumbāṣ*, the compass rose for bearings), the monsoon and other seasonal winds.[63] At the core of his treatise, Ibn Mājid identifies the sailor's two most important navigational elements: Namely, "star altitude measurements and compass bearings, which together enable a route to be laid down."[64] We have seen in earlier pages that the Zheng He navigators combined these two elements. Ibn Mājid provides the exact altitude figures for different stars that help pilots understand their location, and explains how to use compass rhumbs indicators and stars to plot a direction. The pilots used the compass at night to check star locations: "But longitudes (*al-maraqq wa-l-maghzar*) are [calculated] with compass roses and bearings and staying awake at nights and preserving the bearing or in making a dogleg. But astronomers use it in lunar and solar eclipses...."[65]

Ibn Mājid does not mention the shape of the compass or its origin. Some Arabic texts do describe a compass used by the Muslim navigators in the Indian Ocean as "a magnetic needle in the form of a hollow iron fish floating on water," which resembles the mariner's compass used by Chinese sailors since 1100.[66] We can conclude that Muslim sailors combined the Chinese mariner's compass with their indigenous star-location technique to sail on the Indian Ocean safely. We have seen in earlier pages that the sailors of Zheng He's expeditions similarly combined these two techniques. This is a remarkable example of the mutual advancement of technical knowledge.

Ibn Mājid also provides a detailed explanation for sailing from East Africa to Indonesia, but it does not extend to China, probably because he sailed in the Red Sea and the Arabian Sea but never as far as Southeast Asia and China. By consulting other classical geographic works, Ibn Mājid develops a description of the Malay Peninsula's east coast and the route from there to China in a section that paints an overview of the world's coastlines. The description found in this section is somewhat vague, and the author himself admits that the accounts he used do not all agree with each other. Still, the author strived to cover voyages throughout the entire known world from Africa to China based on other accounts.[67] In his explanation of the seasons, he describes the route to China and the route that sailors took to sail back from China to the west:

> From Ṣanf (Champa, modern-day Vietnam) and China to Malacca, Java, Sumatra, Palembang and its surroundings, they travel in al-Tīrmā – Tīrmā means first quarter of the year, that is, the first hundred days of the year. They enter Malacca after the departure of the fleet for Calicut (Kālīkūt) from [Malacca] sometimes come across [the fleet] and sometimes [the fleet] leaves before their arrival, and generally it leaves before their arrival unless a ship is expected from Ṣanf about the New Year or slightly after. So it meets the ships coming from Hormuz and Mecca in Malacca. The latest ships [from Ṣanf] reach Malacca on the 120th [22nd March].[68]

Although lacking detail, this passage gives information that all pilots should have known, such as the season (spring) in which one should start sailing and the total sailing period (100 days) required to sail from China and Vietnam through Southeast Asia to the western coast of India (Calicut). The sailing period described resembles that cited on a Mongol-period Chinese map for sailing from Quanzhou to the area of Calicut (128 days). Other detailed routes follow, such as the passage from India's southwestern coast to the Arabian Peninsula, which according to both

Arabic and Chinese sources were the usual routes taken. Muslims from South and Southeast Asia were also active in the western Indian Ocean. When Vasco da Gama arrived on Africa's eastern coast in 1498, he tried to hire Muslim pilots to guide him to India, and so the ruler of Malindi sent a pilot to help him. The Portuguese texts always report that the Muslim pilot who helped da Gama sail to Asia was from Gujarat.[69]

Gerald Tibbetts, who translated Ibn Mājid's entire prose work, and Sanjay Subrahmanyam, the author of a biography of Vasco da Gama, both argue persuasively that there is no evidence that Ibn Mājid would have been Vasco da Gama's pilot. Ferrand, who first associated Ibn Mājid with Vasco da Gama, cites a poetic line in an Ottoman text – which probably expressed anti-Arab sentiment and makes vague accusations against a Muslim who taught the Indian route to the Europeans. However, the text does not mention Ibn Mājid at all.[70]

Even so, Ibn Mājid's navigational guidance sufficiently represents the high-level of navigational knowledge that Muslims possessed and Europeans desperately needed in order to reach Asia by sailing across the Indian Ocean. Ibn Mājid's guide represents the best navigational work of its time, a work that later Muslim navigators continued to consult, even though other navigational theories by different Muslim navigators circulated as well. Once da Gama rounded the Cape of Good Hope, he arrived at a well-traveled route that he would be able to safely sail with the help of any number of Muslim guides, a route on which commodities, people, and information had been flowing between China and the Islamic world since the eighth century.

Conclusion

Scholars have often assumed that contacts between China and the Islamic world came to a close with the fall of the Mongols because successor states like the Ming dynasty and the Timurids sparked antagonistic political relationships, which is evident in examples from Timur's attempt to invade China to Ming China's sea-ban policy. However, careful examination of Chinese and Islamic sources reveals that the contact and geographic knowledge within both societies peaked in the century that immediately preceded European expansion in the 1500s. Despite the political turmoil that erupted after the fall of the Mongols, Chinese and Muslims gained some new information about the other society by exchanging political embassies, such as that of Chen Cheng from the Ming dynasty and Ghiyāth al-Dīn Naqqāsh from the Timurid dynasty.

They also retained geographic knowledge that they inherited from the Mongol period. Scholars and geographers continued to draw world maps using maps from earlier periods. Ming Chinese scholars inherited Mongol-period maps from which they drew new works of cartography like *The Comprehensive Map of the Great Ming Empire* and *The Broad Terrestrial Map*. Both display fairly accurate representations of the coastlines of West Asia and the East African coast. Meanwhile, throughout the Islamic world, scholars circulated Ibn Khaldūn's description of al-Idrīsī's world map that included China.

From the perspective of the maritime world, Muslims updated their knowledge about China more slowly than Chinese did about the Islamic world. Perhaps China, more politically unified than the Islamic world under the Ming dynasty, could more easily obtain the rich geographic sources about foreign countries that belonged to their Yuan predecessors who actively supported maritime trade. The third Ming ruler, Emperor Yongle, used this information about the maritime route to the Islamic world to carry out an ambitious diplomatic enterprise by sending the largest imperial fleet in world history to West Asia and the East African coast. The seven voyages of Zheng He mark the culmination of Chinese maritime activities in the early fifteenth century.

The Zheng He voyages began in 1405, about a century earlier than Vasco da Gama's adventure around the Cape of Good Hope to reach Calicut in 1498. The main purpose of the Ming voyages was to project China's political power to the foreign countries along the Asian coastline between China and the Islamic world. In order to do so, the Chinese needed good geographic information. Chinese documents, including the Zheng He sea chart and Ma Huan's eyewitness account, reveal that Zheng He's crews acquired new information and commodities during the course of the voyages, and put to use the rich information that they inherited from earlier periods. Even so, the voyages came to a complete close after the deaths of Emperor Yongle and admiral Zheng He, and the Chinese made no further use of their valuable information. Their failure to do so contrasts starkly with later European explorers.

The Islamic world in this post-Mongol period also witnessed the culmination of Muslim navigational knowledge as seen in the publication of navigational treatises by renowned navigators such as Ibn Mājid. For his work, Ibn Mājid consulted navigational and geographic accounts and drew on his own experiences sailing the Indian Ocean in order to provide essential technical details to ship pilots. Unfortunately, his work does not provide much new information about China because he did not sail that far. Nonetheless, his writings synthesized Muslim navigational theory and practice to date, including the combination of the indigenous Muslim navigational technique of measuring stellar altitudes and the Chinese method of using the mariner's compass. Ibn Mājid also laid out the representation of the coastline from the Islamic world to China using Muslim geographic knowledge about China that he extracted from Arabic and Persian geographic accounts.

Soon after the historic voyages of the Chinese in the early 1400s, a new variable began to affect the Sino-Islamic relationship, namely, the arrival of the Europeans on Asian waters. After about 1200, European societies grew increasingly aware of their marginal position in the enormously rich markets of the Indian Ocean and some eventually resolved to gain direct access there. There is little doubt that geographic knowledge flowed gradually from Asia to Europe via intermediaries, and that this contributed to gradually awakening of Europeans from the self-centered worldview that persisted for a millennium. The major significance of Ibn Mājid's work lies in its representation of the sum of Muslim navigational knowledge, or even the sum of knowledge all over the Indian Ocean world, as it had accumulated over the course of several centuries. Much of the information was implemented by Muslim navigators, some of whom were hired by the Portuguese to guide them to Asia.

The coming of the Europeans to Asian waters marks a major turning point in the Indian Ocean trade because they used real military force to dominate the trade market. Therefore, we will conclude our account of the active maritime contact between China and the Islamic world and the resulting increase of mutual knowledge at this point.

Conclusion

Lessons from Pre-modern Sino-Islamic Contact

The history of contact and exchange between China and the Islamic world offers one of the most remarkable cases of pre-European encounter because it involves tremendous wealth, transformative ideas, and great power. This contact was without interruption for eight centuries – despite frequent changes to both regions, from evolving political dynamics to sweeping technological advances – that led to a continuous transfer of geographic information over time, a process that occurred in three distinct stages.

Political Conflict Leads to Commercial and Cultural Exchange

Geographers and cartographers both documented and facilitated the increase of knowledge in their societies, often with government sponsorship. However, the information that provided the basis for this knowledge came from intermediaries who moved between the societies and engaged in a process of cross-cultural exchange. In the recent past, societies often learned about other societies as a result of military powers conquering weaker societies and then studying them in order to control and govern the people.[1] As the evidence demonstrates, the history of contact between China and the Islamic world appears more complicated than this scenario suggests and rarely accords with a general pattern.

True, the most dramatic form of contact between these two worlds began when two expansionist empires in both the east and the west, the ʿAbbāsids and Tang China, grew enmeshed in a complicated political conflict that came to blows in a military showdown at Talas in 751. Political complications continued, however, and led to the gradual decline of overland routes in Central Asia, which turned mercantile attention toward the sea. A more peaceful form of maritime commercial contact flourished as a result. The major driving forces behind this seaborne expansion were Arab, Persian, and other seafaring traders from the Islamic world who, with the help of Islamic political expansion and a new Muslim ethic that encouraged commerce, began to play an important intermediary role in building a new maritime bridge between China and the Islamic world. Maritime trade boomed, and a new nexus of Sino-Islamic interaction developed in the Indian Ocean. Advances in navigation and shipbuilding technologies developed apace, leading to improvements in transportation that in turn led to increased volumes of traffic as more and more people turned to travel and trade by sea. Merchants from the Islamic world were most active in this long-distance traffic (with aid from South and Southeast Asian seafarers), but in time, the sea attracted Chinese as well. This growing population of itinerant merchants and seafarers increasingly settled along trading routes and began to interact and develop bonds with local societies, even as they periodically returned to their home countries. Sailing routes were documented in greater detail, and more people had opportunities to learn about the countries with which they had trade relations, however distant they were.

The evidence of cross-cultural contact between Chinese and Islamic worlds can give the impression that the production and exchange of knowledge produced purely positive results: Merchants and travelers simply recorded their impressions about other societies, which allowed for the straightforward transmission of their knowledge to other merchants and travelers. But states, or rather writers enjoying state support, actively worked to shape the interpretation of knowledge from the very beginning of Sino-Islamic interaction when imperial historians drew from accounts by merchants and travelers in order to compose their own brief description of the other societies. The analysis in this book makes the state's agenda behind the production of geography and cartography abundantly clear: Not only did rulers within both Chinese and Islamic societies want to encourage commerce with other societies and reap its benefits, they also attempted to better place themselves and other countries within a global context in order to advance their own political ambitions and better strategize their security.

Geographic knowledge was not simply conveyed through words, of course; geographers also visualized it on maps. The communication of geographic data and concepts can prove more difficult to draw than write because doing so effectively requires a high level of cartographic skill.

Geographers in both Chinese and Islamic societies succeeded in the production of effective maps, however, because they could look to geographic and cartographic precedents that their societies inherited. Early Islamic geographic works drew on the knowledge of the ancient geographers filtered through the traditions of pre-Islamic predecessors in the territories of the Islamic world, from Greeks like Ptolemy to Byzantine and Sassanid Persian scholars, all of whom shaped the emergent Muslim culture that came to dominate the Islamic world. Muslim geographers who utilized older works updated them with newly acquired knowledge gained from experienced Muslim travelers in order to draw the most accurate world maps of their time. The Chinese developed cartographic techniques beginning no later than the third century, yet until about 1000 CE these early maps merely portray China. Only the ascent of the Mongol empire in the thirteenth century fostered a new sense of geographic understanding among Chinese that rendered this narrow geographic self-perception obsolete and encouraged the creation of maps offering an expanded image of China's geographic place in the world. To realize this new understanding of China in the world, geographers and cartographers needed additional information about the world beyond their borders, much of which they obtained from the Islamic world through Muslim scholars working at the Yuan court.

Direct Transmission of Information in the Integrated World under Mongol Rule

The greatest degree of interaction between China and the Islamic world occurred between 1260 and 1368 when significant parts of both societies fell under the rule of the Mongols. The Mongols' destruction of the ʿAbbāsid capital Baghdad and their conquest of the entire Chinese empire (which no nomadic society had ever done before) changed both societies profoundly. Obviously, the Mongol empire was born in bloodshed. Its military sweep across Eurasia, however, soon gave way to the Pax Mongolica or Mongol Peace that encouraged cross-cultural interaction across the empire and beyond, including the circulation of commodities and information adopted from the cultures of the societies they subjugated. Scholars did not always view the Mongol era this way, of course; in fact, scholars have only recently begun to reassess it.[2] In place of the old negative stereotype that depicts Mongols as single-mindedly destructive, historians have recognized their role in sparking an important transition in world history as they erased boundaries between east and west and integrated once distant and fragmented societies into a single world system. In this capacity, the Mongols transformed the relationship of China and the Islamic world.

One of the most remarkable achievements resulting from long-distance contact between Mongol-ruled Yuan and Il-khanate came with the increase of world geographic knowledge in the two societies, which encouraged them to modify their traditional self-centered worldviews to some degree. Evidence reveals how Mongol rulers exchanged not only politicians and scholars, but also goods and knowledge. The Yuan dynasty in China sponsored the first production of world maps that combined traditional Chinese and newly-acquired Islamic geography. The Mongol government under Khubilai's rule expanded the Chinese worldview by allowing non-Chinese scholars to collaborate with Chinese counterparts in the production of court-sponsored scholarly compilations. Far to the west, a similar phenomenon unfolded in the Il-khanate. Muslims not only inherited the legacies of their geographic forebears, but they also assimilated new information as it became available. This led to one of the Il-khanate's most notable achievements in the first large-scale and systematic world history, a feat made possible thanks to the increased inflow of geographic information. Government sponsorship encouraged the widening of knowledge in the world and the frequent movement of people and their ideas through it. Such an attitude affected both Chinese and Islamic societies, and it probably began to influence their European contemporaries as well. This is reflected in Marco Polo's travelogue, whose information often can be verified by contemporaneous sources from China and the Islamic world. This makes Polo's memoir seem like an expression of collective knowledge circulating throughout the Mongol world and beyond.

Contact between China and the Islamic world increased to new levels because of the growth of close political connections and dynamic trading networks during the Mongol era. Both Chinese and Muslims expanded the body of geographic knowledge in their societies in both state and civilian spheres. Individuals wrote local gazetteers and travelogues in order to bring geographic information about the world's societies and the routes to reach them. Some also claimed to have traveled directly between China and the Islamic world.

Muslims migrated to China in large numbers during the Mongol era, and this too changed China. Muslim immigrants in China during earlier periods of history formed small-scale communities in port cities like Guangzhou, where they lived separately because of the right of autonomy they received from the Chinese court. After the Mongol campaigns to the west ended, many Muslim soldiers went to China and settled in places like Eastern Turkestan. Artisans and merchants soon followed. Many others settled in southeastern seaports like Guangzhou and Quanzhou, and helped to develop them into the major trading emporiums for Chinese commerce with South and Southeast Asia. The famous Muslim traveler Ibn Baṭṭūṭa traced this Muslim network to Quanzhou where he met many Muslims. Although Ibn Baṭṭūṭa says that Muslims in China did not get along with the Chinese, evidence for their collaboration in international trades questions his claim. When at last the Mongols fell, Muslims had to find ways to accommodate and survive in their new political environment, like other collaborators of the Mongols. In doing so, they began to evolve into a distinct ethnic group, beginning a process that would lead to the formation of the Hui people of modern-day China.

The Increasing Spread of World Geographic Knowledge

The age of unprecedented cross-cultural contacts under the Mongol empire did not last long. After Mongol rulers fell from power in both China and the Il-khanate, the two societies grew distant. Tensions between successor regimes culminated in Timur's attempt to attack the new Ming empire, a plan that failed only when he died in 1405. Timur's failure hardly translated into victory for China's empire in Central Asia as it was no longer the suzerain state of the entire Mongol empire. Some previous relationships continued, such as those of Chen Cheng and Ghiyāth al-Dīn Naqqāsh, and contributed to preserving diplomatic relations, yet even these ties gradually fell off. Meanwhile, the new Ming regime dealt a similarly heavy blow to its maritime frontiers when it prohibited private trade along its coast and thereby hindered the region's booming maritime trade and the free flow of ideas that accompanied it. The imprint of the Mongol legacy on Chinese society survived, however, and continued to influence Chinese minds. Many surviving copies of world maps and geographies that include information from the Mongol-Yuan period were actually produced during the Ming. In other words, the circulation of a global geographic perspective continued for several decades. This fact is epitomized by the famed Zheng He voyages.

When the fleets of the Ming emperor Yongle embarked on their expeditions into the Indian Ocean, they followed routes that were established by previous generations of mariners. These magnificent expeditions have often been compared and contrasted to European explorations with regard to both scale and motive. Their scale was much larger than their western counterparts, but unlike the Europeans, the Chinese did not sail into unknown waters. Many studies of pre-modern contacts have highlighted the fleets' remarkable geographic range as an exceptional achievement of the Ming period, exaggerating the scale and achievements of the Zheng He expeditions. However, the actual contact proves to have been more limited than it was during the previous Mongol era and much of the geographic knowledge that circulated through China during the Ming era was produced during the previous dynasty. Therefore, we should give credit to the legacy of the Yuan and earlier eras for their achievements of connecting Chinese to the greater world and expanding Chinese geographic knowledge. In reality, the Ming period marks a point of decline in China's contact with the wider world, including the Islamic world. Contact between the two societies did not cease altogether, of course; informal forms of interaction and exchange persisted. However, Muslim merchants could not travel as freely into China as they once did because of the Ming ban on private trade. The same phenomenon can be observed in the Islamic world. Muslim navigational works produced during the post-Mongol age synthesized previous geographic information about the Indian Ocean with new achievements in navigational techniques, yet provided little new information about China and the eastern edges of the Indian Ocean as previous generations had.

At the same time, Europeans began to appear on the Indian Ocean stage after 1500 and diminished the importance of direct contact between China and the Islamic world because they gradually created a broader system of oceanic global trade connecting the Afro-Eurasian world to the Americas. European nations competed to discover new routes to Asia; in the course of which, they discovered routes to the Americas. Portugal took the lead thanks to the advanced geographic knowledge it acquired, largely through Muslim sources,[3] and guidance from Muslim sailors who possessed a level of practical geographic knowledge and navigational techniques gleaned from centuries of experience. One of these Muslim seafarers eventually guided Vasco da Gama to India after he rounded the Cape of Good Hope.

The Influence of the Asian Geographic Knowledge on the Rise of the Europeans

The Europeans indeed established landmarks in world history in 1492 and 1498. They had prepared the foundations of this achievement many decades earlier, however. Geographic knowledge that accumulated through contact between China and the Islamic world gradually flowed into Europe as well. Those who attained this knowledge first were Italian merchants of the Mongol period. Francesco Pegolotti (flourished 1310–1347) wrote his merchant handbook containing advice for those bound for China based on circulating information that he collected from Asian sources. Marco Polo's account, a best-selling book in Europe at that time, also reflects this historical phenomenon, whether or not he truly did travel to China. The appearance of these works during the Mongol period calls to mind Janet Abu-Lughod's proposal that a world economic system existed in the thirteenth century and functioned as a predecessor to the European system.[4] Perhaps in our endless debates about the veracity of Polo's claims we have missed its most important significance: Quite simply, that his book is the by-product of the great circulation of information that accompanied the culmination of this pre-modern world system. Moreover, the influence of Mongol-era works like Polo's travelogue proved important to Europe's age of expansion. His travelogue, first doubted by his Italian fellows, ultimately caused an enormous sensation in Europe. It is known that Henry the Navigator enjoyed reading Polo and his contemporary, Christopher Columbus, brought the book with him on his voyages to reach India, China, and Japan. In fact, Columbus carried the conviction that that his famous expeditions had reached India to his death.

Thus, agents of European expansion like the Portuguese and Columbus were enabled by the accumulation of systematic geographic knowledge that originated in Asia. New maps made by European cartographers differed from the medieval T-O maps that evolved from the Eurocentric Christian worldview. For example, the Catalan Atlas that circulated widely in the fourteenth century plots many specific places in Asia and includes caravan routes and maritime routes. Newly arrived Islamic maps and reconstructed Greek world maps emboldened Europeans to sail to wider oceans. Indeed, this knowledge transfer was very much a part of the new humanistic spirit of Renaissance that led to the revival of ancient Greek philosophies and science and the transformation of the European world view. Columbus had access to many of these books through collections held in Renaissance cities such as Genova and Venice, and by studying them gained new knowledge about the globe. Ironically, Columbus made his alternate westward trek across the Atlantic in search of Asia because he relied on Ptolemy's inaccurate estimation of a much smaller globe circumference. In contrast, the expeditions of Henry the Navigator set forth on their own search for India equipped with more accurate geographic knowledge of the world based on the professional studies of Islamic and Greek geographies collected in the academies of Portugal; this knowledge proved indispensible to the success of the missions he sponsored to round Africa and sail to Asia.

Contact between Asia and Europe at this crucial point remains a topic in need of further scrutiny. However, it is already clear that Portuguese and other western merchants who began to sail directly to the east after 1500 and subsequently dominated Indian Ocean trade owed their success to the good use they made of Islamic geography, including the accurate information it offered about the coastline between the Islamic world and China. Knowledge about the Asian coastline did not develop instantaneously, however; it gradually accumulated through centuries of continuous contact between China and the Islamic world. People in China and the Islamic world did not know much about each other in 750, when this study begins. From that point on, soldiers, merchants, travelers, and scholars from both worlds moved back and forth, gradually learning more about each other's societies. This long-term uninterrupted process reached its period of most intense contact during the Mongol era. As George Hourani noted half a century ago, the route from Guangzhou (Canton) to the Persian Gulf was the longest and most heavily traveled sea route in regular use before 1492. By 1500, knowledge about the world had developed in Islamic and Chinese geography and transferred to Europe. Clearly, the continuous exchange of goods and people by land and sea led to a substantial transfer of knowledge that profoundly affected not only China and the Islamic world between 750 and 1500, but also Europe and world history after 1500. It was more than a coincidence that a Muslim navigator from Gujarat guided Vasco da Gama into the Indian Ocean in 1498 after he rounded the Cape of Good Hope.

Toward a Multi-centered Model of World History

Let us define the world historical significance of the Asian knowledge that accumulated through Sino-Muslim contact. After 1500, the two Asian societies continued to interact to some degree, mostly through unofficial trade. However, the scale and character of this contact changed profoundly with the active engagement of new European powers in Asia. In fact, the Europeans moved into position as the group that best utilized this inherited understanding of the world. The vicissitudes of long-term Sino-Muslim interaction is important to understanding the history of these societies; however, it is just as important to consider its relevance from the broad perspective of world history. Doing so suggests a better model for studying the history of contact for the coming decades; one that places all forms of cross-cultural contact on an equal level.

Consider the larger picture of this pre-modern Sino-Islamic contact: The pursuit of goods led to interactions of a grand scale that in turn led to the transfer of geographic knowledge. No doubt, newly acquired information about a society's navigational routes, trade goods, history, and cultural customs affected the worldviews of those who acquired this knowledge. People increasingly acknowledged that other societies were worth learning about and trading with, even if they were thought to sit at a distant part of the world. Soon after Chinese and Islamic societies developed contacts with each other, geographers from both sides of the exchange began to map each other's territories, ultimately drawing world maps that placed the two societies and their relationship with each other into geographical context. Conceptually, geographers retained the central position of their own society in the maps they drew, but over time the outlines of the other society gradually gained nuance and accuracy. Scholars continued to obtain new information from those who had actually visited the other place or who had talked to those who had. Many factors – the expansion of commercial markets, the expansion of political control and security, and a growing curiosity about the wider world – all came together to motivate the continued pursuit of knowledge.

In contrast to European world maps produced since the early modern period that often reflect state agendas to conquer new territory,[5] pre-modern Chinese and Islamic world maps offer the opportunity to trace the increase in commercial and scholarly exchange between the two societies over a long period of time. This interaction was not always peaceful, of course, but evidence suggests that many writers in both Chinese and Islamic societies generally regarded each other favorably. Muslim authors examined here depicted the Chinese as good at skills and craftsmanship, and held high regard for their extensive territory, systematic political and legal system, sophisticated culture, and wealth. Chinese authors produced similarly positive portraits, characterizing Muslims as rich and decent people with reputable cultures. In most cases, these characterizations were based in factual knowledge, although sometimes they contained fantastic stories or legends.

Sources for the period show that pre-modern contact between the Chinese and Muslims revolved mainly around trade, and so did the interest of the geographers. In China, there existed the added political motivation of establishing a Chinese-centered world order. This did not spring from an interest in "colonization" in the European sense; Chinese did not possess such a concept traditionally. However, China's approach to the world was often driven by a desire to impose a tribute system that required the subjugation of non-Chinese to a hierarchy that placed Chinese at its political and moral apex. Ideally, then, the exchange of goods, which brought practical economic benefits, operated in this uneven context. The Zheng He voyages provide a good example of this. Despite their clear ability to militarily conquer the countries they visited, the Ming fleets instead sought only the acknowledgment of China's superiority and the promise to send periodic tributes to the imperial capital. By doing so, the Ming court hoped to assert Chinese power and prestige in the Indian Ocean for several centuries and establish Chinese dominion over its trade. In the Islamic world, most of the Muslims who maintained active ties with Chinese were merchants who traveled to China in search of commodities that were highly prized in their home countries. Some of them settled, and in doing so they became a part of an expanding diaspora of Muslim believers (*ummah*). A few, like Ibn Baṭṭūṭa, traveled simply for the sake of knowledge, an important duty of pious Muslims. The waterway that opened between the two societies in the Indian Ocean worked to develop commercial and cultural relations that geographers appear to regard more significant than military conquests.

To conclude, it seems fitting to underscore the fact that the long and dynamic contact between Chinese and Islamic societies depended on many kinds of peoples from many different societies and cultures. The Mongols provide the most remarkable example of this. Connecting Chinese and Islamic societies by force, these nomads from northern Mongolia adopted the sedentary cultures of their subjects quite actively and often in creative ways, which created many opportunities for cultural exchanges "under Mongolian yoke." This is just one significant example among many, of people from the steppes of Central Asia to the seas of South Asia, as well as other ethnic groups in East Asia and West Asia. Many different layers of interaction shaped the entire system of contact and exchange, creating multiple channels through which the transfer of knowledge could take place.

Close connections and exchange of goods and information among different societies in the pre-modern period was often initiated by military conquest such as that of the Mongol empire. In contrast, societies of the twenty-first century characterized by multiple centers and globalized societies tend to interact most through practical commercial contact rather than political and military conflict, although the latter continues to play a role in today's society as well. With this in mind, it can be instructive to overcome Eurocentric models and consider how a multi-centric model may apply to past epochs in world history as well. The pre-modern relationship between China and the Islamic world, two societies who experienced roughly equal levels of development, provides an alternate model for analyzing an intercultural exchange quite different from the pattern of unequal contact often found in colonization encounters. This will provide us with ample ideas and new lessons for understanding both the past as well as the new types of exchanges that shape our globalized world.

Notes

Introduction

1. Some scholars have suggested that the Phoenicians may have voyaged around the Cape of Good Hope in ancient times. See Fuat Sezgin, *Mathematical Geography and Cartography in Islam and Their Continuation in the Occident*, Part 2 (Frankfurt am Main, 2000), 343.
2. The modern-day European expansion that began with Columbus and da Gama has continuously engaged historians, as one can see from the recent surge of work on this topic. This scholarship is gradually breaking with earlier Eurocentric studies that merely emphasized a rapid shift to European dominance. Instead, the new approach attempts to examine dynamic interactions in the maritime history of every part of Asia. John E. Wills, "Maritime Asia, 1500–1800: The Interactive Emergence of European Domination," *The American Historical Review* 98, no. 1 (1993): 83–105.
3. Literally "big eat" in Chinese, the term *Dashi* is a transcription of the Persian word *Tājik* or *Tāzī*. This derives from a nisba of the Arab tribe of Ṭayyiʾ that was located in Iraq. Because the Muslim Ṭayyiʾ tribe was the Arabs most frequently met by the Sassanids, it came to refer to the country of the Arabs or the entire Islamic world. Bosworth, "al-Ṣīn," *EI2*, 9: 618. According to Bernhard Karlgren's *Dictionary of Old and Middle Chinese*, the pronunciation of Dashi around the eighth century is d'âi-dźi̯ək, which was similar to "Tajik" or "Tazi." Tor Ulving, *Dictionary of Old and Middle Chinese: Bernhard Karlgren's Grammata Serica Recensa Alphabetically Arranged* (Göteborg, 1997).
4. When I refer to "precise" or "accurate" depictions, I mean those that are in accord with our modern-day understanding. For a specialized discussion on *precision*, see F. Jamil Ragep, "Islamic Reactions to Ptolemy's Imprecisions," in *Ptolemy in Perspective* (New York: Springer, 2010), 121–134.
5. David Woodward, "Medieval Mappaemundi," in *HC1*, 286–370.
6. R. A. Skelton, *Explorer's Maps: Charters in the Cartographic Record of Geographical Discovery* (New York, 1958), 16–17.

7. Many earlier scholars in this field did pioneering work on examining the contacts in the commercial and cultural connections between China and the Islamic world, translating some important parts of the relevant primary sources. Some works, from which I have benefited, in particular, include the works by Gabriel Ferrand, Kuwabara Jitsuzō, Donald Daniel Leslie, W. M. Thackston, and many more, whom I will cite throughout this book.
8. Wang Q. Edward, "History, Space, and Ethnicity: The Chinese Worldview," *Journal of World History* 10, no. 2 (Fall 1999): 285–289.
9. Patricia Risso, *Merchants & Faith: Muslim Commerce and Culture in the Indian Ocean* (Colorado, 1995), 5–7.
10. For a nuanced discussion about the early relations between the Chinese and their northern neighbors, see Nicola Di Cosmo, *Ancient China and its Enemies: The Rise of Nomadic Power in East Asian History* (New York, 2002).
11. Sogdian traders were the main Central Asian middlemen on the Silk Road between the fifth to the eighth century. Étienne de la Vaissière, *Sogdian Traders: A History* (Leiden, 2005); Jonathan K. Skaff, "The Sogdian Trade Diaspora in East Turkestan during the Seventh and Eighth Centuries," *Journal of the Economic and Social History of the Orient* 46, no. 4 (2003): 475–524. For traces of Sogdians in the cities of north China, see Rong Xinjiang, *Zhonggu Zhongguo yu wailai wenming* (Beijing, 2001). For the archaeology and art excavated in the main oasis towns along the Silk Road, see the lifeworks of Borris Marshak, including *Legends, Tales, and Fables in the Art of Sogdiana* (New York, 2002).
12. C. E. Bosworth, et al., "al-Ṣīn," *EI2*, 9: 616–625.
13. Only two delegations, which took place around 715 and 750, are mentioned by some Muslim sources like the chronicles of al-Ṭabarī, yet they are not documented in Chinese sources. See the chart of embassies from the Arabs based on Chinese official histories in Donald D. Leslie, *Islam in Traditional China: A Short History to 1800* (Belconnen ACT, 1986), 31. The same Chinese sources also record forty-six cases of Persian tributary envoys from 455, some of which came to China even after the fall of the Sassanid Empire in 651, and lasted until 771. See the chart on p.16 of *Islam in Traditional China.*
14. Huichao, *Wang wu tianzhu guo zhuan jian shi* (Beijing, 2000); Leslie, *Islam in Traditional China*, 20.
15. al-Ṭabarī (838–923). *The Periplus Maris Erythraei: Text with Introduction, Translation, and Commentary*, trans. Lionel Casson (Princeton, 1989).
16. Ibid., 90–91, 238. Different transcriptions of the term – *This*, *Thīnai*, *Sīnai* – were used by scholars. See *Periplus Maris Erythraei*, trans. Murakami Kentarō (Tokyo, 1993), 275. Some scholars argue that the two places in the eastern extremity of the inhabitable world appearing in the Greek and Roman sources, Seres in the north (from the overland connections) and Sinai in the south (from the maritime connection), refer to China, but there have been debates among sinologists about the exact identifications and locations of the two place names. For further discussion of the pre-modern western names for China, see Paul Pelliot, "Cin," in *Notes on Marco Polo*, vol.1 (Paris, 1959), 264–278.

17. There were maritime contacts between West Asia and East Asia between third and seventh centuries. Many treasures from the Sassanid Persia including glassware, tapestries, and musical instruments, excavated in Korean tombs (Gyeongju, Korea) and preserved in Shōsōin (in Nara, Japan), were probably brought by maritime routes via China to Korea and Japan. On the archaeological evidence for the Indian Ocean trade network at that time, see Himanshu P. Ray, *The Archaeology of Seafaring in Ancient South Asia* (Cambridge, 2003), 198–213.
18. Chen Gaohua and Wu Tai, *Songyuan shiqi de haiwai maoyi* (Tianjin, 1981), 1–12. Some scholars argued based on some passages from the official histories mentioning people from Persia (Bosi) that many Persian merchants came to China via maritime routes during the Sassanid period (226–651). Wang Gungwu, however, disputes these arguments by suggesting that the state of Wei 魏, which conducted trade with the Persians was located in the northern part of China and thus "most of the possible contacts with Persia must have been overland contacts." Wang Gungwu, *The Nanhai Trade: Early Chinese Trade in the South China Sea* (Singapore, 2003), 123.
19. Since Sugiyama Masaaki suggested in 1995 that the Mongol empire constructed a Eurasian commercial network covering land and sea, recent studies have explored the details of the maritime contacts during the Mongol period. Sugiyama Masaaki, *Kubirai no chōsen: Mongoru kaijō teikoku e no michi* (Tokyo, 1995); Yokkaichi Yasuhiro, "Chinese and Muslim Diasporas and the Indian Ocean Trade Network under Mongol Hegemony," in *The East Asian Mediterranean: Maritime Crossroads of Culture, Commerce and Human Migration* (Wiesbaden, 2008), 73–102.
20. There exist a number of pre-Islamic Arabic (especially South Arabic) texts.
21. The writers in the two societies also documented the societies in-between, such as those in Central Asia and South and Southeast Asia. Because the peoples there did not leave many written accounts about their own societies, Chinese and Muslim sources are crucial. Yet this is not our focus in this book.
22. A noteworthy debate on sources of the period is the European travelogue of Marco Polo. Among many different versions in different languages are only a few that scholars believe are at all close to the original that is lost. See John Larner, *Marco Polo and the Discovery of the World* (New Haven, 1999). Comparative examination of the contents in different versions helps us piece together which parts were added later or distorted in the course of transmission and pinpoint reliable aspects of the thirteenth century and a little later period. We have to be cautious when we deal with similar accounts in Chinese and Arabic, yet we can assume that the degree of variation is much less than that of Polo's account, which was one of the most sensational books in the pre-modern period.
23. The ancient Chinese pronunciation "an-siək" is a transcription of Arsaces, the name of the empire's founder (died 246 or 211 BCE), which was also adopted by succeeding Parthian rulers. Wang Tao, "Parthia in China: a Re-examination of the Historical Records," in *The Age of the Parthians: The Idea of Iran*, vol. II (London, 2007), 87–104. This identification of Anxi is

quite convincing and has had general acceptance, yet those of the following place names are less clear, causing debates among scholars. See D. D. Leslie and K. H. J. Gardiner, "Chinese Knowledge of Western Asia During the Han," *T'oung Pao* LXVIII, 4–5 (1982): 254–308 (287–288 for Anxi).

24. Sima Qian, *Records of the Grand Historian of China, translated from the Shih chi of Ssu-ma Ch'ien, Vol.II: the age of emperor Wu 140 to circa 100 B.C*, trans. Burton Watson (New York, 1961), 268, 278 with some changes to Watson's Romanization. The original is Sima Qian, *Shiji* (Beijing, 1959), 123: 3162–3164, 3172–3173. See also the translation by Leslie in his *Islam in Traditional China*, 7–8.
25. Leslie, "Chinese Knowledge," 268.
26. Anne Birrell, trans., *Classic of Mountains and Seas* (London, 1999). Although other ethnographic information existed in later periods, *Shanhai jing* continued to influence contemporary thought at the same time. Wang Qi's (1565–1614) Ming dynasty encyclopedia *Shancai tuhui* contained several fantastic illustrations similar to those of *Shanhai jing*'s descriptions of foreign peoples. Laura Hostetler, *Qing Colonial Enterprise: Ethnography and Cartography in Early Modern China* (Chicago, 2001), 87–90.
27. Sima Qian, 123:3179.
28. They drew foreign maps and also "illustrations of foreign visitors who arrived for the presentation of tribute" (*zhigong tu*). The earliest extant one, *Liang zhigong tu*, has fifteen texts on foreign countries and twelve "portraits" of the envoys who were sent by those countries. See Kazuo Enoki, "The Liang chih-kung-t'u," in *Studia Asiatica: the Collected Papers in Western Languages of the Late Dr. Kazuo Enoki* (Tokyo, 1998).
29. See S. Maqbul Ahmad, "Djughrāfiyā (Geography)," *EI2*, 2: 575–590, and J. F. R. Hopkins, "Geographic and Navigational Literature," in *The Cambridge History of Arabic Literature: Religion, Learning and Science in the 'Abbāsid Period* (Cambridge, 1991), 301–312.
30. Raoul McLaughlin, *Rome and the Distant East: Trade Routes to the Ancient Lands of Arabia, India, and China* (London, 2010); Ray, *The Archaeology of Seafaring*, 25–26.
31. For a brief survey of ancient Greek cartography before Ptolemy, see Germaine Aujac et al., "Greek Cartography in the Early Roman World," *HC1*, 161–176.
32. O. A. W. Dilke, "The Culmination of Greek Cartography in Ptolemy," *HC1*, 177–200.
33. Arab writers also incorporated non-Muslim materials such as those of Nestorian Christians who have traveled to Southeast Asia at this early period. G. R. Tibbetts, *A Study of the Arabic Texts Containint Material on South-east Asia* (Leiden: Brill, 1979), 2.
34. David A. King, *World-Maps for Finding the Direction and Distance to Mecca* (Leiden: Brill, 1999).
35. Risso, *Merchants & Faith*, 9–54.
36. See Ahmad, "Djughrāfiyā"; Heribert Busse, "Arabische Historiographie und Geographie," in *Grundriss der Arabischen Philologie,* vol. II (Wiesbaden, 1987), 293–296; Hopkins, "Geographic and Navigational

Literature," 301–327; I. Y. Kračkovsky, *Izbrannye Socineniya IV: Arabskaya Geograficeskaya Literature* (Moscow, 1955–1960), and its Arabic translation, I. Y. Kračkovsky, *Tā'rkh al-adab al-jughrāfī al-'Arabī*, trans. Hāshim Ṣalāḥ al-Dīn 'Uthmān (Cairo, 1963–1965); André Miquel, *La Géographie Humaine du Monde Musulman jusqu'au Milieu de 11e Siècle*, 4 vols. (Paris, 1967–1988). There have been partial and occasionally complete translations of the most famous works into other languages. Gabriel Ferrand (1913–1914) introduced some sections of various Arab authors' accounts on the trade in the Indian Ocean in translation. Gabriel Ferrand, *Relations de Voyages et Texts Géographiques Arabes, Persans et Turks Relatifs à l'Extrême-Orient du VIIIe au XVIIIe Siècles* (Paris, 1913–1914).

37. For a systematic argument about how to read illustrated maps of the premodern period to explore changes in people's worldviews, ideals, desires, and space consciousness based on religious beliefs in different periods, see Ohji Toshiaki, *Echizu no sekaizō* (Tokyo, 1996).
38. The first surviving maps of this kind were unearthed in the tombs of the Qin and western Han dynasties in Fangmatan and Mawangdui. See the maps 4–29 in *ZGDJ/Yuan*.
39. Ahmad, "Djughrāfiyā," 5: 576. See the discussion about the account by Ibn al-Faqīh (flourished 902) in Chapter 2.
40. For a succinct overview of the development of traditional Muslim maps, see S. Maqbul Ahmad, "Kharīṭa or Khāriṭa," *EI2*, 4: 1077–1083.
41. A surviving eighteenth-century Chinese sea chart, found by accident in a Shanghai bookstore, shows a primitive and scattered form of sea chart that people used to sail along the Chinese coast from Guangdong to Shandong. The information of the eighteenth-century sea chart was probably transferred from earlier periods, from generation to generation. Zhang Xun, *Gu hanghai tu kaoshi* (Beijing, 1980).
42. The excavations in the Persian Gulf and on the shores of the Arabian Sea in the last twenty years have provided archaeological data to supplement the written evidence about the origins and growth of direct contact with China. George F. Hourani's classical and influential survey on Arab seafaring with neighboring peoples (1951) was revised in 1995 with the annotations for updated scholarship based on new archaeological findings. George F. Hourani, *Arab Seafaring* (Princeton, 1995).
43. David Whitehouse, "'Abbāsid Maritime Trade: the Age of Expansion," in *Cultural and Economic Relations between East and West* (Wiesbaden, 1988), 62–70.
44. See Mikami Tsugio, *Tōjibōeki shi kenkyū, ge, chūkintō hen* (Tokyo, 1988); Michèle Pirazzoli-T'serstevens, "A Commodity in Great Demand: Chinese Ceramics Imported in the Arabo-Persian Gulf from the Ninth to the Fourteenth Century," *Orient* 8 (2004): 26–38; Axelle Rougeulle, "Medieval Trade Networks in the Western Indian Ocean (8–14th centuries)," in *Tradition and Archaeology: Early Maritime Contacts in the Indian Ocean* (New Delhi, 1996), 159–180; Moira Tampoe, *Maritime Trade between China and the West: An Archaeological Study of the Ceramics from Siraf (Persian Gulf), 8th to 15th centuries A.D.* (Oxford, 1989); Yuba Tadanori,

"Ejiputo · Fusutāto Iseki shutsudo no tōji: Ibutsu ichiranhyō," in *Tojiki no tōzai kōryū: Ejiputo · Fusutāto Iseki shutsudo no tōji* (Tokyo, 1984), 84–99.

45. Billy K. L. So, *Prosperity, Region, and Institutions in Maritime China: the South Fukien Pattern, 946–1368* (Cambridge, MA, 2000), 186–201. See also Ho Chuimei, "The Ceramic Boom in Minnan during Song and Yuan Times," in the same volume, 237–281; Richard Pearson, Li Min, and Li Guo, "Port, City, and Hinterlands: Archaeological Perspectives on Quanzhou and its Overseas Trade," in *The Emporium of the World*, 177–235.
46. Jonathan Adams, "Ships and Boats as Archaeological Source Material," *World Archaeology* 32, no. 3 (2001): 299.
47. Michael Flecker, *The Archaeological Excavation of the 10th Century: Intan Shipwreck* (Oxford, 2002); David Gibbins and Jonathan Adams, "Shipwrecks and maritime archaeology," *World Archaeology* 32, no. 3 (2001): 282. For more technical examination on the seafaring in the Indian Ocean and on the ships that sailed on them, see Hourani, 87–122.
48. Mikami Tsugio, *Tōjibōeki shi kenkyū, jō, higashi ajia, tōnan ajia hen* (Tokyo, 1987), 252–276.
49. *QZZJSK.*
50. Fernand Braudel, *La Méditerranée et le Monde Méditerranéen a l'époque de Philippe II* (Paris, 1949).
51. K. N. Chaudhuri, *Trade and Civilisation in the Indian Ocean: An Economic History from the Rise of Islam to 1750* (Cambridge, 1985).
52. Many scholars of Chinese history have devoted their research to the remarkable changes in China during the Tang and Song dynasties. See Peter Bol, *'This Culture of Ours': Intellectual Transitions in T'ang and Sung China* (Stanford, 1992); Mark Elvin, *The Pattern of the Chinese Past* (Stanford, 1973); Miyakawa Hisayuki, "An Outline of the Naitō Hypothesis and Its Effects on Japanese Studies of China," *Far Eastern Quarterly* 14 (1955): 533. Few doubt that the ʿAbbāsid dynasty, when the Islamic empire reached from Central Asia to North Africa, was also one of the most prosperous periods in Islamic history. Although the empire disintegrated gradually into multiple local autonomous states, the cultural development of the Islamic world did not cease. For basic works on Islamic history, see *The Cambridge History of Islam*; Marshall G. S. Hodgson, *The Venture of Islam: Conscience and History in a World Civilization* (Chicago, 1974); and relevant articles in *EI2*.
53. Sugiyama, *Kubirai no chōsen*, 70–73. For a detailed examination of the event, see Reuven Amitai-Preiss, *Mongols and Mamluks: The Mamluk Ilkhanid War, 1260–1281* (Cambridge, 1995), 26–48.

1. From Imperial Encounter to Maritime Trade

1. Du You, *Tongdian* (Beijing, 1988), 193:5279.
2. Ibid.
3. It is the first Chinese institutional history and encyclopedic text that had considerable influence on later works. Denis Twitchett, *The Writing of Official History under the T'ang* (Cambridge, 1992), 84–91.

4. For a detailed analysis of the section about western countries in Du You's *Tongdian*, see Li Jinxiu and Yu Taishan, *"Tongdian" Xiyu wenxian yaozhu* (Beijing, 2009).
5. These include *Jiu Tangshu*, *Xin Tangshu*, *Tang huiyao*, and *Cefu yuangui*.
6. Twitchett, *The Writing of Official History Under the T'ang*, 104–107.
7. A similar passage in *the Old History of the Tang* (*Jiu Tangshu*) says that they are "white." *JTS*, 198:5315.
8. Du You, 193:5279. Compare the translation by Leslie, *Islam in Traditional China*, 23.
9. For Chinese contact with the Persians, see the Introduction of this book.
10. Du You, 193:5279.
11. Ibid.
12. Ibid., 191:5199.
13. For the most detailed discussion of the Battle of Talas using Chinese and Arabic sources, see Maejima, "Tarasu Senkō: Joshō," 657–691, and "Tarasu Senkō: honshō," *Shigaku* 32.1 (1967): 1–37.
14. Christopher I. Beckwith, *The Tibetan Empire in Central Asia* (Princeton, 1987), 37–140.
15. *JTS*, 109:3298.
16. Maejima, "Tarasu Senkō: honshō," 28–29.
17. *JTS*, 198:5316, and *XTS*, 221:6263.
18. An Arabic account, dating to the early eleventh century, confirms the transfer of Chinese papermaking to the Islamic world after the Battle of Talas. ʿAbd al-Malik ibn Muḥammad al-Thaʿālibī, *The Laṭāʾif al-maʿārif of Thaʿālibī: The Book of Curious and Entertaining Information* (Edinburgh, 1968), 140. Several paper mills were built in major cities such as Baghdad in the eighth century. See Jonathan M. Bloom, *Paper before Print: the History and Impact of Paper in the Islamic World* (New Haven, 2001), 47–89. For more Islamic sources about the transfer of the art of papermaking from Chinese craftsmen (taken prisoners in 751) to the people in Samarqand in the eighth century, see W. Barthold, *Turkestan down to the Mongol Invasion* (Frankfurt am Main, 1995 [1928]), 236–237. Similar stories about captives who transferred information and technology to other societies are often found in history; for example, Japanese ceramics (*imari-yaki*) were transferred from Korea to Japan through Korean craftsmen who were brought to Japan as captives. Misugi Takatoshi, *'Gen no sometsuke' umi wo wataru: sekai ni hirogaru yakimono bunka* (Tokyo, 2004), 150–152.
19. Du You, 193:5280.
20. Du Huan mentions Dashi (Arabia), Malin 摩隣 (Malindi?), Daqin 大秦 (The Byzantine empire), Shan 苫 (Syria), Bahanna 拔汗那 (Ferghana), Kang 康 (Samarqand), Shizi 師子 (Sarandib, the modern-day Sri Lanka), Fulin 拂菻 (Western side of Syria), Boshi 波斯 (Persia), Shi 石 (Tashkent), Suiye 碎葉 (Tokmak in Central Asia) and Molu 末祿 (Amol in Central Asia). It is most likely that the original work contained more entries because these eleven countries are not contiguous. Du Huan, *Jingxing ji jianzhu* (Beijing, 2000), 1–66.
21. Du You, 193:5279.

22. See Amira K. Bennison, *The Great Caliphs: The Golden Age of the 'Abbasid Empire* (New Haven, 2009), 62 ; Hichem Djaït, "Al-Kūfa," *EI2*, 5: 345–351.
23. For a concise yet comprehensive survey of the history of the Islamic law as one given from God, implemented by Muslim states and practiced in their societies, see Knut S. Vikor, *Between God and the Sultan: A History of Islamic Law* (New York, 2006).
24. For excavated glass products from this period on, see Stefano Carboni, *Glass from Islamic Lands* (New York, 2001).
25. Du Huan, 5–6.
26. Sugiyama Masa'aki, *Shikkusuru sōgen no seifukusha, Ryō, Seika, Kin, Gen* (Tokyo, 2005), 57–65.
27. De la Vaissière, *Sogdian Traders*, 223–225.
28. Chen Gaohua, *Songyuan shiqi de haiwai maoyi*, 12. Angela Schottenhammer, "Transfer of *Xiangyao* 香藥 from Iran and Arabia to China – A Reinvestigation of Entries in the *Youyang zazu* 酉陽雜俎 (862)," *Aspects of the Maritime Silk Road: From the Persian Gulf to the East China Sea*, ed. Ralph Kauz (Wiesbaden: Harrassowitz Verlag, 2010), 117–149.
29. Wu Chunming, *Huan Zhongguo hai chenchuan: gudai fanchuan, chuanji yu chuanhuo* (Nanchang, 2003), 179–188. Kenneth R. Hall, "Indonesia's Evolving International Relationship in the Ninth to Early Eleventh Centuries: Evidence from Contemporary Shipwrecks and Epigraphy," *Indonesia*, 90 (October 2010): 1–31.
30. Mikami Tsugio, *Tōjiki no michi: tōzai bunmei no setten wo tazunete* (Tokyo, 1969), 68–78.
31. *XTS*, 43:1146, 1153–4.
32. Di Cosmo, *Ancient China and its Enemies*, 284.
33. For a brief English summary of the style and structure of writing official histories established by Sima Qian, see Endymion Porter Wilkinson, *Chinese History: a Manual* (Cambridge, MA, 2000), 501–15. See 150–2 for the monograph on administrative geography (*dilizhi*).
34. *XTS*, 166:5083–5.
35. It is one of the six routes connecting China with foreign regions. *XTS*, 43:1146. It was probably in his lost work *Huanghua sida ji* 皇華四達記 [The Record of the Imperial Glory Reaching Four Directions], which was introduced in *XTS*, 48:1506.
36. For a succinct examination about the ancient maritime trade activities and political dynamics between China and Southeast Asia before 1000, see Wang Gungwu, *The Nanhai Trade.* Early Chinese Buddhist pilgrims since the Six Dynasties period (220–589) traveled to India not only by land routes but also by sea routes between Guangzhou and Southern India. For example, Faxian (circa 337–circa 422) boarded a Persian ship at Sri Lanka to travel back to China. Three centuries later in 671, Yijing (635–713) traveled from Guangzhou via Sumatra and Malay Peninsula to a region in Western India (modern-day Calcutta) by a sea route.
37. *XTS*, 43:1153–4.

38. al-Ṭabarī, *The History of al-Tabarī (Ta'rīkh al-rusul wa'l-mulūk)*, vol. 28 (New York, 1995), 238.
39. Sources written in China, the Islamic world, Korea, and Japan all testify to increasing scale and numbers of special districts of foreigners allowed by Chinese government in port cities. On details of Muslim self-governing districts in important ports like Guanzhou from the Tang to the Song period, see Kuwabara Jitsuzō, *Ho Jukō no jiseki* (Tokyo, 1989), 78–158.
40. "hainei 海内" should be translated as "in the world" or "under the heaven."
41. 3 zhang 丈 in width and 3 zhang 丈 3 chi 尺 in length. *Xin Tangshu* includes a textual description of this now lost map. *XTS*, 166:5083–5. Another source for Jia Dan's map is also found in poems of the Tang dynasty. See Hilde de Weerdt, "Maps and Memory: Readings of Cartography in Twelfth- and Thirteenth-Century Song China," *Imago Mundi* 61, no. 2 (2009): 155–157. Also see Unno, *Tōyō chirigaku shi kenkyū: tairiku hen* (Osaka, 2004), 113.
42. Hilde de Weerdt examines these maps, along with other contemporary surviving maps, to argue that the genre of the empire map in China reached a broad readership of literate elites during the Song period and came to be used by politicians to discuss political strategies in their relations with northern dynasties. In this book, I use her English translation for the original Chinese map titles of this atlas. See De Weerdt, "Maps and Memory," 145–167. For the original sources, see *Songben lidai dili zhizhang tu* (Shanghai, 1989). Also see Cao Wanru, "'Lidai dili zhizhang tu' yanjiu," *ZGDJ/Yuan*, 31–34, and Unno, *Tōyō chirigaku shi kenkyū*, 59–64.
43. The map also portrays other foreign countries in East Asia, South, and Southeast Asia that had some commercial (and for some, close diplomatic) relations with China.
44. Cao Wanru, "Guanyu Huayi tu wenti de tanguo," *ZGDJ/Yuan*, 42–44.
45. Another engraved copy of *The Tracks of Yu* (*Yuji tu* 禹迹圖), which used a different Chinese character with the same pronunciation and meaning for the word "tracks," was carved and set by Yu Chi, a governmental official and also master of the school under Zhenjiang 鎮江 Prefecture in Jiangsu province in 1142 in the Song dynasty, based on the original Chang'an copy of 1136. The two maps are almost identical except that the later one depicted waves in the area of the sea. This map was probably attached to a wall of a school hall, thus did not have the other side carved. For a detailed discussion on this map, see Unno, *Tōyō chirigaku shi kenkyū*, 178–191.
46. D. K. Yee, "Taking the World's Measure: Chinese Maps between Observation and Text," *HC2:2*, 124. See the entire article (pp. 96–127) for what mensurational techniques the Chinese cartographers developed to draw precise maps.
47. Pei Xiu's six principles of cartography are described in the *History of Jin* (*Jinshu*); Fang Xuanling, *Jinshu* (Beijing, 1974), 4:1039. There have been scholarly debates whether his six principles include the use of a grid system. The use of grid perhaps developed even before Pei Xiu and was adopted by Chinese cartographers in a later period to draw precise contours of China. See Wang Yong, *Zhongguo ditu shi gang* (Beijing, 1958), 18–24; see also

Nancy Steinhardt, "Chinese Cartography and Calligraphy," *Oriental Art* 43, no. 1 (1997): 10–11; Yee, "Taking the World's Measure," 110–113.

48. *XTS*, 166:5084.
49. On a detailed discussion about the stone tablet of *The Map of Chinese and Non-Chinese Territories* and *The Tracks of Yu* (*Yuji tu*) engraved in the Song dynasty, see Aoyama Sadao, *Tō Sō Jidai no kōtsū to chisi chizu no Kenkyū* (Tokyo, 1963), 569–593.
50. Cao Wanru, "Guanyu Huayi tu wenti de tanguo," 41–45.
51. The emperor also ordered the ministers to place another copy in the Secretariat for State Affairs (Shangshu xing 尙書省). Fan Sheng, "Songdai dili xue de guannian, tixi yu zhishi xingqu," PhD dissertation: Peking University, 2008), 117; Unno, *Tōyō chirigaku shi kenkyū*, 113–114.
52. A Song author Chen Zhensun (circa 1183–1262) said in his *Zhizhai shulu jieti* that the emperor ordered Shui Anli to compile the atlas. Chen Zhensun continues saying that Shui Anli died before submitting it to the emperor officially, and the publisher still published it without including the author's name and his preface, making the authorship unclear. See the original text by the Song author Chen Zhensun. Chen Zhensun, *Zhizhai shulu jieti* (Shanghai, 1937), 8:233.
53. The earliest Song dynasty wood-block-printed version is preserved in Japan. The earliest surviving wood-block-printed version preserved in China is a Ming dynasty version, which is a little different from the Song version with regards to the content and spellings. For more discussions about the two different versions, see Cao Wanru, "'Lidai dili zhizhang tu' yanjiu," 31.
54. Miya Noriko, *Mongoru teikoku ga unda sekaizu* (Tokyo, 2007), 143.
55. Fan Sheng, "Songdai dili xue de guannian, tixi yu zhishi xingqu." From this, we can naturally assume that these kinds of maps had been circulating among the local elite by the mid-Song period. This process of localization may go along with the general transformations from the northern Song and the southern Song in political and social spheres. See Robert Hartwell, "Demographic, Political, and Social Transformations of China," *Harvard Journal of Asiatic Studies* 42 (1982): 365–442.
56. Jan Yün-hua, *A Chronicle of Buddhism in China, 581-960 A.D.: Translations from Monk Chih-p'an's Fo-tsu t'ung-chi* (Santiniketan, 1966), 8–9.
57. Zheng Xihuang, "Guanyu *Fozu tongji* zhong sanfu ditu dangyi," *ZGDJ/Yuan*, 81–84.
58. These are sections about western regions in *Shiji* [Records of the historian] by Sima Qian (circa 145–86 BCE), *Hanshu* [History of the Former Han] by Ban Gu (32–92 CE), and *Hou Hanshu* [History of the Later Han] by Fan Ye (398–445 CE).
59. Tianzhu means "Sindhu" in Sanskrit, which is an old name for the Indus River.
60. See Xuanzang, *Da Tangxiyu ji jiaozhu* (Beijing, 1985).
61. That is the five zhu (wu zhu 五竺) in the text. Zhu 竺 means Tianzhu 天竺. The text says that the official name of Tianzhu is India (Yindu 印度), so five zhu means East India, West India, South India, North India, Middle India. More detailed explanations about each region is given in the text. See Zhipan, 32:111–14l.

62. Ohji Toshiaki, *Chizu ha kataru: sekai chizu no tanjō* (Tokyo, 2007), 46–50.
63. Jam-bu-dvīpa had originally translated as Yanfu ti 閻浮提 in Chinese. Nakamura Gen, *Iwanami Bukkyō Jiten*, 81r.
64. For a discussion on "India's unique status in the Chinese world order," see Tansen Sen, *Buddhism, Diplomacy, and Trade: the Realignment of Sino-Indian Relations, 600-1400* (Honolulu, 2003), 8–12. For a detailed discussion on Buddhist worldview and its gradual acceptance by the Chinese, see also Unno, *Tōyō Chirigaku shi kenkyū*, 18–30. For maps with India at the center, see Unno, *Chizu no bunkashi – sekai to nihon* (Tokyo, 1996), 19–21.
65. Baida 白達 is pronounced b´wâng-d´ăt according to Karlgren.
66. Baghdad is transcribed differently here as Fuda 縛達.
67. Huang Shengzhang, "Songke *Yu ditu* congkao," *ZGDJ/Yuan*, 56–60.
68. No paintings of Chinese seagoing vessels in the Tang dynasty survived, yet the Japanese scroll preserved in Kōyasan 高野山 temple, which dates back to the fourteenth century, depicts Japanese seagoing vessels for the eighteenth imperial embassy to China (Kentōshi sen) in 804. Yamagata Kinya, *Rekishi no umi wo hashiru: Chūgoku zōsen gijutsu no kōseki* (Tokyo, 2004), 97. The Chinese and Japanese probably influenced each other regarding shipbuilding technology. Many written sources also testify to Chinese construction of large seagoing vessels during the Tang period. Sun Guangqi, *Zhongguo gudai hanghai shi* (Beijing, 2005), 196–199.
69. On the contact between China and Japan during the Tang period, including the Japanese imperial embassies to the Tang dynasty (Kentōshi, eighteen to twenty times in 630–894 CE), see Sun Guangqi, *Zhongguo gudai hanghai shi*, 218–240.
70. Chen Gaohua, *Songyuan shiqi de haiwai maoyi*, 99–122.
71. Sanfoqi was a large commercial hub/center in the maritime route that was connected to the east and the west. Kuwabara, *Ho Jukō no jiseki*, 162, 182–184.
72. The place-names along the eastern coast are even more precise and rich than those along the southern coast. Aoyama points out that it is because the Chinese in the Song period had more contacts with the countries in East Asia including Japan and Korea than with those in Southeast, South, and West Asia. Aoyama, *Tō Sō Jidai no kōtsu to chishi chizu no Kenkyū*, 610. It is true that the contact between China and the countries in East Asia dramatically increased in the Song period, yet the trade in the South China Sea also flourished considerably according to contemporary written and archeological evidence. The cartographer of the map may have not possessed the best knowledge about the southern coast of China.
73. Shen Gua, *Mengxi bitan*, 2:768–771; Joseph Needham, et al., *Science and Civilisation in China*, vol. 4, Part III (Cambridge, 1971), 563–564.
74. Xu Song, *Songhuiyao jigao* (Beijing, 1957), 7:22, 4:91.
75. The Song dynasty, which was politically-weaker than the Tang dynasty, had already compromised with strong northern peoples such as the Liao and Xixia the traditional hierarchical principles of the tributary system in order to maintain peace. Chaffee, "Diasporic Identities," 400–401.
76. See Tuo Tuo, *Songshi* (Beijing, 1977), 167:3971. For a succinct English summary of the duties of the Office of the Superintendent of Merchant Shipping

(shibosi) and further information about Chinese and Japanese scholarship on this topic, see So, *Prosperity, Region, and Institutions in Maritime China*, 46–7.

77. Chaffee, "Diasporic Identities," 395–420; see also Hugh R. Clark's essay about Quanzhou as China's maritime frontier and Muslim communities there from the tenth to the thirteenth century. Hugh R. Clark, "Muslims and Hindus in the Culture and Morphology of Quanzhou from the Tenth to the Thirteenth century," *Journal of World History* 6, no. 1 (Spring 1995): 49–74. See also Chen Dasheng and Denys Lombard, "Foreign Merchants in Maritime Trade in Quanzhou ('Zaitun'): Thirteenth and Fourteenth Centuries," in *Asian Merchants and Businessmen in the Indian Ocean and the China Sea* (Oxford, 2000), 19–24.
78. For some examples such as the Arab merchant Pu Ximi (Abu Hamid?), see Chaffee, "Diasporic Identities," 401–403. Also see Kuwabara, *Ho Jukō no jiseki*, 92, 161–162.
79. For more details about this case, Zhang Jun-yan, "Relations between China and the Arabs in Early Times," *The Journal of Oman Studies* 6 (1980): 102.
80. See John W. Chaffee, "The Impact of the Song: Imperial Clan on the Overseas Trade of Quanzhou," in *The Emporium of the World*, 13–46; Robert M. Hartwell, "Foreign Trade, Monetary Policy and Chinese 'Mercantilism'," in *Collected Studies on Sung History Dedicated to Professor James T. C. Liu in Celebration of his Seventieth Birthday* (Kyoto, 1989); Jung-pang Lo, "The Emergence of China as a Sea Power During the Late Sung and Early Yüan Periods," *Far Eastern Quarterly* 14, no. 4 (1955): 489–503.
81. Fujian sheng Quanzhou haiwai jiaotongshi bowuguan, *Quanzhou wan Songdai haichuan de fajue yu janjiu* (Beijing, 1987).
82. On discussions about technological breakthroughs in shipbuilding and in the art of seafaring during the Song period, see Needham, *Science and Civilisation in China,* vol. 4, Part III, 563–564. Chen Xinxiong updates Needham's classical work on technological breakthroughs in shipbuilding and in the art of seafaring. Chen Xinxiong, "Song Yuan de yuanyang maoyi chuan," in *Zhongguo Haiyang fazhan shi lunwen ji*, vol.2 (Taipei, 1986).
83. See my discussion on the descriptions about advantages of the watertight compartments in the accounts of Marco Polo and Ibn Baṭṭūṭa in Chapter 4.
84. Some of the things on the ships were made earlier such as the first-century coins found on the fourteenth-century shipwreck from Sinan that were apparently still on circulation. *Conservation and Restoration Report of Shinan Ship* (Mokpo, 2004), 196–204.
85. So, *Prosperity, Region, and Institutions in Maritime China*, 186–201. See also many articles in Angela Schottenhammer, ed., *The Emporium of the World*, most of which attest to the boom of Chinese maritime trade centering around Quanzhou in the Song period based on recent archeological findings.
86. He says in his preface that he summarized 400 sections first that he later lost, and therefore, the information he collected was more than that in the Notes from the *Land beyond the Passes*. Zhou Qufei, *Lingwai daida* (Beijing, 1999), 7. There are four surviving editions for Zhou Qufei's *Lingwai daida*. All of them are from the Ming dynasty *Yongle dadian* [Great Encyclopedia

of the Yongle Reign], which contains collected texts that are quite close to the originals. The final Zhonghua shuju volume edited and commented by Yang Wuquan compares the earlier three editions and provides the most reliable text, and therefore, I mainly used that in this study.

87. We can also find some valuable accounts about sailing and ships in other chapters. Due to the book's rich contents, many scholars have used the work to research the maritime contacts of the Song period.
88. Zhou Qufei, 126.
89. Ibid., 99.
90. There are debates about the exact location of this country. Some scholars identify it with Malabar Coast in southern India, yet because the text says people can reach Mecca from Maliba for eighty-day journey west on foot, Mirbat in the Arabian Peninsula is more convincing than Malabar from which people have to sail to reach Mecca. Zhou Qufei, 99, 101.
91. In the section about Lumei 盧眉 in *Zhufan zhi*, Zhao Rugua says Meilugudun 眉路骨惇 is Lumei 盧眉 (the Roman empire). *Zhufan zhi*, 116.
92. Zhou Qufei, 74–75.
93. Ibid., 126–127.
94. Ibid., 91.
95. Shen Gua, *Mengxi bitan*, 2:768–771.
96. Zhou Qufei, 216–217. Compare Zhu Yu, *Pingzhou ketan* (Shanghai, 1989), 26–7.
97. Although Zhao Rugua does not mention the title, he cites much from the *Notes from the Land beyond the Passes*. The edition that Hirth used did not contain Zhao Rugua's own preface. I also used Zhonghua shuju edition and the Japanese translation, which scholars agree are the best annotated editions.
98. Zhao Rugua himself says in his preface that he used some free time to inquire foreign merchants about their countries' products, customs, and travel itineraries. Yet Fujiyoshi argues that Zhao Rugua's term in office was only one and a half years, which was too short to do all of inquiries, and that he probably used previous works. *Zhufan zhi*/Fujiyoshi, 1, 330.
99. *Zhufan zhi*, 1; *Zhufan zhi*/Fujiyoshi, 1, 339.
100. *Zhufan zhi*, 91; Compare *Zhufan zhi*/Fujiyoshi, 158, and *Zhufan zhi*/Hirth, 119.
101. Although Lin Zhiqi used different Chinese characters for Shi Nawei 試那圍 (not 施那幃) in his book, the Chinese pronunciation is the same; Chinese authors often transcribed the Arabic name of an identical foreign merchant to Chinese names using different Chinese characters that have the same pronunciations. Lin Zhiqi (1112–76), *Zhuozhai wenji* (Taipei, 1971), 15:13. For a brief discussion about an original name for the Arab merchant Shi Nawei (Shilāvi: from Sirāf) and the Chinese author Lin Zhiqi, see *Zhufan zhi*/Fujiyoshi, 168.
102. See Kuwabara, *Ho Jukō no jiseki*, 88, 200–201.
103. *Zhufan zhi*/Hirth, 124.
104. See Chapter 3 for more details on the Muslim stone inscriptions in the most recent publication, *QZZJSK*. A few surviving Muslim tombstones date back to the Song period. The Muslim communities flourished in the ports

of southeastern China since the tenth century as part of a trade diaspora. Chaffee, "Diasporic Identities," 395–420.

105. *Zhufan zhi*, 120–123; Compare *Zhufan zhi*/Fujiyoshi, 192–195, and *Zhufan zhi*/Hirth, 114.
106. The traditional sources of the Nile River were thought to be in a mountain range called Mountains of the Moon by ancient Greek and Muslim geographers. See Chapters 2, 3, and 4 for its depictions in Muslim and Chinese maps. The real sources of the White Nile were found only in the mid-nineteenth century by the exploration of Sir Richard Francis Burton and John Hanning Speke. On this topic, also see Christopher Ondaatje, *Journey to the Source of the Nile* (Toronto, 1998).
107. The story in the Qur'ān is from that of the Hebrew Bible (Genesis, Chapters 30–7).
108. *Zhufan zhi*, 123.

2. The Representation of China and the World

1. Ibn al-Nadīm, *The Fihrist of al-Nadīm* (New York, 1970), 31.
2. Ibid., 32.
3. J. W. Fück, "Ibn al-Nadīm," *EI2*, 3: 895–896. Jonathan M. Bloom. *Paper Before Print: The History and Impact of Paper in the Islamic World* (New Haven, 2001).
4. For the translation movement, see Dimitri Gutas, *Greek Thought, Arab Culture: the Graeco-Arabic Translation Movement in Baghdad and Early Abbasid Society* (New York, 1998).
5. Busse, "Arabische Historiographie und Geographie," 293–296.
6. Ragep, "Islamic Reactions to Ptolemy's Imprecisions," 124–125.
7. Abū Dja'far Muḥammad b. Mūsā al-Khwārizmī is more famous for writing many scientific works from which modern terms like algebra and algorithm originate. See J. Vernet, "Al-Khwārazmī," *EI2*, 4: 1070–1071.
8. Ptolemy, *Ptolemy, Geography, Book 6: Middle East, Central and North Asia, China*, trans. Helmut Humbach (Wiesbaden, 1998–2002), vol.1, 201–211, vol.2, 102–104.
9. Wilhelm Spita discovered the only surviving manuscript of *The Shape of the Earth* in Cairo in 1878. It mentions three cities in China, one of which, according to Kuwabara Jitsuzō, was Khantū (probably Yangzhou). Takahashi Tadashi, "Aru-kuwārizumī zusetsu [gaihō]," *Chiri gakushi kenkyū* 2 (1962): 52. Also see Kuwabara, *Ho Jukō no jiseki*, 33, 49, for his discussion about Khantu.
10. Ibn Khurradādhbih, *Kitāb al-Masālik wa-l-mamālik* (Leiden, 1889).
11. Ibid. For reliable English translations of sample passages, see S. Maqbul Ahmad, *Arabic Classical Accounts of India and China* (Shimla, 1989), and Pier Giovanni Donini, *Arab Travelers and Geographers* (London, 1991).
12. This view is probably based on the common doctrine of both Judeo-Christian and Islamic beliefs that all of us are descended from Adam and Eve. This belief showed Muslims' open attitude towards the Chinese, whom they saw as their brothers. "Faghfūr," *EI2*, 2: 738.

13. Bosworth et al., "al-Ṣīn."
14. See L. Hambis, "Khānfū," *EI2*, 4: 1024. For a detailed discussion about the identification and location of Khānfū, see Kuwabara, *Ho Jukō no jiseki*, 39–42.
15. Kuwabara, *Ho Jukō no jiseki*, 47–48.
16. Walther Hinz, *Islamische Masse und Gewichte* (Leiden, 1970), 62.
17. Ibn Khurradādhbih, 69. For a detailed discussion of the entire route from Ceylon to Qānṭū, see Aloya Sprenger, *Die Post- und Reiserouten des Orients* (Nendeln, Liechtenstein, 1966).
18. Bosworth et al., "al-Ṣīn." See an example of al-Idrīsī in the discussion about al-Idrīsī's geographic works at the end of this chapter.
19. A recent archaeological find demonstrates the importance of Yangzhou in the maritime trade with the Islamic world. See Hsieh Ming-liang, "Ji heishi hao (Batu Hitam) chenchuan zhong de Zhongguo taociqi (Batu Hitam)," *Meishu shi yanjiu jikan* 13 (2002): 1–60.
20. For Wāqwāq, see F. Viré, "Wāḳwāḳ," *EI2*, 11: 103–109. For al-Shīlā, see the article about Korea Kei Won Chung and George F. Hourani, "Arab Geographers on Korea," *Journal of the American Oriental Society* 58.4 (December 1983): 658–661.
21. Ibn Khurradādhbih, 70.
22. For an illustration of the wāqwāq tree in a later Muslim account, see Figure 33 in E. Edson and E. Savage-Smith, eds., *Medieval Views of the Cosmos* (Oxford, 2004), 66.
23. The most important case is that of al-Jayhānī, a vizier of the Sāmānid dynasty (875–999) in Central Asia and eastern Iran. His *Book of Routes and Realms* is not extant, yet we can assume, based on some later accounts that frequently cited its coverage of eastern countries, that his book was similar to Ibn Khurradādhbih's or perhaps even richer because he expanded on it by using more travelers as sources. Some scholars argue that the version of Ibn Khurradādhbih's book that we have now is abridged and that there was a more complete version (Ibn Khurradādhbih himself revised his first text after forty years passed) which al-Jayhānī copied. Later writers who cited Ibn Khurradādhbih's book kept describing it as brief in order to justify their own more detailed works, which were in fact, based on other available sources at their disposal. Marwazī, *Sharaf al-Zamān Ṭāhir Marvazī on China, the Turks, and India: Arabic Text (circa A.D. 1120) with an English Translation and Commentary*, trans. V. Minorsky (Frankfurt am Main, 1993), 6–8. See an example of such discussions in De la Vaissière, *Sogdian Traders*, 312–313.
24. I agree with their argument because the name Sulaymān is only mentioned once in the middle of the entire volume. See Ahmad, *Arabic Classical Accounts*, xv, and Hourani, 68.
25. Buzurg b. Shahriyar, *The Book of the Wonders of India*, trans. G. S. P. Freeman-Grenville (London, 1981), see especially 62–64. *Arabian Nights: The Marvels and Wonders of the Thousand and One Nights*, vol.1, trans. Richard F. Burton (New York, 1991).
26. I mainly used the original Arabic text compiled by Jean Sauvaget to translate the passages in the first volume because it is a clearer edition with vowels,

and I compared them with another original Arabic text compiled by Reinaud and also with English and French translations. Sauvaget's Arabic text does not contain the second volume by Abū Zayd, so I had to use Reinaud's Arabic text to translate the passages in the second volume and compare them with English and French translations.

27. Another source is a passage in al-Mas'ūdī's *The Meadows of Gold and Mines of Gems* (*Murūj al-dhahab wa-ma'ādin al-jawāhir*) where al-Mas'ūdī directly cites him.
28. The name "al-'Irāq" (also spelled "Iraq") in medieval Arabic sources denoted the region of the Tigris and Euphrates river valleys rather than a discreet political unit.
29. Abū Zayd explains this in his second volume. Reinaud, 61; Renaudot, 31.
30. The author used the term "Chinese ships (al-Sufun al-Ṣīnīyah)" to refer to "ships that sail to China," not ships from China as some have assumed. Al-Mas'ūdī's *Murūj al-dhahab wa-ma'ādin al-jawāhir* also mentions "Chinese ships" in the Persian Gulf. Al-Mas'ūdī, *Les prairies d'or,* trans. Barbier de Meynard and Pavet de Courteille, vol. 1, (Paris, 1962) 216; some scholars interpret this usage to mean that the Chinese used to sail to the Persian Gulf. However, as Hourani pointed out, no other evidence clearly supports the sailing of Chinese ships as far as the Persian Gulf. Hourani, *Arab Seafaring,* 75–76.
31. Reinaud, 88; Renaudot, 46.
32. For more detail about the Intan ship found in 1998–1999, see Flecker, *The Archaeological Excavation of the 10th Century: Intan Shipwreck,* (Oxford, 2002).
33. Michael Flecker, "A Ninth-Century AD Arab or Indian Shipwreck in Indonesia," *World Archaeology* 32, no. 3 (2001): 340, Plate 4.
34. We can gain some clearer sense about what the ancient sewn boats of the Indian Ocean looked like from a surviving sewn boat found in the mid-nineteenth century on India's east coast. Ray, 59–64. Eric Kentley, "The Sewn Boats of India's East Coast," in *Tradition and Archaeology*, 254; see page 260 for a mid-19th century model of a *masula.*
35. Denis Twitchett and Janice Stargardt, "Chinese Siver Bullion in a Tenth-Century Indonesian Wreck," *Asia Major* (3rd series), 15, no. 1 (2002): 35–60.
36. Twitchett and Stargardt, "Chinese Siver Bullion," 25–26.
37. Flecker, "A Ninth-Century AD Arab or Indian Shipwreck in Indonesia," 339–342.
38. Tampoe, *Maritime Trade between China and the West*, 54–57, 65–66. Whitehouse, "'Abbāsid Maritime Trade," 64–67.
39. Sauvaget, 7–9; Ahmad, *Arabic Classical Accounts*, 38–40.
40. Sauvaget, 9.
41. Sauvaget, 16; Ahmad, *Arabic Classical Accounts*, 46.
42. Sauvaget, 7.
43. Kuwabara, *Ho Jukō no jiseki*, 97–98.
44. Sauvaget, 16; Ahmad, *Arabic Classical Accounts*, 46.
45. Sauvaget, 11–27; Ahmad, *Arabic Classical Accounts*, 42–57.

46. Sauvaget, 18–19; Ahmad, *Arabic Classical Accounts*, 49.
47. Chunyan Huang, "Songdai dengwengu zhidu," *Zhongzhou xuekan* 6 (November 2004): 112–116; Edward A. Kracke, "Early Visions of Justice for the Humble in East and West," *Journal of the American Oriental Society* 96, no. 4 (October-December 1976): 493–495.
48. On a comparative and comprehensive discussion of the tort redress conducted in China, the Sassanid dynasty, and the Islamic world, see Beatrice Gruendler, "Tawqīʿ (Apostille)," in *The Evolution of Artistic Classical Arabic P*, (Beirut), 3–6.
49. Reinaud, 75–77; Renaudot, 39–40.
50. Abu Ḥāyyan al-Tawḥīdī, "Al-Tawḥīdī," in *The Book of Entertainment and Good Company*, 353–357 (the quotation on p. 354).
51. For classical works on the contacts between Chinese and the Persians of the Sassanid dynasty, Ishida Mikinosuke, *Chōan no haru* (Tokyo, 1979) for Persian influence on Chinese, and Berthold Laufer, *Sino-Iranica* (Chicago, 1919) for Chinese influence on Persians. In his *Chōan no haru*, Ishida Mikinoske reconstructed the lively and "cosmopolitan" scenes of the Chang'an including many business transactions of Persian- or Arabic-speaking, non-Chinese merchants using the Tang period collections of stories and poems including *Taiping guangji* (Extensive Records of the Taiping Era). According to the sources, the Chinese during the Sui and Tang dynasties enjoyed Iranian-style wine, clothes, music, and dances. The Iranians built Zoroastrian temples in Chang'an to keep their religious lives. Ishida, 163–205. For exotic goods that came from Central Asia to Chang'an, see Edward H. Schafer, *The Golden Peaches of Samarkand: A Study of T'ang Exotics* (Berkeley, 1963).
52. Reinaud, 77–85; Renaudot, 40–45.
53. Reinaud, 85–86; Renaudot, 45. Heng Chye Kiang reconstructed a hypothetical walk through Chang'an taken Ibn Wahb based on these sources. Heng Chye Kiang, *Cities of Aristocrats and Bureaucrats: the Development of Medieval Chinese Cityscapes* (Honolulu, 1999), 1–16. See page five of the book for the reconstructed plan of Chang'an and hypothetical route taken by Ibn Wahab in Figure A.
54. Ishida, *Chōan no haru*, 214–215.
55. Ibid., 163–196.
56. Huang Chao occupied Guangzhou in 879. For more details, see Ouyang Xiu, *Biography of Huang Ch'ao [Hsīn T'ang-shū 225C.1a-9a]*, trans. Howard S. Levy (Berkeley, 1955).
57. Reinaud, 62–63; Renaudot, 32–33.
58. Another Arabic source about the same event estimates the casualties at 200,000. For the original text, see al-Masʿūdī, *Murūj al-dhahab wa-maʿādin al- jawhar* (Bayrūt), 106. Compare a French translation, al-Masʿūdī, *Les prairies d'or*, trans. Barbier de Meynard and Pavet de Courteille, vol. 1, 125; and an English translation, al-Masʿūdī, *El-Mas'udi's Historical Encyclopedia: entitled "Meadows of Gold and Mines of Gems"*, trans. Aloys Sprenger (London, 1841), 325. Chinese sources about the Huang Chao Rebellion seem not to mention the massacre of foreigners, although another Chinese source about 100 years earlier relates a similar event of a massacre of 4,000

Persian merchants when Tang general Tian Shengong rebelled and entered Yangzhou in 760. *JTS*, 124:3533.

59. S. D. Goitein, *Letters of Medieval Jewish Traders* (Princeton, 1973).
60. Kenneth R. Hall, "Local and International Trade and Traders in the Straits of Melaka Region: 600–1500," *Journal of the Economic and Social History of the Orient*, 47, no. 3 (2004): 213–260.
61. S. Maqbul Ahmed, "Travels of Abu 'l Hasan 'Ali b. al Husayn al-Mas'udi," *Islamic Culture: An English Quarterly* 28, no. 1 (January 1954): 523.
62. Born in Baghdad, he traveled widely during his lifetime and settled down in Cairo before his death. For more about al-Mas'ūdī, see S. Maqbul Ahmad, ed., *Al-Mas'ūdī: Millenary Commemoration Volume* (Aligarh, 1960).
63. He consulted Ptolemy's *Geography* and *Almagest*, and he often shows his interest in geography in his books. See the discussion of al-Mas'ūdī.
64. The first sea, Sea of Fārs, begins from Basra and al-Ubullah in the Persian Gulf and continues via the five intervening seas – the Sea of Lārwī لاروي, the Sea of Harkand, the Sea of Kālah Bār [كلاه بار] (Also called Sea of Kalah) كله, the Sea of Kundranj كندرنج, the Sea of al-Ṣanf – and ends in the seventh and final sea, that is, the Sea of China. Al-Masūdī, *Murūj al-dhahab*, vol.1, 114–122. An earlier Muslim geographer al-Ya'qūbī (died 897) gives a slightly different sea division that has the fifth sea as the Sea of Salāhiṭ and the sixth sea as the Sea of Kundranj. Ferrand, *Relations de Voyages*, 49–50.
65. Many other passages in *Accounts of China and India* are the same as, or similar to, those in al-Mas'ūdī's account. *The Accounts of China and India*, however, contains richer information not found in al-Mas'ūdī's account; similar summarized descriptions about the seven seas are found in other contemporary accounts.
66. Al-Masūdī, *Murūj al-dhahab*, 129. Compare Abū Zayd's account in Reinaud, 87–88 for Arabic with French translation; Renaudot, 46 for English.
67. Al-Iṣṭakhrī based his works on those of al-Balkhī (died 934?), which are not extant. Al-Mas'ūdī says he has seen a world map of Caliph al-Ma'mūn, which he considered was superior to the maps of Ptolemy and Marinos of Tyre. None of these maps survive, yet some extant maps whose originals date back to the tenth century may reflect an initial template similar to the earlier maps.
68. Abū Zayd al-Balkhī's map is lost. Hopkins, "Geographic and Navigational Literature," 312–315. Ahmad, "Djughrāfiyā," 2: 581–582.
69. Ibn al-Faqīh, *Compendium libri Kitāb al-Boldān* (Lugduni-Batavorum, 1885), 3–4 for Arabic. Compare Ferrand, *Relations de Voyages*, 55 for French translation.
70. There were other famous geographers such as al-Ya'qūbī who authored books with the same title. See Hopkins, "Geographic and Navigational Literature," 309–312.
71. Bosworth, "al-Ṣīn."
72. The many later manuscripts suggest that the Balkhī School maps were popular in the succeeding centuries. See Gerald R. Tibbetts, "The Balkhī School of Geographers" and "Later Cartographic Developments," *HC2:1*.

73. The Balkhī School maps also contain sectional maps that do not include China but show the Sea of China (the present-day Indian Ocean). Tibbetts, "The Balkhī School of Geographers," 112–122.
74. Early ʿAbbāsid scholars, including al-Khwārizmī, had tried to draw the world or locate regions based on longitude-latitude coordinate systems influenced by the Greco-Roman geographic tradition, but none of their maps survive (see Chapter 4 for further discussion of a possible copy of al-Maʾmūn's map).
75. *MGC1*, 95–108.
76. See a reconstruction of the world of Ptolemy in Dilke, "The Culmination of Greek Cartography in Ptolemy," 184.
77. Al-Muqaddasī (circa 946), *The Best Divisions for Knowledge of the Regions: a Translation of Ahsan al-Taqasim fi Maʿrifat al-Aqalim*, trans. Basil Anthony Collins (Reading, UK, 1994), 10–11. Compare al-Muqaddasī, *Aḥsan al-taqāsīm fī maʿrifat al-āqālīm* (Leiden, 1976 [1877]), 10–11 for Arabic.
78. Al-Muqaddasī, *The Best Divisions for Knowledge of the Regions*, 10–24; al-Muqaddasī, *Aḥsan al-taqāsīm fī maʿrifat al-āqālīm*, 10–24.
79. For the Indian mathematical geographic tradition, including the *Zīj* book and the Muslim scholars who were influenced by such traditional scholars as al-Fazārī and al-Bīrūnī, see *MGC1*, 64–74.
80. Anya H. King, "Beyond the Geographers: Information on Asia in Early Medieval Arabic Writers on Pharmacology and Perfumery," unpublished paper presented at the AAS annual conference, Philadelphia, March 27, 2010.
81. Al-Bīrūnī's sketch map was occasionally cited by later authors (for instance, al-Qazwīnī in his cosmographical work), but its influence was very clear in practically all future Islamic maps of the world. See Tibbetts, "Later Cartographic Developments," 141–142.
82. Al-Kāshgharī illustrates each word with a sentence, idiomatic expression, proverb, or piece of poetry that provides precious insights into Turkish life during the eleventh century. Andreas Kaplony, "Comparing al-Kāshgharī's Map to his Text: On the Visual Language, Purpose, and Transmission of Arabic-Islamic Maps," in *The Journey of Maps and Images on the Silk Road* (Leiden, 2008), 143.
83. Maḥmūd al-Kāshgharī, Compendium of the Turkic Dialects *(Dīwān luγāt at-Turk)*, trans. Robert Dankoff (Cambridge, MA, 1982–1985), 82.
84. Kaplony, "Comparing al-Kāshgharī's Map to his Text," 144–148.
85. For the changes in the meaning of the terms about China that originated from India and for the appearance of more specific terms for a Chinese northern dynasty such as Tawjāch (Toba in Chinese) that originated from the ruling family of the Northern Wei dynasty (386–534), see Michal Biran, *The Qara Khitai Empire in Eurasian History: Between China and the Islamic World* (Cambridge, 2005), 98.
86. Kaplony, "Comparing al-Kāshgharī's Map to his Text," 144.
87. It was included in *The Book of Curiosities of the Sciences and Marvels for the Eyes* (*Kitāb Gharāʾib al-funūn wa-mulaḥ al-ʿuyūn*). For this newly discovered

manuscript and its remarkable series of early maps and astronomical diagrams, see Jeremy Johns and Emilie Savage-Smith, "The Book of Curiosities: A Newly Discovered Series of Islamic Maps," *Imago Mundi* 55 (2003), and Yossef Rapoport, "The Book of Curiosities: A Medieval Islamic View of the East," in *The Journey of Maps and Images on the Silk Road*, 155–171.

88. *Ḥudūd al-ʿĀlam "The Regions of the World": A Persian Geography 372 A.H.–982 A.D.*, trans. V. Minorsky (Frankfurt am Main, 1993), xvi.
89. Pavel B. Lurje, "Description of the Overland Route to China in *Hudud al-ʿAlam*," *Ouya xuekan* 6 (2007): 179–197.
90. Marwazī, *Sharaf al-Zamān Ṭahir Marwazī*, 13–29.
91. We have seen in Chapter 1 that Zhao Rugua's *Records of Foreign People* also had a section about it.
92. Al-Idrīsī, *Nuzhat al-mushtāq fī ikhtirāq al-āfāq* (Napoli, 1970). Only a French translation is available. Al-Idrīsī, *Géographie d'Edrisi*, trans. P. Amédée Jaubert (Frankfurt am Main, 1992 [1836–1840]).
93. Frances Carney Gies, "Al-Idrisi and Roger's Book," *Saudi Aramco World* 28.4 (July/August 1977): 14–19.
94. Al-Idrīsī, *Nuzhat al-mushtāq fī ikhtirāq al-āfāq*, 4–6.
95. Ibid., 7–9.
96. Ibid., 9.
97. Ibid., 6.
98. Miller created a detailed reconstructed map of the Middle Kingdom as it appeared to al-Idrīsī. See Miller, vol. 3, 44–45.
99. For a discussion about the weaknesses of al-Idrīsī's geography on India, see Al-Idrīsī, *India and the Neighboring Territories in the Kitāb Nuzhat al-Mushtāq fi khtirāq al-āfāq of al-Sharīf al-Idrīsī*, trans. S. Maqbul Ahmad (Leiden, 1960).
100. On Gog and Magog, see E. Van Donzel and Claudia Ott, "Yādjūdj wa-Mādjūdj," *EI2*, 11: 231–234.
101. Herrlee G. Creel and Robert Hartwell have cited al-Idrīsī's treatise to also claim that Chinese institutional forms spread as far as Sicily and that Roger II, for example, adopted the civil service examinations. Robert M. Hartwell, "Foreign Trade, Monetary Policy and Chinese 'Mercantilism,'" in *Collected Studies on Sung History Dedicated to Professor James T. C. Liu in Celebration of his Seventieth Birthday* (Kyoto, 1989), 461.
102. This is the same as Ibn Khurradādhbih's route. See the place-names of slightly different spellings in the previous discussion. The maps are similar to a contemporary Chinese map, *The Map of the Five Indian States in the West,* that shows relative location of cities in India and the pilgrimage route of Chinese monk Xuanzang.
103. Al-Idrīsī, *Nuzhat al-mushtāq fī ikhtirāq al-āfāq*, 98.
104. Ibid., 210.
105. For the China entry in original texts, see Yāqūt ibn ʿAbd Allāh al- Ḥamawī, *Muʿjam al-buldān* (Bayrūt, 1990), 500–509, and Yāqūt ibn ʿAbd Allāh al-Ḥamawī, *Yāqūt's Geographisches Wörterbuch: herausgegeben von Ferdinand Wüstenfeld* (Frankfurt am Main, 1994 [1866–1873]), 444–458.

106. For more information about Yāqūt and his works, see Khandkar M. ʻAbdur Rahman, "The Arab Geographer Yāqūt al-Rūmi," *Journal of the Asiatic Society* 3 (1958); Barbara Ostafin, "Yāqūt-Geographer, Compiler or Adīb? According to the Preface to his Dictionary," *Folia Orientalia* 30 (1994); Fuat Sezgin, ed., *Studies on Yāqūt al-Ḥamawī (d. 1229)* (Frankfurt am Main, 1994).
107. See Biran, *The Qara Khitai Empire in Eurasian History.*
108. Muḥammad ibn Najīb Bākran (flourished 1208), *Jahān-nāmah* (Tehran: Ibn-I Sīnā, 1963 [1342]), 15.
109. Ibid., 71–72.

3. Interpreting the Mongol World

1. On Jin dynasty rule in northern China, see Tao Jing-shen, *The Jurchen in Twelfth-Century China: a Study of Sinicization* (Seattle: University of Washington Press, 1977); and Hoyt Cleveland Tillman and Stephen West, eds., *China under Jurchen Rule* (Albany: State University of New York Press, 1995).
2. There were diplomatic exchanges between the Jin dynasty and the Mongols from the early 1200s. Some of those who traveled to the Mongol regions provide valuable information about the Mongols and other peoples, including Muslims living in the regions conquered by the Mongols. One surviving account is *Beishi ji* [Notes on an Embassy to the North] (early thirteenth century) by Liu Yu, who recorded Wugusun Zhongdan's description of his travels to see Chinggis Khan in Central Asia for peace negotiations. A more detailed informant was the Daoist monk Qiu Chuji 邱處機 (1148–1227), also called Changchun 長春, who around 1220 traveled by invitation from China via Samarkand to Chinggis Khan's camp in the north of Hindu Kush Mountains. One of his disciples, Li Zhichang, wrote *Changchun zhenren xiyou ji* [The Travels of an Alchemist] (1224?) based on Qiu's trip. Li Zhichang's account provides vivid details about Muslim society and cultures in Samarkand, including Muslim practices such as not depicting people in temple decoration, the orientation of the heads of the deceased towards the west for burial, the role of *Dashima* 大石馬 (Danishmand, meaning scholars or monks in Persian?) in Samarkand as *Muaddin* [a person who leads the call (*adhan*) to Friday service and the five daily prayers from one of the mosque's minarets], and fasting during Ramadan. See Li Chih-Ch'ang, *The Travels of an Alchemist – The Journey of the Taoist Ch'ang-Ch'un From China to the Hindukush at the Summons of Chingiz Khan*, trans. Arthur Waley (London, 1931).
3. The travel account was included in Wang Yun's *Qiujian xuansheng da quanwen ji: Yutang jiahua*, and Tao Zongyi's *Shuofu*, both published in the Mongol period, and in several later works. Bretschneider compared the texts of four different editions of the account and reconstructed the complete original account in order to translate it. See Bretschneider, vol.1, 109–156, which provides an introduction to the text and an English translation

with annotations and footnotes. For an English translation of direct quotations in the book, I used the Zhonghua shuju edition of Wang Yun's *Yutang jiahua*, which is the first Yuan dynasty text that contained this account. Compare also Liu Yu, *Xishi ji* (Shanghai, 1936), 1–4.

4. Wang Yun, 60. Compare Bretschneider, vol.1, 138–139.
5. For other contemporaneous sources on this event, see J. A. Boyle, "The Death of the Last 'Abbāsid Caliph: a Contemporary Muslim Account," *Journal of Semitic Studies* 6 (1961), 145–161; David Morgan, *The Mongols* (Oxford, 2007 [1986]), 132–133. Liu Yu's calculation of the years of the Caliphate as "more than six hundred years under forty rulers" probably includes the period of the four caliphsand both the Ummayad and Abbasid caliphates (total 627 years under fifty rulers).
6. Wang Yun, 60–61.
7. We have seen in earlier chapters that, soon after the 'Abbāsid dynasty's apogee in the ninth century, it began to lose control. Around 900, many regional Islamic provinces, which had been established in the course of the Muslim conquests, began to ignore the political authority of the Abbasid caliphate. The Islamic world unified under the authority of the Abbasid caliphs, which could be considered an ideal *umma*, began to decentralize. Different political entities, however, continued to acknowledge the religious, but not political, authority of the caliph in Baghdad.
8. Wang Yun, 61.
9. For more details about the history of this region from the seventh century to the fourteenth century, see John Limbert, *Shiraz in the Age of Hafez: The Glory of a Medieval Persian City* (Seattle, 2004).
10. R. A. Donkin, *Beyond Price: Pearls and Pearl-fishing: Origins to the Age of Discoveries* (Philadelphia, 1998), 119–129.
11. Bretschneider argued that Liu Yu mistakenly considered Egypt as the country of *Fulin* 拂秣 (the Byzantine empire), mentioned in the official history of the Tang dynasty. Bretschneider, vol. 1, 156. Egypt had belonged to the Byzantine empire until it was conquered by the Arabs in the seventh century; Liu Yu probably used an outdated source for this.
12. See endnote3 in Chapter 3.
13. *YS*, 149:3523–3526; Bretschneider, vol. 1, 111–156.
14. After making a comparison between the two accounts regarding some major differences in the descriptions, Bretschneider thinks both reports were probably written independently. His point about the spelling differences of some proper names is valid. Bretschneider, vol.1, 111. For example, *Bao-da* 報達 (Baghdad; here the 'Abbāsid dynasty) and *Mi-qi-er* 密乞兒 (Misr; Egypt) in *Xishi ji* are presented as *Xirong* (Western "barbarians") and *Mi-xi-er* 密昔兒 in *The History of the Yuan*. *YS*, 149:3524.
15. Bretschneider, vol. 1, 139; *YS*, 149:3524. Qiu Yihao suggests that Zhou-da-er 紂答儿 is probably a misspelling of 討答儿 Tao-da-er, which could be an official title called Dawatdar (literally, Holder of Sultan's ink bottle). A contemporaneous Persian source (Naṣir al-Din Ṭūsi's report on the collapse of Baghdad) testifies that, when Baghdad collapsed, a Dawatdar tried to escape by ship yet failed and was eventually killed. "Ze͟yl K͟hwāja Naṣir

al-Dīn Ṭūsī bar Jahāngūshā'ī-yi Juwaynī," *Tārīkh-i Jahāngūšā'ī*, ed. Qazwīnī (Leyden: Brill, 1937), 384–385.

16. For a succinct overview of the Mongol conquest of the Islamic world and the continuing Mongol influences and legacy in the subsequent periods, see Michal Biran, *Chinggis Khan: Makers of the Muslim World* (Oxford, 2007).
17. Michal Biran, "The Mongols in Central Asia from Chinggis Khan's invasion to the rise of Temür: Ögödeid and Chaghadaid realms," in *The Cambridge History of Inner Asia,* vol. 2: *The Chinggisid Age* (Cambridge, 2009), 46–66.
18. Morgan, *The Mongols*, 138–139. For another of Khubilai's rivals, Qaidu (died 1301: a grandson of the second Mongol Khan Ögedei), and the wars between different Mongol khanates leading to Qaidu, see Michal Biran, *Qaidu and the Rise of the Independent Mongol State in Central Asia* (Richmond, 1997).
19. For a succinct overview of the continuing political, diplomatic, and economic relations of the Yuan dynasty and the Il-khanate throughout these regimes, see Thomas T. Allsen, *Culture and Conquest in Mongol Eurasia* (Cambridge, 2001), 17–56. Allsen explains that an important factor to maintaining economic ties between the two societies was the fact that the Il-khanate kept land assigned by the Great Khans from earlier Mongol conquests in China, such as that in Zhangde (Chang-te) in Hunan province, and maintained formalized economic exchanges between the two courts. See Allsen, *Culture and Conquest*, 43–50. As Allsen has continually shown in the second half of this volume, there were many exchanges in various fields between the Yuan and the Il-khanate in Iran.
20. Sugiyama, *Yūbokumin kara mita sekaishi* (Tokyo, 1997), 314–317.
21. When the Mongols attacked the Song, Pu Shougeng shifted sides by providing them with the strong naval forces under his control. Due to the crucial role that Pu Shougeng played in the final victory of the Mongols against the Song navy, the Mongol government promoted him to supervisor of the Maritime Trade Superintendency (*tiju shibo* 提擧市舶), the most important position in charge of maritime trade.
22. Most scholars agree that Pu Shougeng was Muslim. For opinions about his origins, see Leslie, *Islam in Traditional China*, 66. For more details about Pu Shougeng, see Kuwabara Jitsuzō, "On P'u Shou-keng," *Memoirs of the Research Department of the Tōyō Bunko* 2 (1928): 1–79 and (1935):1–104, as well as a new edition of collected articles in original Japanese, *Ho Jukō no jiseki*; Luo Xianglin, *Pu Shougeng yanjiu* (Hong Kong, 1959); Geoff Wade, "The Li (李) and Pu (蒲) 'surnames' in East Asia-Middle East Maritime Silkroad Interactions during the 10th-20th Centuries," *Aspects of the Maritime Silk Road*, ed. Ralph Kauz (Wiesbaden, 2010), 181–193.
23. Instead of following Kuwabara Jitsuzō's accepted theory (1928) about the crucial role of Pu in the fall of the southern Song, Billy So emphasizes the support of the influential local elite. His argument adds a new insight on the recently re-envisioned Song local elite: With close connections to the foreign residents of Quanzhou, they cooperated with the Mongol invaders in order

to preserve their family interests. In his reassessment of socio-political economic studies, So draws on broader literature about Quanzhou during the Song and Yuan periods, as is seen in his incorporation of memorials, local gazetteers, and poems for the wine industry. See So, *Prosperity, Region, and Institutions in Maritime China*, 80–81.

24. David Bade, *Khubilai Khan and the Beautiful Princess of Tumapel* (Ulaanbaatar, 2002), 18–32.
25. Allsen, *Culture and Conquest*, 189.
26. See Wang Jianping, *Concord and Conflict: the Hui Communities of Yunnan Society* (Stockholm, 1996), 43–53.
27. Thomas Allsen, *Commodity and Exchange in the Mongol Empire: A Cultural History of Islamic Textiles* (Cambridge, 1997).
28. Although Khubilai invited Chinese elites into the Mongol government and adopted much Chinese tradition such as dramas and arts, he also kept Mongol customs and consulted with many foreigners. See Morris Rossabi, *Khubilai Khan: His Life and Times* (Berkeley, 1988), 177–205.
29. The two officials previously mentioned had a large impact on Chinese society for both good and bad. Scholars like Yang Zhijiu began to reassess Aḥmad, stressing his contribution to the Yuan fiscal policy as well as his personal virtues such as steady spirit, honesty, concern for relationships, and elegant taste. See a biography of Aḥmad in Yang Zhijiu, *Yuanshi sanlun* (Beijing, 1985). Also see H. Franke, "Aḥmad (?–1282)," in *In the Service of the Khan* (Wiesbaden, 1993), 539–557. For a detailed discussion of Sayyid ʿAjall Shams al-Dīn, see Jacqueline Misty Armijo-Hussein, "Sayyid ʿAjall Shams al-Dīn: A Muslim From Central Asia, Serving the Mongols in China, and Bringing 'Civilization' to Yunnan" (PhD dissertation: Harvard University, MA, 1996). For an examination of the Muslims in the early Yuan dynasty, see Morris Rossabi, "The Muslims in the Early Yuan Dynasty," in *China under Mongol Rule* (Princeton, 1981), 257–295. For biographies of more Muslims working in the Yuan court, see Bai Shouyi and Yang Huaizhong, eds., *Huizu renwu zhi*, vol. 1 (Yinchuan, 1985).
30. *Huihui* probably stemmed from *Huihe* 回紇 or *Huihu* 回回鶻, indicating the Turkish Uighurs, who also came to China and served the Mongols in core administrative roles. Sometimes the word Huihui seems to include people from the western ethnic origins in a broader sense. The official history of the Yuan dynasty also called the countries of Muslims coming to China for trade via the sea route the country of Huihui instead of an earlier designation, the country of Dashi. See *YS*, 210:4671. For a detailed discussion about the conditions and process of the migration of the Muslims to China, see Ma Jianchun, *Yuandai dongqian xiyuren jiqi wenhuayanjiu* (Beijing, 2003). For a brief discussion about changes in the names of the Muslims designated by the Chinese from the Tang to the Yuan dynasty, see E. Bretschneider, "Chinese Medieval Notices of Islam," *The Moslem World* 19, no. 1 (January 1929): 52–61. For a discussion about the changing circulation of the name "Huihui" among the Chinese and the Muslims during the Yuan period, see Wang Jianping, 125–126. For overall details about the Muslims in China during the Yuan dynasty, see the classic work by Tazaka Kōdō, *Chūgoku ni okeru kaikyō no denrai to sono gutsū*, vol.1 (Tokyo, 1964), 557–852.

31. Liu Yingsheng, "A Lingua Franca along the Silk Road: Persian Language in China between the 14th and the 16th Centuries," *Aspects of the Maritime Silk Road*, ed. Ralph Kauz (Wiesbaden, 2010), 87–95.
32. YS, 40:2297. A well-known contemporaneous source, the *Compendium of Chronicles* (*Jāmiʿ al-tawārīkh*) by the Persian historian Rashīd al-Dīn (1247–1318), which we will examine in Chapter 4, mentions a certain Jamāl al-Dīn Muḥammad ibn Ṭāhir ibn Muḥammad al-Zaydī from Bukhara (in modern-day Uzbekistan) who was active during the reign of the fourth grand Khan Möngke (1251–1259). It is possible that the two Jamāl al-Dīn's are the same person. *JT*, 502.
33. Based on the fact that Jamāl al-Dīn was already active in the Islamic Astronomical Bureau in 1267, he probably came to China from the Islamic world in the early years of the Mongol conquest or right after the establishment of the Il-khanate in 1259. For a discussion about his activities and works based on fragmented information in the documents of the Yuan dynasty, see Bai Shouyi, *Huizu renwu zhi*, 73–88.
34. Wang Shidian, *Mishujian zhi* (Hangzhou, 1992).
35. Miyajima Kazuhiko, "Genshi tenmonshi kisai no isuramu tenmongiki ni tsuite," in *Tōyō no kagaku to gijutsu* (Kyoto, 1982), 410.
36. See *YS*, 48:998–999.
37. For more discussion about why Wei Yuan collected this map, see Hyunhee Park, "Cross-Cultural Exchange and Geographic Knowledge of the World in Yuan China," in *Eurasian Influences on Yuan China: Cross-Cultural Transmissions in the 13th and 14th Centuries* (Singapore, 2011).
38. Its grids are described as follows: "[The surface of] it [the globe] is divided into small grids, by which we can measure the size of the entire area and the distance of the space." *YS*, 48:999. For more details about the globe, see Ma Jianchun, "Yuandai dongchuan huihui dili xue kaoshu," *Huihui yanjiu* 45, no. 1 (2002): 15–16.
39. These are Tianzhu (India), Tubote 土伯特 (Tibet), Yutian 于闐 (Khotan in Xinjiang), and Shazhou 沙州 (Dunhuang). Wei Yuan, *Haiguo tuzhi*, 221.
40. See the preface of *Da yitong zhi* in Xu Youren, *Zhizheng ji* (Taipei, 1978), 35: 41–61. For discussions on the compilation of *Dayuan da yitong zhi*, see Ma Jianchun, "Yuandai dongchuan huihui dili xue kaoshu," 14–18; Miya Noriko, "'Kon'itsu kyōri rekidai kokuto no zu' eno michi: 14 seiki shimei chiho no 'chi' no yukue," *Mongoru jidai no shuppan bunka* (Nagoya, 2006), 517–523.
41. Wang Shidian, *Mishujian zhi*, 4:74. The original text is written in colloquial Chinese, a translation of the Mongolian language. I consulted Miya Noriko's Japanese translation and Kim Hodong's Korean translation into English. Compare Kim Hodong, "A Portrait of a Christian Official in China under the Mongol Rule: Life and Career of 'Isa Kelemechi (1227–1308)," *Chung'ang Asia Yŏn'gu* 11 (2006):102, and Miya Noriko, *Mongoru jidai no shuppan bunka*, 520.
42. The original copy is lost, yet two later copies have been preserved in Japan – the earliest one dated 1470 is preserved in the library of Ryūkoku University, and the second one dated between 1673 and 1680 is preserved in the Honkō Temple in the city of Shimabara. Two later maps entitled "the map of the

great Ming Empire" (*Dai Ming koku chizu / Dai Ming koku zu*), also preserved in Japan, are almost the same as the copies of the 1402 map except for a few minor differences – one dated the late sixteenth century preserved in the Honmyō Temple in the city of Kumamoto and the other one preserved in the library of the Tenri University whose date is unknown. These maps do not have Gwon Geun's afterword, and they do contain place-names not found in the copies of the 1402 map, such as the Arctic Ocean and some islands in the Indian Ocean. Despite these differences, the contours of the continents in these maps are almost identical to the copies of the 1402 map, and therefore, it is possible that Japanese cartographers used a copy of the 1402 map to draw these later maps and added information obtained from foreigners, probably Europeans. For the most detailed analysis of the copies of the 1402 map, its sources, and possible transfer routes of the original Chinese geographic information into Korea and Japan, see Miya, "'Kon'itsu kyōri rekidai kokuto no zu' eno michi," 487–651. See also Sugiyama Masa'aki, "Tōzai no sekaizu ga kataru jinrui saisho no dai chihei," *Daichi no Shōzō – Ezu・Chizu ga kataru sekai* (Kyoto, 2007), 54–69; see also color maps in the volume. Also see Walter Fuchs, *The "Mongol atlas" of China by Chu Ssu-pen, and the Kuang-yü-t'u* (Peiping, 1946), 10; Gari Ledyard, "Cartography in Korea," in *The History of Cartography, Volume Two, Book Two*, 244–249; Unno, *Tōyō chirigaku shi kenkyū*, 211–223 for a brief introduction and analyses in English.

43. Gwon Geun's afterword is also in his literary collection. Gwon Geun, *Yangchon jip* (Seoul: Sol, 1997), 22: 2 [60] (Chinese), 165–166 (Korean).
44. See further discussions about this possibility in Chapter 4.
45. See endnote 18in Chapter 5.
46. According to traditional Chinese cosmology, the world is divided into the heaven (*tian*) and the earth (*di*), and the earth is again divided into China (*Hua*) and non-China (*Yi*). The heaven is spherical and the earth is quadrangle (*Tianyuan difang*). Ohji Toshiaki, "Indo yō no rikufū to kaihō," in *Daichi no Shōzō*, 46–47.
47. Zhao Rugua also mentioned the Pharos lighthouse of Alexandria in his *Zhufan zhi* (see Chapter 1); al-Khwārizmī's representation of the sources of Nile was influenced by that of Ptolemy's geographic works. Florian Mittenhuber, "The Tradition of Texts and Maps in Ptolemy's Geography," in *Ptolemy in Perspective*, 114–115.
48. *Ma-li-xi-li-na* 麻里昔里那.
49. The names in original Chinese are *Shan-ma-na-si* 山麻那思, *Bu-he-la* 不哈剌, *Ma-na-he* 麻那合, *Da-la-bu-luo-si* 達剌不羅思, *Pa-he-da* 八合打, *Ma-he* 馬喝, *He-dan* 哈丹, and *Shi-la-si* 失剌思. The transliteration of the place-names into Chinese is quite accurate. For example, Marseille was called Massalia in Latin at that time. For a detailed analysis of the place-names and their locations in West Asia, Central Asia, and Europe, see the chart in Sugiyama, "Tōzai no sekaizu ga kataru jinrui saisho no dai chihei," 58–59.
50. Wang Shidian, *Mishujian zhi*, 4:72–91.
51. Popular circulating copies of *Shuidong riji* (*The Diary from East of the River*) by Ye Sheng (1420–1474) only mention this map, yet do not contain

a copy. Recently Miya Noriko found copies of the map in some versions of the account including one preserved in the Library of Congress. She identified this map with the lost *Hunyi jiangli tu* [Map of Integrated Regions and Terrains], which was a source for the Korean map. For more discussion, see Miya Noriko, *Mongoru jidai no shuppan bunka*, Plate 12, 489–503.

52. The island of Hormuz as "New-Hormuz" is different from "Old-Hormuz," the former capital of the Hormuzian kingdom on the mainland near Mīnāb that was more exposed to external raids. Ralph Kauz and Roderich Ptak, "Hormuz in Yuan and Ming Sources," *Bulletin de l'École Française d'Extrême-Orient* 88 (2001): 31–35. See the entire article (27–75) for a detailed discussion of Hormuz before 1500 using both Chinese and West Asian sources. Also see Jean Aubin, "Les princes d'Ormuz du XIIIe au XVe siècle," *Journal Asiatique* 241 (1953): 77–138.

53. Marco Polo also visited Hormuz, which he describes as a flourishing international sea port to which merchants from all different parts of the world traveled with their ships for trade. Hormuz was also a point where both the maritime and the revived overland portions of long-distance trade merged. Ralph Kauz and Roderick Ptak point out that this description of Marco Polo's account is very similar to that of a contemporaneous account by Waṣṣāf. Kauz and Ptak, "Hormuz in Yuan and Ming Sources," 35–36.

54. Before the Yuan dynasty, only the sea shipping system had been used to transfer many goods during times of war or emergency. For more details on the sea shipping system of the Yuan dynasty, see Aritaka Iwao, "Gendai no Kaiun to Dai Gen Kaiun ki," *Tōyō gakuhō* 7 (1917), 411–424.

55. Chen Gaohua, *Yuan Dadu* (Beijing, 1982); Sugiyama, *Bunmei no michi*, 74–87; Sugiyama Masa'aki, *Shikkusuru sōgen no seifukusha, Ryō, Seika, Kin, Gen* (Tokyo, 2005), 341–343.

56. Khubilai dispatched Yang Tingbi and a Uighur Yiheimishi (Yighmish) to Malabar, in South India, as envoys between 1279 and 1283. See *YS*, 12:245 and 210:4669–4670 for Yang Tingbi and 131:3198–3200 for Yiheimishi. For an examination of the dispatch of these envoys to India by the Yuan government in the broader context of the relations between the Yuan dynasty and India, see Tansen Sen, "The Yuan Khanate and India: Cross-Cultural Diplomacy in the Thirteenth and Fourteenth Centuries," *Asia Major* 1/2, part 1/2 (2006): 299–326. These are also cited in Chen Gaohua, "Yuandai de hanghai shijia Ganpu yangshi," *Haijiaoshi yanjiu* 1 (1995): 4–18.

57. *Ortaq* in Persian and *wotuo* in Chinese. For more detailed arguments on the *ortagh*, see Allsen, "Mongolian Princes and Their Merchant Partners," 83–126; Endicott-West, "Merchants Associations in Yüan China: The *Ortoγ*," 127–154; Sugiyama Masa'aki, *Mongoru teikoku no kōbō*, vol. 2 (Tokyo, 1996), 187–191.

58. *JT*, vol. II.

59. We should also check Persian sources to understand their activities. Chinese sources do not provide detailed information about the *ortagh* merchants, yet some sources, such as *Yuandianzhang*, hint at concrete activities of these merchants, for example, the pearl trade. See Yokkaichi Yasuhiro, "Gen-chō no chūbai hōka: sono igi oyobi nankai bō'eki-orutoku tono kakawarini

tsu'ite," *Nairiku Ajia shi kenkyū* 17 (2002): 41–59. Another contemporaneous source *Tongzhitiaoge* mentions the *ortagh* merchants in Quanzhou who voyaged and traded through the ocean to the Islamic world. *Tongzhi tiaoge* 通制条格, 27:45–46. The legal document forbids the merchants from buying the Mongol men or women to the Islamic world or India as slaves by maritime trade.

60. Some large *ortagh* merchant associations even functioned as general trading companies that deal with a wide range of products and materials as well as transportation and banking throughout the Mongol empire in Eurasia. Sugiyama, *Kubirai no chōsen*, 203–204.
61. See *YS*, 134:3266. See also Yokkaichi, "Gen-chō no chūbai hōka."
62. For a succinct argument about special characteristics that the Muslim communities gained thanks to the preferential Mongol policies toward Muslims and expanded maritime networks in the Yuan period, see Chaffee, "Diasporic Identities," 412–416.
63. I used the most recent publication of Muslim stone inscriptions to calculate this. Of a total of thirty-seven tombstones, only one inscription dates back to 1171 (the Song period), thirty-one date to the Yuan (1260–1368), and five to the first two decades of the Ming period (1368–1644). See *QZZJSK*.
64. See *QZZJSK*, 64–68.
65. See *QZZJSK*, 42–45. Wu located the tombstone among the Muslim graves in Lingshan 靈山, Dongtangtou 東塘頭, in the eastern suburb (*dongjiao* 東郊) of Quanzhou.
66. Chen Gaohua, "Yuandai de hanghai shijia Ganpu yangshi," 243. Many works, including those of Sugiyama Masa'aki and Yokkaichi Yasuhiro, discuss detailed evidence for the active involvement of the Yuan government in maritime trade, which far exceeded that of the previous southern Song government. A good example is the Yuan governmental-ship (*guanben chuan*) system, in which the government constructed sea-going vessels, funded, and recruited traders, and received 70 percent of the profit, the managers receiving 30 percent. The original purpose was to prohibit private merchants from trading, yet it did not work. *YS*, 94:2402.
67. For a detailed discussion of Yang Shu's family, see Wilt L. Idema, "The Tza-jiu of Yang Tz: An International Tycoon in Defense of Collaboration?" in *Proceedings on the Second International Conference on Sinology* (Taipei, 1989), 523–529.
68. Chen Gaohua, "Yuandai de hanghai shijia Ganpu yangshi," 243; Idema, "The Tza-jiu of Yang Tz," 526.
69. Chen Gaohua, "Yuandai de hanghai shijia Ganpu yangshi," 243. His epitaph, entitled "Songjiang jiaxing dengchu haiyun qianhu Yang jun muzhi ming 松江嘉興等處海運千戶楊君墓志銘," survived by virtue of its inclusion in Huang Jin's *Jinhua Huang xuansheng wenji* (The Collection of Mr. Huang of Jinhua), Juan 35.
70. Sir Henry Miers Elliot, *The History of India, as Told by Its Own Historians: the Muhammadan Period* (Frankfurt am Main, 1997), 45–47.
71. Chen Dazhen, *Dade Nanhai zhi canben* (Guangzhou, 1986), 37–38.
72. The Chinese of the Yuan dynasty saw the East and West as divided by Java. See Liu Yingsheng, *Silu wenhua: Haishang juan* (Hangzhou, 1995), 146–148.

73. The book originally had a total twenty juan, yet only five juan (6–10) survive, by virtue of being included in *Guangzhou fu zhi* in the Ming dynasty *Yongle dadian*, juan 11905–11907. Although the first part treats the general situation of the society in Canton during the Yuan period, the remainder describes maritime traffic and foreign countries.
74. Chen Dazhen, 31.
75. Wang Dayuan, *Daoyi zhilüe* (Beijing, 1981), 1–11, 385.
76. He Qiaoyuan, *Minshu* (Fuzhou, 1995), 4362.
77. Ibid., 1. The following passage is from Sima Qian's biography of Zou Yan. "China that Confucian scholars call is one of eighty one parts of the world. China is called 'the godly province of red prefecture' (*chixian shenzhou* 赤縣神州). Inside 'the godly province of read prefecture' are nine provinces, and these are the nine provinces that is mentioned in the preface of the king of Wu 禹 ... Outside China are nine provinces like 'the godly province of read prefecture' and they are the nine provinces. Here, the sea of Pi 裨 is surrounding it, and people and beasts cannot not contact each other. One quarter forms one province, and things like this are nine. Inside these is the sea of the Great Sea (Daying hai 大瀛海) which surrounds them, and this is the border between the heaven and the earth." Sima Qian, 74:2344.
78. The authoritative Chinese-centered worldview had been influential since the ancient geographic account of *Yugong*. Yee, "Chinese Maps in Political Culture," *HC2:2*, 76.
79. Wang Dayuan, *Daoyi zhilüe*, 385.
80. Ibid., 5.
81. Roderich Ptak, "Wang Dayuan on Kerala," *Explorations in the History of South Asia: Essays in Honour of Eietmar Rothermund* (New Delhi, 2001), 40; Philip Snow, *The Star Raft: China's Encounter with Africa* (New York, 1988), 17; William Rockhill, however, considered the book a personal and trustworthy account, thus distinguished from similar Chinese works in the earlier periods such as *Lingwai daida* [1178] and *Zhufan zhi* [1226]. William Rockhill, "Notes on the Relations and Trade of China with the Eastern Archipelago and the Coast of the Indian Ocean during the Fourteenth Century," Part II, *T'oung Pao 15* (1914), 62.
82. He Qiaoyuan, 4362.
83. Rossabi, "Mongol Empire and its Impact on the Arts of China," prepared for Conference at the Hebrew University, June, 2006.
84. Ibid. For an argument about the creation of blue-and-white porcelain caused by the Mongol conquest of Eurasia and China's increased contacts with the Islamic world, see Yuba, "Gen seika jiki to Mongoru teikoku."
85. See Misugi Takatoshi, *'Gen no sometsuke' umi wo wataru: sekai ni hirogaru yakimono bunka* (Tokyo, 2004); Priscilla Soucek, "Ceramic Production as Exemplar of Yuan-Ilkhanid Relations," *Res* 35 (Spring 1999): 125–141.
86. About debates on interpreting the Chinese name Ganmaili 甘埋里 into Hormuz, see Kauz and Ptak, "Hormuz in Yuan and Ming Sources," 29–30, 42–45.
87. Wang Dayuan, *Daoyi zhilüe*, 364. Also compare an updated English translation of the section about Hormuz in "Hormuz in Yuan and Ming Sources," 39–40.
88. Ptak, "Wang Dayuan on Kerala," 47. Compare Wang Dayuan, 321.

89. Wang Dayuan, *Daoyi zhilüe*, 364.
90. *The Official History of the Ming* (Mingshi) says, "during the Yuan period, the Muslims had spread to all over China." *MS*, 332:8598.
91. Zheng Sixiao (1241–1318), *Zheng Sixiao ji*, 184. Another Chinese writer, Tao Zongyi (1329–1412), also includes similar disdaining descriptions about Muslims whom he observed. Leslie, *Islam in Traditional China*, 92–93. Also see Tazaka, *Chūgoku ni okeru kaikyō no denrai to sono gutsū*, 813–852, for the Chinese accounts of the Muslim communities.
92. Zhou Mi, *Guixin zashi* (Beijing, 1988), 138, 142–143, 254.
93. The Chinese characters Dashi 大實 have a similar pronunciation to 大食, that are used more frequently. There are other similar cases, such as 大石.
94. *QZZJSK*, 17; *QZIJSK*, 9 (for classical Chinese text) of the Chinese section and 13–14 (for English translation) of the English section. For detailed information on when and how the stele was found, see Maejima, "The Muslims in Ch'üan-chou at the End of the Yüan dynasty, Part 1," *Memoirs of the Research Department of the Tōyō Bunko* 31 (1973): 27–51.
95. *QZZJSK*, 17; *QZIJSK*, 9 and 14.
96. *She* 摄 *Silian* 思廉 *Buluhanding* 不魯罕丁.
97. *Shelafuding* 舍剌甫丁 *Hetibu* 哈悌卜.
98. *QZZJSK*, 17; *QZIJSK*, 9 and 14.
99. *QZZJSK*, 17–18; *QZIJSK*, 9 and 15.

4. Beyond Marco Polo

1. B. Spuler, "The Disintegration of the Caliphate in the East," in *The Cambridge History of Islam*, vol. 1A (Cambridge, 1970), 143–174.
2. Morgan, *The Mongols*, 15–16.
3. Interestingly, this was only three years before the Chinese scholar produced the first Chinese description of the event, *Xishi ji*.
4. "'Alā' al-Dīn 'Aṭā Malik Juwaynī", *The History of the World-Conqueror*, translated from the text of Mirza Muhammad Qazvini by John Andrew Boyle (Cambridge, MA, 1958).
5. Bernard Lewis, "Egypt and Syria," in *The Cambridge History of Islam*, vol. 1A, 175–230.
6. Allsen, *Culture and Conquest*, 43–50.
7. A. Bausani, "Religion under the Mongols," in *The Cambridge History of Islam*, vol. 5, 541–543.
8. For the patronage to the Maragheh observatory given by Hülegü long before Mongol Islamization, see George Lane, *Early Mongol Rule in Thirteenth-Century Iran: A Persian Renaissance* (London, 2003), 213–225.
9. George Saliba, *A History of Arabic Astronomy: Planetary Theories during the Golden Age of Islam* (New York, 1995).
10. For a comprehensive study of Persian and Arabic literature during the Mongol period, see Edward G. Browne, *A History of Persian Literature under Tartar Ddominion (A.D. 1265–1502)* (Cambridge, 1920).
11. See G. Lazard, "The Rise of the New Persian Language," in *The Cambridge History of Islam*, vol. 4, 595–632.

12. See the many Arabic maps made since the Mongol period in Miller, vol. 5.
13. Hopkins, "Geographic and Navigational Literature," 320–321.
14. Filled with illustrations, this treatise enjoyed great popularity and therefore was frequently reproduced, so that copies exist today. Its novelty lies in its methodical arrangement. The two parts of the work deal with celestial and terrestrial matters. See T. Lewicki, "Ḳazwīnī," *EI2*, 4: 865–867.
15. See Tibbetts, "Later Cartographic Developments," 144–145.
16. Morgan, *The Mongols*, 16–17.
17. For a short biography of Rashīd al-Dīn, see Dorothea Krawulsky, *The Mongol Īlkhāns and their Vizier Rashīd al-Dīn* (Frankfurt am Main: Peter Lang, 2011), 119–134.
18. For its value as the first systematic and comprehensive history of the known world, see Allsen, *Culture and Conquest*, 83–102.
19. *JT*, 6. The Arabic version of Rashīd al-Dīn does not survive, and I am unable to read the book in the original Persian. Therefore, I have used W. M. Thackston's English translation for direct quotations. I have also consulted Hodong Kim's Korean translation which is based on a manuscript held in the Topkapi Palace, Istanbul, which many scholars regard as the best available edition. There is no significant discrepancy in meaning between the passages from Thackston's translation that I quoted in this book and those of Hodong Kim's Korean translation based on the Topkapi manuscript. Compare Rashīd al-Dīn, *Rasid at din ui jipsa*, trans. Hodong Kim (Paju, 2002–2005).
20. For more details about the unity retained between the four Mongol khanates and occasional diplomatic contacts among them, see Kim Hodong, "The Unity of the Mongol Empire and Continental Exchanges over Eurasia," *Journal of Central Eurasian Studies* 1 (December 2009): 15–42.
21. *JT*, 11. The first volume is called *The History of Ghazan* and the second volume consists of "The History of Öljeitü" and histories of all the peoples in the earth since Adam.
22. For more details about the possible content of this geographic section and scholarly debates about whether the section was completed or not, see Allsen, *Culture and Conquest*, 103–104.
23. *JT*, 113.
24. Di Cosmo, *Ancient China and its Enemies*, 138–158.
25. *JT*, 113.
26. *JT*, 153.
27. See the sections about Khubilai Khan and his sons in *JT*, 421–470.
28. *JT*, 440.
29. During the Mongol period, the Mongols also called Māchīn Nankiyas and the Cathaians called it Manzī. For more discussions on various designations about China in medieval Islamic and European accounts, see *JT*, 154, and Paul Pelliot, *Notes on Marco Polo*, vol. 1 (Paris, 1959), 264–278.
30. Marco Polo, *The Travels of Marco Polo*, trans. Ronald Latham, 118.
31. On a discussion and city plan of Dadu, see Nancy Shatzman Steinhardt, *Chinese Imperial City Planning* (Honolulu, 1990), 154–160.
32. *JT*, 440.
33. *JT*, 441.

34. Charles O. Hucker, "shěng," in *A Dictionary of Official Titles in Imperial China*, 1st ed.
35. *JT*, 444.
36. *Da Yuan shengzheng guochao dianzhang* (Beijing, 1998), 22:943–954.
37. H. Franke, "Aḥmad (?-1282)," 539–557. See Chapter 3 for the Chinese accounts about Aḥmad.
38. ʿAlāʾ al-Dīn ʿAṭā Malik Juwaynī, *The History of the World-Conqueror*.
39. Allsen argues that he was a "cultural broker" and gives details about his coming to, and activities in, the Il-khanate. Allsen, *Culture and Conquest*, 59–80, 90–91.
40. Rashīd al-Dīn (1247–1318), *Die Chinageschichte des Rasīd al-Dīn*, trans. ed. by Karl Jahn (Vienna, 1971), Table 36. We can find more Chinese-style paintings in Iran in later periods. For example, a Persian miniature painting of the Turcoman school (circa 1470–1480) depicts in color not only Chinese people wearing Chinese-style dresses but also Chinese blue-and-white ware, one of the most important Chinese imports of the Mongol period. See the painting in Robert Irwin, "The Emergence of the Islamic World System: 1000–1500," in *The Cambridge Illustrated History of the Islamic World* (New York, 1996), 51.
41. For a biography of Rabban Sauma that places his journeys in the dynamic historical context of east-west contact during his time, see Morris Rossabi, *Voyager from Xanadu* (New York, 1992).
42. E. A. Wallis Budge, *The Monks of Ḳublai Khan, Emperor of China* (London, 1928), 56–57. The two monks ended up remaining in Baghdad for good.
43. For Marco Polo's account of a Mongol princess Kokaqin, who went from China to Iran around 1292 in order to become the consort of Ghazan Khan of the Il-khanate, see Igor de Rachewiltz, "Marco Polo Went to China," *Zentralasiatische Studien* 27 (1997): 34–92.
44. Elliot, *The History of India, as Told by Its Own Historians*, 45–47.
45. Qiu Yihao, "Yutu yuanzi haixi lai – Taolisi wenxuan jizhen suozai shijie ditu kao," *Xiyu yanjiu* 82, no. 2 (2011): 23–143.
46. It is not known whether Ḥamd Allāh Mustawfī had full access to Rashīd al-Dīn's *Compendium of Chronicles*.
47. Jonathan M. Bloom, "Lost in Translation: Gridded Plans and Maps along the Silk Road," in *The Journey of Maps and Images on the Silk Road*, 83–96; for more on the use of the grid in Chinese architecture, maps, printed books, and calligraphy in premodern China, see Ahmad, "Kharīṭa or Khāriṭa," *EI2*, 4:1081; Steinhardt, "Chinese Cartography and Calligraphy," 10–20.
48. Needham, "Geography and Cartography," 564.
49. Allsen, *Culture and Conquest*, 113.
50. Unno Kazutaka suggests the possibility of the direct influence of Ḥamd Allāh Mustawfī's map on the geographical map from *The Encyclopedia of Yuan-Dynasty Institutions*. Unno, *Chizu no bunkashi – sekai to nihon* (Tokyo, 1996), 51–52.
51. *NQ2*, 250.
52. Ibid.
53. Ibid., 250–251.

54. Ibid., 254.
55. Marco Polo, *The Description of the World,* trans. A. C. Moule and Paul Pelliot (London, 1938), 213.
56. Abū al-Fidā' al-Ḥamawī, *Kitāb Taqwīm al-buldān* (Frankfurt, 1985), 363–367. Compare Abū al-Fidā', *Géographie d'Aboulféda*, trans. Joseph-Toussaint Reinaud and annotated by Fuat Sezgin (Frankfurt am Main, 1998), 122–125.
57. Shams al-Dīn Muḥammad ibn Abī Ṭālib Dimashqī, *Nukhbat al-dahr fī 'ajā'ib al-barr wa-'l-baḥr* (Frankfurt am Main, 1994), 167–169, 265–266. Compare a French translation, *Manuel de la Cosmographie du Moyen Age,* trans. Mehren, M. A. F. (Frankfurt am Main, 1994), 226–230, 383–384.
58. Al-Idrīsī mentioned a similar place name, Ṣīniyyat al-Ṣīn, two centuries earlier, yet he meant a city in China by the place-name.
59. Dimashqī, *Nukhbat al-dahr fī 'ajā'ib al-barr wa-'l-baḥr*, 265–266. Compare Dimashqī, *Manuel de la Cosmographie du Moyen Age*, 384–385.
60. Ibn Faḍlallāh al-'Umarī's another volume on the Mongols includes a description of the "land of the great Khan." Ibn Faḍlallāh al-'Umarī (1301–1349), *Das mongolische Weltreich: al-'Umarīs Darstellung der mongolischen Reiche in seinem Werk Masālik al-abṣar fī mamālik al-amṣaār,* edited and translated by Klaus Lech (Wiesbaden: Otto Harrassowitz verlag, 1968). Lech identifies in his notes informants for al-'Umarī's information, many of which operated on the land routes with the Il-khanate.
61. The map for Caliph al-Ma'mūn was most likely drawn based on al-Khwārizmī's geographic treatise because al-Khwārizmī was one of the major scholars in Caliph al-Ma'mūn's academic institute, "The House of Wisdom." Fuat Sezgin argues that the map is an exact copy of the world map of Caliph al-Ma'mūn in the ninth century. *MGC1*, 86–90.
62. See the discussion of al-Khwārizmī's *Ṣūrat al-arḍ* (Shape of the Earth) in Chapter 2.
63. Ibn Faḍlallāh al-'Umarī, *Masālik al-abṣār fī mamālik al-amṣār* (Casablanca, 1988), 69–70.
64. Herodotus, *The Histories* (London, 2003), 253.
65. Fuat Sezgin thinks that Muslim seafarers traveled to West Africa before Bartolomeu Dias went to South Africa and found the Cape of Good Hope. He even argues that "[w]hen Portugal was still under Muslim protection, many Islamic explorers attempted to reach China from Lisbon on the western route across the Atlantic." Sezgin, *Science and Technology in Islam,* 20–21. Yet we could expect Islamic maps to show Africa more accurately if they had frequently traveled along the west coast of Africa.
66. *MGC1*, 565.
67. See the articles in Kenneth R. Hall, ed., *Secondary Cities and Urban Networking in the Indian Ocean Realm, c. 1400–1800* (Lanham, MD, 2008) and *The Growth of Non-Western Cities: Primary and Secondary Urban Networking, c. 900–1900* (Lanham, MD, 2011). These studies demonstrate that networks of small cities in the Indian Ocean realm, based not only on commercial trade but also on other factors such as political and religious ties, played an important role in integrating and maintaining regional connections and eventually contributing to global trade systems.

68. Aubin, "Les princes d'Ormuz du XIIIe au XVe siècle," 89–91; Kauz and Ptak, "Hormuz in Yuan and Ming Sources," 36; V. F. Piacentini, *Merchants – Merchandise and Military Power in the Persian Gulf (Sūriyānj/Shahriyāj – Sīrāf)* (Rome, 1992), 110–189.
69. Engseng Ho, *The Graves of Tarim. Genealogy and Mobility across the Indian Ocean* (Berkeley, 2006); Elizabeth Lambourn, "India from Aden: *Khuṭba* and Muslim Urban Networks in Late Thirteenth-Century India," in *Secondary Cities and Urban Networking in the Indian Ocean Realm, c. 1400–1800* (Lanham, MD, 2008), 55–97.
70. Kārimī merchants were active in earlier periods. Subhi Y. Labib, "Kārimī," *EI2*, 4: 640–643. For several Arabic sources that mention Kārimī's trade with China, see E. Ashtor, "The Kārimī Merchants," *Journal of the Royal Asiatic Society* (1956): 45–56.
71. For more details about the Kāzarūnī Sufi order and their role in Indian Ocean trade, see Ralph Kauz, "A Kāzarūnī Network?," *Aspects of the Maritime Silk Road* (Wiesbaden, 2010), 61–69.
72. J. N. Mattock, "Ibn Baṭṭūṭa's Use of Ibn Jubayr's Riḥla," in *Proceedings of the Ninth Congress of the Union Europeenne des arabisants et Islamisants* (Leiden, 1981), 211.
73. See Ross E. Dunn, *The Adventures of Ibn Battuta: A Muslim Traveler of the 14th Century* (Berkeley, 1986), 260.
74. Scholars generally accept the veracity of his trip to India. Yajima Hikoichi, *Ibun Battūta no sekai dai ryokō – 14 seiki Isurāmu no jikū wo ikiru* (Tokyo, 2003).
75. Ibn Baṭṭūṭa, 92. Compare Ibn Baṭṭūṭa/Gibb, 813–814.
76. The dates of these shipwrecks have been determined on the basis of the style of ceramics, dates on the coins they carried, and dates written on the wooden tags on the cargos they carried. After analyzing some of the artifacts found in the vessel, Korean archaeologists assume that the Sinan ship is a Mongol-Yuan dynasty ship that departed from Ningbo, Jiangsu, in China. On the way to its final destination (the port of Hakata in Japan), it was shipwrecked on the southwest coast of Korea. *The Conservation and Restoration of Shinan Ship, the 20 Years History* (Mokpo, 2004).
77. Yuan Xiaocun, "A study of the differences between the Sinan ship and ancient Chinese ships," in *The Conservation and Restoration of Shinan Ship, the 20 Years History*. This article includes a list of ancient Chinese shipwrecks. Also see Donald H. Keith and Christian J Buys, "New Light on Medieval Chinese Seagoing Ship Construction," *The International Journal of Nautical Archaeology and Underwater Exploration* 10, no. 2 (May 1981): 119–132.
78. Needham, "Nautical Technology," 420–422.
79. Marco Polo, *The description of the world*, 354–355. Compare Marco Polo, *The Travels of Marco Polo* (London, 1958), 241.
80. About some technical problems in the observation, see Yamagata, *Rekishi no umi wo hashiru*, 54–66.
81. Ibn Baṭṭūṭa, 93–94. Compare Ibn Baṭṭūṭa/Gibb, 814.
82. A total of 20,661 Chinese porcelains were found with the sunken Sinan ship, and many of these vessels were fired in famous kilns throughout China:

Jizhou kiln porcelain from Jiangxi province, Jingdezhen kiln porcelain from Jiangxi province, and Longquan kiln porcelain from Zhejiang province. *Conservation and Restoration Report of Shinan Ship*, 161–169.

83. Ibn Baṭṭūṭa, 254–268. Compare Ibn Baṭṭūṭa/Gibb, 888–894.
84. Hsiao Ch'i-ch'ing, "Mid-Yuan Politics," in *The Cambridge History of China*, vol. 6: *Alien Regimes and Border States, 907–1368* (Cambridge, 1994), 500–501.
85. J. A. Boyle, "Dynastic and Political History of the Īl-Khāns," in *The Cambridge History of Iran*, vol. 5 (London, 1968), 374–377.
86. Ibn Baṭṭūṭa, 268–269. Compare Ibn Baṭṭūṭa/Gibb, 894.
87. This was first noted by Zhang Xinglang in Zhang Xinglang, "Quanzhou fanggu ji," *Dili zazhi* 17, no. 1 (1928): 3–22. See Donald Daniel Leslie, *Islam in Traditional China*, 82. Some scholars like Donald Daniel Leslie and H. A. R. Gibb argue that this accurate report proves that Ibn Battuta went to China, yet I think he could as easily have learned these famous names from a secondhand source.
88. Ibn Baṭṭūṭa, 287. Compare Ibn Baṭṭūṭa/Gibb, 902.
89. Ibn Baṭṭūṭa, *The Travels of Ibn Battutah*, ed. Tim Mackintosh-Smith (London, 2003), xii-xiii.
90. *Muqaddimah*/Rosenthal, vol. 1, 369–372. Compare *Muqaddimah*, vol. 1, 310–311.

5. Legacy from Half the Globe before 1492

1. See Beatrice F. Manz, *The Rise and Rule of Tamerlane* (Cambridge, 1989).
2. Ma Huan/Mills, 69–70; for the original Chinese text, see Ma Huan, 1. Wan Ming argues that the *Account of the Non-Chinese Island Peoples* mentioned by Ma Huan here is a lost book by a Song-period author and is different from Wang Dayuan's *Daoyi zhilüe*. Yet Wan Ming also agrees that Wang Dayuan of the Yuan dynasty expanded the Song work based on his own sailing experiences. It is possible that Ma Huan had access to Wang Dayuan's work.
3. Robert Finlay, "The Treasure Ships of Zheng He: Chinese Maritime Imperialism in the Age of Discovery," *Terrae Incognitae* 23 (1991): 1–12.
4. On the Ottoman Turks's active struggle for global dominance during the Age of Exploration, and its efforts to launch a systematic ideological, military, and commercial challenge to Portugal in a contest for control over the lucrative trade routes of maritime Asia, see Giancarlo Casale, *The Ottoman Age of Exploration* (New York, 2010).
5. Hidehiro Okada, "China as a Successor State to the Mongol Empire," in *The Mongol Empire and its Legacy* (Leiden, 1999), 260–272; Frederick Mote and Denis Twitchett, eds., *The Cambridge History of China*, vol. 7: *The Ming Dynasty, 1368–1644*, Part 1 (Cambridge, 1988); David M. Robinson, "The Ming Court and the Legacy of the Yuan Mongols," in *Culture, Courtiers and Competition: the Ming Court (1368–1644)* (Cambridge MA, 2008), 365–421; Denis Twitchett and Frederick Mote, eds., *The Cambridge History of China*, Vol. 8: *The Ming Dynasty, 1368–1644*, Part 2 (Cambridge, 1998).

6. Wang Qianjin, Hu Qisong, and Liu Ruofang, "Juanben caihui daming hunyi yitu yanjiu," *ZGDJ/Ming*, 51–55.
7. The Manchus changed the Chinese names into the Manchu language by pasting new labels with Manchu place-names on the maps that were originally written in Chinese. See Wang Qianjin, "Juanben caihui daming hunyi yitu yanjiu," 51–52. The scholars in Kyoto University are currently interpreting the Manchu place-names and notes attached to the map. Miya Noriko, *Mongoru teikoku ga unda sekaizu* (Tokyo, 2007), 285–293.
8. Fuchs, *The "Mongol atlas" of China by Chu Ssu-pen, and the Kuang-yü-t'u;* Miya, "'Kon'itsu kyōri rekidai kokuto no zu' eno michi," 487–568. See also a reprint of the original maps and texts in Luo Hongxian, *Guang yutu.*
9. Zheng Hesheng and Zheng Yijun, eds., *Zheng He xiaxiyang ziliao huibian*, an expanded edition, 3 vols. (Jinan, 2005)], 1244, 1259.
10. During the period of political disunity in Japan from 1336 to 1392, many Japanese pirates came to plunder Chinese coasts. The remnants of the defeated rivals of the Ming emperor Hongwu also joined the pirates, and therefore, the Ming emperor had to enact strict maritime bans as defense measures. For further discussion of this topic and other diplomatic and economic reasons for the sea ban, see Chao Zhongchen, *Mingdai haijin yu haiwai maoyi* (Beijing, 2005), 30–45; Roderich Ptak, "Ming Maritime Trade to Southeast Asia, 1368–1567: Visions of a 'System,'" in *From the Mediterranean to the China Sea: Miscellaneous Notes* (Wiesbaden, 1998),159–160.
11. Ptak, "Ming Maritime Trade to Southeast Asia, 1368–1567," 157–191; Wang Gungwu, "Merchants without Empire: The Hokkien Sojourning Communities," in *The Rise of Merchant Empires. Long Distance-Trade in the Early Modern World, 1350–1750* (Cambridge, 1990), 400–421.
12. He Qiaoyuan, *Minshu*, 4362.
13. Manz, *The Rise and Rule of Tamerlane*, 73.
14. Morris Rossabi, "Two Ming Envoys to Inner Asia," *T'oung Pao* 62.1–3 (1976): 16–17.
15. For Chen Cheng's missions, see ibid., 1–34; Chan Hok-lam, "The Chien-wen, Yung-lo, Hung-his, and Hsüan-te reigns, 1399–1435," in *The Cambridge History of China,* vol. 7, 203–282, 223, 256–272; for the relations between the Ming and Inner Asia, see Morris Rossabi, "The Ming and Inner Asia," in *The Cambridge History of China,* vol. 8, 221–271.
16. Morris Rossabi, "From Chen Cheng to Ma Wensheng: Changing Chinese Visions of Central Asia," *Crossroads – Studies on the History of Exchange Relations in the East Asian World* 1 (Sept. 2010): 23–31.
17. An enormous quantity of primary sources and relevant secondary sources about Zheng He are already available in many languages, and Zheng He and his voyages have become a hotly debated topic in recent years. Among the many books about the topic published in China in 2005 to mark the 600th anniversary of the Zheng He voyages is an expanded edition of the collection of the source materials for Zheng He's travels to the Western Ocean. Zheng Hesheng, *Zheng He xiaxiyang ziliao huibian*. For the most recent English work on Zheng He, see Edward L. Dreyer, *Zheng He: China and the Oceans in the Early Ming Dynasty, 1405–1433* (New York, 2007).

18. For a discussion about Hormuz, one of the major destinations of Zheng He's last four voyages, see Kauz and Ptak, "Hormuz in Yuan and Ming Sources." See footnote 2 on page 28 for literature about the concrete evidence; in 2002, the retired British submarine commander Gavin Menzies argued in his best-seller *1421: The Year China Discovered America* that squadrons from the Zheng He fleets, between 1421 and 1423, did get to the Americas before Christopher Columbus – as well as to Greenland, Antarctica, Australia, and New Zealand. Gavin Menzies, *1421: The Year China Discovered America* (London, 2002). Although his claim brought the topic about Zheng He's voyages to sensation, many historians have refuted that because no extant sources tell its voyage to the Americas. For such a discussion, see Robert Finlay, "How Now to (Re)Write World History: Gavin Menzies and the Chinese Discovery of America," *Journal of World History* 15:2 (2004), 229–242.
19. Yamagata, *Rekishi no umi wo hashiru*, 68–70.
20. Chao Zhongchen, *Mingdai haijin yu haiwai maoyi*, 78–91.
21. We have seen in Chapter 3 that the Yuan government obtained a Muslim sea chart submitted by Muslim sailors.
22. Zheng He was a descendent of the famous governor Sayyid ʿAjall Shams al-Dīn during Khubilai's reign.
23. Ptak, "Ming Maritime Trade to Southeast Asia, 1368–1567," 160–165.
24. Kauz and Ptak, "Hormuz in Yuan and Ming Sources," 37.
25. The section about "going down to the Western Ocean (*xia xiyang*)" in Zhu Yunming's (1460–1526) *Qianwen ji* (Record about What I Heard Before) reports that the crew of the seventh voyage totaled 27,550 that included soldiers, pilots, steersmen, interpreters and translators, physicians, ship carpenters, and sailors. Miyazaki Masakatsu, *Te'iwa no nankai dai ensei: eiraku tei no sekai chitsujo saihen* (Tokyo, 1997), 93.
26. See Nanjing shi bowuguan, *Baochuanchang yizhi* (Beijing, 2006).
27. See Tang Zhiba, "Zheng He baochuan chidu zhi wojian," *Chuanshi yanjiu* 17 (2002): 21–27; Yamagata, *Rekishi no umi wo hashiru*, 67–75.
28. For the debates about the size of the Zheng He ships, see Finlay, "How Now to (Re)Write World History," 229–242; and Andre Wegener Sleeswyk, "The Liao and the Displacement of Ships in the Ming Navy," *The Mariner's Mirror* 82, no. 1 (February 1996): 3–13. Chinese and Japanese scholars including Yang You and Yamagata Kinya concur.
29. *Zheng He hanghai tu* (Beijing, 1961), 23–66.
30. Miyazaki, *Te'iwa no nankai dai ensei*, 172–174.
31. Ibid., 165–167. For more details about the Arab method of determining latitude by stellar measuring, see Alfred Clark, "Medieval Arab Navigation on the Indian Ocean: Latitude Determinations," *The Journal of the American Oriental Society* 113 (1993): 360–373; H. Congreve, "A Brief Notice of Some Contrivances Practiced by the Native Mariners of the Coromandel Coast, in Navigating, Sailing and Repairing their Vessels," in *Introduction: à L'astronomie Nautique Arabe* (Paris, 1928), 25–30; J. Prinsep, "Note on the Nautical Instrument of the Arabs," in *Introduction: à l'astronomie Nautique Arabe* (Paris, 1928), 1–24 (The article is originally from *JASB*, vol.5, 1836).

32. Congreve, "A Brief Notice of Some Contrivances," 26; Guangqi Sun and Chen Ying, "Shilun Zheng He suoxingshu zhongde alabo tianwen hanghai yinsu," in *Zheng He yanjiu lunwen ji*, vol.1 (Dalian, 1993), 389–399; also see Miyazaki, *Te'iwa no nankai dai ensei*, 163–167, 231; and Yamagata, *Rekishi no umi wo hashiru*, 75–79.
33. Fei Xin, *Xing cha sheng lan: the Overall Survey of the Star Raft*, trans. J. V. G. Mills (Wiesbaden, 1996), 30. Compare Fei Xin, *Xingcha shenglan jiaozuo* (Taibei, 1962), 10.
34. Fei Xin, *Xingcha shenglan Jiaozuo*, 25–37; Mikami Tsugio, *Ceramic Road*, 68–78; Misugi Takatoshi, *'Gen no sometsuke' umi wo wataru*, 172–174.
35. Ma Huan, 100–101. Compare Ma Huan/Mills, 174–176.
36. Ma Huan, 77–79. Compare Ma Huan/Mills, 152–153.
37. On the Arabic manuscript that Yajima Hikoichi found in *Bibliothèque Nationale* (Paris MS Arabe 4609, ff. 8b–74b) and its information about foreign vessels, including Chinese ships that came to Aden in the fifteenth century, see Yajima Hikoichi, "Jūgo seiki ni okeru indo yō tsūshōshi no hitokoma: teiwa'ensei buntai no iemen hōmon ni tsuite," *Ajia Afurika Gengo Bunka Kenkyū* 8 (1974): 137–155, see especially 139–148.
38. Ma Huan, 84. Compare Ma Huan/Mills, 158. Nine *chi*, which is around 28cm in the Ming period, is too short for two fore-feet of a giraffe, and the figure was probably a mistake.
39. Zheng Hesheng and Zheng Yijun, eds., *Zheng He xiaxiyang ziliao huibian*, 1361.
40. Ma Huan, 92. Compare Ma Huan/Mills, 165.
41. Piacentini, *Merchants – Merchandise and Military Power in the Persian Gulf*, 174–176.
42. Ma Huan, 1. Compare Ma Huan/Mills, 69–70.
43. See Map 3 at a front page of this volume.
44. Wang Gungwu, "Ming Foreign Relations: Southeast Asia," *The Cambridge History of China*, Vol. 8, 320–322.
45. Geoff Wade, The *Ming Shi-lu* as a source for Southeast Asian History, to accompany *Southeast Asia in the Ming Shi-lu: an open access resource* <http://epress.nus.edu.sg/msl>, 2005, 31.
46. Morgan, *The Mongols*, 139–151.
47. *Muqaddimah*/Rosenthal, vol.1, lxiii–lxiv.
48. *Muqaddimah*/Rosenthal, vol.1, 63–65. Compare *Muqaddimah*, vol.1, 45–47.
49. Except for some stylistic differences in the depiction of sea waves and mountains and a more crudely drawn coastline, this map looks nearly identical to the earlier version of al-Idrīsī's world map. *Muqaddimah*/Rosenthal, vol.1, a front page.
50. *Muqaddimah*/Rosenthal, vol.1, 109–127. Compare *Muqaddimah*, vol.1, 83–97.
51. *Muqaddimah*, vol.1, 90. Compare *Muqaddimah*/Rosenthal, vol.1, 117.
52. John Mercer, "The Canary Islanders in Western Mediterranean Politics," *African Affairs* 78, no. 311 (April 1979): 159.
53. *Muqaddimah*, vol.1, 90. Compare *Muqaddimah*/Rosenthal, vol.1, 117.

54. Ferrand, *Relations de Voyages*, 473–474. Compare an English translation in R. H. Major, *India in the Fifteenth Century: Being a Collection of Narratives of Voyages to India* (London, 1857), 5–7.
55. ʿAbd al-Razzāq also visited the Persian Gulf and India. See Sanjay Subrahmanyam, *The Career and Legend of Vasco da Gama* (New York, 1997), 100; W. M. Thackston, *A Century of Princes: Sources on Timurid History and Art* (Cambridge, MA, 1989), 299–321.
56. William C. Brice, "Early Muslim Sea-Charts," *Journal of the Royal Asiatic Society of Great Britain and Ireland* 1 (1977): 53–61.
57. Buzurg b. Shahriyar, *The Book of the Wonders of India.*
58. Ibn Mājid/Tibbetts, 3–4.
59. Hopkins, "Geographic and Navigational Literature," 324–327.
60. Ibn Mājid/Tibbetts, 9–10.
61. For a detailed discussion of Ibn Mājid's works, see Ibn Mājid/Tibbetts, 7–41.
62. Gabriel Ferrand, *Instructions Nautiques et Routiers Arabes et Portugais des XVe et XVIe siècles* (Paris, 1921).
63. Ibn Mājid/Tibbetts, 29. Of twelve sections, sections 1–8 and 11 show complicated science of navigation, difficult for general readers to follow if not familiar with basic navigational technical terms. Fuat Sezgin argues that the authors of the navigational accounts like Ibn Mājid preferred astronomical and mathematical procedures to knowledge acquired by experience. For further details and discussion, see Sezgin, *Mathematical Geography and Cartography in Islam and Their Continuation in the Occident*, Part 2, 157–264.
64. Ibn Mājid/Tibbetts, 272.
65. Ibn Mājid, 56–57. Compare Ibn Mājid/Tibbetts, 91–92.
66. Ibn Mājid/Tibbetts, 290. The Chinese float a fish-shaped piece of wood with magnetic content in a water basin to find out the direction that their ship should follow. For three types of compasses used in the Indian Ocean after 1500, see figures 47–52 in Sezgin, *Mathematical Geography and Cartography*, Part 2, 253–259.
67. See the ninth section for descriptions of the coasts of the world. Ibn Mājid, 265–288. Compare Ibn Mājid/Tibbetts, 204–216.
68. Ibn Mājid, 324–325. Compare Ibn Mājid/Tibbetts, 233.
69. Ibn Mājid/Tibbetts, 10; Subrahmanyam, 8–9.
70. Ibn Mājid/Tibbetts, 10; Subrahmanyam, 112–128.

Conclusion

1. An example is Chinese travel literature on Taiwan in the eighteenth and nineteenth centuries. See Emma Jinhua Teng, *Taiwan's Imagined Geography: Chinese Colonial Travel Writing and Pictures, 1683–1895* (Cambridge, MA: Harvard University Press, 2004).
2. For succinct reviews on the studies of the Mongol empire, see Peter Jackson, "The State of Research: The Mongol Empire, 1986–1999," *Journal of Medieval History* 26, no. 2 (2000): 189–210, and Morgan, *The Mongols*,

181–227. On a project to connect the pre-Mongol and post-Mongol periods, see Paul Smith and Richard von Glahn, eds., *The Song-Yuan-Ming Transition in Chinese History* (Cambridge, MA: Harvard University Press, 2003).

3. Sezgin, *Mathematical Geography and Cartography in Islam and Their Continuation in the Occident*, Part 2.
4. In her book *Before European Hegemony,* Janet Abu-Lughod described the flourishing Eurasian world economic system that peaked in the thirteenth and fourteenth centuries when a large number of Eurasian societies were under Mongol domination. This ambitious work, which covers many different societies, posed significant challenges to the existing Eurocentric world system theories (such as that by Wallerstein) that assumed that the world system had its origins in the sixteenth century under the lead of the Europeans. Despite its ambitious thesis, this work was less successful in using concrete examples, especially from Asia, to prove how societies were connected to the entire world system of the thirteenth century. Janet L. Abu-Lughod, *Before European Hegemony: the World System A.D. 1250–1350* (New York, 1989).
5. Skelton, *Explorer's Maps.*

Works Cited

Primary sources

ʿAbd al-Malik ibn Muḥammad Thaʿālibī (961 or 962–1037 or 1038). *The Book of Curious and Entertaining Information*. Translated by C. E. Bosworth. Edinburgh: Edinburgh University Press, 1968.

Abū al-Fidā' al-Ḥamawī (died 1331). *Géographie d'Aboulféda*. Translated by Joseph-Toussaint Reinaud and annotated by Fuat Sezgin. Frankfurt am Main: Institute for the History of Arabic-Islamic Science at the Johann Wolfgang Goethe University, 1998.

Kitāb Taqwīm al-buldān [The book of survey of the lands, circa 1321]. Frankfurt am Main: Institute for the History of Arabic-Islamic Science at the Johann Wolfgang Goethe University, 1985.

Abū-Zayd Ḥasan al-Ṣīrāfī (tenth century). *Aḫbar aṣ-Ṣin wa l-Hind. Relation de la Chine et de l'Inde rédigée en 851*. Translated by Jean Sauvaget. Paris: Belles Lettres, 1948.

Ancient Accounts of India and China by Two Mohammedan Travellers, Who Went to Those Parts in the 9th Century. Translated by Eusebius Renaudot. London: Sam. Harding at the Bible and Anchor on the Pavement in St. Martins-Lane, 1733.

Chūgoku to Indo no shojōhō 中国とインドの諸情報 [Various information about China and India]. Translated and annotated by Yajima Hikoichi 家島彦一. Tokyo: Heibonsha, 2007. 2 vols.

Relation des voyages faits par les Arabes et les Persans dans l'Inde et à la Chine dans le IXe siècle de l'ère chrétienne, Arabic text with French translation and commentary. Translated by M. Reinaud. Osnabruck: O. Zeller, 1988.

Aḥmad b. Mājid al-Najdī (flourished 1462–1498). *Arab Navigation in the Indian Ocean before the Coming of the Portuguese, being a translation of Kitāb al-fawā'id fī uṣūl 'ilm al-baḥr wa-l-qawā'id of Aḥmad b. Mājid al-Najdī*. Translated by G. R. Tibbetts. London: The Royal Asiatic Society of Great Britain and Ireland, 1971.

Kitāb al-fawā'id fī uṣūl 'ilm al-baḥr wa-l-qawā'id [The book of profitable things concerning the first principles and rules of navigation]. Dimashq: al-Maṭba'ah al-Ta'āwunīyah, 1971.

Ahmad, S. Maqbul. *Arabic Classical Accounts of India and China.* Shimla: Indian Institute of Advanced Study, 1989.

Ahmad, S. Maqbul, ed. *Al-Mas'ūdī: Millenary Commemoration Volume.* Aligarh: Indian Society for the History of Science, 1960.

Arabian Nights: The Marvels and Wonders of the Thousand and One Nights. Translated by Richard F. Burton, and edited by Zack Zipes. New York: Signet Classic, 1991. 2 vols.

Bākran, Muḥammad ibn Najīb (flourished 1208). *Dzhakhān name (Kniga o mire)* [World book]. Edited by Iu. E. Borshchevskii. Moscow: Izdatel'stvo vostochnoi literatury, 1960.

Jahān-nāmah [World book]. Tehran: Ibn-I Sīnā, 1963.

Bretschneider, Emil (1833–1901). *Mediaeval Researches from Eastern Asiatic Sources: Fragments towards the Knowledge of the Geography and History of Central and Western Asia from the 13th to the 17th Century.* London: Routledge & Kegan, 1910 [1888]. 2 vols.

Budge, E. A. Wallis, Sir (1857–1934). *The Monks of Kûblâi Khân, Emperor of China.* London: The Religious Tract Society, 1928.

Buzurg b. Shahriyār (tenth century). *The Book of the Wonders of India: Mainland, Sea and Islands.* Translated by G. S. P. Freeman-Grenville. London: East-West Publications, 1981.

Chen Dazhen 陳大震. *Dade Nanhai zhi canben* 大德南海志残本 [The surviving fragments of the Nanhai (Southern Seas) gazetteer, written in the Dade reign (1297–1307) of the Yuan dynasty]. Guangzhou: Guangzhou shi difang zhi yanjiusuo, 1986.

Chen Zhensun 陳振孫 (circa 1183–1262). *Zhizhai shulu jieti* 直齋書錄解題 [Zhizhai's Bibliographical Introduction of Books]. Shanghai: Shangwu, 1937.

Da Yuan shengzheng guochao dianzhang 大元聖政國朝典章 [Compendium of statutes and substatutes of the Yuan]. Beijing: Xinhua shudian, 1998. 3 vols.

Dimashqī, Shams al-Dīn Muḥammad ibn Abī Ṭālib (1256–1327). *Manuel de la cosmographie du Moyen âge (Nukhbat al-dahr fī 'ajā'ib al-barr wa-'l-baḥr).* Translated and annotated by M. A. F. Mehren. Copenhagen: Institute for the History of Arabic-Islamic Science at the Johann Wolfgang Goethe University, 1994 [1874].

Nukhbat al-dahr fī 'ajā'ib al-barr wa-'l-baḥr [The choice of the age, on the marvels of land and sea]. Frankfurt am Main: Institute for the History of Arabic-Islamic Science at the Johann Wolfgang Goethe University, 1994 [1865–1866].

Du Huan 杜環 (flourished 751–761). *Jingxing ji jianzhu* 經行記箋注 [Traveling records, with annotations]. Annotated by Zhang Yichun 張一純. Beijing: Zhonghua shuju, 2000.

Du You 杜佑 (735–812). *Tongdian* 通典 [The encyclopedic history of institutions]. Beijing: Zhonghua shu ju, 1988.

Elliot, Henry Miers (1808–1853). *The History of India, as Told by Its Own Historians: the Muhammadan Period.* Edited from the posthumous papers of Sir Henry Miers Elliot by John Dowson. Frankfurt am Main: Institute for the History of Arabic-Islamic Science at the Johann Wolfgang Goethe University, 1997.

Fang Xuanling 房玄齡 (579–648), ed. *Jinshu* 晉書 [The official history of the Jin dynasty]. Beijing: Zhonghua Shuju, 1974.

Faxian 法顯 (circa 337–422). *Faxian zhuan jiaozuo* 法顯傳校注 [Biographies of Faxian, with annotations and footnotes]. Edited by Zhang Xun 章巽. Shanghai: Shanghai guji, 1985.

Fei Xin 費信 (flourished 1409–1430). *Xingcha shenglan jiaozuo* 星槎勝覽校注 [The overall survey of the star raft, with annotations and footnotes]. Edited by Feng Chengjun 馮承鈞. Taibei: Taiwan shangwu yinshuguan, 1962.

Xing cha sheng lan: the Overall Survey of the Star Raft. Translated by J. V. G. Mills. Wiesbaden: Harrassowitz, 1996.

Ferrand, Gabriel. *Relations de voyages et texts géographiques arabes, persans et turks relatifs a l'extrême-orient du VIIIe au XVIIIe siècles*. Paris: E. Leroux, 1913–1914.

Gwon Geun 權近 (1352–1409). *Yangchon jip* 陽村集 [The collection of Yangchon]. Seoul: Sol, 1997.

Ḥamd Allāh Mustawfī al-Qazwīnī (circa1281–1339). *Geographical Part of the Nuzhat al-Qulub composed by Hamd-Allah Mustawfi of Qazwin in 740 (1340)*. Edited and translated by G. Le Strange. Leyden: E. J. Brill, 1919. Vol.1 in Persian and Vol.2 in English.

He Qiaoyuan 何喬遠 (1558-1632). *Minshu* 閩書 [Book of Min]. Fuzhou: Fujian renmin, 1995. 5 Vols.

Herodotus (fifth century BCE). *The Histories*. Translated by Aubrey De Sélincourt. London: Penguin Books, 2003.

Ḥudūd al-ʿĀlam. "The Regions of the World": A Persian Geography 372 A.H.-982 A.D. Translated by V. Minorsky. Frankfurt am Main: Institute for the History of Arabic-Islamic Science at the Johann Wolfgang Goethe University, 1993.

Hui Chao 慧超 (704–783). *Wang ocheonchukguk jeon* 往五天竺國傳箋釋 [Record of travels in Five Indic Regions]. Annotated by Zhang Yi 張毅. Beijing: Zhonghua shuju, 2000.

Ibn al-Faqīh (flourished 902). *Compendium libri Kitāb al-Boldān* [A book of the countries]. *Bibliotheca Geographorum Arabicorum*, Vol. 5, edited by M. J. de Goeje, Lugduni-Batavorum, 1885.

Ibn al-Nadīm, Muḥammad b. Isāaq (flourished 987). *The Fihrist of al-Nadīm: a Tenth-Century Survey of Muslim Culture*. Edited and translated by Bayard Dodge. New York: Columbia University Press, 1970.

Ibn Baṭṭūṭa (1304–1378). *Dai ryokōki* 大旅行記 [The great travelogue]. Translated by Yajima Hikoichi 家島彦一. Tokyo: Heibonsha, 1996–2002. 8 vols.

The Travels of Ibn Battutah. Edited by Tim Mackintosh-Smith. London: Picador, 2003.

The Travels of Ibn Battuta A.D. 1325–1354. Translated with Revisions and Notes from the Arabic Text Edited by C. Défrémery and B. R. Sanguinetti. Translated, revised, and annotated by H. A. R. Gibb. Cambridge: The Hakluyt Society, 1958–2000. 5 vols.

Voyages d'Ibn Batoutah: texte arabe, accompagné d'une traduction. Edited by C. Defrémery and B. R. Sanguinetti. Paris: Imprimerie impériale, 1853–1858.

Ibn Khaldūn (1332–1406). *Al-Muqaddimah* [The introduction]. Al-Dār al-Bayḍa (Casablanca): Khizānat Ibn Khaldūn, Bayt al-Funūn wa-l-ʿUlūm wa-l-Ādāb, 2005. 3 vols.

Muqaddimah, an Introduction to History. Translated by Franz Rosenthal. Princeton, NJ: Princeton University Press, 1967.

Ibn Khurradādhbih (flourished 848). *Kitāb al-Masālik wa ʾl-mamālik* [Book of routes and realms]. Edited by M. J. de Goeje. Leiden: E. J. Brill, 1889.

al-Idrīsī, al-Sharīf (1100–1165 or 1166). *Géographie d'Edrisi*. Translated by P. Amédée Jaubert. Frankfurt am Main: Institute for the History of Arabic-Islamic Science at the Johann Wolfgang Goethe University, 1992 [1836–1840].

India and the Neighboring Territories in the Kitāb Nuzhat al-Mushtāq fi'khtirāq al-ʿafāq of al-Sharīf al-Idrīsī. Translated by S. Maqbul Ahmad. Leiden: E. J. Brill, 1960.

Nuzhat al-mushtāq fī ikhtirāq al-āfāq [The pleasure of him who longs to cross the horizons]. Edited by R. Rubinacci and U. Rizzitano. Napoli: Istituto Universitario Orientale, repr. Port Said, n.d, 1970.

Jahn, Karl. *Die Chinageschichte des Rašīd ad-Dīn*. Vienne: Österreichischen Akademie der Wissenschaften, 1971.

Jan Yün-hua. *A Chronicle of Buddhism in China, 581–960 A.D.: Translations from Monk Chih-p'an's Fo-tsu t'ung-chi*. Santiniketan, 1966.

Juwaynī, ʿAlāʾ al-Dinʾ ʿAṭā Malik (1226–1283). *The History of the World-Conqueror*, translated from the text of Mirza Muhammad Qazvini by John Andrew Boyle. Cambridge, MA: Harvard University Press, 1958.

al-Kāshgharī, Maḥmu'd (eleventh century). *Compendium of the Turkic Dialects (Diw'anʾ Luγat at-Turk)*. Translated by Robert Dankoff. Cambridge, MA: The Harvard University Printing Office, 1982–1985.

Lin Zhiqi 林之奇 (1112–1176). *Zhuozhai wenji* 拙齋文集 [Literary collection of Zhuozhai]. Taibei: Taiwan shangwu yinshuguan, 1971.

Li Tao 李燾 (1114–1183). *Xu Zizhi tongjian changbian* 續資治通鑑長編 [Long draft of the continuation of the Zizhi tongjian]. Beijing: Zhonghua shuju, 1279–1295.

Liu Xu 劉煦 (887–946). *Jiu Tangshu* 舊唐書 [Old history of the Tang]. Beijing: Zhonghua shuju, 1975.

Liu Yu 劉郁 (flourished 1260s). *Xishi ji* 西使記 [The record of an embassy to the regions in the west]. *Congshu jicheng chubian* 叢書集成初編. Shanghai: Shangwu yinshuguan, 1936.

Li Zhichang 李志常 (1193–1256). *The Travels of an Alchemist: the Journey of the Taoist, Ch'ang-ch'un, from China to the Hindukush at the Summons of Chingiz Khan, recorded by his disciple, Li Chih-ch'ang*. Translated by Arthur Waley. London: George Routledge & Sons, Ltd, 1931.

Luo Hongxian 羅洪先 (1504–1564). *Guangyu tu* 廣輿圖 [The broad terrestrial map]. Taibei: Xuehai, 1969.

Ma Huan 馬歡 (flourished 1414–1451). *Ming chaoben "Yingyai shenglan" Jiaozuo* 明钞本《瀛涯 胜览》校注 [Ming-period manuscript of "Yingyai shenglan," with annotations and footnotes]. Edited by Wan Ming 万明. Beijing: Haiyang, 2005.

Ying-yai Sheng-lan: The Overall Survey of the Ocean's Shores. Translated by J. V. G. Mills. London: Hakluyt Society, 1970.

Major, R. H. *India in the Fifteenth Century: Being a Collection of Narratives of Voyages to India*. London: The Hakluyt Society, 1857.

Marwazī (flourished 1056–1120). *Sharaf al-Zamān Ṭāhir Marvazī on China, the Turks, and India: Arabic Text (circa A.D. 1120) with an English Translation and Commentary*. Translated by V. Minorsky. Frankfurt am Main: Institute for the History of Arabic-Islamic Science at the Johann Wolfgang Goethe University, 1993 [1942].

al-Mas'ūdī, Abū al-Ḥasan 'Alī b. al-Ḥusayn b. 'Alī (896–956). *El-Mas'udi's Historical Encyclopedia: entitled "Meadows of Gold and Mines of Gems."* Translated by Aloys Sprenger. London: Printed for the Oriental Translation Fund of Great Britain and Ireland, 1841.

Les prairies d'or [Meadows of gold]. Translated by Barbier de Meynard and Pavet de Courteille, revised and corrected by Charles Pellat. Paris: Société asiatique, 1962–1989. 5 vols.

Murūj al-dhahab wa-ma'ādin al-jawāhir [Meadows of gold and mines of gems]. Bayrūt: Dār Ṣādir, 2005. 4 vols.

Miller, Konrad. *Mappae Arabicae: Arabische Welt- und Länderkarten*. Reprinted by Fuat Sezgin. Frankfurt am Main: Institute for the History of Arabic-Islamic Science at the Johann Wolfgang Goethe University, 1994 [1926–1931]. 2 vols.

al-Muqaddasī, Muḥammad b. Aḥmad Shams al-Dīn. (circa 946). *Aḥsan al-taqāsīm fī ma'rifat al-āqālīm* [The best divisions for knowledge of the climates (regions)]. *Bibliotheca Geographorum Arabicorum*, Vol. 3, edited by M. J. de Goeje, Leiden: Brill, 1976 [1877].

The Best Divisions for Knowledge of the Regions: a Translation of Ahsan al-Taqasim fi Ma'rifat al-Aqalim. Translated by Basil Anthony Collins. Reading, UK: Centre for Muslim Contribution to Civilization, Garnet Publishing, 1994.

Ouyang Xiu 歐陽修 (1007–1072). *Biography of Huang Ch'ao [Hsīn T'ang-shū 225C.1a–9a]*. Translated by Howard S. Levy. Berkeley: University of California Press, 1955.

Xin Tangshu 新唐書 [New history of the Tang]. Beijing: Zhonghua shuju, 1975.

The Periplus Maris Erythraei: Text with Introduction, Translation, and Commentary. Translated by Lionel Casson. Princeton, NJ: Princeton University Press, 1989.

Polo, Marco (1254–1324). *The Description of the World*. Translated and annotated by A. C. Moule and Paul Pelliot. London: G. Routledge, 1938.

The Travels of Marco Polo. Translated by Ronald Latham. London: Penguin Books, 1958.

Ptolemy (circa 90–160). *Ptolemy, Geography, Book 6: Middle East, Central and North Asia, China*. Translated by Helmut Humbach. Wiesbaden: L. Reichert, 1998–2002.

Rashīd al-Dīn (1247–1318). "Jāmi' al-tawārīkh [The compendium of chronicles]." 1518. Istanbul, Topkapi Sarayi Müzesi, Revan.

Die Chinageschichte des Rasīd al-Dīn. Translated and edited by Karl Jahn. Vienna: Herman Böhlaus, 1971.

Rashiduddin Fazlullah's Jamiʿu't-tawarikh: Compendium of Chronicles. Translated by W. M. Thackston. Cambridge, MA: Harvard University, Dept. of Near Eastern Languages and Civilizations, 1998. 3 vols.

Rasid at din ui jipsa 라시드 앗 딘의 집사 [The compendium of chronicles]. Translated by Hodong Kim. Paju: Sakyejul, 2002–2005. 3 vols.

Rockhill, William. "Notes on the Relations and Trade of China with the Eastern Archipelago and the Coast of the Indian Ocean during the Fourteenth Century," Part II. *T'oung Pao* 15 (1914) and 16 (1915).

Shen Gua 沈括 (1031–1095). *Mengxi bitan jiaozheng* 夢溪筆談校證 [The dream pool essays, with complete annotations and collations]. Taibei: Shijie shuju, 1961.

Sima Guang 司馬光 (1019–1086). *Zizhi tongjian* 資治通鑑 [*Comprehensive mirror for aid in government*]. Beijing: Zhonghua shuju, 1995.

Sima Qian 司馬遷 (circa 145–86 BCE). *Records of the Grand Historian of China, translated from the Shi chi of Ssu-ma Ch'ien, Vol.II: the age of emperor Wu 140 to circa 100 B.C.* Translated by Burton Watson. New York: Columbia University Press, 1961.

Shiji 史記 [Records of the historian]. Beijing: Zhonghua shuju, 1959.

Song Lian 宋廉 (1310–1381), ed. *Yuanshi* 元史 [The history of the Yuan]. Beijing: Zhonghua shuju, 1976.

al-Ṭabarī (838–923). *The History of al-Tabarī (Taʾrīkh al-rusul waʾl-mulūk): An Annotated Translation.* Translated by Jane Dammen McAuliffe. New York: State University of New York Press, 1985–2007. 40 vols.

Tuo Tuo 脫脫 (1313–1355). *Songshi* 宋史 [History of the Song]. Beijing: Zhonghua shuju, 1977.

Al-ʿUmarī, Ibn Faḍlallāh (1301–1349). *Das mongolische Weltreich: al-ʿUmarī's Darstellung der mongolischen Reiche in seinem Werk Masālik al-abṣār fī mamālik al-amṣār: mit Paraphrase und Kommentar.* Edited and translated by Klaus Lech. Wiesbaden: Otto Harrassowitz Verlag, 1968.

Masālik al-abṣār fi mamālik al-amṣār [Ways of perception concerning the most populous (civilized) provinces]. Casablanca: Tawzīʿ Sūshibrīs, 1988.

Wang Dayuan 汪大淵 (1311–1350). *Daoyi zhilüe* 島夷誌略校釋 [A shortened account of the non-Chinese island peoples, with annotations and footnotes]. Edited by Su Jiqing 蘇繼廎. Beijing: Zhonghua shuju, 1981.

Wang Shidian 王士點 (died 1358). *Mishujian zhi* 秘書監志 [The account of the palace library]. Edited by Gao Rongsheng 高榮盛. Hangzhou: Zhejiang guji, 1992.

Wang Yun 王惲 (1227–1304). *Yutang jiahua* 玉堂嘉話 [Pleasant talks in the jade house, with annotations and footnotes]. Edited by Yang Xiaochun 杨晓春. Beijing: Zhonghua shuju, 2006.

Wei Yuan 魏源 (1794–1856). *Haiguo tuzhi* 海國圖志 [Illustrated treatise on the sea kingdoms]. Taibei: Chengwen, 1967.

Wu Wenliang 吴文良, ed. *Quanzhou zongjiao shike* 泉州宗教石刻 [Religious inscriptions in Quanzhou]. Edited and expanded by Wu Youxiong 吴幼雄. Beijing: Kexue 科学, 2005.

Xuanzang 玄奘 (602–664). *Da Tang xiyu ji jiaozhu* 大唐西域記校注 [The great Tang records on the western regions, with annotations and footnotes]. Anotated by Ji Xianlin 季羡林. Beijing: Zhonghua shuju, 1985.

Xu Song 徐松 (1781–1848). *Songhuiyao jigao* 宋會要輯稿 [Draft recovered edition of the Song huiyao]. Beijing: Zhonghua shuju, 1957.

Xu Youren 許有壬 (1287–1364). *Zhizheng ji* 至正集 [The collection of Zhizheng]. Taibei: shangwu yinshuguan, 1978.

Yao Guangxiao 姚廣孝 (1335–1418). *Yongle dadian* 永樂大典 [Yongle encyclopedia]. Beijing: Zhonghua shuju, 1959.

Yāqūt ibn ʿAbd Allāh al-Ḥamawī (1179–1229). *Muʿjam al-buldān* [Dictionary of countries]. Bayrūt: Dār al-Kutub al-ʿIlmīyah, 1990. 7 vols.

Yāqūt's Geographisches Wörterbuch: herausgegeben von Ferdinand Wüstenfeld. Frankfurt am Main: Institute for the History of Arabic-Islamic Science at the Johann Wolfgang Goethe University, 1994 [1866–1873]. 6 vols.

Yijing 義淨 (635–713). *Nanhai jigui neifa zhuan* 南海寄歸內法傳 [A record of Buddhist practices sent home from the Southern Sea, with annotations and footnotes]. Edited by Wang Bangwei 王邦維. Beijing: Zhonghua shuju, 1995.

"Zeyl Khwāja Naṣir al-Dīn Ṭūsī bar Jahāngūshā'ī-yi Juwaynī." In *Tārīkh-i Jahāngūšā'ī*, ed. Qazwīnī. Leyden: Brill, 1937.

Zhang Tingyu 張廷玉 (1672–1755). *Mingshi* 明史 [The history of the Ming]. Beijing: Zhonghua shuju, 1974.

Zhang Xun 章巽. *Gu hanghai tu kaoshi* 古航海图考释 [An atlas of old nautical charts of China with detailed annotations]. Beijing: Haiyang, 1980.

Zhao Rugua 趙汝适 (1170–1228). *Chau Ju-Kua: his work on the Chinese and Arab trade in the twelfth and thirteenth centuries entitled Chu-fan-chi (Description of foreign peoples).* Translated and annotated by Friedrich F. Hirth and W. W. Rockhill. St. Petersburg: Printing Office of the Imperial Academy of Sciences, 1911.

Shoban shi 諸蕃志 [Description of the foreign lands]. Translated by Fujiyoshi Masumi 藤善真澄. Osaka: Kansai daigaku, 1991.

Zhufan zhi jiaoshi 諸蕃志校释 [Description of the foreign lands, with annotations and footnotes]. Edited by Yang Bowen 楊博文. Beijing: Zhonghua shuju, 1996.

Zheng He hanghai tu 鄭和航海圖 [The sea chart of Zheng He]. Edited by Xiang Da 向達. Beijing: Zhonghua shuju, 1961.

Zheng Hesheng 郑鹤声and Zheng Yijun 郑一钧, eds. *Zheng He xiaxiyang ziliao huibian* 郑和下西洋资料汇编 [Collection of the source materials for Zheng He's going down to the Western Ocean], an expanded edition. Jinan 济南: Qilu shushe 齐鲁书社, 2005. 3 vols.

Zheng Sixiao 鄭思肖 (1241–1318). *Zheng Sixiao ji* 鄭思肖集 [Collection of Zheng Sixiao]. Shanghai: Shanghai Guji, 1991.

Zhipan (13th century). *Fozu tongji* [The General Records of the Founders of Buddhism]. Yangzhou: Jiangsu Guangling guji, 1991.

Zhou Mi 周密 (1232–1298). *Guixin zashi* 癸辛雜誌 [Miscellaneous notes from the Guixin quarter, Hangzhou]. Beijing: Zhonghua shuju, 1988.

Zhou Qufei 周去非 (12th century). *Lingwai daida* 嶺外代答校注 [Notes from the land beyond the passes, with annotations and footnotes]. Edited by Yang wuquan 楊武泉. Beijing: Zhonghua shuju, 1999.

Zhu Yu 朱彧 (eleventh to twelfth centuries). *Pingzhou ketan* 萍洲可談 [Pingzhou table talks]. Shanghai: Shanghai guji, 1989.

Studies

ʿAbdur Rahman, Khandkar M. "The Arab Geographer Yāqūt al-Rūmi." *Journal of the Asiatic Society* 3 (1958): 23–28.

Abu-Lughod, Janet L. *Before European Hegemony: the World System A.D. 1250–1350*. New York: Oxford University Press, 1989.

Adams, Jonathan. "Ships and Boats as Archaeological Source Material." *World Archaeology* 32.3 (2001): 292–310.

Ahmad, Nafis. *Muslim Contribution to Geography*. Lahore: Ashraf Press, 1965.

Ahmad, S. Maqbul. "Cartography of al-Sharīf al-Idrīsī." In *The History of Cartography: Volume Two, Book One, Cartography in the Traditional Islamic and South Asian Societies*, edited by J. B. Harley and David Woodward, 156–174. Chicago: University of Chicago Press, 1992.

ed. *Al-Masʿūdī: Millenary Commemoration Volume*. Aligarh: Indian Society for the History of Science, 1960.

"Travels of Abu 'l Hasan ʿAli b. al Husayn al-Masʿudi." *Islamic Culture: An English Quarterly* 28, no. 1 (January 1954): 509–524.

Allen, Roger M. A. *An Introduction to Arabic Literature*. New York: Cambridge University Press, 2000.

Allsen, Thomas T. *Commodity and Exchange in the Mongol Empire: A Cultural History of Islamic Textiles*. Cambridge: Cambridge University Press, 1997.

Culture and Conquest in Mongol Eurasia. Cambridge: Cambridge University Press, 2001.

"Ever Closer Encounters: the Appropriation of Culture and the Apportionment of Peoples in the Mongol Empire." *Journal of Early Modern History* 1 (1997): 2–23.

"Mongolian Princes and Their Merchant Partners." *Asia Major* 2 (1989): 83–126.

"Mongols as vectors for cultural transmission." In *The Cambridge History of Inner Asia*: Vol. 2: *The Chinggisid Age*, ed. Nicola Di Cosmo and Allen J. Frank, 135–154. Cambridge: Cambridge University Press, 2009.

Amitai-Preiss, Reuven. *Mongols and Mamluks: The Mamluk Ilkhanid War, 1260–1281*. Cambridge: Cambridge University Press, 1995.

Aoyama Sadao 青山定雄. *Tō Sō Jidai no kōtsu to chisi chizu no Kenkyu* 唐宋時代の交通と地誌地圖の研究 [Study of the communication systems of the Tang and Song China and the development of their topographies and maps]. Tokyo: Yoshikawa Kōbunkan, 1963.

Aritaka Iwao 有高巖. "Gendai no Kaiun to Dai Gen Kaiun ki 元代の海運と大元海運記 [The sea shipping of the Yuan dynasty and the account of the sea shipping of the Great Yuan dynasty]." *Tōyō gakuhō*東洋学報7 (1917): 411–424.

Armijo-Hussein, Jacqueline Misty. "Sayyid ʿAjall Shams al-Dīn: A Muslim From Central Asia, Serving the Mongols in China, and Bringing 'Civilization' to Yunnan (A thesis presented to the committee on Inner Asian and Altaic studies)." Ph.D. diss., Harvard University, Cambridge. 1996.

Ashtor, E. "The Kārimī Merchants." *Journal of the Royal Asiatic Society* (1956): 45–56.

Aubin, Jean. "Les princes d'Ormuz du XIIIe au XVe siècle." *Journal Asiatique* 241 (1953): 77–138.

Aujac, Germaine, et al. "Greek Cartography in the Early Roman World." In *The History of Cartography: Volume One: Cartography in Prehistoric, Ancient and Medieval Europe and the Mediterranean*, edited by J. B. Harley and David Woodward, 161–176. Chicago: University of Chicago Press, 1987.

Ayres, John. "The Discovery of a Yuan Ship at Sinan, South-West Korea: A First Report." *Oriental Art* 24, no. 1 (Spring 1978): 79–85.

Bade, David. *Khubilai Khan and the Beautiful Princess of Tumapel*. Ulaanbaatar: A. Chuluunbat. 2002.

Bai Shouyi "Songshi Yisilan jiaotu di xiangliao maoyi" 宋時伊斯蘭教徒底香料貿易 [The spicy trade by the Muslims in the Song period]. *Yugong* 禹貢 7 (1937): 47–77.

Bai Shouyi 白寿彝, and Yang Huaizhong 杨怀中, eds. *Huizu renwu zhi* 回族人物志 [Biographies of the Muslims]. Yinchuan: Ningxia renmin, 1985. 2 vols.

Barfield, Thomas J. *The Perilous Frontier: Nomadic Empires and China, 221 BC to AD 1757*. Cambridge: Blackwell, 1989.

Barthold, W. *Turkestan down to the Mongol Invasion*. Translated from the original Russian and revised by the author with the assistance of H. A. R. Gibb. Frankfurt am Main: Institute for the History of Arabic-Islamic Science at the Johann Wolfgang Goethe University, 1995 [1928].

Bausani, A. "Religion under the Mongols." In *The Cambridge History of Iran*, Vol. 5, edited by J. A. Boyle, 538–549. London: Cambridge University Press, 1968.

Bearman, P. J. et al., eds. *The Encyclopaedia of Islam*, 2nd Edition. Leiden: Brill, 1954–2005. 12 vols.

Beckingham, C. F. "The Riḥla: Fact of Fiction?" In *Golden Roads: Migration, Pilgrimage and Travel in Mediaeval and Modern Islam*, edited by I. Netton, 86–94. Richmond, UK: Curzon Press, 1993.

Beckwith, Christopher I. *The Tibetan Empire in Central Asia: a History of the Struggle for Great Power among Tibetans, Turks, Arabs, and Chinese during the Early Middle Ages*. Princeton, NJ: Princeton University Press, 1987.

Bennison, Amira K. *The Great Caliphs: The Golden Age of the 'Abbasid Empire*. New Haven & London: Yale University Press, 2009.

Bentley, Jerry H. *Old World Encounter: Cross-Cultural Contacts and Exchanges in Pre-Modern Times*. New York: Oxford University Press, 1993.

Biran, Michal. *Chinggis Khan*. Oxford: Oneworld, 2007.

Qaidu and the Rise of the Independent Mongol State in Central Asia. Richmond: Curzon, 1997.

"The Mongols in Central Asia from Chinggis Khan's invasion to the rise of Temür: Ögödeid and Chaghadaid realms." In *The Cambridge History of Inner Asia*: Vol. 2: *The Chinggisid Age*, ed. Nicola Di Cosmo and Allen J. Frank, 46–66. Cambridge: Cambridge University Press, 2009.

The Qara Khitai Empire in Eurasian History: Between China and the Islamic World. Cambridge: Cambridge University Press, 2005.

Birrell, Anne, trans. *Classic of Mountains and Seas*. London: Penguin Books, 1999.

Black, Jeremy. *Visions of the World: A History of Maps*. London: Octopus Publishing Group Ltd, 2003.

Bloom, Jonathan M. "Lost in Translation: Gridded Plans and Maps along the Silk Road." In *The Journey of Maps and Images on the Silk Road*, edited by Philippe Forêt and Andreas Kaplony, 83–96. Leiden: Brill, 2008.

Paper before Print: the History and Impact of Paper in the Islamic World. New Haven, CT: Yale University Press, 2001.

Bol, Peter. *'This Culture of Ours': Intellectual Transitions in T'ang and Sung China*. Stanford, CA: Stanford University Press, 1992.

Bosworth, C. E. "An Alleged Embassy from the Emperor of China to the Amir Naṣr b. Ahmad: a Contribution to Sâmânid Military History." In *Yâd-nâme-ye īrānī-ye Minorsky*, edited by M. Minovi and I. Afshar, 17–29. Tehran: Uden Forlag, 1969.

Boyle, John. A. "Dynastic and Political History of the Īl-Khāns." In *The Cambridge History of Iran*, Vol. 5, edited by J. A. Boyle, 303–421. London: Cambridge University Press, 1968.

"The Death of the Last ʿAbbāsid Caliph: a Contemporary Muslim Account." *Journal of Semitic Studies* 6 (1961): 145–161.

Braudel, Fernand. *La Méditerranée et le Monde Méditerranéen a l'époque de Philippe II*. Paris: Colin, 1949.

Bretschneider, Emil. "Chinese Medieval Notices of Islam." *The Moslem World* 19, no. 1 (January 1929): 52–61.

Brice, William C. "Early Muslim Sea-Charts." *Journal of the Royal Asiatic Society of Great Britain and Ireland* 1 (1977): 53–61.

Browne, Edward G. *A History of Persian Literature under Tartar Dominion (A.D. 1265–1502)*. Cambridge: Cambridge University Press, 1920.

Busse, Heribert. "Arabische Historiographie und Geographie." In *Grundriss der Arabischen Philologie*, Vol. II, *Literaturwissenschaft*, edited by Helmut Gätje, 293–296. Wiesbaden: Reichert, 1987.

Campbell, Tony. "Portolan Charts from the Late Thirteenth Century to 1500." In *The History of Cartography: Volume One: Cartography in Prehistoric, Ancient and Medieval Europe and the Mediterranean*, ed. J. B. Harley and David Woodward, 371–463. Chicago: University of Chicago Press, 1987.

Cao Wanru 曹婉如 et al. *Zhongguo gudai ditu ji: Zhanguo – Yuan* 中国古代地图集: 战国 – 元 [An atlas of ancient maps in China – From the Warring States period to the Yuan dynasty (476 BCE –1368 CE)]. Beijing: Wenwu, 1990.

Carboni, Stefano. *Glass from Islamic Lands*. New York: Thames & Hudson Inc. 2001.

Casale, Giancarlo. *The Ottoman Age of Exploration*. New York: Oxford University Press, 2010.

Chaffee, John W. "Diasporic Identities in the Historical Development of the Maritime Muslim Communities of Song-Yuan China." *The Journal of the Economic and Social History of the Orient* 49.4 (2006): 395–420.

"Maritime Tribute and Maritime Trade from the Southern Seas in the Early Song." Unpublished paper presented at the annual meetings of the Association for Asian Studies, Boston, March 2007.

"The Impact of the Song: Imperial Clan on the Overseas Trade of Quanzhou." In *The Emporium of the World: Maritime Quanzhou, 1000–1400*, edited by Angela Schottenhammer, 13–46. Leiden: Brill, 2001.

Chan, Hok-lam. "The Chien-wen, Yung-lo, Hung-his, and Hsüan-te reigns, 1399–1435." In *The Cambridge History of China*. Vol. 7: *The Ming Dynasty, 1368–1644*, Part 1, edited by Denis Twitchett and Frederick W. Mote, 182–304. Cambridge: Cambridge University Press, 1988.

Chao Zhongchen 晁中辰. *Mingdai haijin yu haiwai maoyi* 明代海禁与海外贸易 [The Sea Ban and the maritime trade during the Ming dynasty]. Beijing: Renmin, 2005.

Chaudhuri, K. N. *Trade and Civilisation in the Indian Ocean: An Economic History from the Rise of Islam to 1750*. Cambridge: Cambridge University Press, 1985.

Chen Dasheng 陈达生. *Quanzhou Yisilan jiao shi ke* 泉州伊斯兰教石刻 [Islamic inscriptions in Quanzhou (Zaitun)]. Fuzhou: Fujian renmin, 1984.

Chen Dasheng, and Denys Lombard. "Foreign Merchants in Maritime Trade in Quanzhou ('Zaitun'): Thirteenth and Fourteenth Centuries." In *Asian Merchants and Businessmen in the Indian Ocean and the China Sea*, edited by Denys Lombard and Jean Aubin, 19–24. Oxford: Oxford University Press, 2000.

Chen Gaohua 陈高华. *Yuan Dadu* 元大都 [Dadu of the Yuan dynasty]. Beijing: Beijing chubanshe, 1982.

"Yuandai de hanghai shijia Ganpu yangshi 元代的航海世家 浦杨氏 [The Yang family of Ganpu: A distinguished family of navigation in the Yuan period]." *Haijiaoshi yanjiu* 1 (1995): 4–18.

Chen Gaohua 陈高华 and Chen Shangsheng 陈尚胜. *Zhongguo haiwai Jiaotong shi* 中国海外交通史 [The history of Chinese overseas contacts]. Taibei: Wenjin 文津, 1997.

Chen Gaohua 陈高华 and Wu Tai 吴泰. *Songyuan shiqi de haiwai maoyi* 宋元时期的海外贸易 [The overseas trade in the Song-Yuan period]. Tianjin: Tianjin renmin, 1981.

Chen Gaohua 陈高华, Wu Tai 吴泰, and Guo Songyi 郭松义, *Haishang sichou zhi lu* 海上丝绸之路 [Maritime Silk Road]. Beijing: Haiyang, 1991.

Chen Jiarong 陈佳荣, Xie Fang 谢方, Lu Junling 陆峻岭. *Gudai nanhai diming huishi* 古代南海地名汇释 [Collected interpretation of ancient place-names in the Southern Sea]. Beijing: Zhonghua shuju, 1986.

Chen Xinxiong 陳信雄. "Song Yuan de yuanyang maoyi chuan 宋元的遠洋贸易船 [The long-range merchant vessels of the Song and Yuan dynasties]." In *Zhongguo Haiyang fazhan shi lunwen ji* 中国海洋发展史论文集 [Chinese Maritime Development]. Vol. 2, edited by Academia Sinica, Committee for the Study of Chinese Maritime Development. Taibei: Zhongyang yanjiuyuan sanmin zhuyi yanjiusuo, 1986.

Chung Kei Won and George F. Jourani. "Arab Geographers on Korea." *Journal of the American Oriental Society* 58, no. 4 (December 1983): 658–661.

Clark, Alfred. "Medieval Arab Navigation on the Indian Ocean: Latitude Determinations." *The Journal of the American Oriental Society* 113 (1993): 360–373.

Clark, Hugh R. "Muslims and Hindus in the Culture and Morphology of Quanzhou from the Tenth to the Thirteenth century." *Journal of World History* 6, no. 1 (Spring 1995): 49–74.

Congreve, H. "A Brief Notice of Some Contrivances Practiced by the Native Mariners of the Coromandel Coast, in Navigating, Sailing and Repairing their Vessels." In *Introduction: à L'astronomie Nautique Arabe*, edited by Gabriel Ferrand, 25–30. Paris: Librairie Orientaliste Paul Geuthner, 1928.

Conservation and Restoration Report of Shinan Ship. Mokpo: Kungnip Haeyang Yumul Chŏnsigwan 국립해양유물전시관, 2004.

Curtin, Philip D. *Cross-Cultural Trade in World History (Studies in Comparative World History)*. Cambridge: Cambridge University Press, 1984.

Dalen, Benno van. "Islamic and Chinese Astronomy under the Mongols: A Little - Known Case of Transmission." In *From China to Paris: 2000 Years Transmission of Mathematical Ideas*, edited by Yvonne Dold - Samplonius et al., 327–356. Stuttgart: Steiner, 2002.

de la Vaissière, Étienne. *Sogdian Traders: A History (Handbook of Oriental Studies)*. Boston: Brill, 2005.

De Weerdt, Hilde. "Maps and Memory: Readings of Cartography in Twelfth- and Thirteenth-Century Song China." *Imago Mundi* 61, no. 2 (2009): 155–157.

Di Cosmo, Nicola. *Ancient China and its Enemies: The Rise of Nomadic Power in East Asian History*. New York: Cambridge University Press, 2002.

Dilke, O. A. W. "The Culmination of Greek Cartography in Ptolemy." In *The History of Cartography: Volume One: Cartography in Prehistoric, Ancient and Medieval Europe and the Mediterranean*, edited by J. B. Harley and David Woodward, 177–200. Chicago: University of Chicago Press, 1987.

Donini, Pier Giovanni. *Arab Travelers and Geographers*. London: Immel, 1991.

Donkin, R. A. *Beyond Price: Pearls and Pearl-fishing: Origins to the Age of Discoveries*. Philadelphia: American Philosophical Society, 1998.

Drake, F. S. "Mohammedanism in T'ang Dynasty." *Monumenta Serica*, vol. VILI, 1943.

Dreyer, Edward L. *Zheng He: China and the Oceans in the Early Ming Dynasty, 1405–1433*. New York: Pearson Longman, 2007.

Dunn, Ross, E. *The Adventures of Ibn Battuta: A Muslim Traveler of the 14th Century*. Berkeley: University of California Press, 1986.

Edson, Evelyn. *The World Map, 1300–1492: The Persistence of Tradition and Transformation*. Baltimore: The Johns Hopkins University Press, 2007.

Edson, Evelyn and Emilie Savage-Smith. *Medieval Views of the Cosmos*. Oxford: Bodleian Library, 2004.

Elvin, Mark. *The Pattern of the Chinese Past*. Stanford, CA: Stanford University Press, 1973.

Endicott-West, Elizabeth. "Merchants Associations in Yüan China: The Ortoγ." *Asia Major* 2 (1989): 127–154.

Enoki Kazuo. "The Liang chih-kung-t'u 梁職貢圖." In *Studia Asiatica: the collected papers in Western languages of the late Dr. Kazuo Enoki*. Tokyo: Kyuko-Shoin, 1998.

Fan Sheng 潘晟. "Songdai dili xue de guannian, tixi yu zhishi xingqu 宋代地理学的观念. 体系与知识兴趣 [Ideas, System and Interest in the Geography of the Sung Dynasties]." PhD dissertation: Peking University, 2008.

Ferrand, Gabriel. *Instructions Nautiques et Routiers Arabes et Portugais des XVe et XVIe siècles*. Paris: Geuthner, 1921.

Finlay, Robert. "How Now to (Re)Write World History: Gavin Menzies and the Chinese Discovery of America." *Journal of World History* 15, no. 2 (2004): 229–242.

"The Treasure Ships of Zheng He: Chinese Maritime Imperialism in the Age of Discovery." *Terrae Incognitae* 23 (1991): 1–12.

Flecker, Michael. "A Ninth-Century AD Arab or Indian Shipwreck in Indonesia: first evidence for direct trade with China." *World Archaeology* 32, no. 3 (2001): 335–354.

The Archaeological Excavation of the 10th Century: Intan Shipwreck. Oxford: Archaeopress, 2002.

Franke, Herbert. "Aḥmad (?–1282)." In *In the Service of the Khan*, edited by Igor de Rachewiltz, et al, 539–557. Wiesbaden: Harrassowitz Verlag, 1993.

Franke, Herbert and Denis Twitchett. *The Cambridge History of China*. Vol. 6: *Alien Regimes and Border States, 907–1368*. Cambridge: Cambridge University Press, 1994.

Fuchs, Walter. *The "Mongol atlas" of China by Chu Ssu-pen, and the Kuang-yü-t'u*. Peiping: Fu Jen University, 1946.

Fujian sheng Quanzhou haiwai jiaotongshi bowuguan 福建省泉州海外交通史博物馆 [Quanzhou Maritime Museum in Fujian Province]. *Quanzhou wan Songdai haichuan de fajue yu janjiu* 泉州湾宋代海船的发掘与研究 [The Excavation and Studies of the Song Period Shipwreck in the Quanzhou Bay]. Beijing: Haiyang, 1987.

Fuji'i Jōji 藤井譲治, Sugiyama Masa'aki 杉山正明, and Kinda Akihiro 金田章裕, eds. *Ezu・Chizu kara mita sekaizō* 絵図・地図からみた世界像 [Worldview seen from pictorial maps and geographical maps]. Kyoto: Kyoto Daigaku Daigakuin Kenkyūka, 2004.

Gibbins, David and Jonathan Adams. "Shipwrecks and maritime archaeology." *World Archaeology* 32, no. 3 (2001): 279–291.

Gies, Frances Carney. *"Al-Idrisi and Roger's Book." Saudi Aramco World* 28.4 (July/August 1977): 14–19.

Goitein, S. D. *Letters of Medieval Jewish Traders*. Princeton, NJ: Princeton University Press, 1973.

Gruendler, Beatrice. "Tawqīʿ (Apostille)." In *The Evolution of Artistic Classical Arabic P*, edited by Lale Behzadi and Vahid Behmardi, 1–34. Beirut: The German Orient-Institut Beirut, 2008.

Gutas, Dimitri. *Greek thought, Arab Culture: the Graeco-Arabic Translation Movement in Baghdad and Early Abbasid Society (2nd-4th/8th-10th Centuries)*. New York: Routledge, 1998.

Hall, Kenneth R. "Indonesia's Evolving International Relationship in the Ninth to Early Eleventh Centuries: Evidence from Contemporary Shipwrecks and Epigraphy." *Indonesia*, 90 (October 2010): 1–31.

"Local and International Trade and Traders in the Straits of Melaka Region: 600–1500." *Journal of the Economic and Social History of the Orient* 47, no. 3 (2004): 213–260.

"Ports of Trade, Maritime Diasporas, and Networks of Trade and Cultural Integration in the Bay of Bengal Region of the Indian Ocean: c. 1300–1500." In *Empires and Emporia: The Orient in World Historical Space and Time*, edited by Jos Gommans. Leiden: E. J. Brill, 2010.

Secondary Cities and Urban Networking in the Indian Ocean Realm, c. 1400–1800. Lanham, MD: Lexington Books, 2008.

The Growth of Non-Western Cities: Primary and Secondary Urban Networking, c. 900–1900. Lanham, MD: Lexington Books, 2011.

Han Rulin 韩儒林, et al. *Yuanchao shi* 元朝史 [A history of the Yuan dynasty]. Beijing: Renmin, 1986. 2 vols.

Hargett, James M. "Song Dynasty Local Gazetteers and Their Place in the History of Difangzhi Writing." *HJAS* 56, no. 2 (December 1996): 405–442.

Hartner, Willy. "The Astronomical Instruments of Cha - ma - lu - ting, Their Identification, and Their Relations to the Instruments of the Observatory of Marāgha." *Isis* 41 (1950): 184–194.

Hartwell, Robert M. "Demographic, Political, and Social Transformations of China." *HJAS* 42 (1982): 365–442.

"Foreign Trade, Monetary Policy and Chinese 'Mercantilism'." Edited by Kinugawa Tsuyoshi. *Collected Studies on Sung History Dedicated to Professor James T. C. Liu in Celebration of his Seventieth Birthday*. Kyoto: Dōhōsha, 1989.

Heinen, Anton M. *Islamic Cosmology: A Study of As-Suyūṭī's al-Hay'a as-sanīya fī l-hay'a as-sunnīya*. Wiesbaden: F. Steiner Verlag, 1982.

Heng, Chye Kiang. *Cities of Aristocrats and Bureaucrats: the Development of Medieval Chinese Cityscapes*. Honolulu: University of Hawai'i Press, 1999.

Hinz, Walther. *Islamische Masse und Gewichte: Umgerechnet ins Metrische System*. Leiden: E. J. Brill, 1970.

Ho, Chuimei. "The Ceramic Boom in Minnan during Song and Yuan Times." In *The Emporium of the World: Maritime Quanzhou, 1000–1400*, edited by Angela Schottenhammer, 237–281. Leiden: Brill, 2001.

Hodgson, Marshall G. S. *The Venture of Islam: Conscience and History in a World Civilization*. Chicago: University of Chicago Press, 1974.

Holt, P. M., ed. *The Cambridge History of Islam, Vol 1A: the Central Islamic Lands from Pre-Islamic Times to the First World War*. Cambridge: Cambridge University Press, 1970.

Hopkins, J. F. R. "Geographic and Navigational Literature." In *The Cambridge History of Arabic Literature: Religion, Learning and Science in the 'Abbāsid Period*, edited by M. J. L. Young, 301–327. Cambridge: Cambridge University Press, 1991.

Hostetler, Laura. *Qing Colonial Enterprise: Ethnography and Cartography in Early Modern China*. Chicago: University of Chicago Press, 2001.

Hourani, George F. *Arab Seafaring*. Edited by John Carswell. Princeton, NJ: Princeton University Press, 1995.

Hsiao, Ch'i-ch'ing. "Mid-Yuan Politics." In *The Cambridge History of China*. Vol. 6: *Alien Regimes and Border States, 907–1368*, edited by Herbert Franke and Denis Twitchett, 490–560. Cambridge: Cambridge University Press, 1994.

Hsieh Ming-liang 謝明良. "Ji heishi hao (Batu Hitam) chenchuan zhong de Zhongguo taociqi 記黑石號(Batu Hitam)沈船中的中國陶姿器 [A Discussion of the Chinese Ceramics Recovered from the Wreck of the Batu Htam]." *Meishu shi yanjiu jikan* 美術史研究集刊 13 (2002): 1–60.

Huang Chunyan 黄纯艳. "Songdai dengwengu zhidu 宋代登闻鼓 [On Appealing to the Emperor System in Song dynasty]." *Zhongzhou xuekan* 中州学刊 [Academic Journal of Zhongzhou] 6 (November 2004): 112–116.

Huang, Shih-shan Susan. "Daoist Imagery of Body and Cosmos, Part 1: Body Gods and Starry Travel." *Journal of Daoist Studies* 3 (2010): 57–90.

Idema, Wilt L. "The Tza-jiu of Yang Tz: An International Tycoon in Defense of Collaboration?" In *Proceedings on the Second International Conference on Sinology*, edited by Academia Sinica, 523–548. Taipei: Academia Sinica, 1989.

Irwin, Robert. "The Emergence of the Islamic World System: 1000–1500." In *The Cambridge Illustrated History of the Islamic World*, edited by Francis Robinson, 32–61. New York: Cambridge University Press, 1996.

Ishida Mikinosuke 石田幹之助. *Chōan no haru* 長安の春 [The Spring in Chang'an]. Tokyo: Kōdansha, 1979.

Israeli, Raphael. "Medieval Muslim Travellers to China." In *Haishang sichou zhilu yanjiu 1*海上丝绸之路研究 1 [*Maritime Silk Route Studies 1*]. Fuzhou: Fujian Education Publishing House, 1997.

Jackson, Peter. "The State of Research: The Mongol Empire, 1986–1999." *Journal of Medieval History* 26, no. 2 (2000): 189–210.

Johns, Jeremy and Emilie Savage-Smith. "The book of curiosities: a newly discovered series of Islamic maps." *Imago Mundi* 55 (2003): 7–24.

Kaplony, Andreas. "Comparing al-Kāshgharī's Map to his Text: On the Visual Language, Purpose, and Transmission of Arabic-Islamic Maps." In *The Journey of Maps and Images on the Silk Road*, edited by Philippe Forêt and Andreas Kaplony, 137–153. Leiden: Brill, 2008.

Kauz, Ralph. "A Kāzarūnī Network?" *Aspects of the Maritime Silk Road: From the Persian Gulf to the East China Sea*. Wiesbaden: Harrassowitz Verlag, 2010.

Kauz, Ralph and Roderich Ptak. "Hormuz in Yuan and Ming Sources." *Bulletin de l'École Française d'Extrême-Orient*, 88 (2001): 27–75.

Keith, Donald H. and Christian J. Buys. "New Light on Medieval Chinese Seagoing Ship Construction." *The International Journal of Nautical Archaeology and Underwater Exploration* 10, no. 2 (May 1981): 119–132.

Kentley, Eric. "The Sewn Boats of India's East Coast." In *Tradition and Archaeology: Early Maritime Contacts in the Indian Ocean*, edited by Himanshu Prabha Ray and Jean-Francois Salles, 247–260. New Delhi: Manohar, 1996.

Khalidi, Tarif. *Islamic Historiography: the Histories of Masʿūdī*. Albany: State University of New York Press, 1975.

Kim, Hodong. "The Unity of the Mongol Empire and Continental Exchanges over Eurasia," *Journal of Central Eurasian Studies* 1 (2009): 15–42.

"A Portrait of a Christian Official in China under the Mongol Rule: Life and Career of 'Isa Kelemechi (1227–1308)," *Chung'ang Asia Yŏn'gu* 中央아시아研究 [Journal of Central Eurasian Studies] 11 (2006):75–112.

King, Anya H. "Beyond the Geographers: Information on Asia in Early Medieval Arabic Writers on Pharmacology and Perfumery." Unpublished paper presented at the AAS annual conference, Philadelphia, March 27, 2010.

King, David A. *World-Maps for Finding the Direction and Distance to Mecca*. Leiden: Brill, 1999.

Kracke, Edward A. "Early Visions of Justice for the Humble in East and West." *Journal of the American Oriental Society* 96, no. 4 (October-December 1976): 492–498.

Kračkovsky, I. Y. *Izbrannye socineniya IV: Arabskaya geograficeskaya literature*. Moscow: Izd-vo Akademii nauk SSSR, 1955–1960.

Tā'rkh al-adab al-jughrāfi al-ʿArabī. Translated by Hāshim Ṣalāḥ al-Dīn ʿUthmān. Cairo: Lajnat al-Ta'līf wa-al-Tarjamah wa-al-Nash, 1963–1965.

Krawulsky, Dorothea. *The Mongol Īlkhāns and their Vizier Rashīd al-Dīn*. Frankfurt am Main: Peter Lang, 2011.

Kuwabara Jitsuzō 桑原隲蔵. *Bu Jukō no jiseki* 蒲寿庚の事蹟 [Pu Shougeng's achievements]. Tokyo: Heibonsha, 1989 [1922].

"On P'u Shou-keng." *Memoirs of the Research Department of the Tōyō Bunko* 2 (1928): 1–79, 7 (1935):1–104.

Lambourn, Elizabeth. "India from Aden: *Khuṭba* and Muslim Urban Networks in Late Thirteenth-Century India." Edited by Kenneth R. Hall. *Secondary Cities and Urban Networking: in the Indian Ocean Realm, c. 1400–1800*. Lanham, MD: Lexington Books, 2008.

Lane, George. *Early Mongol Rule in Thirteenth-Century Iran: A Persian Renaissance*. London: RoutledgeCurzon, 2003.

Langlois, Jr. John D. ed. *China under Mongol Rule*. Princeton, NJ: Princeton University Press, 1981.

Larner, John. *Marco Polo and the Discovery of the World*. New Haven, CT: Yale University Press, 1999.

Laufer, Berthold (1874–1934). *Sino-Iranica; Chinese Contributions to the History of Civilization in Ancient Iran, with Special Reference to the History of Cultivated Plants and Products*. Chicago, 1919.

Lazard, G. "The Rise of the New Persian Language." In *The Cambridge History of Iran*, Vol. 4, edited by R. N. Frye, 595–632. London: Cambridge University Press, 1975.

Ledyard, Gari. "Cartography in Korea." In *The History of Cartography, Volume Two, Book Two: Cartography in the Traditional East and Southeast Asian Societies*, edited by J. B. Harley and David Woodward, 235–345. Chicago: University of Chicago Press, 1994.

Leslie, Donald Daniel. *Islam in Traditional China: A Short History to 1800*. Belconnen ACT: Canberra College of Advanced Education, 1986.

Leslie, Donald Daniel and K. H. J. Gardiner. "Chinese Knowledge of Western Asia During the Han." *T'oung Pao* LXVIII, no. 4–5 (1982): 254–308.

Lewis, Bernard. "Egypt and Syria." In *The Cambridge History of Islam, Vol 1A: the Central Islamic Lands from Pre-Islamic Times to the First World War*, edited by P. M. Holt, Ann K. S. Lambton, and Bernard Lewis, 175–230. Cambridge: Cambridge University Press, 1970.

Li Jinxiu 李锦绣, and Yu Taishan 余太山. *"Tong dian" Xiyu wenxian yaozhu* 《通典》 西域文献要注 [Main annotations on the accounts about western regions in Tong dian]. Beijing: Shanghai renmin. 2009.

Limbert, John. *Shiraz in the Age of Hafez: The Glory of a Medieval Persian City*. Seattle: University of Washington Press, 2004.

Liu Yingsheng 刘迎胜. "A Lingua Franca along the Silk Road: Persian Language in China between the 14th and the 16th Centuries." In *Aspects of the Maritime Silk Road*, ed. Ralph Kauz, 87–95. Wiesbaden: Harrassowitz Verlag, 2010.

Silu wenhua: Haishang juan 丝路文化: 海上卷 [The culture of Silk Road: Maritime route]. Hangzhou 杭州: Zhejiang renmin, 1995.

"Youguan Yuandai Huihui ren yuyan wenti 有关元代回回人语言问题 [The language of Hui Muslims in the Yuan China]." *Yuanshi luncong* 元史论从 *(Studies in Yuan History)* 10 (2005): 19–38.

Lo, Jung-pang. "The Emergence of China as a Sea Power during the Late Sung and Early Yüan Periods." *Far Eastern Quarterly* 14, no. 4 (1955): 489–503.

Luo Xianglin 罗香林. *Pu Shougeng yanjiu* 蒲壽庚研究 [A study of Pu Shougeng]. Hong Kong: Zhongguo xueshe, 1959.

Lurje, Pavel B. "Description of the Overland Route to China in *Hudud al-ʿAlam*: Dates of the Underlying Itinerary." *Ouya xuekan* 欧亚学刊 [Eurasian Studies] 6 (2007): 179–197.

Maejima Shinji 前嶋信次. "Tarasu Senkō タラス戦ž [A Study of the Battle of Talas]." *Shigaku* 史学 32, no. 1 (1967): 1–37.

"The Muslims in Chʻüan-chou 泉州 at the End of the Yüan Dynasty, Part 1." *Memoirs of the Research Department of the Tōyō Bunko* 31 (1973): 27–51.

Ma Jianchun 马建春. "Yuandai dongchuan huihui dili xue kaoshu 元代东传回回地理学考述 [An examination of the Huihui (Muslim) geographic studies in the Yuan dynasty]." *Huihui yanjiu* 回族研究 [The study of the Hui people] 45, no. 1 (2002): 14–19.

Yuandai dongqian xiyuren jiqi wenhuayanjiu 元代东迁西域人及其文化研究 [A study of the western peoples who migrated to the east and their cultures during the Yuan dynasty]. Beijing: Minzu, 2003.

Manz, Beatrice Forbes. *The Rise and Rule of Tamerlane*. Cambridge: Cambridge University Press, 1989.

Marshak, Borris. *Legends, Tales, and Fables in the Art of Sogdiana*. New York: Biblioteca Persica Press, 2002.

Ma Qiang 马强. *Tang Song shiqi Zhongguo xibu dili renshi yanjiu* 唐宋时期中国西部地理认识研究 [Study of the geographical understanding of the western area of China during the Tang-Song periods]. Beijing: Renmin, 2009.

Mattock, J. N. "Ibn Baṭṭūṭa's Use of Ibn Jubayr's Riḥla." In *Proceedings of the Ninth Congress of the Union Europeenne des arabisants et Islamisants*, edited by Rudolph Peters, 209–218. Leiden: E. J. Brill, 1981.

McLaughlin, Raoul. *Rome and the Distant East: Trade Routes to the Ancient Lands of Arabia, India, and China*. London: Continuum, 2010.

Menzies, Gavin. *1421: The Year China Discovered America*. London: Bantam Dell Pub Group, 2002.

Mercer, John. "The Canary Islanders in Western Mediterranean Politics." *African Affairs* 78, no. 311 (April 1979): 159–176.

Mikami Tsugio 三上次男. *Tōjibōeki shi kenkyū, ge, chūkintō hen* 陶磁貿易史研究, 下, 中近東編 [A study of the ceramic trade, Vol.3, Middle East]. Tokyo: Chūō kōron bijutsu, 1988.

Tōjibōeki shi kenkyū, jō, higashi ajia, tōnan ajia hen 陶磁貿易史研究, 上, 東アジア・東南アジア編 [A study of the ceramic trade, Vol.1, East Asia and Southeast Asia]. Tokyo: Chūō kōron bijutsu, 1987.

Tōjiki no michi: tōzai bunmei no setten wo tazunete 陶磁の道: 東西文明の接点をたずねて [Ceramic road: a visit to the intersection of East-West civilizations]. Tokyo: Iwanami 岩波, 1969.

Miquel, André. *La Géographie Humaine du Monde Musulman jusqu'au Milieu de 11e Siècle*. Paris: La Hay, Mouton & Co, 1967–1988. 4 vols.

"L'Inde et la Chine vues du cote de l'Islam." In *As Others See Us: Mutual Perceptions, East and West*, edited by B. Lewis and E. Leites, 284–300. New York, 1985.

Misugi Takatoshi 三杉隆敏. *'Gen no sometsuke' umi wo wataru: sekai ni hirogaru yakimono bunka* '元の染付'海を渡る：世界に拡がる焼物文化 [Maritime trade of the Yuan period blue-and-white porcelains: worldwide spread of ceramic culture]. Tokyo: Nōsan gyoson bunka kyōkai, 2004.

Mittenhuber, Florian. "The Tradition of Texts and Maps in Ptolemy's Geography." In *Ptolemy in Perspective: Use and Criticism of his Work from Antiquity to the Nineteenth Century*, edited by Alexander Jones, 95–119. New York: Springer, 2010.

Miya Noriko 宮紀子. "'Konitsu kyōri rekidai kokuto no zu' eno michi: 14 seiki shimei chihō no 'chi' no yukue" 「混一疆理歴代国都之図」への道 – 14世紀四明地方の「知」の行方 [An approach to the 'Map of Integrated Regions and Terrains and of Historical Countries and Capitals': The traces of the "knowledge" in the fourteenth-century Siming region], *Mongoru jidai no shuppan bunka* モンゴル時代の出版文化 [The publishing culture of the Mongol period]. Nagoya: Nagoya daigaku shuppankai, 2006, 517–523.

Mongoru teikoku ga unda sekaizu モンゴル帝国が生んだ世界図 [The world map that the Mongol empire created]. Tokyo: Nihon keizai shimbun shuppansha, 2007.

Miyajima Kazuhiko. "Genshi tenmonshi kisai no isuramu tenmongiki ni tsuite [New Identification of Islamic astronomical instruments described in the Yuan-shi]." In *Tōyō no kagaku to gijutsu* [Science and skills in Asia], 407-427. Kyoto: Dōhōsha Shuppan, 1982.

Miyakawa, Hisayuki. "An Outline of the Naitō Hypothesis and its effects on Japanese Studies of China." *Far Eastern Quarterly* 14 (1955): 533–552.

Miyazaki Masakatsu 宮崎正勝. *Te'iwa no nankai dai ensei: eiraku tei no sekai chitsujo saihen* 鄭和の南海大遠征：永楽帝の世界秩序再編 [The maritime grand expeditions of Zheng He: The reorganization of the world by Emperor Yongle]. Tokyo: Chūō kōronsha, 1997.

Morgan, David. *The Mongols*. Oxford: B. Blackwell, 2007 [1986].

Mote, Frederick W. and Denis Twitchett. *The Cambridge History of China*. Vol. 7: *The Ming Dynasty, 1368–1644*, Part 1. Cambridge: Cambridge University Press, 1988.

Nanjing shi bowuguan 南京市博物馆. *Baochuanchang yizhi* 宝船厂遗址 [Baochuanchang Shipyard in Nanjing]. Beijing: Wenwu, 2006.

Needham, Joseph and Wang Ling. *Science and Civilisation in China*. Vol. 3: *Mathematics and the Sciences of the Heavens and the Earth*. Cambridge: Cambridge University Press, 1959.

Needham, Joseph, Wang Ling, and Lu Gwei-djen. *Science and Civilisation in China*. Vol. 4: *Physics and Physical Technology: Part III. Civil Engineering and Nautics*. Cambridge: Cambridge University Press, 1971.

Netton, I. R. "Myth, Miracle and Magic in the Rihla of Ibn Battuta." *Journal of Semitic Studies* 29 (1984): 131–140.

"Basic Structures and Signs of Alienation in the Riḥla of Ibn Jubayr." In *Golden Roads: Migration, Pilgrimage and Travel in Mediaeval and Modern Islam*, 57–63.

Ohji Toshiaki 応地利明. *Chizu ha kataru: sekai chizu no tanjō* 地図は語る「世界地図」の誕生 [The map speaks out: the birth of the world map]. Tokyo: Nihon keizai shimbun shuppansha 日本経済新聞出版社, 2007.

Echizu no sekaizō 絵地図の世界像 [The portraits of the world in illustrated maps]. Tokyo: Iwanami 岩波, 1996.

"Indo yō no rikufū to kaihō インド洋の陸封と解放 [Landlocking and Unlocking of the Indian Ocean]." In *Daichi no Shōzō – Ezu・Chizu ga kataru sekai* 大地の肖像 – 絵図・地図が語る世界 [Portrait of the earth: the world described by pictorial maps and geographical maps], edited by Fuji'i Jōji 藤井譲治, Kinda Akihiro 金田章裕, and Sugiyama Masa'aki 杉山正明, 29–53. Kyoto: Kyoto Daigaku Gakujutsu Shuppankai, 2007.

Okada, Hidehiro. "China as a Successor State to the Mongol Empire." In *The Mongol Empire and its Legacy*, edited by Reuven Amitai-Preiss and David O. Morgan, 260–272. Leiden: Brill, 1999.

Ondaatje, Christopher. *Journey to the Source of the Nile*. Toronto: HarperCollins Publishers Ltd., 1998.

Ostafin, Barbara. "Yāqūt-Geographer, Compiler or Adīb? According to the Preface to his Dictionary." *Folia Orientalia* 30 (1994): 119–123.

Park, Hyunhee. "A Buddhist Woodblock-Printed Map and Geographic Knowledge in 13th Century China," *Crossroads – Studies on the History of Exchange Relations in the East Asian World* 1 (September 2010): 55–78.

"Cross-Cultural Exchange and Geographic Knowledge of the World in Yuan China." In *Eurasian Influences on Yuan China: Cross-Cultural Transmissions in the 13th and 14th Centuries*, edited by Morris Rossabi and John Chaffee, 125-157. Singapore: The Institute for Southeast Asian Studies, 2012.

"Port-City Networking in the Indian Ocean Commercial System Represented in Geographic and Cartographic Works in China and the Islamic World from 750 to 1500." In *The Growth of Non-Western Cities: Primary and Secondary Urban Networking, c. 900–1900*, edited by Kenneth Hall (Lanham, MD: Lexington Books, 2011), 21–53.

Pearson, Richard, Li Min, and Li Guo. "Port, City, and Hinterlands: Archaeological Perspectives on Quanzhou and its Overseas Trade." In *The Emporium of the World: Maritime Quanzhou, 1000–1400*, edited by Angela Schottenhammer, 177–235. Leiden: Brill, 2001.

Pelliot, Paul (1878–1945). *Notes on Marco Polo*. Paris: Impr. nationale, 1959. 3 vols.

Piacentini, V. F. *Merchants – Merchandise and Military Power in the Persian Gulf (Sūriyānj/Shahriyāj – Sīrāf)*. Rome: Accademia Nazionale Dei Lincei, 1992.

Pirazzoli-T'serstevens, Michèle. "A Commodity in Great Demand: Chinese Ceramics Imported in the Arabo-Persian Gulf from the Ninth to the Fourteenth Century." *Orient* 8 (2004): 26–38.

Prinsep. J. "Note on the Nautical Instrument of the Arabs." In *Introduction: à L'astronomie Nautique Arabe*, edited by Gabriel Ferrand, 1–24. Paris: Librairie Orientaliste Paul Geuthner, 1928.

Ptak, Roderich. *China's Seaborne Trade with South and Southeast Asia (1200–1750)*. Aldershot: Ashgate, 1999.

"Glosses on Wang Dayuan's *Daoyi zhilüe*." In *Récits de Voyages Asiatiques: Genres, Mentalistés, Conception de l'Espace, Actes du Colloque EFEO-EHESS de Décembre 1994*, edited by Claudine Salmon. Paris: Ecole française d'Extrême-Orient, 1996.

"Merchants and Maximization: Notes on Chinese and Portuguese Entrepreneurship in Maritime Asia, c. 1350–1600." In *Maritime Asia: Profit Maximization, Ethics and Trade Structure, c. 1300–1800*, edited by Karl Anton Sprengard and Roderich Ptak. Wiesbaden: Harrassowitz, 1994.

"Ming Maritime Trade to Southeast Asia, 1368–1567: Visions of a 'System.'" In *From the Mediterranean to the China Sea: Miscellaneous Notes*, edited by Claude Guillot, Denys Lombard and Roderich Ptak, 157–191. Wiesbaden: Harrassowitz, 1998.

"Wang Dayuan on Kerala." In *Explorations in the History of South Asia: Essays in Honour of Eietmar Rothermund*, edited by Georg Berkemer, Tilman Frasch, Hermann Kulke, and Jürgen Lütt. New Delhi: Manohar, 2001.

Qiu Yihao 邱轶皓. "Yutu yuanzi haixi lai – Taolisi wenxuan jizhen suozai shijie ditu kao 舆图原自海西来 – <桃里寺文献集珍>所载世界地图考 [The Exotic Geography Knowledge from Ilkhanate – A study on the world map in *Safineh-yi Tabrīz*]." *Xiyu yanjiu*西域研究 [Studies of the Western Regions] 82, no. 2 (2011): 23–143.

Rachewiltz, Igor de. "Marco Polo Went to China." *Zentralasiatische Studien* 27 (1997): 34–92.

Ragep, F. Jamil. "Islamic Reactions to Ptolemy's Imprecisions." In *Ptolemy in Perspective: Use and Criticism of his Work from Antiquity to the Nineteenth Century*, edited by Alexander Jones, 121–134. New York: Springer, 2010.

Rapoport, Yossef. "The Book of Curiosities: A medieval Islamic view of the East." In *The Journey of Maps and Images on the Silk Road*, edited by Philippe Forêt and Andreas Kaplony, 155–171. Leiden: Brill, 2008.

Ray, Himanshu P. *The Archaeology of Seafaring in Ancient South Asia*. Cambridge: Cambridge University Press. 2003.

Richards, D. S. ed. *Islam and the Trade of Asia*. London: Spottiswoode, Ballantyne & Co. Ltd, 1970.

Risso, Patricia. *Merchants & Faith: Muslim Commerce and Culture in the Indian Ocean*. Colorado: Westview Press. 1995.

Robinson, David M. ed. *Culture, Courtiers and Competition: the Ming Court (1368–1644)*. Cambridge, MA: Harvard University Asian Center, 2008.

Rong Xinjiang 榮新江. *Zhonggu Zhongguo yu wailai wenming* 中古中國與外來文明 [Middle-period China and outside cultures]. Beijing: Shenghuo dushu xinzhi Sanlian shudian, 2001.

Rossabi, Morris. ed. *China among Equals: The Middle Kingdom and Its Neighbors, 10th-14th Centuries*. Berkeley: University of California Press, 1983.

"From Chen Cheng to Ma Wensheng: Changing Chinese Visions of Central Asia." *Crossroads – Studies on the History of Exchange Relations in the East Asian World* 1 (September 2010).

Khubilai Khan: His Life and Times. Berkeley: University of California Press, 1988.

"Mongol Empire and its Impact on the Arts of China." Unpublished paper prepared for the conference at the Hebrew University of Jerusalem, June 2006.

"The Ming and Inner Asia." In *The Cambridge History of China*. Vol. 8: *The Ming Dynasty, 1368–1644*, Part 2, edited by Denis Twitchett and Frederick W. Mote, 221–271. Cambridge: Cambridge University Press, 1998.

"Two Ming Envoys to Inner Asia." *T'oung Pao* 62, no. 1–3 (1976): 1–34.

Voyager from Xanadu. Tokyo: Kōdansha International, 1992.

Rougeulle, Axelle. "Medieval Trade Networks in the Western Indian Ocean (8–14th cent.): Some Reflections from the Distribution Pattern of Chinese Imports in the Islamic World." In *Tradition and Archaeology: Early Maritime Contacts in the Indian Ocean*, edited by Himanshu Prabha Ray and Jean-Francois Salles, 159–180. New Delhi: Manohar, 1996.

Saguchi Toru 佐口透. *Mongoru teikoku to seiyou: Tozaibunnmei no koryu* モンゴル帝國と西洋: 東西文明の交流 [The Mongol Empire and the West: The Cultural Exchange between the East and the West]. Tokyo: Heibonsha, 1998.

Saliba, George. *A History of Arabic Astronomy: Planetary Theories during the Golden Age of Islam*. New York: NYU Press, 1995.

Schafer, Edward H. *The Golden Peaches of Samarkand: A Study of T'ang Exotics*. Berkeley: University of California Press, 1963.

Schottenhammer, Angela, ed. *The Emporium of the World: Maritime Quanzhou, 1000–1400*. Leiden: Brill, 2001.

"Transfer of *Xiangyao* 香藥 from Iran and Arabia to China – A Reinvestigation of Entries in the *Youyang zazu* 酉陽雜俎 (862)." *Aspects of the Maritime Silk Road: From the Persian Gulf to the East China Sea*. Wiesbaden: Harrassowitz Verlag, 2010.

Sen, Tansen. *Buddhism, Diplomacy, and Trade: the Realignment of Sino-Indian Relations, 600–1400*. Honolulu: University of Hawai'i Press, 2003.

"The Yuan Khanate and India: Cross-Cultural Diplomacy in the Thirteenth and Fourteenth Centuries." *Asia Major* 1/2, part 1/2 (2006): 299–326.

Sezgin, Fuat. ed. *Studies on Yāqūt al-Ḥamawī (d. 1229)*. Frankfurt am Main: Institute for the History of Arabic-Islamic Science at the Johann Wolfgang Goethe University, 1994.

Mathematical Geography and Cartography in Islam and Their Continuation in the Occident. Parts 1–3 (Being an English Version of Volume X, XI, and XII of *Geschichte des Arabischen Schrifttums*), translated by Guy Moore and Geoff Sammon. Frankfurt am Main: Institute for the History of Arabic-

Islamic Science at the Johann Wolfgang Goethe University, 2000–2007. 3 vols.

Science and Technology in Islam: Catalogue of the Exhibition of the Institute for the History of Arabic-Islamic Science (Johann Wolfgang Goethe University in Frankfurt, Germany) at the Frankfurt Book Fair 2004. Frankfurt am Main: Institut für Geschichte der Arabisch-Islamischen Wissenschaften, 2004.

Skaff, Jonathan K. "The Sogdian Trade Diaspora in East Turkestan during the Seventh and Eighth Centuries." *Journal of the Economic and Social History of the Orient* 46, no. 4 (2003): 475–524.

Skelton, R. A. *Explorer's Maps: Charters in the Cartographic Record of Geographical Discovery*. New York: Praeger, 1958.

Sleeswyk, Andre Wegener. "The Liao and the Displacement of Ships in the Ming Navy." *The Mariner's Mirror* 82, no. 1 (February 1996): 3–13.

Smith, Paul, and Richard von Glahn, eds. *The Song-Yuan-Ming Transition in Chinese History*. Cambridge, MA: Harvard University Press, 2003.

Smith, Richard J. *Chinese Maps: Images of "All Under Heaven."* Hong Kong: Oxford University Press, 1996.

Snow, Philip. *The Star Raft: China's Encounter with Africa*. New York: Weidenfeld and Nicolson, 1988.

So, Billy K. L. *Prosperity, Region, and Institutions in Maritime China: the South Fukien Pattern, 946–1368*. Cambridge, MA: Harvard University Asia Center, 2000.

Soucek, Priscilla. "Ceramic Production as Exemplar of Yuan-Ilkhanid Relations." *Res* 35 (Spring 1999): 125–141.

Sprenger, Aloya. *Die Post- und Reiserouten des Orients*. Nendeln, Liechtenstein: Kraus Reprint, 1966.

Spuler, B. "The Disintegration of the Caliphate in the East." In *The Cambridge History of Islam, Vol. 1A: the Central Islamic Lands from Pre-Islamic Times to the First World War*, edited by P. M. Holt, Ann K. S. Lambton, and Bernard Lewis, 143–174. Cambridge: Cambridge University Press, 1970.

Steinhardt, Nancy Shatzman. "Chinese Cartography and Calligraphy." *Oriental Art* 43, no. 1 (1997): 10–20.

Chinese Imperial City Planning. Honolulu: University of Hawaii Press, 1990.

Subrahmanyam, Sanjay. *The Career and Legend of Vasco da Gama*. New York: Cambridge University Press, 1997.

Sugiyama Masa'aki 杉山正明. *Bunmei no michi*, Vol 5, *Mongoru teikoku* 文明の道, 第5巻, モンゴル帝国 [The road of civilization, Vol 5, the Mongol empire]. Tokyo: Nihon hōsō kyōkai, 2004.

Kubirai no chōsen: Mongoru kaijō teikoku e no michi クビライの挑戦: モンゴル海上帝国への道 [Challenge of Kubirai: The road to the Mongol maritime empire]. Tokyo: Asahi Shinbunsha, 1995.

Mongoru teikoku no kōbō モンゴル帝國の興亡 [The rise and fall of the Mongol empire]. Tokyo: Kōdansha, 1996. 2 vols.

Mongoru teikoku to daigen urusu モンゴル帝国と大元ウルス [The Mongol empire and the Great Yuan Ulus]. Kyoto: Kyoto Daigaku Gakujutsu Shuppankai, 2004.

Shikkusuru sōgen no seifukusha, Ryō, Seika, Kin, Gen 疾駆する草原の征服者：遼、西夏、金、元 [The sweeping conqueror of the steppe, the dynasties of Liao, Xixia, Jin, and Yuan]. Tokyo: Kōdansha, 2005.

"Tōzai no sekaizu ga kataru jinrui saisho no dai chihei 東西の世界図が語る人類最初の大地平 [The first portrait of the world depicted in the world maps in the East and the West]." In *Daichi no Shōzō – Ezu・Chizu ga kataru sekai* 大地の肖像 – 絵図・地図が語る世界 [Portrait of the earth: The world described by pictorial maps and geographical maps], edited by Fuji'i Jōji 藤井譲治, Kinda Akihiro 金田章裕, and Sugiyama Masa'aki 杉山正明, 54–69. Kyoto: Kyoto Daigaku Gakujutsu Shuppankai, 2007.

Yūbokumin kara mita sekaishi 遊牧民から見た世界史 – 民族も国境もこえて [The world history seen from the nomads – Beyond the nations and borders]. Tokyo: Nihon Keizai shimbun sha 日本經濟新聞社, 1997.

Sun Guangqi 孙光圻. *Zhongguo gudai hanghai shi* 中国古代航海史 [History of ancient Chinese navigation]. Beijing: Haijun 海军, 2005.

Sun Guangqi 孙光圻 and Chen Ying 金陈鹰. "Shilun Zheng He suoxingshu zhongde alabo tianwen hanghai yinsu 试论郑和索星术中的阿拉伯天文航海因素 [An attempt to discuss factors of the Arab astronomical navigation in Zheng He voyages observing the stellar location technique]." In *Zheng He yanjiu lunwen ji* [The collection of academic articles about Zheng He]. Vol. 1. Dalian: Dalian haiyun xueyuan 大连海运学院, 1993.

Taiwan Zhongyanyuan lishi yuyan yanjiusuo bianjiao 臺灣中研院歷史語言研究所編校. *Ming shilu jiaokan ji* 明實錄校勘記 [A collated edition of the veritable records of the Ming dynasty]. Beijing: Xianzhuang shuju 綫裝書局, 2005.

Takahashi Tadashi 高橋正. "Aru-kuwārizumī zusetsu [gaiho] アル・クワーリズミー図説 [概報] [A report on the illustration of al-Khuārizmī's geography]." *Chiri gakushi kenkyū* 地理學史研究 2 (1962): 7–58.

Tampoe, Moira. *Maritime Trade between China and the West: An Archaeological Study of the Ceramics from Siraf (Persian Gulf), 8th to 15th centuries A.D.* Oxford: B. A. R., 1989.

Tang Zhiba 唐志拔. "Zheng He baochuan chidu zhi wojian 郑和宝船尺度之我见 [My opinion about the size of the Zheng He treasure ships]." *Chuanshi yanjiu* 船史研究 [The study of the history of ships] 17 (2002): 21–27.

Tazaka Kōdō 田坂興道. "An Aspect of Islam Culture Introduced into China." *Memoirs of the Research Department of the Tōyō Bunko* 16 (1957): 75–160.

Chūgoku ni okeru kaikyō no denrai to sono gutsū 中國における回教の傳來とその弘通 [Islam in China: its introduction and development]. Tokyo: Tōyō Bunko, 1964. 2 vols.

Teng, Emma Jinhua. *Taiwan's Imagined Geography: Chinese Colonial Travel Writing and Pictures, 1683 – 1895*. Cambridge, MA: Harvard University Press, 2004.

Thackston, W. M. *A Century of Princes: Sources on Timurid History and Art.* Cambridge, MA: The Aga Khan Program for Islamic Architecture, 1989.

Tibbetts, G. R. *A Study of the Arabic Texts Containing Material on South-east Asia*. Leiden: Brill, 1979.

"Later Cartographic Developments." In *The History of Cartography: Volume Two, Book One, Cartography in the Traditional Islamic and South Asian Societies*, edited by J. B. Harley and David Woodward, 137–155. Chicago: University of Chicago Press, 1992.

"The Balkhī School of Geographers." In *The History of Cartography: Volume Two, Book One, Cartography in the Traditional Islamic and South Asian Societies*, edited by J. B. Harley and David Woodward, 108–136. Chicago: University of Chicago Press, 1992.

Tillman, Hoyt Cleveland and Stephen West, eds. *China under Jurchen Rule*. Albany: State University of New York Press, 1995.

Twitchett, Denis. *The Writing of Official History Under the T'ang*. New York: Cambridge University Press, 1992.

Twitchett, Denis and Frederick W. Mote. *The Cambridge History of China*. Vol. 8: *The Ming Dynasty, 1368–1644*, Part 2. Cambridge: Cambridge University Press, 1998.

Twitchett, Denis and Janice Stargardt. "Chinese Silver Bullion in a Tenth-Century Indonesian Wreck." *Asia Major* (3rd series), 15, no. 1 (2002), 23–72.

Ulving, Tor. *Dictionary of Old and Middle Chinese: Bernhard Karlgren's Grammata Serica Recensa Alphabetically Arranged*. Gōteborg: Acta Universitatis Gothoburgensis, 1997.

Unno Kazutaka 海野一隆. *Chizu no bunkashi – sekai to nihon* 地図の文化史 – 世界と日本 [The cultural history of maps – the world and Japan]. Tokyo: Yasaka shobō 八坂書房, 1996.

Tōyō Chirigaku shi kenkyū: Tairiku hen 東洋地理学史研究: 大陸篇 [Monographs on the history of geography in the East: volume on continental Asian societies]. Osaka: Seibundō, 2004.

Vikor, Knut S. *Between God and the Sultan: A History of Islamic Law*. New York: Oxford University Press, 2006.

Wade, Geoff. "The Li (李) and Pu (蒲) 'surnames' in East Asia-Middle East Maritime Silkroad Interactions during the 10th-20th Centuries." In *Aspects of the Maritime Silk Road*, ed. Ralph Kauz, 181–193. Wiesbaden: Harrassowitz Verlag, 2010.

Wade, Geoff and Sun Laichen, eds. *Southeast Asia in the Fifteenth Century: The Ming Factor*. Singapore: University of Singapore Press, 2010.

"The *Ming Shi-lu* as a source for Southeast Asian History, to accompany *Southeast Asia in the Ming Shi-lu: an open access resource* <http://epress.nus.edu.sg/msl>, 2005.

Wang Gungwu. "Merchants without Empire: The Hokkien Sojourning Communities." In *The Rise of Merchant Empires. Long Distance-Trade in the Early Modern World, 1350–1750*, edited by James D. Tracy, 400–421. Cambridge: Cambridge University Press, 1990.

"Ming Foreign Relations: Southeast Asia." In *The Cambridge History of China*. Vol. 8: *The Ming Dynasty, 1368–1644*, Part 2, edited by Denis Twitchett and Frederick W. Mote, 301–332. Cambridge: Cambridge University Press, 1998.

The Nanhai Trade: Early Chinese Trade in the South China Sea. Singapore: Eastern Universities Press, 2003.

Wang Jianping. *Concord and Conflict: the Hui Communities of Yunnan Society.* Stockholm: Almqvist & Wiksell, 1996.
Wang Q. Edward. "History, Space, and Ethnicity: The Chinese Worldview." *Journal of World History* 10, no. 2 (Fall 1999): 285–305.
Wang Qianjin 汪前进, Hu Qisong 胡启松, and Liu Ruofang 刘若芳. "Juanben caihui daming hunyi yitu yanjiu 绢本彩绘大明混一图研究 [As regards the Da Ming Hun Yi Tu (Amalgamated map of the Great Ming Dynasty) drawn in colors on stiff silk]." In *Zhongguo gudai ditu ji: Ming* 中国古代地图集: 明 [An atlas of ancient maps in China – the Ming Dynasty (1368–1644)], edited by Cao Wanru 曹婉如 et al, 51–55. Beijing: Wenwu, 1994.
Wang Tao. "Parthia in China: a Re-examination of the Historical Records." In *The Age of the Parthians: The Idea of Iran*: Vol. 2, edited by Vesta S. Curtis and Sarah Stewart, 87-104. London: I. B.Tauris, 2007.
Wang Yong 王庸. *Zhongguo ditu shi gang* 中国地图史纲 [Outline of the history of Chinese maps]. Beijing: Xinhua, 1958.
Wheatley, Paul. "Geographical Notes on Some Communities Involved in Sung Maritime Trade." *Journal of the Malayan Branch of the Royal Asiatic Society* 32, no. 2 (1961): 5–140.
Whitehouse, David. "'Abbāsid Maritime Trade: the Age of Expansion." In *Cultural and Economic Relations between East and West*, edited by H. I. H. Prince Takahito Mikasa. Wiesbaden: Otto Harrassowitz, 1988.
Wilkinson, Endymion Porter. *Chinese History: a Manual.* Cambridge, MA: Harvard University Press, 2000.
Wills, John E. "Maritime Asia, 1500–1800: The Interactive Emergence of European Domination." *The American Historical Review* 98, no. 1 (1993): 83–105.
Woodward, David. "Medieval Mappaemundi." In *The History of Cartography: Volume One: Cartography in Prehistoric, Ancient and Medieval Europe and the Mediterranean*, ed. J. B. Harley and David Woodward, 286–370. Chicago: University of Chicago Press, 1987.
Wu Chunming 吴春明. *Huan Zhongguo hai chenchuan: gudai fanchuan, chuanji yu chuanhuo* 环中国海沉船: 古代帆船、船技与船货 [Shipwrecks from China Sea: Ancient sailing boats, navigation techniques and merchandise]. Nanchang: Jiangxi gaoxiao, 2003.
Yajima Hikoichi 家島彦一. *Ibun Battūta no sekai dai ryokō – 14 seiki Isurāmu no jikū wo ikiru* イブン・バットゥータの世界大旅行 – 14世紀イスラームの時空を生きる [The great world travel of Ibn Baṭṭūṭa – Living in the Islamic world in the fourteenth century]. Tokyo: Heibon sha, 2003.
"Jūgo seiki ni okeru indo yō tsūshōshi no hitokoma: teiwa'ensei buntai no iemen hōmon ni tsuite 十五世紀におけるインド洋通商史の一齣: 鄭和遠征分隊のイエメン訪問について [Some aspects of the Indian Ocean trade in the 15th century: On the arrivals of Chinese Junks at 'Adan]." *Ajia Afurika Gengo Bunka Kenkyū* アジア・アフリカ言語文化研究 [Journal of Asian and African Studies] 8 (1974): 137–155.
Yamagata Kinya 山形欣哉. *Rekishi no umi wo hashiru: Chūgoku zōsen gijutsu no kōseki* 歴史の海を走る 中国造船技術の航跡 [Sailing on the sea of history: A survey of Chinese shipbuilding technology]. Tokyo: Nōbun kyō, 2004.

Yang Zhijiu 杨志玖. *Yuanshi sanlun* 元史三語 [Three discussions on the history of the Yuan]. Beijing: Renmin, 1985.
Yee, Cordell D. K. "Chinese Maps in Political Culture." In *The History of Cartography, Volume Two, Book Two: Cartography in the Traditional East and Southeast Asian Societies*, edited by J. B. Harley and David Woodward, 71–95. Chicago: University of Chicago Press, 1994.
"Reinterpreting Traditional Chinese Geographic Maps." In *The History of Cartography, Volume Two, Book Two: Cartography in the Traditional East and Southeast Asian Societies*, edited by J. B. Harley and David Woodward, 35–70. Chicago: University of Chicago Press, 1994.
"Taking the World's Measure: Chinese Maps between Observation and Text." In *The History of Cartography: Volume Two, Book Two: Cartography in the Traditional East and Southeast Asian Societies*, edited by J. B. Harley and David Woodward, 96–127. Chicago: University of Chicago Press, 1995.
Yokkaichi Yasuhiro 四日市康博. "Chinese and Muslim Diasporas and the Indian Ocean Trade Network under Mongol Hegemony." In *The East Asian Mediterranean: Maritime Crossroads of Culture, Commerce and Human Migration*, edited by Angela Schottenhammer, 73-102. Wiesbaden: Harrassowitz Verlag, 2008.
"Gen-chō no chūbai hōka: sono igi oyobi nankai bō'eki-orutoku tono kakawarini tsu'ite 元朝の中賣寶貨: その意義および南海交易・オルトクとの関わりについて [Yuan-period Zhongmai baohua: its significance and relationship between south sea trading and ortagh]." *Nairiku Ajia shi kenkyū* 内陸アジア史研究 [Study of Inner Asian history] 17 (2002): 41–59.
Yuan Xiaocun 袁晓春. "A study of the differences between the Sinan ship and ancient Chinese ships 韩国新安沉船与中国古代沉船比较研究." *The Conservation and Restoration of Shinan Ship, the 20 Years History*. Mokpo: Kungnip Haeyang Yumul Chŏnsigwan 국립해양유물전시관, 2004.
Yuba Tadanori 弓場紀知. "Ejiputo・Fusutāto Iseki shutsudo no tōji: Ibutsu ichiranhyō エジプト・フスタート遺跡出土の陶磁: 遺物一覧表 [A chart of porcelains found in Fustat excavation sites]." In *Tōjiki no tōzai kōryū: Ejiputo・Fusutāto Iseki shutsudo no tōji* 陶磁器の東西交流: エジプト・フスタート遺跡出土の陶磁 [The inter-influence of ceramic art in East and West]. Tokyo: Idemitsu bijutsukan, 1984.
"Gen seika jiki to Mongoru teikoku 元青花磁器とモンゴル帝国" [Yuan blue-and-white porcelain and the Mongol empire]. In *Tōjiki no tōzai kōryū: Ejiputo・Fusutāto Iseki shutsudo no tōji* 陶磁器の東西交流:エジプト・フスタート遺跡出土の陶磁 [The inter-influence of ceramic art in East and West]. Tokyo: Idemitsu bijutsukan, 1984.
Zhang Jun-yan. "Relations between China and the Arabs in Early Times." *The Journal of Oman Studies*, no. 6 (1980): 91–109.
Zhang Xinglang 張星烺. "Quanzhou fanggu ji 泉州访古记 [Account of visiting historical remains in Quanzhou]." *Dili zazhi* 地理杂志 [Journal of geography] 17, no. 1 (1928): 3–22.

Index

'Abbāsids, 'Abbāsid caliphate, 7
  breakup of, 90
  conflicts with the Tang army in Central Asia, 11, 24–25
  Du You's section about, 26
  fall of, 17, 96
  in Jia Dan's Route, 32
  updating their geographic knowledge, 12
'Abd al-Razzāq al-Samarqandī, 183
Abū al-Fidā', 147
Abu-Lughod, Janet, 197
Abū Zayd al-Sīrāfī, 52, 65–74, 77, 84, 86, 87, 89
Abyssinian Sea. *See* Indian Ocean
Account of Foreign Countries in the Western Regions (Xiyu fanguo zhi). *See* Chen Cheng
Account of the Palace Library (*Mishujian zhi*), 99, 103, 107
Accounts of China and India (*Akhbār al-Ṣīn wa-l-Hind*), 63–72, 86, 155, 157
Achaemenids, 128
Aḥmad, Yuan minister, 99, 138
Alexander the Great
  wall of, 134
Alexandria, 53
  Lighthouse of, 53, 106
Allsen, Thomas, 98
Amīr Sayyid Toghān Shāh, 111
An Lushan rebellion, 29
Anxi. See Parthian Empire
Arabs, 2, 6, 11, 20, 22, 28, 29, 60, 119, 181
archeological excavations
  in Aden, 30
  in Arikamedu, 30
  in Banbhore, 30
  in Sīrāf, 30, 66
  in Suhar, 30
  of Zheng He shipyards in Nanjing, 171
Arigh Böke, 97
atabeg, 95
'AṭāMalik. *See History of the World Conqueror*
Ayyubids, 52

Baghdad, 21
  Chinese craftsmen in, 68
  commercial connection of, to China, 57, 64
  fall of, 94, 126
  as the new 'Abbāsid capital, 27, 32
al-Balkhī, 73, 75
Balkhī School, 73, 75, 76, 77, 78, 80, 84, 90, 129, 148
Ban Gu, legendary first emperor of China, 138
Basra, 32, 61
Battle of 'Ayn Jālūt, 19, 127
Battle of Talas, 21, 25
Bayt al-Ḥikmah (House of Wisdom), 59
Beijing. *See* Dadu (Daidu) and Khanbaliq
al-Bīrūnī, 78–80, 84, 87, 130, 147
  Zīj of, 78
blue-and-white porcelain, 117, 176
Bolad, 125, 138
Book of Curiosities, 80

Book of Min (Minshu), 115, 116, 167
Book of Profitable Things Concerning the First Principles and Rules of Navigation (*Kitāb al-fawā'id fī uṣūl 'ilm al-baḥr wa-l-qawā'id*). *See* Ibn Mājid
Book of Roger, 82–83, 86, 181
Book of Routes and Realms (*Kitāb al-Masālik wa-'l-mamālik*), 60–64, 71
Book of the Lands (Kitāb al-Buldān), 76
Book of the Wonders of India, 64
Branch Quanzhou Prefecture Office (*xing Quanfu si*), 110, 137
Branch Secretariats (*Xing zhongshu sheng*), 137
Braudel, Fernand, 17
Broad Terrestrial Map (*Guang yutu*), 165–167, 189. *See also* Luo Hongxian
Bureau for the Procurement of Necessities (*zhiyong yuan*), 112
Buyids, 75, 126
Byzantine empire, 163

Caliph al-Ma'mūn, 59, 76, 148
 commissioning a geodetic survey, 59
 world map of, 59, 76
Caliph al-Manṣūr, 57
Caliph al-Mu'tamid, 60
Caliph Amir al-Mu'minin, 26, 32
Canary Islands, 181
cartography. *See* maps
 development of, ancient China, 14
 development of, Islamic world, 74
Chaffee, John, 44
Chagatai Khanate, 102
Chain of the Histories (Silsilat al-tawarīkh), 65
Chang De. *See Record of an Embassy to the Regions in the West* (*Xishi ji*)
Chang'an, 21, 68
 Western Market, 69
Chaudhuri, K. N., 17
Chen Cheng, 168, 188, 195
Chen Dazhen. *See Record of the Southern Sea* (*Nanhai zhi*)
Chīn. *See* China
China
 Chīn [China], 6, 80
 definition of, in this book, 5, 19
 Māchīn[greater China], 80
 Manzi, 135
 and the Silk Road, 5
 al-Ṣīn, 6, 81, 87, 144
 Ṣīn al-Ṣīn, 148, 155
China-centered "world order", 22
Chinggis Khan, 18, 93
Chinistan. See China
Choice of the Age, on the Marvels of Land and Sea (Nukhbat al-dahr fī 'ajā'ib al-barr wa-'l-baḥr). *See* Dimashqī, Shams al-Dīn
Classic of Mountains and Seas (Shanhai jing), 10
Columbus, Christopher, 4, 162, 197
Compendium of Chronicles (*Jāmi' al-tawārīkh*). *See* Rashīd al-Dīn
Comprehensive Map of the Great Ming Empire (Daming hunyi tu), 164, 172, 173, 189
Continuation of the History and Topography of Quanzhou (Qingyuan xuzhi). See Wu Jian
country of Shi, 25

da Gama, Vasco, 1, 188, 189, 196
Dadu (Daidu), 108, 135, 136
Daibul, 32
Dār al-Islām (the land of Islam), 59
Dar es Salaam, 33
Dashi, 2, 6, 20, 23
 countries of, 47
Description of the Foreign Lands (Zhufan zhi), 46, 50–54
dhow ships
 characteristics of, 65
 Chinese description about the shipbuilding technology of, 118
 shipwrecks in Belitung, 16
Dimashqī, Shams al-Dīn, 147
Ding Jiezhai, 111
Du Huan, 56, 68, 91, 113, 116, 119
Du You, 62. *See also Encyclopedic History of Institutions* (*Tongdian*)

"Eastern Sea of the Muslims" (Dong Dashi hai), 48, 49
Egypt, 47, 52
Emperor Yongle, 168–169, 179, 182, 189, 195
Encompassing Sea, 76
Encyclopedia of Yuan Dynasty Institutions(Yuan Jingshi dadian), 100, 102
 geographical map of, 100, 142

Encyclopedic History of Institutions (Tongdian), 11, 50. *See also* Du You
Euphrates, 32
European exploration and discovery, 4

Fakhr al-Dīn, 140
Fatimids, 52
Fei Xin, 175–176

Ganpu, 112
Gaozong, Song Dynasty, 134
Gaozong, Tang Dynasty, 35
Gathering of the Summarizing Concerning the First Principles of the Knowledge of the Seas (Ḥāwiyat al-ikhtiṣār fī uṣūl ʿilm al-biḥār). *See* Ibn Mājid
General Map of China (Yu ditu), 42–43
General Records of the Founders of Buddhism(Fozu tongji), 38–41
"General Survey Map of Chinese and Non-Chinese Territories from the Past through the Present" (Gujin huayi quyu zongyao tu), 34, 37
Geniza records, 71
"Geographic Map of the Land of China to the East" (Dong zhendan dili tu), 41, 51
Geographical Dictionary (Muʿjam al-buldān), 86
  of al-Qazwīnī, 129
  of Yāqūt, 86–87, 129
geography
  descriptive, in China, 34
  descriptive, of Abū al-Fidā', 147
  descriptive, of Ibn al-Faqīh, 76
  descriptive, of Ibn Khurradādhbih, 60
  physical and mathematical, as a field, 11
  physical and mathematical, of Caliph al-Ma'mūn, 59
Ghazan, 112, 128, 131, 133, 139, 140
  conversion to Islam during the reign of, 180
  envoys to China dispatched by, 112, 140
  and Rashīd al-Dīn, 131
Ghazni, 47, 113
Ghiyāth al-Dīn Naqqāsh, 182–183, 188, 195
glass, 28
Go Seonji [Chinese: Gao Xianzhi], 24
Gog and Magog, 84, 134
Golden Horde, 102
Governmental Ship (*guanben chuan*), 111
Grand Canal, 136
Great Wall, 133
grid maps, in China, 100
Guangxi, 46
Guangzhou, 6, 44, 61, 66
  Huang Chao Rebellion in, 70
  Ibn Baṭṭūṭa's journey to, 154
  local gazetteer from, 113
  Office of the Superintendent of Merchant Shipping in, 48
  self-governing districts in, 34, 67
  Ṣīn Kalān, 155
Guo Kan, 96
Guo Ziyi, 96

hajj, 47, 152, 176
Ḥamd Allāh Mustawfīal-Qazwīnī, 141–146
Handy Geographical Maps throughout the Ages (Lidai dili zhizhang tu), 34
Hanoi, 61
Hearts' Bliss (Nuzhat al-Qulūb). *See* Ḥamd Allāh Mustawfīal-Qazwīnī
Henry the Navigator, 4, 162, 197
History of Ghazan. *See* Rashīd al-Dīn
History of the Former Han (Hanshu), 31
History of the World Conqueror, 127
Hormuz, 92, 107, 117
  described by ʿAbd al-Razzāq al-Samarqandī, 183
  Ma Huan's section about, 178
  rivalry of, with Qais, 107, 151
  route to, in a Chinese map, 107
  Yang Shu's trip to, 112, 113
  in the Zheng He sea chart, 174
  Zheng He's voyages to, 170
Hourani, George, 198
Huang Chao Rebellion, 69, 87
Huihui (Muslim), 99
Huihui calendar (*Huihui li*), 100
Hülegü, 18, 94, 96
Hyecho [Chinese: Huichao], 6

Ibn al-Faqīh, 75
Ibn al-Nadīm. *See Kitāb al-Fihrist*
Ibn Amīr Ḥājib, a sultan of Mali, 149
Ibn Baṭṭūṭa, 114, 124, 137, 152–160, 185, 195, 200
Ibn Faḍlallāh al-ʿUmarī, 148–150
Ibn Ḥawqal, 75
Ibn Jubayr, 153
Ibn Juzayy, 153, 155, 157
Ibn Khaldūn, 158, 161, 180–182, 189
Ibn Khazar, 152

Ibn Khurradādhbih, 58, 76, 133, 144, *See also Book of Routes and Realms* (*Kitāb al-Masālik wa-'l-mamālik*)
Ibn Mājid, 162, 174, 184–190
Ibn Wahab, 68–69
al-Idrīsī, 2, 82–86, 89, 95, 129, 133, 141, 148, 181, 189
Il-Khanate, 18
Illustrated Treatise on the Sea Kingdoms(Haiguo tuzhi), 100
Indian Ocean, 72
  ancient Greek and Roman sailors in, 7, 12
  Muslim merchants in, 12
  seven seas of, 72
  Zhou Qufei's five great seas in, 48
Introduction (Muqaddimah). See Ibn Khaldūn
Islamic Astronomical Bureau and Observatory (*Huihui Sitiantai*), 99
Islamic Imperial Academy (Huihui Guozijian), 99
the Islamic world. *See also* Dashi and Huihui (Chinese terms for the Muslims)
  breakup of, in the Late 'Abbāsid Period, 75
  definition of, in this book, 5, 19
  rise of, 6
al-Iṣṭakhrī, 74, 75, 84

Jamāl al-Dīn (*Zhamaluding*), Yuan scholar, 99–104, 125, 142
  astronomical work of, 100
Jamāl al-Dīn Ibrāhīm b. Muḥammad al-Ṭībī in Qais, 151
Japan, 63, 183
Jia Dan, 31–37, 45, 48, 65
  Map of Chinese and Non-Chinese Territories in the World (Hainei huayi tu), 34
  "The Route to the Foreign Countries across the Sea from Guangzhou" (Guangzhou tong haiyi dao), 31–34
Jin Dynasty. *See* Jurchens
Jingdezhen, 117
Jipangu. *See* Japan
Jishui tan, 108
junk ships, 43, 49
  construction technology of, 154, 170
Jurchens, 46, 93
Juwaynī, 'AṭāMalik. *See History of the World Conqueror*

Ka'bah, 177
kamāl, 174
Kangnido, 104–107, 173
Kārimī, 152
Kāshgharī, 80, 87
Khanbaliq, 135–137, 184
Khānfū. *See* Guangzhou
Khānjū. *See* Quanzhou
Khara Khorum, 94
kharāj (land tax), 170
Khitan Liao Empire, 87
Khitans, 46, 78, 81
Khubilai, 18, 102, 132
  and Bolad, 138
  building the new capital Daidu (Dadu), 135
  conflict with Arigh Böke, 97
  conquest of the Southern Song of, 98
  elected as the fifth grand Khan of the Mongol empire, 19, 97
  facilitating China's sea trade, 98
  Grand Canal of, 108, 136
  and Jamāl al-Dīn, 100, 103
  and Prime Minister Aḥmad, 138
  proclaiming the Yuan dynasty, 97
  and Sayyid 'Ajall Shams al-Dīn, 99, 111
Khumdān. *See* Chang'an
khuṭba (Friday prayers), 67, 151
Khwārazm Shāh, 93, 126–128
al-Khwārizmī, 84, 142, 148. *See also Shape of the Earth* (*Ṣūrat al-arḍ*)
Kim Sahyung, 105
Kitāb al-Fihrist, 56–57, 63
Korea, 2, 73
  Goryeo, 135, 147
  Silla (al-Shīlā, Sīlā), 62–63, 73, 135
Kūfa, 21, 26–27, 29

Lambourn, Elizabeth, 151
lemon (limu), 114
Li Zemin, 105, 166
Liao Dynasty. *See* Khitans
Lin Zhiqi, 51, 52
Liu Yu. *See Record of an Embassy to the Regions in the West* (*Xishi ji*)
Lumei. *See* Rūm, the Roman [Byzantine] Empire

Luo Hongxian, 165, 166, 167
Lūqīn, 86. *See also* Hanoi

Ma Huan, 161, 176–179
Machīn. *See* China
Maḥmūd of Ghazna, 78, 81
Malindi, 174
Mamlūks, 19, 53, 127, 147, 152
al-Manṣūr, 32
Manzi. *See* China
"Mao Kun map" (Zheng He Hanghai tu), 15
Map of Chinese and Non-Chinese Territories (Huayi tu), 35–37, 100, 133
Map of Foreign Countries (Zhufan tu), 50
"Map of Foreign Lands in Southeast Sea" (Dongnan haiyi tu), 165
"Map of Foreign Lands in Southwest Sea" (Xinan haiyi tu), 165
Map of Integrated Regions and Terrains (Hunyi jiangli tu). *See* Qing Jun
Map of Integrated Regions and Terrains and of Historical Countries and Capitals (Honil gangli yeokdae gukdo jido), 165. *See also Kangnido*
"Map of the Five Indian States in the West" (Xitu wuyin zhi tu), 38–41
Map of the Resounding Teaching (of the Khan) Prevailing All Over the World (Shengjiao guangbei tu). *See* Li Zemin
"Map of the States in the Western Regions in the Han Dynasty" (Han xiyu zhuguo tu), 38–40
"Map of the World Regions" (Guanglun jiangli tu), 107, 112
maps
  as a historical source, 14–15
Mar Yaballaha III, Rabban Markos, 139
Maragheh
  observatory at, 128
Marvels of India ('Ajā'ib al-Hind), 185
Marvels of Things Created and Miraculous Aspects of Things Existing'Ajā'ib al-makhlūqāt wa-gharā'ib al-mawjūdāt), 129. *See also* al-Qazwīnī, Zakariyā' b. Muhammad
Marwazī, 81, 87
al-Mas'ūdī, 70–75, 76, 77, 84, 89, 95, 148, 180
Meadows of Gold and Mines of Gems (Murūj al-dhahab wa-ma'ādin al-jawhar). *See* al-Mas'ūdī
Mecca, 47, 59, 76, 95, 113, 116, 152, 176, 185
"Middle Kingdom" (*zhongguo*), 5
Min, Fujian, 112
Ming Dynasty, 19
  establishment of, 163
Möngke, 97, 109, 132, 135, 138, 140
Mongols, 8, 18
  conquest of Eurasia by, 93
  fall of the Mongol empire, 19
  the Mongol empire established by, 18, 91, 97
Mountain of the Moon, 130, 141, 144
Muḥammad, the Prophet, 6, 20, 68, 111, 120
Muḥammad ibn Najīb Bākran. *See World Book (Jahān-nāmah)*
Muḥammad Ibn Tughluq, 153
al-Muqaddasī, 75, 77
Muslim communities
  in China, 118, 123, 125, 155
  in Hangzhou, 118, 157
  over the Indian Ocean, 44, 110
  in Quanzhou, 110, 121
  in South and Southeast Asia, 92, 152
  in South Asia, 111, 151
  in Southeast Asia, 87, 170
  in the ports of southeastern China, 44, 159

Needham, Joseph, 154
New History of the Tang Dynasty (Xin Tangshu), 31, 34
  geography (*dili*) section, 31
Nile River, 53
nisba, 111
Notes from the Land beyond the Passes (Lingwai daida), 46–50, 172

Office of the Court of State Ceremonial (*Honglü si*), 11, 31
Office of the Superintendent of Merchant Shipping (*shibosi*), 44, 48
Ögödei, 135
Ohji, Toshiaki, 84
Öljeitü, 140, 180
  sponsoring Rashīd al-Dīn's *Compendium of Chronicles*, 131
One Thousand and One Nights (Arabian Nights), 64, 89

ortagh, 109, 152
Ottoman Empire, 162
Overall Survey of the Ocean's Shores (Yingyai shenglan). *See* Ma Huan
Overall Survey of the Star Raft (Xingcha shenglan). *See* Fei Xin

Palace Library (*xing mishujianshi*), 99
paper money, 156
Parthian Empire, 10, 38
Pax Mongolica, 19, 193
Pei Xiu, 35
Periplus of the Erythraean Sea, 7
Pleasure of He who Longs to Cross the Horizons (Nuzhat al-mushtāq fī ikhtirāq al-āfāq). *See Book of Roger*
Polo, Marco, 4, 124–126, 194, 197
  accompanying a Mongol princess named Kokaqin from China to Iran, 139
  compared to Bolad, 138
  compared to Wang Dayuan, 91, 114, 115
  description about China by, 145, 157
  description of a grand canal by, 136
  exchange of envoys between the Yuan Dynasty and the Il-Khanate mentioned by, 112
  inspiring Henry the Navigator and Christopher Columbus, 162
  junk ship's advantages described by, 154
  the last days of the Abbasid Caliphate confirmed by, 95
  skepticism on the account by, 153
  use of paper money in China referred to by, 156
Portuguese, 150, 162, 163, 182, 197
Ptolemy of Alexandria, 12, 76, 83, 142, 193, 197
  Geography, 12, 15, 59
Pu Shougeng, 98, 111

Qara Khitai (Western Liao), 87, 93, 126, 131
al-Qazwīnī, Zakariyā' b. Muḥammad, 129–131, 141
Qibla, 185
Qin Dynasty, 133
Qing Dynasty, 165
Qing Jun, 105
Quanzhou, 61, 115, 137
  ceramic production of, 45
  Chinese shipwreck in, 45
  Ibn Baṭṭūṭa's descriptions of, 156
  Ibn Baṭṭūṭa's stay in, 153
  local gazetteer from, 115
  mosque in, 120
  Muslim tombstones in, 52, 110, 111
  Office of the Superintendent of Merchant Shipping in, 48, 50, 98
Quilon, 48, 49, 117
Qur'ān, 8, 11, 12, 27, 67, 120

Rabban Bar Sauma, 139
Rashīd al-Dīn, 131–141, 146, 147, 157
Record of an Embassy to the Regions in the West (*Xishi ji*), 94–96
Record of Routes to the Western Regions (Xiyu xingcheng ji). *See* Chen Cheng
Record of the Southern Sea (Nanhai zhi), 113–114
Records of the Grand Historian (*Shiji*), 9–11, 116. *See also Sima Qian*
Regions of the World (*Ḥudūd al-ʿĀlam*), 81
Renaissance, 197
riḥla, 153. *See also* travel accounts
Rise of the Two Auspicious Constellations and the Confluence of the Two Oceans (*Maṭlaʿ-i Saʿdayn wa-Majmaʿ-i Baḥrayn*). *See* ʿAbd al-Razzāq al-Samarqandī
Roger II of Sicily, 83, 86
Roman Empire, 6
"The Route to the Foreign Countries across the Sea from Guangzhou" (Guangzhou tong haiyi dao). *See* Jia Dan
Rūm, the Roman [Byzantine] Empire, 51, 65
  sea of, 73

Saʿd b. Abī Waqqās, 6
Safineh-yi Tabrīz, 140, 144
ṣaḥīfah (compass chart), 182
Sanfoqi. *See* Srivijaya
Sassanids, 5, 60
Sayyid ʿAjall Shams al-Dīn, 99, 111
sea bans (*haijin*), 167, 188
Seljuks, 126
semuren, 98
Serica [*Sērikē*]. *See* China
Shangdu (Xanadu), 139
Shape of the Earth (*Ṣūrat al-arḍ*), 59–60
Sharia, 27
Shenzhong, Northern Song Dynasty, 44

Shi Nawei, 51–52, 110
Shīʿa Ismāʿīlīs, 127, 128
al-Shīlā. *See* Korea
shipwrecks
in Belitung, 65
in Quanzhou Bay, Song Dynasty, 16, 45
in Sinan, Korea, 45
Shiraz, 95
Shortened Account of the Non-Chinese Island Peoples (Daoyi zhilüe), 114–118
Sīlā. *See* Korea
Silk Road, 2, 5, 7, 21
Silla. *See* Korea
Sima Qian, 91, 116. *See also Records of the Grand Historian* (*Shiji*)
al-Ṣīn. *See* China
Ṣīn al-Ṣīn. *See* China
Ṣin Kalān. *See* Guangzhou
Sīrāf, 33, 65, 66, 68, 107
excavations at, 16
So, Billy K. L., 45
Sogdians, 5, 6, 29
geographical knowledge possessed by, 60
Song Dynasty
Northern Song, 44
Southern Song, 46, 93, 97–98, 110–111
Srivijaya, 46, 70
Sugiyama Masaaki, 18
Sunnah, 27
Survey of the Lands (Taqwīm al-buldān). *See* Abū al-Fidāʾ

"T-in-the-O" map, 4, 197
Taizong, Tang Dynasty, 35
Taizu, Ming Dynasty, 178
Talas
Battle of, 53, 56, 191
Tang Code, 67
Tangiers, Morocco, 152
al-Tawḥīdī, 68
terra cognita, 63, 89
terra incognita, 9, 76, 78, 89
Thīnai (*Sinae*). *See* China
Tibbetts, Gerald, 188
Tibet, 29
Tigris, 32
Timur (Tamerlane), 161, 167, 180, 188, 195
recruiting Ibn Khaldūn, 180
setting out to conquer China, 168
Timurid Dynasty, 19, 162, 182, 188
Tiyu. *See* Daibul
Toghun Temür, 157
Tracks of Yu (Yuji tu), 35, 100
transfer of Islamic cartographic techniques into China, 100–107
transfer of Islamic scholarship into China, 99–100
transfer of papermaking, 56, 57
travel accounts, 13
reliability of, as sources of historical geographical information, 13
Travels of Ibn Batuta. *See* Ibn Baṭṭūṭa
Treatise of Military Preparation (*Wubei zhi*), 172–175
Treatise on the Great Unified Realm of the Great Yuan (Dayuan da yitong zhi), 103–104
tribute-based diplomatic order, 169
Tufan. *See Tibet*
Ṭūsī, Naṣīr al-Dīn, 128

al-Ubullah, 32–33
Umayyads, Umayyad caliphate, 7, 27, 29
ummah, 6
Unno Kazutaka, 142

Wang Dayuan, 91, 161, 176, 178, *See also Shortened Account of the Non-Chinese Island Peoples* (*Daoyi zhilüe*)
skepticism on the travel of, to West Asia, 153
Wang Yinglin, 37
Wang Yun, 96
al-Wāqwāq, 62, 63
Waṣṣāf, 139, 151
Ways of Perception Concerning the Most Populous [Civilized] Provinces (*Masālik al-abṣār fi mamālik al-amṣār*). *See* Ibn Faḍlallāh al-ʿUmarī
Wei Yuan. *See Illustrated Treatise on the Sea Kingdoms(Haiguo tuzhi)*
Western Barbarians (*Xirong*), 22, 23
Western Regions (*Xiyu*), 9
Western Sea, 24
Western Sea (*Xihai*), 24
"Western Sea of the Muslims" (Xi Dashi hai), 48
World Book (*Jahān-nāmah*), 88, 142
Wu Jian, 91, 115, 119
Wusili. *See* Egypt

Xinya Tuoluo, 44

Yamagata Kinya, 171
Yang Shu, 92, 112–113, 140, 170
Yang You, 171
Yangzhou, 61
Yāqūt. *See Geographical Dictionary (Mu'jam al-buldān)*
Yeke Mongol Ulus. *See* Mongol empire
Yongle Encyclopaedia (Yongle dadian), 102
Yuan Dynasty, 18, 97
"Yugong tu", 14

Zaitūn. *See* Quanzhou
Zhang Qian, 96
Zhao Rugua, 89, 93, 113. *See also Description of the Foreign Lands* (*Zhufan zhi*)
Zheng He, 15, 19, 161, 169–179, 184, 189, 196, 200
  treasure ships (*baochuan*) of, 171
Zheng Sixiao, 118
Zhipan, 38–41
Zhou Mi, 118
Zhou Qufei, 53, 75, 89, 114. *See also Notes from the Land beyond the Passes* (*Lingwai daida*)
Zhu Siben, 165
Zhu Yuanzhang, 163
Zīj-i Īlkhānī, 128
Zou Yan, 115

Lightning Source UK Ltd.
Milton Keynes UK
UKHW021958191021
392485UK00009B/1920

9 781107 547834